Not the violent conflict between parts of the truth, but the quiet suppression of half of it, is the formidable evil; there is always hope when people are forced to listen to both sides; it is when they attend to only one that errors harden into prejudices, and truth itself ceases to have the effect of truth, by being exaggerated into falsehood.

John Stuart Mill

Since I've started debating I have fewer opinions.

Y8 student

ISBN 978-1-8381543-3-2

First paperback edition August 2024

Published by Debating For Everyone

www.debatingforeveryone.com

About the author

From 2000 to 2021 Julian Bell was Head of English and Debating at Godolphin and Latymer School in London. In September 2021, he retired from teaching to devote himself full-time to his passion for debating. He provides training in debating to students in prep, primary and secondary schools both in person and online across the UK and overseas, including schools in Spain and the USA, as well as offering consultancy and training services for teachers. He also runs a number of debating competitions both online and in person.

Julian Bell is the author of *The Debating Book: Everything You Ever Need to Know About Debating*, a textbook for student debaters and their teachers, as well as *Win Every Debate: Extended Mace* and *Win Every Debate: British Parliamentary*, workbooks to help students prepare for and analyse debates. You can contact Julian Bell via his website, **www.debatingforeveryone.com**, which holds over a hundred free debating resources.

Debating for Everyone

www.debatingforeveryone.com

CONTENTS

Introduction

This is the sequel to my first title, *The Debating Book: Everything You Ever Need to Know About Debating*.

There is another book much used by debaters, often seen at debating competitions, called *Pros and Cons*. It was first published in 1896, and the most recent edition (the nineteenth) came out in 2014. *Pros and Cons* essentially consists of lists of arguments on either side for the most common debate motions. It is a useful book, and every debater should have a copy.

Think Like A Debater also has lists of arguments, along with much else besides. It offers historical background to every topic; an array of useful facts and statistics; lists of possible motions for debate; and recommended further reading, listening and watching. Most importantly, it offers a searching analysis of the fundamental issues for every topic, helping you to understand how and why the two sides disagree, so you can grasp what debaters call 'the point of clash'. *Think Like A Debater* aspires to be, in the words of one of my students, '*Pros and Cons* on steroids'.

The book is divided into sections, covering Society, Justice, Money, Science and Technology, Life and Death. Each of these sections is then split into chapters, covering topics like free speech, climate change, abortion, etc. Each chapter opens with a survey of the historical background of the topic. How far back the history goes depends on the topic. The chapter on economic inequality opens with the experience of prehistoric hunter-gatherer tribes; the one on the internet doesn't begin until the twenty-first century. The chapters on the welfare state and immigration both start around the end of the Second World War in 1945, as this period saw the birth of the NHS and the beginnings of mass immigration to the UK from Britain's former colonies. And so on.

Think Like A Debater is very broad in scope. My research for each of the topics has largely been based on reading books by people who have spent many years – in some cases their whole lives – studying just one subject, and still haven't come to the end of it. This book makes no claims whatsoever to be a comprehensive study of any of the topics. It is designed to be a general introduction, and hopefully an encouragement to you to explore any or all of the issues further.

I have tried to make the book as accurate as possible; if you spot any errors, please let me know. The text was last checked in the summer of 2024. Given that many of the issues discussed are live, current and constantly changing, it is highly likely that some of it will be out of date by the time you read it. This is one reason why I open by giving you advice on how to do your own research and fact-checking when preparing for debates.

Researching and writing this book has left me feeling that I now understand the world much better than I did when I started. It has also made me both clearer and, at the same time, less certain about my own beliefs. I started out with very strong personal convictions about some of the issues; on others, I was undecided. I am now much more undecided about the issues I was once certain on, and have firmer opinions on the issues I was unsure about. I hope reading this book will have the same effect on you: that it will give you a better understanding of the world, and will help you to challenge and clarify your own beliefs. Read it carefully, and it will make you a better debater and a better person.

Julian Bell
Director, Debating For Everyone
September 2024

1

PART ONE

Thinking like a debater

How and why to think like a debater

In this section, we think about thinking; in particular, thinking like a debater. How can we have better debates? How can we express our own beliefs, while understanding other points of view? How can we find out what's really going on? How can we think more clearly? How can we avoid our own bias? How can debating make the world a better place?

CHAPTER 1

Why You Should Think Like a Debater

We need less debate

Ridicule, abuse, threats of violence

I've lost count of the number of times I've read or heard variations on this statement, in articles in the press, on radio, on TV, on social media, in private conversation. Do I agree with it? Well, obviously not, or I wouldn't have devoted many years of my life to teaching and promoting debate, nor would I have written two books about debate. But I can't just say, no, that's wrong, we don't need less debate, we need more debate. That simple denial would make me a very poor debater. What's more, it would contradict the entire point of this book. So, here goes.

Why do people say we need less debate? When you look at how debate is conducted in the mainstream media, you can understand why. Debate, in most news and discussion programmes, is presented as a kind of combat sport, the purpose of which is to destroy the other side. Any and all issues are split neatly down the middle by producers who sometimes instruct contributors on the positions they should take, as if they were directing a scripted drama. Go to social media and it's even worse. At least in the mainstream media, a reasonable length of time is given to develop ideas; online, complex issues are reduced to tweets and one-sentence posts, with no time to consider complexity. Ridicule and abuse at best, threats of violence at worst, are considered normal ways of responding to different points of view. Algorithms direct users to posts that support their own side, reinforcing tribal loyalties, making mutual understanding even harder. When it seems that everyone else agrees with you, it's hard not to think that people who don't see things your way are stupid or ignorant or evil or all of the above.

And what of our leaders? Tune into Prime Minister's Questions in the House of Commons, and you may think that you have wandered into an unruly Year Nine class presided over by an inexperienced supply teacher on the verge of a nervous breakdown. Shouted insults, personal attacks, speakers constantly interrupted, archaic and pointless rituals. Look across the Atlantic in recent years and it's not much better: the once great nation of America has split into two irreconcilable, mutually uncomprehending tribes, so fearful and mistrusting of each other that they would not let their children marry someone from the other side, agreeing only that they are good and that the other side is evil. The low point (so far) was surely the first 2020 presidential debate between Donald

Will you shut up, man?

Trump and Joe Biden, in which Trump refused to allow Biden to speak, talking over his answers with a non-stop barrage of insults, prompting Biden to cry out in despair, 'Will you shut up, man?'

What's more, those who dominate debate tend to be those who dominate other areas of life. You can barely open a newspaper or turn on the television without hearing a white middle-aged man complain to millions of readers or viewers, in return for a handsome fee, that he is never allowed to say what he thinks. Take what Richard Dawkins once said about his fellow militant atheist, the late Christopher Hitchens: 'If you are a religious believer invited to debate against Christopher Hitchens, decline.' Why? Not, the implication is, because atheism is more intellectually and ethically valid than faith, but because Mr Hitchens will be bigger and stronger and nastier than you. This is the language of the bully.

So, to sum up, debate is divisive, aggressive, ill-informed, uninformative, and reinforces existing unjust power structures. Clearly we need less of it.

But there is another way. What if we had not **less** debate, but **better** debate?

What does good debate look like? You can find it, away from the public arena, in any well-run school debating club or competition. A structured debate following one of the recognised formats for competition will show you speakers treating each other with equality and respect; developing their arguments with diligence, detail and evidence; listening to each other and responding with engagement and honesty to the position of the other side; attacking the arguments, not the person. You'll hear people empathising with points of view not their own, because they have to argue for the side they've been given, not the side they are tribally committed to.

Obviously not all school debaters live up to this ideal all the time. The point is that formal competitive debate is structured such that it is necessary to behave in this way to succeed at it. Yes, it is a competitive and binary format. But the side that the judge or judges give victory to will be the one that has argued more honestly, fairly and thoroughly. Watch a really good debate in this format, and you will come away understanding more about an issue. You may stay on the side of the argument you started with – or you may change your mind. Either way, you will have more comprehension of and respect for people who are not like you.

Debating makes it harder to have opinions

As one of my students said to me, 'Since I've started debating, I have fewer opinions.' By which he meant he found it easier to understand people who disagreed with him.

That's good debate, and we need more of it, for the health of our public life. Good debate is partly a matter of techniques and skills which can be taught and learnt. I covered these techniques and skills in my first book, *The Debating Book: everything you ever need to know about debating*. But good debate also depends on an attitude of mind, a way of looking at the world. Someone who thinks like this – who thinks like a debater – will, when faced with a difficult or controversial question or issue, first ensure they know the facts about the issue, even if these facts are uncomfortable, difficult to understand, or don't reinforce their point of view. Then, they will try to truly understand what the question is about, and why good people can take different positions on it. They will not just tick off lists of arguments on both sides, but will go further, and will search for the essence, the crux, what debaters call 'the point of clash': what exactly do people disagree about, and why?

That way of thinking requires honesty, openness, empathy, mental flexibility and a commitment to the truth. It's hard work. But it's worth it. It will make you a much better competitive debater. It will also make you a better person. Two good arguments for thinking like a debater.

Convinced? Then it's time to look at **how** you can think like a debater.

CHAPTER 2

How to Think Like a Debater

There are three key tasks for a successful debater (and also for anyone who wants to understand and engage with the world).

- **Learn about the world.**
- **Analyse the issues.**
- **Keep learning; keep analysing.**

1. How to learn about the world

Inform yourself about the world

When Donald Trump was inaugurated as 45th President of the United States on January 20th, 2017, it rained during his speech. Mr Trump said it didn't rain during his speech. Journalists accused him of lying (because it did rain during his speech). Mr Trump accused them of bias. A popular line much quoted at the time stated: 'It isn't the job of a journalist to report that some people think it's raining, and that some people think it isn't. It's the job of a journalist to stick his head out of the window and find out if it's raining.'

That, in a nutshell, is also the job of a debater – or, at least, one of the jobs of a debater. Yes, once the debate starts, you have to argue passionately for your side of the debate, and to challenge equally passionately the other side of the debate. But first you have to base what you say in accurate knowledge of the world. This might require some effort. It might require you to metaphorically open the window and stick your head out, even if that means getting a bit wet. But you will be a much better debater (and a far better citizen) if you take the trouble to inform yourself as thoroughly and precisely as possible about the facts.

Here are some tips to help you acquire a full and accurate understanding of the world:

- **Check your sources.**
- **Multiply your sources.**
- **Check your bias.**
- **Take the long view.**
- **Be curious.**
- **Keep a notebook.**

Check your sources

Not everything written down, either in print or online, is true. Nor is everything that is said true. How can you check whether something

Not everything written or said is true

is true or not? One way is to consider what kind of source it is. Ask these three questions:

1. **Who wrote it / said it?**

   The answer to this question will help you identify if the writer / speaker has **expertise**. People with expertise on a topic are more likely to have accurate information about it. If someone writing or speaking about the impact of climate change is a scientist who has spent years studying the subject, they are likely to have first-hand knowledge and therefore expertise; if they have never studied the science of climate change, their knowledge will be at best second hand.

2. **Why did they write it / say it?**

   The answer to this question will help you identify the **motivation** of the writer / speaker. People have many motivations for writing and speaking. They may want to discover and present the truth, or they may want to advance their own or someone else's interests. An article demonstrating the harm to health of eating fried chicken from fast-food shops every day published by a medical journal is likely to be motivated by a search for the truth about the health impacts of junk food. An article published by a fast-food fried chicken company saying there are no health harms from eating fried chicken from fast-food shops every day is likely to be motivated by a wish to keep people buying fried chicken.

3. **When and how was it produced?**

   When something was written or said changes how you read it or hear it. A book or article written about immigration before the enlargement of the European Union allowed more people from Eastern Europe to come to the UK to work will not consider the impact of this kind of immigration. One written more recently may give the impact of Eastern European immigration more weight, only because it is more recent.

   How something is written or said will help you evaluate its accuracy. In general, the longer it took to produce, the more accurate it is likely to be. A tweet can be fired off in seconds with no checking, and (if the handle is anonymous) may be beyond the reach of laws against libel (libel means the publication of inaccurate and malicious statements). A longer post on a blog or a clip on YouTube may be a little more considered, but has the same issues about the lack of checking / accountability. An article in a daily newspaper will have been checked by an editor, who will also want to protect the newspaper against legal action for libel, but will have been written to a short deadline. An article in a weekly magazine will have gone through a similar editing process, but will have allowed the author longer to research and compose it. An article in a monthly magazine will have given the author even longer. A published book is likely to have gone through an extensive process of commissioning, editing and proofreading, making it even more likely to be accurate. Of course, it is possible to give completely accurate information in a tweet, and for a published book to be full of lies and inaccuracies. Even so, length of production is a relevant consideration.

Be hungry and restless for knowledge

Multiply your sources

Investors in the stock market often opt for a 'balanced portfolio'. That is, they buy stocks in many different companies so that the ones that do badly are balanced out by the ones that do well. It's a good idea to do the same with the sources for your facts.

If you want to know more about a particular topic, seek out as many different sources of information on it as possible in as many different genres as possible. A Google search for websites might start you off, but then look out for articles in newspapers, magazines and journals, and track down as many relevant books as you can lay your hands on. Use your school, university or local library. Make friends with the librarian – librarians are usually delighted to have the opportunity to show off how wonderful their collection is, and will be pleased to help you with your quest. Be hungry and restless for knowledge. Even if you find yourself reading the same thing twice (or three times), that's no bad thing, as it will help you remember it.

And don't just multiply your sources of information. Multiply your perspectives on a topic as well. Topics which are likely to be debated are, by their very nature, going to be controversial, and will be open to many different interpretations – expose yourself to as many of those as you can. Above all, challenge your own preconceptions. If you and everyone you know is convinced that the police are institutionally racist, seek out articles in *The Daily Telegraph* denouncing political correctness and calling for coppers to be left alone to do their job. If, on the other hand, you and everyone you know is convinced that billionaire heads of tech companies deserve every penny they earn because they add so much value to the world, make yourself read some books by left-

Give people a fair hearing

wing economists arguing that excessive economic inequality is corrosive for society. Try not to get angry as you read. Try instead to understand why these writers say what they say; try to empathise intellectually with where they are coming from. Imagine as you read that you are debating against them: how would you rebut them? You know you don't agree with them: why? How would you answer them? Reading different points of view may change your mind, or it may not. But you must give people on the other side – on all sides – a fair hearing. It will make you a better person as well as a better citizen. What's more, it will make you a better debater: you might get assigned the other side of the argument in a debate.

Check your bias

We all have our biases: impediments to clear vision that lead us to dismiss points of view not our own without considering them properly. Don't be ashamed of having a bias – it's normal. Just be aware of your bias and don't act on it.

Here are some kinds of bias that can get in the way of understanding different points of view.

Emotional involvement

Soon after students returned to school following the Covid lockdown of 2020, I led a discussion with a class about how strict restrictions should continue to be. The class was leaning towards a more liberal view. Then one girl put her hand up and told us her grandmother had been in hospital with Covid and had nearly died. Suddenly everyone was for stricter restrictions.

This reaction came from a good place. The class wanted to show solidarity with their friend in her distress over her grandmother. But that emotion of shock and sadness got in the way of considering the arguments for loosening restrictions; however affecting the girl's story, it was only a sample of one. And it could have gone the other way. What if another student had put her hand up and told the class that her family's business had gone bankrupt because of lockdown restrictions?

The more personally an issue touches you, the more you need to step back from your own involvement. If you or someone you love has been the victim of racism by the police, you actually need to look even harder for evidence that the police may not be institutionally racist. If your father is a policeman and you feel loyal to him and supportive of his work, you need to look even harder for evidence that the police may be institutionally racist (even if your dad isn't).

When people talk about 'my truth', what they really mean is 'my experience'. Your experience is very important and should be respected, but it is not the same as the truth.

Your experience is not the same as the truth

Tribal bias

Human beings are evolutionarily hardwired to want to belong. They feel safer when they know they are accepted as part of a group. It would take a lot of courage to speak up for the benefits of Brexit at a middle-class dinner party in North London, or to defend abortion rights in an evangelical church in the Deep South of America. It's hard to challenge, even in your head, what everyone around you believes. All the more reason to do it. You don't necessarily have to change your mind, just be aware that peer pressure might be more of a factor in your beliefs than you would like to admit.

Confirmation bias

The psychologist Steven Pinker observes that humans have evolved to be lawyers, not scientists. That is, out of an instinct for survival and self-preservation we are naturally inclined not to seek the truth by considering all the evidence, but to seek out only evidence which confirms our own position as well as that of our group. Obviously when you are preparing for a debate you do want to prioritise evidence that supports your side of the case. However, you also need to consider and respect evidence from the other side, in order to rebut it. You need to do this even more when you are outside of debate preparation mode, learning about the world in the rest of your life. Check you are not ignoring facts that do not support your pre-existing beliefs.

Take the long view

Barack Obama used to talk about the 'fierce urgency of now' (a phrase originally coined by Martin Luther King). He had a point, but there are times when 'now' is a bit too urgent, when we can forget that where we are now is the product of a lot of 'then'.

A good debater will collect facts not just about the current state of an issue, but about what came before; about how we got to where we are. She will enjoy history as much as current affairs. If you're debating immigration policy, you'll be on much stronger ground if

What happened then matters now

you know not just about the government's latest announcement on asylum seekers, but also about the arrival of West Indian immigrants on the *Empire Windrush* in 1948 and how they were received; about Enoch Powell's inflammatory 'Rivers of Blood' speech in 1968 and why he was so popular; about how and why Ugandan Asians came to Britain in 1971, and how they changed British society; and about how and why we joined the Common Market in 1973, and how and why we left the EU in 2020, and what that meant for immigration policy. All of this knowledge will help you understand the mix of fear, need and welcome with which British people have responded, and still respond, to immigrants to the UK, whether you are arguing for more generous or stricter policies on immigration.

What happened then matters now.

Keep a notebook

This is all very well, I hear you say, telling me to learn about the world. The trouble is that my brain isn't that big. I can't remember all this stuff. And in a debate, we've only got fifteen minutes to prepare, and we're not allowed to look stuff up.

That's not quite true. You are allowed to look stuff up, just in hard copy resources. So keep a notebook.

Divide it into categories, separated by index tabs. Helpful categories might be:

- Politics
- Education
- The economy
- Healthcare
- Ethical issues
- Technology
- Identity
- Faith and religion
- Environment
- Crime, punishment, violence

Say you read an interesting article on moves in the USA to restrict abortion rights; flip to your 'Ethical issues' section and make a few notes. If you decide to dive a bit deeper and find out how abortion came to be legalised across the USA in 1973, you can make some notes on *Roe vs Wade* in the same section. Then, if you find yourself taking part in a debate about abortion rights, you can (entirely legally) refresh your memory, and perhaps educate your debating partner, with some useful facts to bolster your arguments.

Educate your debating partner with useful facts

2. Analyse the issues

Let's start with a story.

Ameena and Bryony are best friends. They've been best friends ever since they met in the first session of the Year Seven debating club at school. They bonded over their shared love of debating, and whenever they get together they love to talk over the issues of the day for hours on end.

They graduated from uni a couple of years ago, and are just starting out in their first jobs. They've been really busy with work and haven't seen each other in a while, so they're looking forward to a night out together. They've agreed to see a film. It's Bryony's choice of film. She arrives at the cinema first. She gets a message from Ameena. Ameena's going to be late, because her bus has been held up by climate change protesters blocking the road. Ameena doesn't seem too bothered about the delay. In fact, she's very excited and sends Bryony lots of pictures of the protesters with smiley and thumbs up emojis attached. Bryony is none too impressed. She really wants to see the film. By the time Ameena arrives at the cinema, she's 45 minutes late, the film has long since started, and Bryony is in a foul mood.

'Why are you so happy about those protesters?' says Bryony. 'They've ruined our evening.'

Ameena is about to answer, but she can see the mood her friend is in, so she says, 'Let's go and have dinner at Luigi's instead.' She knows Luigi's will cheer Bryony up. Luigi's cheers everyone up. It's well known as the best Italian restaurant in town. No debate about that.

Seated at the window table in Luigi's with Bryony, a glass of wine each and some olives, Ameena feels it is now safe to breach the subject of the climate protesters who delayed her journey. She was excited to see them because it meant that people would not forget about the urgency of dealing with climate change. 'It's an issue that threatens our very survival.'

The law is the law

'I know that,' says Bryony, 'but they were breaking the law.'

'Well,' says Ameena, 'it's worth breaking the law if it saves the world from destruction.'

'No, it isn't,' says Bryony. 'The law is the law. Maintaining the rule of law is the foundation of a civilised society. Once you allow people to break the law, no matter what the reason, you undermine what keeps us safe. I agree with the protesters about climate change; I just don't agree with them breaking the law.'

The waiter comes. Ameena orders a margherita pizza, and Bryony has spaghetti carbonara. They pour some more wine.

'Well,' says Ameena, 'what if the law is wrong? Isn't it right to break it then? Wasn't it right for civil rights protesters in America in the 1960s to break the laws that made black people use separate (and worse) facilities?'

'Those laws were wrong, yes,' agrees Bryony. 'But America is a democracy, and the way to change those laws was by campaigning peacefully and legally, not by breaking the law.'

'So,' says Ameena, between mouthfuls of pizza, 'what would you have done in South Africa under apartheid, where black people weren't allowed to vote or take any part in public life?'

Bryony concedes that those laws and that system were wrong, but maintains that peaceful protest is still the best way. 'Look,' she says, twirling her spaghetti on her fork, 'at Gandhi in India – he led an entirely peaceful campaign to free India from British rule.'

'Yes,' replies Ameena, 'and he did it by breaking the law. That's what these protesters are doing: breaking the law to stop us forgetting about climate change, and to make the government take action.'

The waiter comes to clear their plates and take their dessert orders. Ameena picks the tiramisu, and Bryony opts for the gelato.

'All right,' says Bryony, 'so maybe these protesters are like Gandhi. But what if it doesn't work? I know you were happy to see them, but what if the other people on the bus, and all the people in cars, were so angry at being delayed that it alienated them, and turned them off support for action on climate change? Wouldn't it be better to protest in a way that doesn't inconvenience people?'

'But,' says Ameena, 'if it doesn't inconvenience people, no one will take any notice. This is too important an issue. We need to inconvenience people. Climate change is going to be a lot more inconvenient. Better to sit on a bus for 45 minutes now than have your city flooded in 20 years' time.'

You always make me think

'No,' says Bryony. 'Better to find other ways to make the government fight climate change than remove the rule of law that keeps us all safe. These climate protesters might be cuddly and nice, but what if next week your bus is blocked by racists? Do you then say they can break the law to make their point, even though you don't agree with them?'

The desserts come. Silence falls for a moment as they each take a mouthful, and reflect on what has been said.

'We're not going to agree on this, are we?' says Bryony.

'No, we aren't,' says Ameena, 'but that's one of the things I love about you, Bryony. You always make me think. You always have, ever since that first discussion about whether homework should be compulsory in the Year Seven debating club.'

'I remember that,' says Bryony. 'You make me think, too. That's one of the things I love about you.'

'So,' says Ameena, pushing away her plate with a contented sigh, 'the difference between us on this one is that you think that the security provided by the rule of law is the most important thing; that once you remove that, chaos will come, which is bad for everyone, and the strong will have power over the weak.'

'That's right,' says Bryony. 'And what you're saying is that the threat of climate change is so fundamental and so existential, in the same way that the racism of the segregated states in America and apartheid South Africa were so fundamentally evil, that the rule of law has to be set aside in order to tackle that threat.'

'That's about it,' says Ameena.

Then they order coffee and catch up with all their other news. And make a plan to see the film next week instead.

See what they did there? They took the issue of when it is and isn't all right to break the law, and analysed it. They ran through the arguments on both sides, and this led them to find out what it was they fundamentally disagreed on (and what they agreed on); why it was that Ameena was excited by the protesters and Bryony was annoyed by them. They found, as debaters would say, the **point of clash**. Ameena believes that some issues, such as climate change and racism, are so fundamental that they take priority over the rule of law; Bryony believes that the rule of law is such a fundamental principle for everyone's well-being that it cannot be compromised for anything. And they managed to realise this disagreement and stay friends.

Know as much about the world as you can manage

Ameena and Bryony were thinking like debaters. They took a topic, analysed it (using, did you notice, their knowledge about the world, including history, e.g. US civil rights, apartheid, Gandhi), and discovered what the fundamental issues were. They did more than just shout slogans at each other, or list arguments for their own side without listening to arguments for the other side. They engaged and they understood. That's what successful debaters – successful citizens – do. And that's what we're going to be doing in this book.

3. Keep learning, keep analysing

This is both an attitude of mind and a collection of habits. A good debater – a good citizen – wants to know as much about the world as she can manage. She will enjoy learning about it. She will often be found with a book or a magazine or a newspaper in her hand. Long train or bus journeys will not be boring; they will be an opportunity for reading. If she's online, she will be prioritising sites that help her understand what is happening and why over sites that stir up an emotional response and reinforce her existing beliefs. (She'll also try not to watch too many clips of cats doing funny things. Well, all right, just a few. We all need to relax sometimes.)

Cultivate this habit of curiosity, and after a while it will not feel difficult. Someone who goes for a five-mile run once a year will find it hard. Someone who goes for a five-mile run every day will hardly notice it, and will also get a lot fitter. Intellectual curiosity is like that – the more you do it, the better you get at it.

Keep thinking...

Here are some books that will help you to keep learning and keep analysing; to keep thinking like a debater.

Critical Thinking Skills for Dummies, Martin Cohen (Dummies, 2015)

Written in a very reader-friendly and accessible style, with an easy-to-follow layout, Cohen gives an excellent introduction to the basic concepts and skills that will enable you to think critically. This doesn't mean criticising everything; it means questioning everything and taking nothing for granted (including your own beliefs), a vital skill for a debater. He has an unfortunate blind spot about climate change, but you can forgive him that for the clarity and helpfulness of this guide.

The Irrational Ape: Why We Fall for Conspiracy Theory, Disinformation and Propaganda, David Robert Grimes (Simon & Schuster, 2019)

Like a lot of arguments for rationality, this book is highly emotional. Grimes is passionate about the need for clear thinking. In a particularly striking story, he relates how the willingness of the commander of a Soviet nuclear submarine at the height of the Cuban Missile Crisis to check the evidence before launching his weapons saved the world from nuclear war. He is uncompromising about the need for critical thinking, but also very helpful in his guidance on how to do it. His no holds barred demolition of anti-vaxxers, written before the Covid-19 pandemic, is all the more relevant now.

The Righteous Mind: Why Good People are Divided by Politics and Religion, Jonathan Haidt (Penguin, 2013)

This book will change the way you see the world. Haidt controversially but convincingly makes the case that our beliefs are very often not, in fact, based on reason, but on our need to belong to and protect our personal tribe. Moreover, beliefs that seem repugnant to liberal Westerners are not immoral, they just appeal to different parts of morality. Far from being a pessimistic theory, this enables us to approach people with whom we disagree profoundly with sympathy and understanding, and also be more critical and sceptical about our own beliefs – both excellent skills for a debater.

How to Make the World Add Up: Ten Rules for Thinking Differently About Numbers, Tim Harford (The Bridge Street Press, 2020)

Statistics are both one of the most valuable tools for understanding the world, and one of the most misused and misunderstood. Harford, who has a weekly column in the *Financial Times* and presents the excellent BBC Radio 4 programme *More Or Less*, gives a superb introduction to using statistics and data in an intelligent and helpful way. You will use statistics in your next debate with much greater confidence after reading this book.

Thinking, Fast and Slow, Daniel Kahneman (Penguin, 2011)

Kahneman has spent a lifetime studying how people come to decisions. His fundamental insight is that there are two kinds of thinking: fast thinking, which is intuitive and unreflective, and slow thinking, which considers the evidence carefully, step by step. Neither is better than the other; each has its place for different purposes. He also explains different 'heuristics': shortcuts to making decisions, which we often use without realising it, and how they work in our minds. Understanding what kind of thinking you (and your opponents) are using will help you think and argue more clearly as a debater.

Rationality: What it is, Why it Seems Scarce, Why it Matters, Steven Pinker (Allen Lane, 2021)

Pinker is a passionate believer in the value of clear, rational thinking as a way of making the world a better place. He is perhaps rather uncompromising in his argument, and his vision of humans all turning into efficient thinking machines risks being a little inhuman in its intolerance for any way of responding to the world that is not entirely logical. However, his guidelines and examples of how to think logically make this book an invaluable primer for any debater.

CHAPTER 3

How to use this book

Each chapter covers a different topic, and is divided into the following sections:

1. The Facts

An introduction to the relevant facts and information connected with the topic, including historical context where appropriate.

2. The Issues

An analysis of the issues the topic gives rise to, considering what key questions it raises.

3. The Point of Clash

Discovering the point of clash; what is / are the fundamental point or points of disagreement on this issue?

4. The Arguments

A summary of the arguments that might be made for and against different responses to the issue.

5. The Motions

Suggested motions connected with the topic.

6. Keep thinking ...

Suggestions for further reading / research; recommendations of books and films.

Here are some suggestions for different ways to use this book:

1. In a debating club

- Take a topic, and have each member of the debating club read the relevant chapter in advance, making notes on it in their debating notebook.
- At the next meeting, discuss what they have learnt about the topic.

- Pick a motion from the list of suggestions and plan speeches together for and against the motion.
- Run a debate on this motion. You will find the debate will be of much higher quality after your period of research and preparation. What's more, should a motion on this topic come up in a competition, the team will be very well prepared.

2. Read the book by yourself

If you have the kind of intellectual curiosity a debater should have, you will find this book very interesting to read. You will be much better informed about all the key issues, and able to approach them in debates (and in general conversation) with greater confidence. Read as many of the books suggested for wider reading as you can manage, and you will be even better informed.

3. Take the book to debating competitions

Remember that hard copy resources are allowed in preparation time. You should already have your debating notebook(s) to hand, as recommended in the previous chapter. You can also have this book. If the motion is on, say, immigration, flip to the chapter on immigration, and you will find material to help you prepare. If you have already studied the chapters, annotating them and making notes, you will be even better prepared. If the competition is long prep, you will have more time to use this book. Do as much of the wider reading recommended at the end of each chapter as you can.

2

PART TWO

Society

How to think about society

Society is about how we live together.

So, in this section, we think about **free speech**. What should we be allowed to say? What should we not be allowed to say? Should we be allowed to cause offence?

We think about **democracy**. How do we make decisions? How can there be such a thing as 'the will of the people' when there are millions of different people, each with their own opinions? How can we disagree in a way that respects difference, but doesn't tear society apart?

We think about **education**. What should children learn at school? What should schools be like? Should all schools be the same? How much should be decided by parents, and how much by the state?

We think about **immigration**. Who should we let into our country? Who should we keep out? What do we want our country to look like?

CHAPTER 4

Free Speech

In this chapter we're thinking about...

- **What should people be allowed to say or write?**
- **What should people not be allowed to say or write?**
- **What should happen to people who say or write things they shouldn't?**

1. THE FACTS

Free speech? Or equal speech?

A short history of free speech

This history focuses primarily on Europe and America, as it is from there that most of our current ideas about free speech originated.

The Ancient World (c. 600 BCE – 300 CE)

Democracy was famously invented in **ancient Athens** (democracy is originally a Greek word). You can learn much more about it in Chapter 5, **Democracy**, but for the purposes of this chapter you need to know that free speech was highly valued by the ancient Greeks. They regularly held city assemblies which all (male, adult, non-enslaved) citizens were expected to attend, where important decisions were made about the city. In these assemblies, anyone was allowed to speak, and they could say pretty much whatever they wanted.

The main reason for promoting free speech was to ensure the widest possible variety of opinions and ideas, in the hope that this would lead to the best possible decisions being taken. As the Greek philosopher Aristotle put it:

'There is this to be said for the many … when there are many, each has his share of goodness and practical wisdom.'

Two guiding principles were central to the practice of free speech in democratic Athens, principles which are still very relevant to contemporary debates about free speech. The first is ***parrhesia***, which means **freedom** of speech: the right to say what you think regardless of whether or not it offends someone. The second is ***isegoria***, which means **equal access** to speech: the right for all citizens to be heard in the assembly, for no one to be excluded. These two ideas are both connected to what we now think of as free speech, but can also be in tension. If you focus more on *parrhesia*, you open the door to a wider range of ideas, and guarantee a more lively discussion, but at the risk of favouring those who make the most noise over those who are quieter or more marginalised and vulnerable. If you focus more on *isegoria*, you ensure that everyone will be heard, but at the risk of potentially restricting access for some louder voices in the interests of protecting the voices of the less powerful. You might say that *parrhesia* guarantees **freedom to**

speak, while *isegoria* guarantees **freedom from being silenced**. This is a subtle distinction but an important one.

There were limits to Athenian tolerance, though; the philosopher Socrates was sentenced to death for allegedly 'corrupting youth' by expressing unorthodox ideas.

Ancient Rome

Ancient Rome was never a fully democratic society in the way that ancient Athens was. However, the art of **rhetoric** (the use of words to persuade people, which the Athenians had developed) was very highly prized. Learning how to speak well was an essential part of a young man's education. (As in ancient Athens – as in almost all societies until quite recently – women were almost entirely excluded from public life.) Different factions and rulers came and went, and the political situation was often tumultuous and unstable. For a politician to achieve power – or in some cases simply to stay alive – he needed to be able to sway his audience with an eloquent speech, whether that was his fellow members of the Senate, or a mob on the streets. These speeches, many of which survive, were often brutally frank in their criticisms of rivals. A famous example of a very consequential debate in Ancient Rome came at the funeral of Julius Caesar, following his assassination in 44 BCE. Brutus, one of the assassins, spoke first. He justified the killing of Caesar in a calm, measured and rational way. Mark Antony, an ally of Caesar's, spoke next, and, by appealing to emotion, stirred up the mob to turn against Brutus and his allies, sparking a civil war which ended with Mark Antony seizing power. This debate is brilliantly dramatised in Shakespeare's play, *Julius Caesar*. It would not be the last time in history that a speaker would use free speech to manipulate their listeners for their own ends.

The pre-modern age (c. 300–1500)

The Ancient Athenian experiment with democracy, and the encouragement of the free exchange of opinions and ideas that went with it, ended in around the fourth century BCE; that was it for democracy for another two thousand years. Democracy was replaced in almost all societies by **monarchy**.

Under a monarchy (an absolute monarchy, that is – not the constitutional monarchy that we have in the UK today), the monarch is the source of all earthly power. What he or she says goes, without contradiction. This applies also to those chosen by him or her to support his or her rule. So there really isn't any room for free speech, in the sense of criticising, or having different opinions from, those in power. In the pre-modern world, criticising those in power was regarded as **sedition**. If you were found guilty of sedition you could face imprisonment, torture or death.

Don't argue with God

Where did the monarch get his or her power from? **God**. Who was responsible for interpreting God's will to people? In Europe, it was the Christian **Church**. From the adoption of Christianity by the Emperor Constantine in the fourth century, until the Reformation in the sixteenth century, the church in Europe meant the Roman Catholic Church. This was (is) a highly hierarchical organisation, with a clear chain of command down from the Pope in Rome, via bishops and then priests to ordinary lay people. The Pope is chosen by the Holy Spirit (who is God), and is the direct successor of Saint Peter, who was chosen by Jesus Christ (who is also God). So if you had your own opinions about religion (or anything else the church pronounced on), and those opinions were different from what the church taught, you were essentially saying that God had got it wrong. This was not a good idea. Challenging the teachings of the church was called **heresy**. If you criticised – or even worse denied the existence of – God, that was **blasphemy**. Like sedition, both heresy and blasphemy could have you imprisoned, tortured or killed. And even if you got away with these crimes in this life, you would go straight to hell if you died without repenting of them.

Of course, it was all a little more complicated than that. In reality, there were many disputes and discussions, often leading to significant changes, within both politics and religion. There were factions at court, each arguing their point of view. Trainee priests were taught theology using debating techniques, and there were numerous disputes about theology (how we should understand God). However, the default assumption was that there was a final, absolute truth, and that the purpose of debate and discussion was to find that final truth.

The early modern age (c. 1500–1776)

In the end, it was religion that got everyone thinking for themselves. The emergence in the early sixteenth century of **Protestantism** led to the **Reformation**, in which churches across Europe broke with the authority of Rome, and started going their own way. In England, the Church of England was established, with the monarch as its Supreme Governor (he still is).

Protestantism originally referred to those who 'protested' against the authority of the Catholic Church. It opened the door to the possibility that people might discover the truth by their own efforts,

What is God saying?

rather than simply by obeying the direction of their superiors. No longer did you have to believe what the priest told you. You could read the Bible for yourself, in your own language, and work out what God was saying to you.

It turned out that God was saying different things to different people. It would have been nice if everyone could have exchanged their different interpretations in a spirit of mutual tolerance, trying to find the truth together, or at least respecting each others' opinions. It didn't work out like that. Across Europe, people were imprisoned, tortured and killed for having heretical opinions (that is, opinions different from whoever happened to be in power at that moment in that country), and brutal wars broke out across Europe between followers of different versions of Christianity. In England, the Civil Wars of the mid-seventeenth century pitted royalists with a version of Christianity more sympathetic to Catholicism against the more severe and uncompromising Puritans. People spoke freely, often with great passion and at great length, but they also suffered terrible consequences for doing so.

A later development was more hopeful for free speech, however. The eighteenth century is often described as the Age of Enlightenment. The **Enlightenment** emphasised the use of reason and observation over the blind acceptance of the dogmas of the church, and as such, positively encouraged free discussion, individual opinion and tolerance of difference. Free speech was a central value of the Enlightenment, and many of the ideas we now have about the value of free speech derive from that period. Enlightenment ideas did much to inspire the American and French Revolutions.

The modern era (c. 1776 – the present)

With the Declaration of Independence in 1776, the United States of America became the first democracy in the modern world (with serious limitations – only rich white men were allowed to vote). In 1789, the French Revolution overthrew the monarchy, similarly paving the way for democracy in France, at least until the next emperor (a kind of super-monarch) came along.

You can read more about both these revolutions and their impact in Chapter 5, **Democracy**. They matter in relation to free speech because free speech was (and is) given high status by both America and France. Free speech was exalted as one of the ideals of the French Revolution, as expressed in the 1789 Declaration of the Rights of Man and Citizens:

No laws against free speech

'The free communication of ideas and opinions is one of the most precious rights of man. Any citizen may therefore speak, write and publish freely …'

The newly formed United States enshrined its right to free speech in the First Amendment to the Constitution, passed in 1791, which states:

'Congress shall make no law … abridging the freedom of speech, or of the press.'

This tradition continues in the contemporary US, which has one of the most liberal free speech regimes in the world.

These noble ideals were tarnished, however, in the aftermath of both revolutions. In America, the practice of slavery, and the stubborn persistence of institutional racism even after slavery was outlawed, systematically denied black Americans the right to speak (or indeed live) freely. In France, the Terror saw thousands of people brutally murdered for expressing opinions which marked them out as 'enemies of the people'. But at least the idea of free speech was out there.

As democracy gradually spread and developed across the world in the nineteenth and twentieth centuries, free speech came to be more highly valued and protected. However, democracy has never gone unchallenged. During the twentieth century, many democracies around the world were replaced by **dictatorships**, giving absolute power to either one person or a very small group of people, and putting an end to the practice of free speech. Imprisonment, torture and death once again lay in store for anyone who criticised those in power.

Some dictatorships were overthrown. Nazism collapsed following Germany's defeat in the Second World War in 1945; the fascist regimes in Spain, Portugal and Greece transitioned peacefully to democracy in the 1970s; the communist regimes in Russia and Eastern Europe imploded in 1989–1990. However, this does not mean that free speech now rules the world. Russia has replaced a communist dictatorship with a regime which can fairly be described as fascist, brutally suppressing any criticism of the government. China, with a population of nearly one and a half billion, has a leadership which rigidly controls what its people can and cannot say, write or read. Dictatorships or near dictatorships control many other countries, silencing criticism from their opponents and denying the right to say what you want.

I am Charlie

The return of religion

The restriction of speech on religious grounds has not gone away in the modern era. The rise in particular of Islamic fundamentalism has seen many regimes practise an extreme form of **censorship**, banning texts which contradict or are seen to criticise the teachings of Islam. This has also impacted on non-Muslim-majority countries. In 1989, following the publication of his novel *The Satanic Verses*, which was perceived to be disrespectful of the Prophet Muhammad, the British writer Salman Rushdie was forced into hiding after the Iranian government issued a *fatwa* calling for his assassination. He eventually emerged from hiding, but in August 2022 he was stabbed and seriously injured by an Islamist extremist while giving a lecture in New York. In January 2015, the office of the French satirical magazine *Charlie Hebdo*, which had published cartoons mocking the Prophet Muhammad, was attacked by Islamist gunmen who killed twelve people and injured eleven more. Following the attack, thousands of French people took to the streets holding up placards saying '*Je suis Charlie*' ('I am Charlie'), expressing solidarity with both the victims of the gunmen and the right to free speech, which is one of the founding principles of the French Republic.

Until quite recently, censorship of writing that showed disrespect for Christianity was still possible in the UK, thanks to a rarely used but still existing law against blasphemy. In 1977, the campaigner Mary Whitehouse successfully launched a private prosecution under this law of the magazine *Gay News* for publishing a poem, 'The Love That Dares To Speak Its Name', which imagined Jesus having gay relationships with his disciples, his guards, a centurion and Pontius Pilate. Unsuccessful attempts were made in 2005 to sue the BBC for its programme *Jerry Springer: The Opera* under the same law for what many Christians saw as a disrespectful presentation of Jesus. The blasphemy law was abolished in England and Wales in 2008, in Northern Ireland in 2020, and in Scotland in 2021.

In the US, school districts are largely controlled by local officials who are elected and are therefore obliged to respond to popular pressure. A very significant number of books have been banned from school syllabuses and libraries following organised protests from fundamentalist Christian campaigners, on the grounds that they are immoral and / or contradict Christian teaching.

Social media

The arrival of social media in the early years of the twenty-first century has changed the free speech landscape dramatically. People are no longer dependent on 'gatekeepers' such as publishers and editors. Anyone can now publish anything at any time at little or no cost in a way that is accessible to anyone with an internet connection anywhere in the world.

Social media can play a significant part in uprisings against tyrannical governments, for example in the so-called 'Arab Spring' of the early 2010s, allowing people to share safely and effectively criticism of the powerful and plans for protest, in a way that protects their identity and location. However, some governments, such as those of Russia, China, Afghanistan and Iran, have found ways to shut down platforms that are too critical of them.

Social media spreads hate

The rise of social media has nonetheless also brought problems for free speech. Anonymous accounts can be used to bombard people with racist, misogynistic or homophobic abuse, known as trolling, sometimes along with threats of violence or even death. Fear of such abuse has prompted many people to withdraw from debate on social media, and there is a case for saying that its prevalence online can change the way people behave in real life towards women and ethnic and sexual minorities, leading to an increase in online persecution and real-life violent assaults. Young and vulnerable people can be put in danger by the dissemination of sites and posts celebrating eating disorders, or advocating suicide or self-harm. The use of algorithms by social media tends to drive people towards more and more extreme content, keeping everyone in a bubble of people who think the same way they do. The brevity and immediacy of social media, while facilitating ease of communication, is not favourable to thoughtful, measured reflection.

Social media can also lead to dangerous falsehoods, known as fake news, being spread without challenge. Millions of people have put their lives at risk by refusing the Covid-19 vaccine, having believed false claims on social media that it is harmful. Similarly, social media played a large part in disseminating the lie that the 2020 US presidential election was stolen from Donald Trump. This led ultimately to the storming of the Capitol in Washington by a violent mob on January 6th, 2021, which left five people dead and posed a serious threat to the stability of American democracy. Following this attack, Facebook, Twitter and YouTube banned President Trump (though he was restored to all three platforms by March 2023). The Trump ban was an exception, though. Social media is daily filled with lies, abuse and threats, without the companies that own them taking any action – perhaps because this kind of content means clicks, and clicks mean cash.

Social media brings more clearly into focus both the opportunities and the dangers of unlimited free speech.

Political correctness, no-platforming, safe spaces and cancel culture

The twenty-first century has also seen the emergence of new debates around limitations on free speech. **Political correctness** is the term commonly given to the attempt to police language in a way which ensures that minority groups are protected from offence, by banning the use of certain words or phrases. **No-platforming** is the practice (most common in universities) of excluding speakers who are perceived to have opinions which are offensive to certain groups. Some institutions have a **safe space** policy, which is designed to ensure that members of certain minority groups are protected from speech which might cause offence to them. Allied to these moves is the rise of so-called **cancel culture**. People (particularly those with a high public profile) who have said or written something that causes offence find themselves subjected to concerted attacks on social media, and may end up losing their jobs or even their careers. One particularly strict form of censorship of offensive opinions is the criminalisation of **Holocaust denial** (making the claim that the murder of six million Jews by the Nazis never happened). Holocaust denial is not against the law in the UK, but it is illegal in Israel, Canada and sixteen European countries, including Germany. Elsewhere, such views may be prosecuted under laws governing public communication of hatred or grossly offensive views, promotion of racist or xenophobic attitudes, the denial of war crimes, or justification of genocide.

Critics of restrictions on offensive speech argue that the answer to bad speech is more speech: offensive opinions should be allowed, but vigorously rebutted. Defenders of these practices argue that they are a way of ensuring that the least powerful in society are protected from those who would attack and exclude them. You could say that one side prioritises *parrhesia*, while the other prioritises *isegoria* (see pages 39-40).

What you can and can't say or write in the UK

You can't say what you like

There never has been, and almost certainly never will be, a time when you could say or write anything you wanted. Although the UK is a democracy, there are significant limitations on what you can say and write.

Legal restrictions on free speech

Libel

Libel is defaming someone through the publication in writing – in a book, magazine or newspaper, or on social media, in a text message or website – of something about another person which tends to bring them into 'hatred, ridicule or contempt, or to lower them in the estimation of right-thinking members of society'. Libel is normally a civil offence – that is, if someone has libelled you, rather than the police seeking a prosecution, you have to sue them at your own cost. If someone is successfully sued for libel, they have to pay compensation to the plaintiff (the person suing them) and also their legal costs. There is also a (more serious) offence of criminal libel, for libels which are considered by a judge to be against the public interest. People accused of criminal libel are prosecuted in court in the same way as someone accused of any other crime, and may face fines or imprisonment.

How can you defend yourself against an accusation of libel? The best defence is to prove that what you said is true. The other main defence is to prove that what you said was a matter of opinion: that it is 'fair comment on a matter of public interest'.

A couple of (fictional) examples to illustrate these defences. A newspaper publishes a story about a famous (married) actor's affair with his make-up assistant. The actor sues for libel. If the newspaper can prove he has been having an affair with his make-up assistant, they win, and the actor has to pay their legal costs. But if it turns out the story was a pack of lies printed only to win readers, the actor wins, and the newspaper has to pay both his legal costs and a sum in compensation. Then the newspaper publishes a review of the actor's latest film, saying that his performance is so wooden that Pinocchio could have done a better job. The actor sues again. The newspaper argues that the review is 'fair comment' (an aesthetic judgement) on 'a matter of public interest' (a high-profile new film). The newspaper wins, and this time the actor has to pay the newspaper's legal costs.

Libel laws silence people

The UK law on libel has many flaws. Some awards for compensation are extremely high, and can ruin individuals or publishers. Even if someone successfully defends themselves against libel, the experience of doing so can be stressful and time-consuming. There are many examples of wealthy and powerful people, who can afford to hire the best lawyers, using the threat of libel to silence individuals who might otherwise have exposed their wrongdoing. Similarly, tabloid newspapers can get away with printing untrue stories about vulnerable people because they know that their victims are unlikely to want to take them on in the courts. Even if their victims sue and win, the newspapers may not be deterred, as their big budgets can absorb the costs.

One distinctive feature of the UK libel law is that, unlike in most other countries, the burden of proof is on the defendant. That is, the defendant has to prove that what was written is true, rather than the plaintiff having to prove that it is false. This has led to the growth of 'libel tourism'. Wealthy and powerful people will try to silence their critics by suing them for libel in the UK. They can do this if even no more than one copy of the offending newspaper, magazine or book has been sold in the UK.

Libel can only be committed against a living person. So you can say or write what you like about someone once they're dead.

Slander

Slander means defaming someone (damaging their good name or reputation) through a passing speech or gesture – one which has not been recorded. Defamatory speech in the course of a film or the performance of a play, the broadcast of a TV or radio programme, or a voicemail or recorded message is still treated as libel. Like libel, slander is a civil offence: if you believe you have been slandered, the burden is on you to sue the person you claim has slandered you.

The principal reasons for accusing someone of slander are:

1. Falsely accusing them of committing a serious crime.
2. Falsely accusing them of having a contagious disease.
3. Making false and damaging accusations about their work or business affairs.

What is obscene?

Hate speech

The Race Relations Act, passed in 1965, made it illegal to stir up hatred or allow discrimination against any section of the public '... on the ground of colour, race, or ethnic or national origins.' In 1986, the Public Order Act included defamation on grounds of religion, amplified in the 2006 Racial and Religious Hatred Act as: 'A person who uses threatening words or behaviour, or displays any written material which is threatening, is guilty of an offence if he intends thereby to stir up religious hatred.' The 2008 Criminal Justice and Immigration Act broadened the scope and made it illegal to use language which expresses hatred towards someone on the grounds of their colour, race, sex, disability, nationality (including citizenship), ethnic or national origin, religion, gender identity or reassignment or sexual orientation.

Obscenity

Under the Obscene Publications Act of 1959, it is against the law to publish material which has 'a tendency ... to deprave and corrupt'. The most famous case under this law came in 1960 when Penguin Books was prosecuted for publishing D.H. Lawrence's novel *Lady Chatterley's Lover*. Several high-profile writers and teachers gave evidence in court to support the defence that it was a work of literature, not pornography. Penguin Books was found not guilty. The trial is often seen as heralding the beginning of a more tolerant, open society in Britain.

During the twentieth century, the act was frequently used to prosecute makers and distributors of pornography. This tended to drive the pornography industry underground, which had the result of turning porn into a profitable business opportunity for criminal gangs (and not a few corrupt police officers). However, the rise of the internet and changing attitudes towards sexual freedom in the twenty-first century made it harder to enforce this law, and in 2019 the Crown Prosecution Service issued guidance that no one should be prosecuted for depicting any legal act taking place between consenting adults.

The Protection of Children Act, passed in 1978, made it illegal to make, distribute or possess pornographic images of children. This continues to be rigorously enforced with universal support.

Speak out and lose your job

Contempt of court

Writing or saying anything which could prejudice a fair trial (for example, implying or stating that the accused is guilty before the jury have given their verdict) is against the law.

National security

Writing or saying anything that could prejudice national security (for example, revealing details of an anti-terrorist operation) is against the law.

Professional restrictions

Many professions have explicit codes of conduct that restrict what they can say. Doctors, lawyers, bankers, priests, therapists and counsellors are all expected to respect the confidentiality of those they serve. Repeating something told them in confidence could mean the end of their career, though this duty of confidentiality is usually suspended if they have reason to believe that a vulnerable person may be in danger. Teachers are expected to conceal their political opinions for fear of influencing young people. BBC journalists reporting on political issues are not allowed to reveal their own views. When he was Prince of Wales, King Charles III would often speak out on issues he felt strongly about. Since becoming king, he has a constitutional duty not to express any controversial opinions. Many businesses require employees to sign a contract preventing them from sharing commercial secrets with rivals. In most professions it is wise not to say exactly what you think of your clients or customers if you want them to keep coming back, or to express your honest opinion of your boss if you want to keep your job.

Non-disclosure agreements

'Non-disclosure agreements' (NDAs) are a legal way of restricting what someone can say or write about a particular matter. They can be used for valid commercial reasons, to prevent someone who has left a business from passing on confidential information about the business to its rivals. Less ethically, NDAs can be used to prevent employees who have been victims of bullying or sexual harassment from speaking out and damaging a company's reputation, often in return for a substantial pay-off. Harvey Weinstein, a prominent producer in Hollywood, was a prolific user of NDAs to silence the many women in the film industry whom he had sexually assaulted. In a powerful example of the way in which free speech, expressed through a free press, can be used to uncover wrongdoing, his crimes were eventually exposed by investigative journalists from *The New*

York Times. In 2020, Weinstein was found guilty of multiple counts of rape and sexual assault and sentenced to 23 years in jail. Free speech helped to achieve justice for the women Weinstein had abused.

Censor yourself

Reputational damage

Saying or writing something which causes offence can be fatal to your career or livelihood. This is especially the case for those in the public eye. Many people have made ill-advised comments on social media in an unthinking moment, only to find those remarks going viral and leading to a campaign to have them sacked, even though they have broken no law. Such remarks may have been posted many years earlier, long before the person concerned was even in the public eye. A tasteless joke which would once have disappeared into the smoky ether of a student bar, never to be heard again, is now up there forever and can come back to haunt its author. Fear of this kind of reaction can lead people to practise **self-censorship**. This is a more subtle, and in some ways more insidious, form of restriction on free speech. People aren't imprisoned, tortured or killed for saying certain things – they just stop saying them. Or, to look at it another way, society's norms teach people respect for vulnerable groups.

2. THE ISSUES

The right to free speech is one of the greatest benefits that a society can confer on its citizens. It's one of the first things that dictators get rid of, and one of the first things that democracies defend. Why? Two reasons:

1. **Free speech makes us more fully human.**
2. **Free speech helps society to function better.**

1. Free speech makes us more fully human.

Free speech helps us to be ourselves. In a society that supports free speech, people can say what they truly think. This means they can be who they truly are. Societies that support free speech are better places to live in. No one likes being silenced; being silenced means losing a part of your identity. People who live in dictatorships report feeling that they can never be fully themselves. A world where you are worried that you may lose your job or be sent to prison for saying the wrong thing is not somewhere you want to live.

Free speech is never really free

2. It helps society to function better.

Societies that support free speech work better. A free exchange of views is more likely to lead to effective decisions being made. Why? Because all the options will be given a hearing; bad ideas will be exposed and rejected; good ideas will be made better by being refined. If those in power make mistakes, they will be challenged and corrected, and we will be better led as a result.

So, free speech is clearly a good thing. It makes us happier, and it makes society run better. We can't get too much of it, surely? What is there even to debate about here?

Well, free speech may not always be a good thing. Here's an analogy.

No one but the most hardcore environmentalist would call for an absolute ban on the use of cars. It is clearly necessary and reasonable for people sometimes to drive to go places. They may need cars to get to work, to visit family and friends, to run their businesses. But, equally, we have rules about how cars can be used. We don't let people drive cars on pavements. We don't let them drive at 200 miles an hour. We don't let them drive in a way that threatens other people's safety. We don't let them drive when they're under the influence of alcohol or drugs. We don't let them go through red lights. We don't let children, or people who haven't passed their driving test, drive a car. We can debate what the rules around car use should be. But, just as no one can reasonably argue for the complete abolition of cars, no one can reasonably argue that there should be no rules, that anyone should be allowed to use their car in any way without any form of restriction. Cars can do a lot of good if used well; they can also do a lot of bad if used badly. That's why we need rules about their use.

Speech, too, can do both good and harm, as we've seen already from some of the examples so far in this chapter. So it's not unreasonable to say there should be rules about its use. Free speech can never be absolutely free.

The two key questions about free speech are:

- **What limits should be set on free speech?**
- **How should these be enforced?**

These questions can be broken down even further:

1. **What should we do with speech that is not true?**
2. **What should we do with speech that causes offence?**
3. **How can we make sure that everyone has equal access to free speech?**

Let the truth prevail

1. What should we do with speech that is not true?

Some lies are fairly harmless. Some 'white lies', such as 'That hairstyle really suits you', 'Father Christmas is coming tonight', or 'It's so nice to see you!' may actually be acts of kindness. Other lies are more dangerous.

We've seen above that there is recourse in the UK law on libel for someone whose reputation has been damaged by a lie (though suing someone for libel is not cheap and not easy). However, there are other lies which are not covered by the law of libel, and which may cause great damage if widely believed.

Let's take one example: 'Climate change is a fraud.'

This is a lie. The existence and dangers of climate change have been proved beyond doubt. If everyone believed this lie – even if enough people believed this lie – it would make it even harder to take concerted action against climate change than it already is. The consequences of this inaction could be literally fatal for millions of people and even potentially for the whole of humanity.

So, what should we do with this dangerous lie? There is an obvious answer: rebut it. Show that it is wrong. There is ample evidence to prove the reality of climate change. All we have to do is to get the facts out there and let them speak for themselves. The answer to bad speech is not less speech, it is more speech. The way to limit falsehood is to lift all limits on the means of challenging falsehood. Let everyone speak, and in the end the lies will be exposed and the truth will prevail.

This – sometimes known as the **absolutist** argument – undoubtedly makes a powerful case for having no restrictions on free speech. There are a couple of problems with it, though.

The first is that it depends on the assumption that all sides of the case will be **heard equally**. That doesn't always happen. Thanks to social media, lies about climate change (and many other issues) can spread as fast as a virus (and infect people just

Should dangerous lies be illegal?

as easily and dangerously). Although the internet was set up to be a free space for open debate, in practice it pushes people into echo chambers where they only hear views that confirm their own prejudices. Even in the mainstream media, people will choose outlets that repeat back to them what they already think, even if it is (dangerously) untrue. So perhaps dangerous lies need to be treated like dangerous driving, by making them against the law. This is the thinking behind the criminalisation of Holocaust denial in many countries: the dangers of denying the reality of the Nazi-led genocide are greater than the benefits of untrammelled free speech. Should climate change denial be made illegal for similar reasons?

The other problem with the argument for unrestricted free speech is that it assumes that people are all entirely **rational** and can be convinced by **facts** and **logic**. You don't have to look at other people (or, let's be honest, yourself) for very long to realise that this is not always the case. We've already looked in Chapter Two, **How to think like a debater**, at some of the ways in which bias and emotion can cloud our thinking. Dangerous conspiracy theories can become widely believed because they tap into very basic and powerful human insecurities. If you can't bear to think of what climate change might do to the world (or face up to what we need to do to combat it), it's easier to pretend it's not happening. You might, for very good reasons, feel left out, forgotten, marginalised, and that your life is out of control. If you can convince yourself that the government is imposing environmental restrictions as part of a plot to control you, the world makes more sense. Paranoia, paradoxically, makes us feel safer, as it turns a chaotic, meaningless world into one which has a recognisable pattern. Like hard drugs, this sort of lie is consoling, but also powerful, addictive and destructive; so perhaps, like hard drugs, these lies should be made illegal in the interests of protecting people.

But then we run into another problem. Who gets to decide which lies are dangerous? Who, come to that, gets to decide whether something is true or not? Dictators and tyrants down the ages have used the protection of the people as an excuse for restricting speech, when in fact they are only protecting their own power. So how do we find out what is true and what is not? Back to the absolutist argument: let everything be said by everyone, and surely the truth will emerge. However, the absolutist approach depends on everyone having equal access to the arguments, and everyone being entirely rational. All right, says the free speech absolutist, I agree we haven't achieved either of those desirable conditions yet; the answer is not to give up, but to keep trying to achieve them.

The argument for unrestricted free speech as a way of dealing with falsehood is more **optimistic**; the argument for banning dangerous lies is more **pessimistic**. The first values **freedom to** speak; the second values **freedom from** falsehood. Both are valid arguments.

Do you have a right not to be offended?

2. What should we do with speech that causes offence?

'Sticks and stones may break my bones, but words will never hurt me.'

That's what I was told to say to bullies when I was younger. It's not true. Unkind words do cause hurt. But does that mean people should not be allowed to use speech that causes **offence** to other people?

You could say no one has the right not to be offended. That asserting such a right means taking away someone else's right to free expression. That (returning to the 'absolutist' free speech argument) the answer to offensive speech is more speech, challenging the offence, engaging with it, not shutting it down. That banning hate speech simply makes martyrs out of the haters, allowing them to present themselves as the victims. Let the haters speak, so we can expose their prejudice for what it is.

As with the argument about tackling dangerous lies through unrestricted free speech, this argument assumes that there is an **equality of power** between the different speakers. A gay boy being bullied at school; a Muslim girl in a hijab who has abuse shouted at her in the street; a woman bombarded on social media with threats of sexual assault – none of these people will feel that they are engaged in a rational discussion with an opponent whose arguments they can calmly disprove. They will feel that they are under attack from people bigger and nastier and more powerful than themselves, from whom they need protection. Such language may put them in physical danger; there is substantial evidence to suggest that abusive language legitimises and encourages violence against those targeted by it. Even if the offensive language does not immediately lead to violence, it can be argued that hate speech is itself a kind of violence. Being on the receiving end of a barrage of abuse can induce a physical response, making it feel like a physical attack.

Challenge or ignore?

So here we see similar issues to the ones we confronted with the issues around false speech. A free speech absolutist would say that good speech will drive out bad speech, and that restricting even the most hateful speech is counterproductive as it makes a martyr out of the hater. Either challenge the hate or ignore it. A supporter of restrictions on hate speech would say that sometimes the circumstances mean that good speech doesn't get a chance, because the terms are so unequal, and that sometimes the right of protection for vulnerable people is a higher good than the right to free speech. You couldn't reasonably object to a man who runs at another man with a knife being knocked down by a policeman, handcuffed and arrested on the grounds that his right to liberty has been taken away from him. He forfeited that right when he threatened another person's safety. Similarly, people who use their right to free speech to abuse people weaker than themselves have forfeited that right.

Then there is a further complication when dealing with language that people find offensive. Who gets to decide what is offensive? Is it the person who considers themselves offended? What happens when people have different, or even contradictory, views on what is offensive? When a person's opinions become a part of their identity, any challenge to these opinions may feel like a personal attack, an expression of hatred, and therefore something that should not be allowed. But if another person holds different opinions, not being allowed to express those opinions for fear of being accused of causing offence may itself seem like a kind of hatred.

Let's take an example to explore these issues.

Ayesha and Ben are both in Year 12. Ayesha is a Muslim. Her family's Muslim faith is a fundamental part of her identity. Ben has recently come out as gay.

Ayesha and Ben are both in Miss Harris's A-Level Philosophy and Religion class. One day the class is discussing religion and sexual morality. Ayesha says that her Muslim faith teaches her that same-sex relationships are against nature.

Ben goes to see Miss Harris after the lesson to complain. He says that he found what Ayesha said offensive, and that he does not feel safe being in a lesson with someone with these views. He asks if Ayesha can be moved out of the class.

Miss Harris calls Ayesha into her office. She tells Ayesha that Ben found what she said about same-sex relationships offensive. Ayesha says she didn't mean to cause anyone offence, she was simply saying what she believed. Miss Harris says that Ben's sexuality is a fundamental part of his identity, and that he should be allowed to express it within the school freely and without fear. Ayesha replies that her Muslim faith is a fundamental part of her identity, and that she should be entitled to express it within the school freely and without fear. Miss Harris tells Ayesha that Ben has been the victim of homophobic bullying. Ayesha tells Miss Harris that she has been the victim of Islamophobic bullying. Miss Harris tells Ayesha that Ben doesn't feel safe being in a class with someone who denies his gay identity. Ayesha tells Miss Harris that she doesn't feel safe being in a class with someone who denies her Muslim identity.

What's Miss Harris to do?

Who's right? Which is more important, Ben's sexual identity or Ayesha's religious identity? Should Ayesha be moved out of the class? Should she be allowed to stay on the understanding that she does not express her beliefs about same-sex relationships? Or should Ben be told not to challenge what Ayesha's faith teaches her about same-sex relationships? What's Miss Harris to do? What would you do if you were her?

When I was at school, homophobic, misogynistic and racist language (often under the guise of humour) was everywhere: in the playground, in the lunchroom, in the classroom (sometimes from teachers), and on television every night. Virtually no one would ever challenge this language. Life was much harder for gay people, women and people of colour as a result. We are well rid of those days, and no one would want them back. But how to deal with language and views that cause offence is not a simple matter.

3. How can we make sure that everyone has equal access to free speech?

A free press is one of the cornerstones of democracy. It allows for the free exchange of views in a public arena, in newspapers, on radio or TV, which can be accessed by anyone, and so ensures a full and open discussion of important issues. Dictatorships and tyrannies fear and censor the press, which shows how important it is. A free press can speak the truth to power, challenging incompetent and corrupt leaders and exposing wrongdoers.

The problem with the free press is that … it isn't really free. It costs a lot of money to produce a newspaper or to run a radio or TV channel. Who pays? Often it is companies who advertise in the newspaper or on the radio or TV channel. Will that newspaper

Free speech is expensive

or radio or TV channel be willing to run stories critical of any of the companies who provide them with their income? Unlikely.

And don't forget that newspapers and radio and TV channels are themselves commercial enterprises, which can be bought and sold. It is perfectly possible (and very common) for a wealthy person to buy a newspaper or broadcasting organisation and then instruct the editors to broadcast news and commentary with a bias that favours the owner's interests. If the editors protest, they can be fired and new ones hired who will do what they are told. If one person is rich enough, they can buy up almost all the news outlets in a country and ensure that only one way of seeing the world is ever heard. Governments may find it difficult to prevent this from happening, as they may face an unanswered storm of criticism from the news outlets if they do.

One solution to the problem of media ownership is to have public broadcasting organisations which are not owned by private individuals, and which are instructed to be politically neutral. In the UK, the BBC operates in this way. However, this way of doing things brings further issues.

False equivalence

The BBC is obliged to give both sides of any question that is discussed. But what if one side is manifestly wrong? For many years, the BBC gave equal time both to people who were concerned about climate change and to people who denied that climate change existed. It has now changed that policy, but not until a lot of airtime had been given to positions that were not supported by facts or evidence, and which encouraged complacency in the face of an emergency. This is called **false equivalence**.

State control

If the government provides the funding for a national broadcasting organisation, it has a lot of power over that organisation. In the UK, the BBC is funded by a licence fee, which everyone who owns a TV set or who accesses BBC content online has to pay, with very few exceptions. But the government gets to choose the level that fee is set at. Even if the government of the day does not issue direct threats to the BBC, fear of having the licence fee cut might make editors and journalists think twice before being too critical of the government. So a supposedly impartial media outlet may, at least implicitly, be under more state control than it should be. In countries which are not democracies, the state-controlled media will be very explicitly supportive of the government and will not criticise them.

The internet

The internet isn't free

But all this talk about newspapers and broadcasting is hopelessly out of date, isn't it? We have the internet now. We don't need to own newspapers or TV or radio companies; we don't need wealthy backers any more to enable us to say what needs to be said. Just get your phone out of your pocket and tell the world what you think. The internet has set us all free.

Or has it?

If you want to spread your views online, it's not enough to just fire off a tweet or an Instagram post and then sit back and wait for the world to change. To do the job properly, you need to buy vast quantities of data from tech companies and then pay rooms full of clever people to use this data to target and manipulate the people you want to persuade. This approach can be (and has been) used to manipulate elections and referendums, often in a way that can be much harder to detect than overt bias in newspapers or broadcasters. Acting on this scale costs a lot of money, so we are back with the problem that the private ownership of print and broadcast outlets presents. The internet might be free to use. But using it effectively doesn't come cheap.

So, free speech isn't really free: it costs a lot of money to spread your views, and this gives ownership of speech to those who already have wealth and power. You can deal with this problem by taking speech into government ownership, but this runs the risk of giving the government excessive power over speech.

If you leave debate in the media to the free market, you can end up with it being dominated by the views of the wealthy and powerful. If you regulate debate in the media to ensure balance and lack of bias, you can end up giving undue exposure to false or dangerous opinions. Free speech absolutists favour a free market in the media, and deal with the issue of a bias towards the wealthy and powerful by setting up their own alternative voices. Supporters of media regulation would impose restrictions to ensure both sides are heard, and would deal with the problem of false equivalence by ensuring that only arguments that are supported by evidence are heard.

The question is, which is more important: **freedom of speech** or **equality of access to speech**? Back to the ancient Greeks; back to ***parrhesia*** versus ***isegoria***.

Rebut or ban?

3. THE POINT OF CLASH

How can we best choose between alternative views on how society should be run? By letting anyone say anything **without restriction**, and allowing the truth to emerge from the contest? Will no-holds-barred debate ensure the survival of only the fittest ideas? Or does debate need **rules** and **restrictions** to ensure that (as in a formal debate) each side has equal exposure?

Can we trust people to come to the best conclusion using their **rationality**? Or do we need to be protected from our own **biases** and **blind spots**?

Which works better: debate **with rules** or debate **without rules**?

What should we do with dangerous lies? **Rebut** them or **ban** them?

What's the best response to offensive speech? Challenging it? Meeting it with a dignified silence? Or protecting vulnerable people from it? Which is more important: freedom to speak or freedom from abuse? Should we **rebut** offence or **restrict** offence?

How **free** is free speech? How do we stop it being dominated by the wealthy and powerful? How do we ensure all voices are heard? Which is more important: **freedom to express** ideas, or **equality of exposure** to ideas?

What is the answer to bad speech? **More speech** or **less speech**?

4. THE ARGUMENTS

For unrestricted free speech	Against unrestricted free speech
In unrestricted discussion, true and good ideas will thrive and false and bad ideas will fail.	Unrestricted discussion will be dominated by the most powerful, who will exclude the less powerful.
The best response to lies is to challenge them, not ban them.	Some lies are so dangerous they need to be banned for our protection.
No one has the right not to be offended.	Everyone is entitled to be protected from abuse.
Verbal abuse is not the same as physical abuse.	Verbal abuse can be as bad as physical abuse, and can also lead to physical violence.
The best response to prejudice is to use free speech to challenge it.	The best response to prejudice is to make it unacceptable and / or illegal.
An unrestricted media is our best guarantee of our freedom.	An unrestricted media is likely to end up being dominated by the wealthy and powerful.
Rules about impartiality in the media interfere with our freedom; we should be allowed to make up our own minds.	Rules about impartiality in the media are necessary to ensure all voices are heard.
Freedom to express ourselves is a fundamental part of being human.	Protecting vulnerable people from abuse and lies is a fundamental part of being humane.
The answer to bad speech is more speech.	The answer to bad speech is less speech.

5. THE MOTIONS

1. This house would ban anyone guilty of using homophobic / misogynistic / racist language from schools / universities.
2. This house would ban anyone guilty of using homophobic / misogynistic / racist language from public office.
3. This house would ban the study in schools of texts which contain racial stereotypes.
4. This house would prevent schools and universities from banning speakers on the grounds of their beliefs.
5. This house would make it a legal requirement for social media companies to take down abusive content.
6. This house would make it illegal for any one person to own more than 10% of media outlets in a country.
7. This house would make the BBC a subscription-only service.
8. This house would abolish the requirement for the BBC to be impartial.
9. This house would ban the use of anonymous accounts on social media.
10. This house would make Holocaust denial a criminal offence.
11. This house would make climate change denial a criminal offence.
12. This house would abolish the law of libel.
13. This house opposes all restrictions on free speech.

Keep thinking…

A selection of further reading and viewing to help you think more deeply about the issues around free speech.

Free Speech: Ten Principles for a Connected World, Timothy Garton Ash (Atlantic, 2016)

Garton Ash played a heroic role in covering the fall of communism across Eastern Europe in 1989, and has therefore had a lot of experience of living in a society which crushes free speech. In this book, he covers the history of free speech and its enemies, and proposes a ten-point charter for its protection in the modern world. Garton Ash fervently believes in the value of unrestricted free speech as a way of promoting liberty and progress, and makes a well-supported, thorough and compelling case for the absolutist approach.

We Need New Stories: Challenging the Toxic Myths behind our Age of Discontent, Nesrine Malik (Weidenfeld & Nicolson, 2019)

This is an excellent book to read next to Garton Ash's *Free Speech* as it makes a strong counterargument to free speech absolutism. Malik persuasively challenges the notion that there is a 'free speech crisis' and that 'political correctness means you can't say anything any more'. What people are objecting to, she argues, is that they are no longer allowed to abuse without consequence people who are weaker than them. Interactions between people have always been (and should always be) policed by social convention and / or the law. So-called 'political correctness' is nothing more than a necessary precondition for a respectful and cohesive society in which the weak are protected from the strong.

On Liberty, John Stuart Mill (1859)

This is the original and best defence of free speech. It is regarded as sacred scripture by advocates of free speech absolutism (or would be if they believed in sacred scripture, which obviously they don't). It is stuffed full of highly quotable arguments in support of unrestricted free speech, expressed with great clarity and force. A must-read for anyone debating free speech issues.

Denial, directed by Mick Jackson (BBC Films, 2016)

Based on the true story of Deborah Lipstadt (Rachel Weisz), a Jewish American academic who in 1996 was sued for libel by the Holocaust-denying British historian David Irving (Timothy Spall), this film dramatises the dilemma faced by many people whose careers, finances and even personal safety are put in jeopardy when they dare to speak a dangerous truth. It also provokes a lot of thought about what should be done about malicious lies like Holocaust denial: confront them or ignore them? Lipstadt won her case, but Irving won a lot of publicity for his repellent views.

She Said, directed by Maria Schrader (Universal Pictures, 2022)

In 2017, two women journalists at *The New York Times*, Jodi Kantor (Zoe Kazan) and Megan Twohey (Carey Mulligan), received a tip-off that the Hollywood producer Harvey Weinstein had for many years been systematically abusing women who worked for him. This film dramatises their struggle to get these women to speak out in the face of his manipulation of the legal system and his status as one of the most powerful men in the industry. The publication of their story ultimately led to Weinstein's prosecution and sparked the worldwide #MeToo movement in which millions of women spoke out about their own experiences of sexual harassment. The film is both an inspirational celebration of the power of the free press in fighting for justice, and a troubling insight into how powerful and wealthy people can silence those who would hold them to account.

CHAPTER 5

Democracy

In this chapter we're thinking about...

- **How did democracy come to be?**
- **What is democracy?**
- **Who should be allowed to vote, and why?**
- **How should we vote, and why?**

1. THE FACTS

Democracy is both very old and very new

How did we get here?

A brief history of democracy around the world

Democracy – rule by the people – is both very old and very new. It was first thought of and practised in Ancient Athens nearly 3,000 years ago. It then dropped out of view for hundreds of years, only re-emerging around two hundred and fifty years ago in America and France.

Full democracy, in the way it would be recognised by most people today, did not really arrive in any country until the early twentieth century. At the same time, the rise of communism, and its parallel ideology fascism, almost stifled modern democracy at birth. It survived, though, enjoying a strong and confident period for several decades after the Second World War, spurred on by the defeat of fascism in that conflict, the granting of independence to many former colonies, and its status as an alternative to communism.

This optimistic period culminated in the abrupt collapse of communist regimes in Russia and Eastern Europe in 1989–90. There were high hopes for a while at the end of the twentieth century that liberal democracy would become the default system for much of the world. The terrorist attacks on the US of September 11, 2001, however, and the subsequent 'war on terror', darkened the picture. Attempts to impose democracy by force on unfriendly countries on the part of the US and its allies ended in chaos and mayhem.

In the second decade of the twenty-first century, democracy is still a long way from being universal. Democracies remain in the minority worldwide, while some countries which claim to be democracies have serious flaws in their model undermining that claim. Many democracies are dangerously polarised (split into two opposing camps), with the democratic values of discussion, open-mindedness and compromise being replaced by hostility, incomprehension and a struggle for control between irreconcilable factions. Nonetheless, Winston Churchill's observation that 'democracy is the worst form of government except for all those other forms that have been tried from time to time' remains true.

Democracy is a Greek word, and it was in Greece that democracy was born, in Athens in eighth-century BCE. In some ways Ancient

Ancient Athens had the purest form of democracy

Athens had the purest and most perfect form of democracy ever seen. In *some* ways. The great gaping hole at the heart of Greek democracy was the absolute exclusion of women, and its dependence on a large population of slaves, who had no rights whatsoever. Leaving aside that democracy was restricted to a very small and entirely male elite, the Ancient Greek system had much to recommend it.

The Ancient Greeks took democracy very seriously. Whenever important decisions had to be made, the entire (male, freeborn, adult) population of Athens was expected to attend a mass meeting or assembly, called an *ekklesia*, held on a hill called the Pnyx. The day would begin with sacrifices to the gods, as the Greeks believed that democracy was a mark of divine favour. Officials would then drag a rope soaked in red paint across the main marketplace to ensure that everyone left and headed for the hill. Anyone found with red smudges on his clothes would be branded as someone neglecting his democratic duty.

Once everyone was on the hill, the order of business would be determined by the Council of Five Hundred, or *boule*, a group of citizens who were chosen randomly by lot to serve for one year only to take day-to-day decisions. Any citizen could address the crowd from a platform. Skills of oratory and persuasion were highly valued, and there was a whole class of people called 'sophists', who made their living from teaching these skills. Political parties and factions were forbidden; everyone was expected to make up their mind as an individual. At the end of the meeting, votes were taken either by a show of hands or by dropping pebbles in urns representing each side of the issue under consideration. Discussions were loud, heated and passionate, but once a decision was made, it was accepted and executed. There was a strong sense of loyalty to and ownership of the democratic system; everyone felt that they had a part to play (except for women and slaves).

Inspiring though it was, Greek democracy was an outlier for most of human history. For the next two thousand years, in almost every society, power was concentrated in the hands of a small group of people (as in Ancient Rome) or in the hands of just one person (as in monarchies). Those people were almost always men, and were almost always much richer than the rest of the people (or if they weren't rich when they started, they quickly became so). This concentration of power was said to be natural, and ordained by God. Strong leadership by very few people, it was claimed, brought order and security, while democracy would only bring chaos.

A government of laws not men

The first stirrings of a return to rule by the people came in the late eighteenth century in the British colonies of America. What began as a protest in 1775 against having to pay tax without having any say in how that tax was spent – expressed in the slogan 'no taxation without representation' – spread into a full-scale **revolution**, a complete overthrow of the existing government. Following a war with the British, what we now know as the United States of America was established. The Declaration of Independence which announced this new society on July 4th, 1776, included a resonant and timeless expression of one of the basic principles of democracy: 'Governments are instituted among Men, deriving their just powers from the **consent of the governed** … whenever any Form of Government becomes destructive of these ends, it is the Right of the People to **alter** or to **abolish** it'. In other words, no one can ever rule over anyone else without their consent; once this consent is withdrawn, those with power must relinquish it.

American democracy was supported by a detailed plan to separate powers more or less equally between the 'legislature' (Congress and the Senate), who made laws; the 'executive' (the President), who carried out the laws; and the 'judiciary' (judges), who interpreted the laws. This separation was meant to ensure that no dictatorship could arise, because no one faction or person would have absolute power. The legislature and the executive were both to be chosen ('elected') by the people. The new constitution also established another important democratic principle: **the rule of law**. This means that decisions should be taken on the basis of laws, not on the whim of those in power, that these laws should have been created by democratically elected bodies chosen by the people, and that they should apply equally to everyone. It was expressed memorably by John Adams, one of the founding fathers, as '**a government of laws not men**.'

The constitution of the United States is one of the foundational documents of democracy. Although it has undergone many amendments since, it remains the basis of all US law, and is still regarded in the US as little short of sacred scripture. Each new President begins his or her term of office by swearing to 'preserve, protect, and defend the constitution of the United States'. The new constitution fundamentally shifted the balance of power away from the few towards the many. The 'many', but not the 'all'. Back in the eighteenth century, there was a 'property qualification' for voting, meaning that only those of a certain level of wealth were allowed to vote, on the grounds that they held a greater stake in society; women could not stand for office, and had no vote; and hundreds of thousands of African slaves were not only not allowed to vote,

Liberty, equality, fraternity

but lacked even the most basic control over their lives. It was a democracy, but a democracy for rich white men only. The US would not become a true democracy, with the full involvement of all citizens regardless of wealth, gender or race, until the passing of civil rights legislation in the 1960s finally granted equal voting rights to black Americans.

Across the Atlantic, the ideas of the American Revolution were stirring things up in France. There, the absolute monarch Louis XVI was in trouble, under pressure because of an economic crisis. Popular discontent led ultimately to an uprising in Paris and the storming of the Bastille prison on July 14th, 1789. A republic was established in place of the monarchy in 1792, and in 1793 Louis XVI was executed. The republic was established on the basis of another famous democratic slogan: **liberty**, **equality**, **fraternity**. These three words sum up the ideals of democracy very neatly, but also express some of the tensions inherent in the democratic project. If **liberty** means the right to acquire and keep more money and power than someone else, how can it be reconciled with **equality**? And what if what you want to do with your **liberty** clashes with what someone else wants to do with theirs? How do you reconcile that with the solidarity implied in **fraternity**?

The revolutionaries were absolutely certain their cause was right. Too certain: any criticism, or implied criticism, of the new order was regarded as an attack on the people. The high hopes of the new regime were soon followed by the 'Reign of Terror' in 1793–4 in which 17,000 people were officially executed in the name of democracy, and many tens of thousands more lost their lives. This would not be the last time in history that high ideals led to horrific actions, with the excuse that 'the ends justify the means'. The French constitution has gone through many rethinks and upheavals ever since, including the brief restoration of the monarchy with the crowning of Napoleon as emperor in 1804, and the rule of the Vichy government, which collaborated with the Nazi occupiers, from 1940 to 1944. The French are currently on their Fifth Republic but, like the Americans, rightly take great pride in their status as pioneers of democracy. Americans hold an annual national holiday, the Fourth of July, to celebrate the signing of the Declaration of Independence; the French do the same each year to mark the storming of the Bastille on the fourteenth of July. Both holidays place democracy at the heart of national identity.

For all their flaws, the American and the French Revolutions set an inspiring precedent for advocates of rule by the people around the world. The year 1848 saw a series of mini-revolutions around

Democracy or class struggle?

Europe. Most were quashed, and rule by the few returned, but the ideas that inspired them did not die. Societies and economies were changing. Towards the end of the nineteenth and the beginning of the twentieth century, the state began to take greater responsibility for people's lives, providing education, healthcare and public services. This meant that higher taxes were levied. Taxation required the consent of the people who were being taxed, and so, little by little, the **franchise** (the category of people allowed to vote) was widened across Europe, the United States, and the 'white dominions' (majority white former countries of the British Empire) of Canada, New Zealand and Australia. First the property qualification was relaxed, and slowly women were then let in. The Isle of Man blazed the trail as the first place in the world to give women the vote in 1881, followed by New Zealand in 1893 and the Australian Commonwealth in 1902. The upheaval of the First World War of 1914–18 also accelerated change: monarchies and empires across Europe tumbled in its aftermath, and were replaced with democratic republics. The significant role women played on the home front during the war prompted many more countries to grant them the vote. Switzerland was the last western country to admit women to the franchise, in 1971.

The military and economic collapse of Russia during the First World War opened the door to one of the greatest rivals to democracy in the twentieth century: communism. A movement that began as a protest against the absolute monarchy of the czar and a demand for democratic reform was hijacked by the Bolsheviks, a small but ruthlessly organised faction, inspired by the teaching of Karl Marx, a nineteenth-century German philosopher. They did not believe in rule by the people as a whole, but rather in a struggle between different social classes, membership of which was determined by your economic status, in which the only outcome was victory for one class over another. They claimed to lead the **proletariat** (the industrial working class) against the **bourgeoisie** (the property-owning class) and the **aristocracy** (who inherited their wealth and status by their birth). Once the proletariat had won this struggle, they would establish a **dictatorship of the proletariat**. At some time in the distant future, the state would wither away and be replaced by a classless society, a kind of earthly paradise where no one would go without anything, and everyone would cooperate naturally without the need for laws. In the meantime, the proletariat – or rather, their representatives leading the Communist Party, which had been taken over by the Bolshevik faction – were entitled to brutally suppress any opposition to their rule. Following a particularly vicious civil war, the Communist Party took control

Democracy or fascism?

across Russia from 1920, establishing the Soviet Union, and ruled there in an utterly undemocratic way until 1990.

The other challenge to democracy in the years between the First and Second World Wars was the rise of **fascism**. A fascist system requires the strong, unchallenged leadership of one ruler, allowing no elections, opposition from other political parties, or criticism of the government. Like communism, it is **totalitarian** in nature, meaning that every aspect of everyone's life, great or small, is controlled by the state. It is strongly **nationalist**, believing in the superiority of its own country, and putting that country first at the expense of the rest of the world. It often launches wars against other countries in order to expand the power and wealth of the nation. It celebrates **violence** both as a way of dealing with opposition and also as a good thing in itself, believing that it helps to purify those involved in it. It is very often associated with **racism**, demonising certain races or ethnic groups as being both inferior and a threat to the nation, often taking violent action against them.

The first fascist government was established when Benito Mussolini declared himself **dictator** (absolute ruler) of Italy in 1925. In Germany, the fledgling democracy established after the Kaiser (Emperor) had abdicated following German's defeat in the First World War collapsed in the midst of economic crisis, and the Nazis under Adolf Hitler took control in 1933. In Spain, an attempted **coup d'état** (violent seizure of power) by the military in 1936 led to a three-year-long civil war, which ended with the establishment of a fascist regime under General Franco. Fascist or quasi-fascist (having many similarities to fascism) governments took over in Portugal and a number of countries in Eastern Europe and South America, while Japan, though still an absolute monarchy, had a government dominated by the military, with many fascist characteristics.

In 1939, Hitler signed a non-aggression pact with the Russian communist leader Josef Stalin, and promptly invaded Poland, triggering the start of the Second World War. This war was (and still is) presented as an existential struggle between democracy and dictatorship, particularly after the Japanese bombing of the American fleet in Pearl Harbour in Hawaii in December 1941 brought the US into the war: on one side, Nazi Germany, Italy and Japan; on the other, the US, Britain and those resisting the Nazi occupation of western Europe. The picture was (and is) complicated by the fact that, following the Nazi invasion of Russia in June 1941, the democracies allied themselves with Stalin's

We are the people!

brutal regime. Although the war ended in the defeat of the Nazi dictatorship, Russia's own invasion of the countries of Eastern Europe brought democracy to an end there, replacing it with communist dictatorship.

The so-called 'Cold War' followed, in which the democratic 'free world', led by the US, faced off against the communist world of Russia, Eastern Europe and, from 1949, following its own upheavals, China. As with the Second World War, the 'Cold War' was presented by the democracies as a great moral struggle between good and evil (though the US actively supported some pretty nasty right-wing dictatorships around the world in the interests of resisting communism). The two sides never descended into open war, but took part in many proxy conflicts in places like Korea and Vietnam. Rebellions against communist rule in Hungary in 1956 and Czechoslovakia in 1968 were both ruthlessly suppressed by Russian invasions, without the West coming to their aid.

In the thirty or so years after 1945, imperial powers such as Britain and France gradually dismantled their empires, granting independence to their former possessions around the world. Most of these became democracies, though others fell into the hands of dictators who ran their countries in the interests of their own tribe, faction or family.

The next great moment in the history of democracy came with the fall of communism in Russia. When Mikhail Gorbachev became General Secretary of the Russian Communist Party in 1985, he began a process of *glasnost* (opening up) and *perestroika* (restructuring), which aimed to modernise the Soviet Union's failing economy. As part of this opening up, he no longer guaranteed that the Soviet Union would come to the aid of eastern European communist regimes facing internal rebellions. As a result, one communist dictatorship after another was peacefully overthrown by popular uprisings. In East Germany, in another great expression of democratic ideals, vast crowds chanted night after night, '*Wir sind das Volk!*' ('We are the people!'), defying the claim of the communist dictatorship to be ruling on behalf of 'the people'. Their protests culminated in the highly symbolic destruction of the wall separating communist East Berlin from democratic West Berlin in November 1989. Not long after, following a failed attempt at a *coup d'etat* by hardliners in Russia, the Russian Communist Party dissolved itself.

The 1990s were a time of unparalleled optimism for supporters of democracy. It seemed as if it was on its way to an inevitable triumph around the world. Then three planes hijacked by terrorists

Democracy can't be imposed at the point of a gun

from the Al-Qaeda organisation, who believed in the most extreme and intolerant form of Islam, were flown into the Twin Towers in New York City and the Pentagon in Washington, D.C., on September 11, 2001, while a fourth hijacked plane crashed in a field in Pennsylvania, killing everyone aboard, after the passengers overpowered the hijackers. Nearly 3,000 American civilians died, in the worst act of terrorism ever seen on American soil. In response, the US, supported by its allies, launched the 'Global War on Terror'. Its first objective, the removal of the Taliban dictatorship in Afghanistan which had protected the hijackers, was uncontroversial and swiftly accomplished. However, victory in this war was not followed by a peaceful transition to democracy. Afghanistan remained torn apart by internal conflict for the next twenty years, until the chaotic withdrawal of US and other forces in the summer of 2021 was followed by the Taliban's immediate return to power. More controversial was the next move in the 'War on Terror': the invasion of Iraq in 2003. Iraq's leader Saddam Hussein was undoubtedly a vicious dictator, but he had no connection with the 9/11 attacks, and posed no real threat to the US. Few European democracies would support the US-led invasion, with the notable exception of the UK, under the leadership of Tony Blair. The invasion was successful in overthrowing Saddam's government, but Iraq quickly descended into blood-soaked chaos, opening the door to the psychopathic brutality of the Islamic State group, which was even more extreme than Al-Qaeda, and which spread fast across the Middle East. The clear lesson of these misadventures was that democracy works best when it evolves naturally from within a society, not when it is imposed from outside at the point of a gun.

While China remained nominally communist, it moved in the twenty-first century towards a capitalist economic system based on private property and profit. This led to a very significant improvement in the living standards of many Chinese, lifting millions out of poverty, but was not accompanied by any increase in democratic rights. Protests in favour of democracy in Hong Kong were ruthlessly suppressed, while President Xi Jinping effectively made himself ruler for life.

In Russia, the end of communism was followed by a form of anarchically unrestrained capitalism which allowed a tiny minority of borderline (and sometimes not so borderline) criminal 'oligarchs' to acquire the vast assets of the Russian state at a small fraction of their true value, thereby making themselves spectacularly rich. Meanwhile, ordinary Russians had to stand by and watch their economy slide into ruin. Many were reduced to selling their

Is populism democratic?

clothes in the street simply to feed their families. When Vladimir Putin came to power in 2000 and promised to restore order and national pride, he became very popular, and won elections easily. Then he took over the media, fixed elections, had opponents killed or jailed, and became as ruthless a dictator as Stalin or the czars.

Popular uprisings in many countries in the Arab world in the early 2010s, in favour of democracy and against dictatorship and corruption, were dubbed the 'Arab Spring'. Social media helped to spread the message and organise protesters. Almost all these countries, however, then returned to some form of dictatorship or descended into chaotic civil war, the conflicts in Libya and Syria being particularly gruesome.

The aftermath of the global financial crisis of 2008 tested the resilience of democracies around the world. The resultant cuts in public spending caused great hardship for many people. Voters wanted someone to blame, and a new breed of politicians were happy to provide them with scapegoats. These **populists** – Donald Trump in the USA, Jair Bolsonaro in Brazil, Viktor Orban in Hungary, Narendra Modi in India, Rodrigo Duterte in the Philippines – all won democratic elections. However, they undermined democratic norms by dismissing their opponents as unpatriotic and alien, attacking and sometimes silencing the free press, sabotaging the impartiality of the justice system, and stirring up prejudice against racial and sexual minorities. They claimed to represent an imaginary 'real people' against an almost equally imaginary self-serving 'elite' which had been in charge for too long, though once in power they quickly set about plundering the state's resources to enrich themselves and their friends and families.

When he lost the US presidential election in 2020, Donald Trump refused to admit defeat and claimed, with no evidence, that the election had been stolen from him. This denial of the truth was believed by millions of his supporters, and was in part the product of a dangerously polarised political culture in which America was split into two bitterly hostile factions, each of which refused to see any good in the other. On January 6th, 2021, two weeks before he was due to leave office, President Trump stirred up a mob to storm the Capitol in Washington, where they held their democratically elected representatives hostage for several hours. Footage of these scenes was played over and over again on Russian and Chinese TV to make the same argument that people in power had made for hundreds of years until the twentieth century: that democracy means chaos, danger and disorder, while the rule of the few keeps everybody safe. Nonetheless, a few days later, Joe Biden was duly sworn in as the 46th President of the United States

Government of the people, by the people, for the people

in a peaceful transition of power. One year into Biden's presidency, he found himself leading an alliance of democracies, unprecedented in modern history, in their support of the Ukrainian people's right to rule themselves, following the invasion of Ukraine in February 2022 by Vladimir Putin's Russia. Now TV screens around the world were filled with images of ordinary Ukrainian people willing to die for democracy. The promise given by Mr Biden's predecessor as President, Abraham Lincoln, at Gettysburg in 1863 over the bodies of men who had died fighting slavery in the American Civil War that 'government of the people, by the people, for the people, shall not vanish from the earth' may yet be kept. But it won't just happen. Democracy is not a natural state of affairs. It takes hard work to succeed. It calls for effort, compromise, determination, and no little sacrifice. And, no less importantly, a great deal of thought.

A brief history of democracy in the UK

The development of democracy in the UK has been a slow incremental progress from absolute monarchy to the fully developed (though still not perfect) democratic state we have today. It is perhaps best understood through the prism of a number of significant moments or movements.

Magna Carta, 1215

This document is often held up and revered as one of the foundations of modern democracy. In fact, it had very little to do with democracy in the sense of elections and political parties. It was more like an agreement between two rival Mafia mobs. It was signed on June 15th, 1215, in a field at Runnymede, just outside Windsor, by the resentful King John, under pressure from a group of powerful barons. They would certainly not have understood, or wished for, democracy in the sense of rule by the people, and were more interested in protecting their own interests against those of the king. Magna Carta did, however, enshrine a couple of key principles of the **rule of law**:

- The right to a **fair trial**, conducted according to the law, not the whim of those in power, with the verdict given by people who are the equals of the accused – the foundation of the modern jury system. As Magna Carta puts it:

  'No free man shall be seized, imprisoned, dispossessed, outlawed, exiled or ruined in any way, nor in any way proceeded against, except by the lawful judgement of his peers and the law of the land.'

- The right to **impartial justice**, free from bribery or obstruction. As Magna Carta puts it:

  'To no one will we sell, to no one will we deny or delay right or justice.'

These principles have echoed down the years, and have inspired many future democratic movements, including the American Revolution and the United Nations Universal Declaration of Human Rights.

The poorest he hath a life to live as the greatest he

The English Civil War and the Putney Debates

During the English Civil Wars of 1642–1651, the country was alive with a ferment of radical ideas, expressed in a torrent of pamphlets and a storm of debates, many of which were remarkably advanced in their conception of democracy. One of the most significant of these was the gathering known as the 'Putney Debates', held in October and November 1647 at the Church of St Mary the Virgin in Putney, which still stands today next to Putney Bridge in London.

At the Putney Debates, soldiers of Oliver Cromwell's New Model Army proposed:

- Universal (male) **suffrage** (the right to vote)
- Equal-sized parliamentary constituencies, where everyone's vote counts equally
- Freedom of religion
- Equality before the law

The guiding principles of democracy were beautifully expressed in the words of Thomas Rainsborough, one of the leading spokesmen for the Levellers: 'For really I think that the poorest he that is in England hath a life to live as the greatest he; and therefore truly, sir, I think it's clear, that every man that is to live under a government ought first by his own consent to put himself under that government; and I do think that the poorest man in England is not at all bound in a strict sense to that government that he hath not had a voice to put himself under.'

Cromwell, however, like many powerful men before and since, believed that democracy would lead to anarchy, particularly if men without property were allowed to vote, and vetoed these radical reforms.

Following the defeat of the Royalists in the Civil War, King Charles I was executed in 1649 and a Commonwealth was instituted, supposedly ruled by Parliament. Parliament split into squabbling

The monarch respects the authority of Parliament

factions, and the government ended up as a virtual dictatorship under Cromwell, styling himself as the Lord Protector. On his death, in a move oddly reminiscent of a monarchical system, Cromwell was followed into power by his son Richard. Richard didn't last long, and in 1660 the monarchy was restored. However, the principle that the monarchy should respect the authority of Parliament had been established, and this arguably paved the way for the constitutional monarchy that the UK has today.

The Great Reform Act

How is Parliament made up? Members of Parliament (**MPs**) are elected to represent a particular area of the country called a **constituency**. It's pretty obvious that for representation to be fair and equal, constituencies should be approximately the same size. In the early nineteenth century, this wasn't the case. The Industrial Revolution of the late eighteenth and early nineteenth century had profoundly changed England, with hundreds of thousands of people moving from the countryside to work in factories in newly established cities, undermining the old order of small, tight-knit rural communities. The electoral and parliamentary system failed to keep up with these changes. As a result, the numbers of voters in constituencies varied wildly, from as few as twelve up to as many as 12,000. What's more, many constituencies were treated essentially as private property, owned by rich and powerful men who handed out places in Parliament to their supporters, shamelessly bribing or threatening voters into supporting their chosen candidates. The **Great Reform Act** of 1832 (passed in the face of considerable opposition from powerful factions) went a long way towards tidying up this system, making it fairer and more rational. It also considerably increased the franchise, so that 20% of men were now eligible to vote. However, women and those without property were still excluded.

Chartism

The Chartist movement took some momentum from the Great Reform Act. It was very different in character, though, since where the Great Reform Act was essentially a reform led by those already in power, Chartism was a mass working-class movement, led by those excluded from power.

Chartism took its name from the 'People's Charter' of 1838, which demanded:

- A universal franchise for all men over 21.
- Equal-sized constituencies.

- Annual elections, to keep governments under constant scrutiny.
- A secret ballot, to ensure no voters could be intimidated or bribed.
- The abolition of property requirements for voters and MPs.
- MPs to be paid a salary, to allow working men to enter politics.

Freedom of assembly is a key democratic right

The Chartists' strategy was to put the government under irresistible moral pressure through sheer force of numbers, via petitions and mass meetings. In 1839, a petition with 1.5 million signatures was presented to the House of Commons; in 1848, a mass meeting of 150,000 people was held on Kennington Common. There was a split within the movement between 'moral force' Chartists who favoured peaceful means, and 'physical force' Chartists, who believed that only violence would bring about change. (Whether the use of violence is justified and / or necessary to bring about democracy has been an ongoing debate throughout history, dividing many movements for democratic change, such as the campaign for votes for women in the UK, the struggle for Indian independence from Britain, the campaign for equal rights for black Americans in the US in the 1960s, and the fight against apartheid in South Africa.) Such was the widespread support for Chartism, that at times it looked as if some sort of revolution might break out. However, the government stifled the movement by banning large gatherings of people. **Freedom of assembly**, denied by the government in this way, is a key part of democracy: it allows people to meet and protest as a way of expressing their views and wishes on the way in which their societies should be run.

Votes for women

The massive elephant in the room in the history of democracy has been the exclusion of slightly over 50% of humanity (women) from the right to vote. In England, this exclusion was made explicit in the Great Reform Act with the naming of voters as 'male persons'. In the late nineteenth century, the 'suffragist' movement began to campaign for votes for women. Initially, the movement favoured peaceful means of persuasion, mostly through mass marches and meetings. However, in the early twentieth century, the movement split, with one faction, the 'suffragettes', turning to violent tactics, vandalising and even burning down public buildings. When arrested for these actions, suffragettes would embark on hunger strikes while in prison. These tactics both raised the profile of

Votes for women (and more men)

the movement and, at the same time, alienated many people. On the outbreak of the First World War in 1914, the suffragettes abandoned their campaign in a spirit of national solidarity. The war greatly increased the activity of women outside the home, as they took on much of the work otherwise carried out by men who were away fighting. This led to a change in thinking on the question of women's suffrage – the vote was seen as a kind of reward for women for their good work during the war. As the Home Secretary, Sir George Cave, somewhat patronisingly put it in 1917, '... is it possible for us, having called upon women for so large a contribution to the work of carrying on the war, and having received so splendid a response to that call, to refuse women a voice in moulding the future of the country?' The working men who had responded to that call (hundreds of thousands of them at the cost of their lives) were also rewarded. In 1918, the Representation of the People Act gave the vote to all men aged over 21, and to women over 30 who met certain property qualifications. Ten years later, in 1928, the experiment of female suffrage was pronounced a success, and women joined men in having the vote from the age of 21, without need for any property qualification. Given that nearly a million British men had been killed in the First World War, women for a while significantly outnumbered men in the electorate. The voting age fell to 18 across the UK in 1970; since 2015, 16-year-olds have been allowed to vote in Scottish national and local elections.

Brexit

Referendums (votes on just one question, with a binary choice between two alternatives) have not normally been a central part of UK democracy. They have mostly been used to authorise changes in the **constitution** (the way in which the country is governed) such as the establishment of national parliaments in Scotland and Wales or the introduction of mayors to lead London or other major cities, and have not attracted much attention. However, the referendum on membership of the European Union held in 2016 had huge consequences for the UK, and raised a number of fundamental issues for British democracy..

In 2014, with an election due the following year, Conservative Prime Minister David Cameron was worried that he would lose votes to the United Kingdom Independence Party (UKIP), which wanted Britain to leave the European Union (the EU). To coax anti-EU voters back to the Conservative Party, he promised that if he won the election, he would hold a referendum on membership of the EU. (A similar referendum on membership of what was then known as the 'Common Market', a predecessor of the EU, had been held in 1975, with a convincing 67% voting in favour of staying in.) Cameron's hope was that voters would opt to remain in the EU, and that the European issue, which had divided the Conservative Party for decades and was now leaking votes to UKIP, would be settled once and for all. The Conservatives duly won the 2015 election, and a referendum on EU membership was scheduled for June 2016, posing the question: *Should the United Kingdom remain a member of the European Union or leave the European Union*?

Take back control

It didn't go according to plan.

The Leave campaign mobilised millions of people who didn't normally bother to vote through some astute manipulation of social media, along with the heavily publicised claim that Britain sent £350 million a week to the EU. (This claim was both inaccurate – the figure had been significantly reduced through a negotiated rebate – and misleading, as it wrongly implied that the UK got nothing back from the EU for this money, when in fact membership conferred many benefits, including subsidies for many poorer parts of the UK.) The Leave campaign also appealed to many voters' resentment at high levels of immigration from countries that had recently joined the EU. Perhaps most powerfully of all, though, it struck an emotional chord with its main slogan: 'Take Back Control'. Following the financial crisis of 2008, austerity measures had led to significant cuts in public spending, leaving many of the poorest members of society, and poorest areas, feeling abandoned, ignored and powerless. Voting Leave gave them the chance to assert themselves against an establishment that seemed to have forgotten them. So they did: a clear (though by no means overwhelming) majority of 52% voted to leave the EU.

Then it all kicked off.

The morning after the referendum, David Cameron announced he would be resigning as Prime Minister. In due course, Theresa May was chosen by Conservative MPs to replace him and became the UK's second woman Prime Minister. Although she announced that 'Brexit [the departure of Britain from the EU] means Brexit', the trouble was that no one actually knew what Brexit meant. Cameron had forbidden any contingency planning by civil servants for a Leave win (on the grounds that it would undermine confidence in a Remain victory), with the result that there were no plans in place – none whatsoever – for this seismic change.

What did Brexit mean?

Another problem was that an overwhelming majority of MPs (including, ironically, Theresa May herself) had backed staying in the EU, so there was a clear divide between the voters' decision and what the MPs themselves had chosen. May tried to resolve this problem by calling a fresh election in 2017, hoping that she would win a decisive victory over a divided Labour Party, led by the controversial far-leftist Jeremy Corbyn.

That didn't go according to plan either.

The Conservatives lost their parliamentary majority, and May was only able to stay in power by patching up an agreement with the Democratic Unionists, a small party from Northern Ireland. Two years of chaos ensued, as May tried again and again to get the exit agreement she had negotiated with the EU through Parliament, constantly defeated by a combination of hardline Leavers who wanted a more decisive break with the EU than she was offering, and hardline Remainers who demanded a second referendum on the agreement (assuming that this second vote would reject Brexit). She twice had to request an extension from the EU for the UK's leaving date. Eventually, she bowed to intense pressure from critics within her own party, and resigned as Prime Minister in the summer of 2019.

Theresa May was now replaced by Boris Johnson. Faced with the same hostile and irreconcilable factions in Parliament, he resorted to more ruthless methods, such as throwing MPs who dared to disagree with him out of the Conservative Party, and asking the Queen to 'prorogue' – that is, shut down – Parliament for an extended period. This last measure was ruled illegal by the Supreme Court of the UK, meaning that the Prime Minister had in effect made the Queen break the law. Finally, Johnson called an election in December 2019. Campaigning on the slogan 'Get Brexit Done', he won a majority of over 80, capturing seats in many areas which had always voted Labour. The UK duly left the EU on January 30th, 2020.

The three and a half years between the EU referendum and the UK's exit from the EU were immensely traumatic for British democracy. The referendum looked like democracy at its most simple and direct: ask people what they want to do, then do what they say – easy. It turned out to be anything but. What went wrong?

The referendum on EU membership presented as very simple something which was in fact enormously complex. The UK's relationship with the EU was based on hundreds of different laws, treaties and agreements, formulated over several decades, expressed in thousands of pages of densely argued legal prose, all of which had to be renegotiated in immense detail. Leaving the EU was not like cancelling a mobile phone contract. It was more like a messy divorce at the end of a long marriage, in which lawyers haggle over every last detail of a couple's life, from ownership of the family home and custody of the children down to splitting up the books and CDs. And we, the British people, were the kids, looking on in sadness and frustration as Mum and Dad spent three years tearing each other apart, too busy arguing to remember to make our packed lunch or help us with our Maths homework.

What went wrong?

Like many (if not most) arguments, the national row over Brexit was not really about what it claimed to be about. In truth, it had very little to do with the fine details of international trade treaties, and more to do with profound questions of identity, of how people thought about themselves and their country. University graduates, young people, and people who lived in cities, who tended to be socially and geographically mobile, voted overwhelmingly for Remain; less educated people, older people, people in poorer parts of the country outside the big cities and the South East, who were often in poorly paid and insecure employment, and tended to be more embedded in their local communities, voted overwhelmingly for Leave. Each side viewed the other with suspicion and resentment. Remainers thought Leavers were ignorant, racist oafs; Leavers thought Remainers were arrogant, entitled snobs who looked down on them. I'm exaggerating, but not much. These divisions already existed, but Brexit brought them out into the open and made them much worse by presenting voters with a binary choice between two irreconcilable alternatives, in which only one side could be the winner, and half the nation had to lose.

The issues that Brexit gave rise to provide a helpful way to think about the pros and cons of different types of democracy, which are discussed later in this chapter.

How does democracy in the UK actually work?

1. Who's in charge?

The UK is a **constitutional monarchy**. The **Head of State** is the monarch (at the time of writing King Charles III), who is chosen by hereditary succession (as the senior child of her or his parents). In theory, the monarch is in charge of everything. In practice, she or he has to do whatever the democratically elected government tells her or him to do. The monarch's role is almost entirely symbolic

Who's in charge?

and ceremonial, acting as a living embodiment of the nation, taking no decisions and expressing no opinions.

The **Head of Government** – the person who is actually in charge, who makes decisions and runs the country – is the Prime Minister ('Prime' means 'First'). The **Prime Minister**, appointed by the monarch, is the leader of the party that has more **MPs** (Ministers of Parliament) in the House of Commons than any other party, and can therefore get laws passed. The leader of the next largest party is the **Leader of the Opposition**. Her or his full title is 'The Leader of His Majesty's Loyal Opposition'. The 'loyal' part says a lot about democracy at its best: challenging the government, holding it to account, presenting a different viewpoint, debating with it, and is in fact an act of loyalty to the nation as a whole, as embodied in the monarch. If the Prime Minister's party has more MPs than all the other parties combined, the government has an **overall majority**, and it should be very easy to get laws passed. If they don't, they will only be able to get laws passed with the agreement of some or all of the opposition parties.

The Prime Minister chooses **ministers** to be responsible for different areas of government, for example, education, health, defence, etc. Together, ministers make up the **Cabinet**, which meets regularly to agree government policy. Meanwhile, the Opposition party forms a matching Shadow Cabinet.

2. Who decides who's in charge?

We do (that's the point of democracy).

All UK citizens (and also Commonwealth citizens resident in the UK) over the age of 18 are allowed to vote in general elections. The only people excluded are prisoners, people who are compulsorily detained in mental health units, and members of the House of Lords. General elections must be held at least every five years, though they are often held more frequently than that. We don't vote directly for the Prime Minister, in the way that Americans or French people vote directly for their President. Instead, we vote for an MP for our **constituency**. There are 650 constituencies across the UK, each one representing approximately 70,000 people. Constituencies in densely populated urban areas are likely to cover a smaller area than those in sparsely populated rural areas. Candidates seeking election as MPs almost all stand as representing a particular **political party**, and voters tend to vote not for the individual MP but more for the party they want to run the government and / or the party leader they want to be Prime Minister. Whichever candidate gets the most votes in a constituency becomes the MP for that constituency.

Who decides who's in charge?

3. What are political parties?

Political parties are organisations of people who broadly share the same views on how the country should be run, and seek power to ensure that it will be run in that way. In the UK, the main political parties are Labour (on the left, favouring greater equality, higher taxes and more public spending), the Conservatives (on the right, favouring greater personal freedoms, lower taxes and lower public spending), and the Liberal Democrats (in the centre, somewhere between Labour and Conservative). In Scotland, the Scottish National Party (SNP) stands for independence for Scotland (and has dominated the national government there since 2007). In Wales, Plaid Cymru campaign for independence for Wales. In Northern Ireland, parties tend to be associated with either the Protestant community (who are more likely to favour keeping Northern Ireland as part of the UK) or the Catholic community (who are more likely to favour a close relationship with the Republic of Ireland to the south), though the Alliance Party makes a point of incorporating both Protestant and Catholic communities.

4. Is the national government in charge of everything?

Not quite. More local concerns, such as parking, rubbish collection, libraries, etc., are run by **local councils**, covering a much smaller area, usually the size of a small town. Councils are run by **councillors**, who are elected for **wards**. Wards are like constituencies, only much smaller; they tend to contain about 7,000 people. Councillors, like MPs, most commonly stand as representatives of a party, though there are also many independent councillors.

Major cities and large areas, such as London or the West of England, may have a **mayor**. The mayor is one person, elected directly. She or he has responsibility for certain local concerns such as transport or policing.

Scotland, Wales and Northern Ireland all have **devolved governments**. They have national parliaments, elected by residents of those countries, and their own First Minister. These governments are responsible for areas such as education, health, etc. (so, for example, during the Covid pandemic of 2020–22, Scotland, Wales and Northern Ireland followed different public health policies from England). However, Scotland, Wales and Northern Ireland are not independent nations. They remain part of the United Kingdom, and the UK government remains responsible for their defence and foreign policy.

Who gets to vote?

2. THE ISSUES

1. Voting

Voting is an essential part of democracy. It's how we choose who has power over us. Although the basic principle of voting is simple – we say what we want – there are a number of issues around how voting should actually work. These come down to two questions. Who gets to vote? How do we vote?

Who gets to vote?

We've seen from the historical summary above that across the world, and in the UK, there has over time been a steady widening of the franchise (the category of people entitled to vote). This is unlikely to go backwards in any significant way: no one would now seriously argue for removing the vote from people because of their colour, gender or economic status. However, that doesn't mean there are no issues left around the franchise.

Who gets to vote when a general election is held in the UK? Obvious, you might think. Everyone who has a stake in the result. That's fair, isn't it? And the result will affect everyone who lives in the UK, so surely everyone who lives in the UK will be allowed to vote.

No they won't.

All British and Commonwealth citizens over the age of 18 resident in the UK are entitled to vote in a general election. (The Commonwealth is a collection of countries that used to be part of the British Empire.) So people who are not British citizens, but come from countries that used to be in the British Empire, can vote, but people who are from other countries, even if they live in the UK, work in the UK, have families in the UK, pay taxes in the UK, obviously have a stake in the future of the UK, can't vote. Why? Is the Commonwealth vote a way of saying 'sorry' to all those countries for having invaded them once?

Prisoners are not allowed to vote. Why not? They may have done something wrong in the past to be put in prison, but don't they have a stake in the future too? In some states in the US, if you commit one crime, you are never allowed to vote again. Is that fair? Is voting a privilege that can be taken away, or a right? Aren't prisoners more likely to want to change their ways and go straight when they get out if they are treated like citizens rather than outcasts?

Should children be allowed to vote?

And why do you have to be 18 or over? Given that the next government could be in power for five years before the next election, what they do will have a big impact on people who will be adults throughout almost all of that time. Even those who won't be adults will be affected by, for example, the government's policy on education – does your school have enough funding from the government? – or transport – are there enough buses to get you to school? – or the economy – will your parents have a job that pays them enough to look after you?

Does everyone miraculously acquire wisdom at midnight on their eighteenth birthday? In Scotland, the vote is granted from the age of 16. But why start at 16? The distinguished Cambridge politics professor David Runciman has argued that six-year-olds should be allowed to vote, as soon as they can read. Surely, though, they're too immature, too ill-informed, too open to influence, have too little stake in the outcome? Professor Runciman makes the point that all those arguments were once made against giving women the vote.

At the other extreme, there were people who said after the EU referendum that people had made a bad decision because they didn't know enough about the facts. It is certainly true that voters with a high level of education tended to vote Remain, and that those with a lower level of education tended to vote Leave. Does that mean that voting Remain was smarter? Does going to university give you better judgement? Should people get extra votes depending on how many exams they have passed? Then again, you're not allowed to drive until you've passed a driving test, to show you know how to drive a car responsibly – shouldn't you have to pass some sort of test to show you know how to vote responsibly?

You could also argue that voting is a civic duty, like jury service, paying your taxes, or putting out the recycling. It's not that hard. For most people, it's a five-minute walk to a polling station. If they don't like any of the candidates when they get there, they can 'spoil' their ballot paper (write on it to show they don't want to vote for anyone). If they can't make it to the polling station for any reason, they can get a postal vote. Shouldn't it be compulsory? That's what they do in Australia. Everyone over 18 is obliged to register for elections and vote. Failure to do so means paying a small fine (about £12). As a result, turnout (the percentage of people voting) in Australian elections is much higher, typically above 90%, whereas in the UK it is more likely to be somewhere above 60%. Doesn't that mean that Australian governments are

Should voting be compulsory?

much more representative of the people, as so many more have voted? Or should democratic freedoms include the freedom not to vote?

How do we vote?

This looks obvious. We choose who we want to vote for, and whoever gets the most votes wins.

In fact, it's not that obvious. There are many different systems for running democratic elections, each of which has its strengths and weaknesses. Here are some of them.

First past the post (FPTP)

This is the system used in general elections in the UK. The votes cast for each candidate in a constituency are added up and whichever candidate has the most is the winner (in the same way that the first horse to pass the winning post in a horse race is the winner) and she or he becomes the MP for that constituency.

This system has the advantage of simplicity. It is very easy to understand. It also means that there is one clearly identifiable person who represents each constituency, to whom constituents can appeal for help. Across the whole country, it has historically tended to lead to parliaments where one party has an overall majority, which supporters of FPTP say ensures stable government with clear, decisive leadership (though this is not guaranteed: the general elections of 2010 and 2017 both resulted in '**hung parliaments**' with no party having an overall majority).

A major issue with FPTP is that the outcome of the election very often does not reflect the number of votes cast for each party. A party whose support is spread thinly across the country might see its candidates come second or third in many constituencies but rarely first, and will therefore have very few MPs; a party whose support is heavily concentrated in a few areas may be able to generate enough MPs in those areas to win a majority in Parliament overall, despite not having a majority of votes cast.

Here are some examples of why this means FPTP is less fair than it looks in practice. In the 1950 election, and in the first election of 1974 (there were two that year), Labour won fewer votes than the Conservatives, but had more MPs elected, and so formed the government. In 1997, Labour won an overwhelming majority in Parliament of 179, though they only had 43.2% of the votes – well ahead of their nearest rivals the Conservatives on 30.7%, but still not a majority. In the 2010 election, in the constituency of Norwich

Is first past the post fair?

South, the Liberal Democrats won the seat with just 29.4% of the vote; some way short of one in three. In the 2015 general election, the United Kingdom Independence Party (UKIP) won 12.6% of the votes in return for precisely one MP – 0.2% of the total. In the 2024 general election, Labour won 63% of the seats with 34% of the vote; Reform (the successor to UKIP) won just 1% of the seats despite receiving 14% of the vote.

You have to be a bit of a nerd to know or care about these sorts of statistics – though let's face it, most debaters are a bit in touch with their inner nerd – but they do illustrate that FPTP, while it (mostly) works in providing a functioning government, is not actually that fair.

So what are the alternatives? They are all variations of **proportional representation**, often known as **PR**. The main idea behind PR is that the outcome of an election should reflect as far as possible the number of votes cast.

Party list voting

In this system, voters vote not for an individual candidate but for a party. Each party is then allocated MPs in proportion to the number of votes cast. So, a party that gets 40% of the vote gets 40% of the MPs, one that gets 30% of the votes gets 30% of the MPs, and so on. The party provides a list of candidates, ranked in order; the more votes a party gets, the further down the list of candidates it goes.

This system is used in the UK to a limited degree for elections to the Scottish Parliament, the Welsh Assembly and the London Assembly. It is also used in many European countries. Its great advantage is that the outcome of elections represents the views of the people much more accurately than any other system. It does however mean that it is much more unlikely that any party will have an overall majority, meaning that governments almost always tend to be some form of coalition (where two or more parties work together in government). An advantage of this is that governments are generally then more representative of the country as a whole, and also that habits of collaboration and compromise are baked into the political system. This approach minimises the sort of toxic polarisation seen in recent years between Republicans and Democrats in the US, or between Leave and Remain following the Brexit referendum in the UK. Germany's use of the party list system has meant that its governments are almost always coalitions, and, as a result, German political culture is much more consensual and less confrontational.

Does PR promote working together or chaos?

This ideal of consensus, collaboration and representativeness is not always achieved, however. A 'hung parliament' can lead to one very small party wielding power far beyond the number of votes it has received because it holds the balance of power, meaning that neither of the two major parties can govern without it. An example of a small party wielding power out of proportion to its support across the country was the agreement between Theresa May and the Democratic Unionist Party (DUP) in the hung parliament that followed the 2017 election. In return for keeping the Conservatives in power, the DUP secured subsidies worth £1 billion for Northern Ireland. Other parts of the UK arguably needed that money more than Northern Ireland, but they weren't represented by a party holding the balance of power.

A disadvantage of the need for consensus is that it can be harder to take swift, decisive action or to enact unpopular but necessary policies. The arrival of a new government can also be delayed by the need for complex negotiations between parties following an election. (The world record for this is held by Belgium, where, following the 2011 election in which no party won more than 20% of the seats, they took 353 days to form a new government). Consensual government works well in stable countries in stable times, but is more problematic in times of crisis.

Another disadvantage of the party list system is that it takes away the choice of MPs from the voters and puts it in the hands of party officials, favouring politicians who are adept at working the party system rather than appealing to ordinary people. In the current UK system, the best MPs have a strong connection with the area which has elected them, live in the area, bring up their families there, are aware of local issues and act as an advocate for the area's needs on the national stage. People may vote for them not on party lines but out of respect for their dedication to serving the local community.

Single transferable vote (STV)

In this system, rather than voting for just one candidate, voters rank them in order, writing one by their first choice, two by their second choice, and so on. (They don't have to put numbers by all the candidates if they don't want to). If a candidate gets more than 50% of first choice votes, she or he is elected. If no candidate gets more than 50% of first choice votes, then the candidate who came last on first choice votes is eliminated, and their second choice votes are allocated to the remaining candidates, for whom they count as first choice votes. If that doesn't result in one candidate getting more than 50% of first choice votes, the next last candidate is eliminated, and their second choice votes are allocated as first choice votes (unless their second choice votes are for a candidate who has already been eliminated, in which case their next choice vote is used). This process continues until only one candidate is left, and she or he is elected.

The single transfer-able vote is like a dating app

STV is (as you can tell from the above explanation) complicated to understand and administer, and counting votes takes a bit longer. However, it's not really that complicated to use. Ranking candidates or parties in order of preference is not that different from the way we often make decisions in ordinary life, e.g. choosing a meal in a restaurant, negotiating with family members about where to go on holiday, or using a dating app. It allows voters to feel more engaged and their views more respected. Under FPTP, voters in a constituency where one party almost always wins sometimes feel forced to vote 'tactically' rather than for their favoured party. So a Labour supporter in a constituency where Labour almost always comes last might vote for the Liberal Democrats, who normally come second, in the hope that this will 'keep the Conservatives out'; under STV, they could put Labour first, the Liberal Democrats second, and the Conservatives last (or nowhere). (Though outcomes are less certain than they once were; in the 2019 election, several constituencies in the north of England and Wales which had always been Labour elected Conservative MPs, something that in previous generations would have been unimaginable.) STV has the greater fairness of PR, while at the same time (unlike the party list system) allowing the retention of MPs elected for particular constituencies, with the consequent sense of personal connection between voters and their MP.

Alternative vote (AV)

This is a simpler version of STV. Voters have a first choice vote and a second choice vote. (They don't have to use the second choice vote if they don't want to.) If one candidate wins more than 50% of first choice votes, they are elected; if not, the lowest scoring candidate is eliminated and their second choice votes are reallocated as first choice votes. This process continues until one candidate has more than 50% of first choice votes.

This system was used in the election of the mayor of London until it was replaced by FPTP in 2024, and is used in national elections in Australia, Fiji and Papua New Guinea. As part of the deal which set up a coalition government comprising the Conservatives and the Liberal Democrats following the 2010 election in which no party won an overall majority, a referendum on introducing AV for general elections in the UK was held in 2011 (the Liberal Democrats have been long-term supporters of PR). AV was decisively rejected, by a margin of two to one.

2. What sort of democracy?

There are four main kinds of democracy:

- Direct democracy
- Plebiscitary democracy
- Representative democracy
- Deliberative democracy

To understand them, let's look at an example of a real-life problem and consider how it might be solved by each type of democracy.

Take a busy road in a residential area. There's constant traffic along it, as it's on the route into town. But there are also houses on either side. Many of these houses are lived in by young children. Their parents are worried about them crossing this busy road on their way to school. So they ask the local council to put in a crossing, with traffic lights. A crossing would make their lives better.

However, there are many people in the area who don't live on that road, but who need to drive along it to get to work or to shops. If there is a crossing, triggering a red light on a regular basis, their journeys will be interrupted and will be much slower. At rush-hour times, existing traffic jams will get even worse. A crossing would make their lives worse.

How would democracy resolve our road crossing problem? Some say that democracy is about enacting the will of the people. The trouble is, the people almost never all think the same thing, as in this case. Some people want a road crossing, other people don't. You can't both have a road crossing and not have it at the same time. So you can't enact the 'will of the people', because there is no one will of the people. A really important thing to understand is that democracy is not actually about enacting the will of the people. It is about finding a way to run society which enables people with different views to carry on getting on with each other, even when decisions are taken that many of them disagree with. This is one of the things that was problematic about the Brexit referendum: because the decision was so binary (in or out) and so irreversible, either result was going to end up alienating half the country.

How would our different types of democracy help a community decide about a road crossing without descending into civil war?

There is no will of the people

1. Direct democracy

Direct democracy is democracy in its purest form. Everyone affected by a particular issue gets together in one place and argues it out until a conclusion is reached, with everyone having an equal voice. As we saw at the start of this chapter, it began in Ancient Greece, and is the oldest type of democracy in the world.

How would it work with our road crossing?

A hall large enough to hold all the residents of the area would be hired. Everyone would be invited to a meeting. Everyone could have their say about the crossing (there would have to be a chair to keep order). At the end of the evening, either an open vote would be taken about whether or not to have a crossing, or, in really advanced direct democracy, it would be clear what the general feeling of the meeting was.

What are the advantages and disadvantages of this type of democracy?

Advantages:

- Everyone is involved.
- Everyone's voice can be heard.
- It operates at a human level, because there is face-to-face interaction.

Disadvantages:

- The practical one. It might be possible to get all the residents of a few streets into one large room; it is not possible to get all the citizens of the United Kingdom into one room.
- The face-to-face interaction and open voting might actually prevent honest discussion, as people may be reluctant to speak candidly to people they have to see every day.
- People may be swayed in their decisions by existing relationships – do you want to publicly disagree with your son's best friend's mother?
- People may be swayed in their decisions by powerful rhetoric, as the sophists of Ancient Greece discovered to their profit.

Direct democracy works best in small groups or communities, such as families or businesses where there are already strong relationships, shared interests and a high level of trust. It's much

Direct democracy works if people trust each other

harder to get it to work in larger groups or ones where there are already problematic relationships.

2. Plebiscitary democracy

Plebiscitary democracy means rule by plebiscite. The word 'plebiscite' originally meant a vote in the plebeians' assembly in Ancient Rome. The plebeians were the lowest class of people in Ancient Rome (hence calling someone you don't much respect a 'pleb'). As with democracy, the word suggests listening to the people directly. In modern times, a plebiscite means a one-off vote on a particular issue, open to all adult citizens of a country. It is more commonly known now as a **referendum**.

So, to resolve our road-crossing controversy, ballot papers are sent to all the houses in the area with a simple question: 'Do you support building a new road crossing?', with the option to vote Yes or No. The votes are collected and counted. If there are more Yes than No votes, the crossing is built; if there are more No than Yes votes, it isn't.

What are the advantages and disadvantages of this type of democracy?

Advantages:

- It is simple and easy to understand.
- Everyone's vote counts equally.
- Because it is a secret ballot, people can vote how they really want to without fear of others' reactions.
- It provides a final resolution of the question.

Disadvantages:

- It reduces complex questions to a simple binary choice.
- Splitting issues in two can cause polarisation, forcing people into two opposing camps, with damaging consequences for social cohesion.
- Particularly in a close result, large numbers of people on the losing side may feel ignored and resentful, with no opportunity of redress.
- It doesn't necessarily provide a final resolution of the question, as circumstances change, and people change their minds.

In most countries, referendums are used only for big constitutional questions such as changing the voting system, or granting independence to a region. They have been used extensively for years in Switzerland, at all levels of government from the highest to the lowest, to decide questions from the opening hours of the local supermarket to whether women should have the vote. There, politicians take great care to ensure that their policies command popular support before they enact them, for fear of having their laws overturned in a further referendum, and citizens feel truly listened to, thereby helping to build a culture of trust and solidarity. The UK's experience with the EU referendum was (for the reasons I have explained above) rather less positive, and did much to undermine trust and solidarity across the UK.

Referendums don't always work

Referendums work best with questions which can and should be reduced to a binary choice, and when the precise course of action following the result is made clear before the vote.

3. Representative democracy

Representative democracy means delegating the job of making decisions. Just as you might take your car to the garage if you don't know how to fix it yourself, so you take your country to Parliament to get it fixed. The people get to choose who makes the decisions, and they then have to trust the people they've chosen. It is the most common form of democracy. Once they are elected, these representative leaders make decisions on behalf of the people, but without the need to consult them. They are however accountable to the people at election time, when the people have the right to remove them.

In our road-crossing example, the local people would vote to choose a small committee of residents who would consider the question of the road-crossing and make a decision on their behalf.

What are the advantages and disadvantages of this type of democracy?

Advantages:

- The representatives have time and energy to concentrate on the issues.
- Decisions are likely to be taken in a more considered and thoughtful way.
- People are freed from having to concern themselves with the decisions and can get on with their lives, while knowing that the people who make the decisions are still accountable to them.

Disadvantages:

- Representatives can seem remote and out of touch.
- People feel less ownership of the decision process.
- Representatives often split on party lines, and waste time and energy in fighting each other.
- If circumstances and opinions change over time, there is little opportunity for the representatives to respond.

Representative democracy is in many ways the most efficient model of democracy, and perhaps that is why it is the most common. However, in recent years it has had something of an image problem, with elected leaders perceived as being out of touch with the people. Specifically in the UK, it has clashed with plebiscitary democracy. The view on the EU expressed in the 2016 referendum (narrowly in favour of leaving) clashed with the view of our elected representatives (overwhelmingly in favour of remaining). This did much to undermine public trust in politicians and, even worse, in democracy itself.

4. Deliberative democracy

Deliberative democracy really just means thinking about things together before you make a decision.

A group of people is selected, not by vote, but in a way that is as representative of the people as possible, by ensuring a balance of age, gender, area, socio-economic background, etc. They are then gathered together in the same room, and given as much evidence as possible on the question to be decided. They listen to this evidence and talk it over and come to a conclusion.

So for the road-crossing, a small committee of residents would be selected, not elected. For example, there might be one parent, one business person, one driver, one non-driver, one older person, one disabled person. They would research evidence on things like traffic flow, pollution, the times of day when most people need to cross the road, etc. They would then come up with a recommended course of action. This would likely be some form of compromise, e.g., only running the crossing at times when children are going to or coming home from school.

What are the advantages and disadvantages of this form of democracy?

Think it through together

Advantages:

- It makes for decisions which are more likely to be based on evidence rather than prejudice.
- If the deliberative panel is well chosen, these decisions will be more representative of the people.
- It often neutralises divisive conflicts, providing more opportunity for compromise.

Disadvantages:

- The panel can seem remote from the people.
- It is very time-consuming.
- Compromise can end up satisfying no one.

The poster child for deliberative democracy is the 2018 referendum in Ireland to repeal the law against abortion. Abortion was a very highly charged and emotional issue in Ireland. The Catholic Church, which opposes abortion under all circumstances, was deeply embedded in Irish culture for hundreds of years, but had recently lost much of its power following a series of abuse scandals. The referendum could easily have split the country down the middle. However, it was preceded by a Citizens' Assembly, which selected a range of people from across Irish society to consider the evidence on abortion in real depth. Many people changed their minds in the process. The vote went two to one in favour of repealing the law against abortion, but, more importantly, unlike the Brexit vote in the UK, the referendum left very little legacy of bitterness: people on both sides felt they had been listened to. While the Catholic Church in Ireland continues to teach that abortion is wrong, it has accepted the change in the law, and is not seeking to overturn it.

Deliberative democracy is probably the highest form of democracy. However, it does require a considerable investment of time and goodwill. As Oscar Wilde said of socialism, it sounds like a good idea, but it takes up too many evenings.

Efficiency or fairness?

3. THE POINT OF CLASH

Who should vote?

Here, the point of clash is really about **what voting is for**.

If the purpose is to **choose the best government**, then you are likely to lean more towards restricting the franchise to those best able to make a good decision. This would mean keeping the current age limit of 18 (children are too immature); continuing to ban convicted criminals from voting (they have shown disrespect for the law and should not be allowed to choose the people who make the law); and excluding foreign nationals resident in the UK (they are not sufficiently invested in the country to take responsible decisions about its future). Be careful with how far you take this line of argument, though; it could shade into the logic which allowed previous generations to argue that women and men without property should be excluded from voting because they did not hold a sufficient interest in the running of the country.

On the other hand, if you see voting as a way of giving people a **stake in society**, then you will want to widen the franchise as much as possible. Children may not know all the ins and outs of all the parties' policies (how many adults do?), but giving them the vote makes them feel responsible and listened to, and increases the chance that they will take an interest in politics; criminals will be more motivated to go straight when they leave prison if they feel they have not been excluded from citizenship; and foreign nationals resident in the UK will feel greater commitment to the country if their views are listened to at elections, and will be more likely to integrate fully into British society. Believers in making voting a key part of citizenship will also lean more towards making it compulsory.

How should we vote?

Do you prioritise **efficiency** or **fairness**?

Efficiency suggests FPTP. It is simple, easy to administer, and is most likely to produce a clear-cut outcome. It can mean a large number of voters are effectively **disenfranchised** (unable to vote) if they live in constituencies where one party almost always wins, but this is a price worth paying for stability and clarity of outcome.

Fairness suggests some form of PR, as it reflects voters' wishes more accurately.

Another question here is whether you most value governments which are **decisive**, or those which are **consensual**.

For **decisive** leadership, FPTP works better, as it is likely to produce majority governments who can carry out their programme without the need for compromise.

For **consensual** and **collaborative** government, some form of PR is preferable, as it is likely to produce non-majority governments who will be obliged to work with their opponents.

Decisive governments can get more things done and more quickly; collaborative governments will command greater support and thus may be more unifying. As the proverb says, 'If you want to go fast, travel alone; if you want to go far, travel together.'

Some decisions need to be made by one person

What kind of democracy?

Similar to the choice of voting system, this question tends to pivot around two points of clash: **efficiency vs fairness**, and **decisiveness vs consensus**.

If you favour **efficiency** in government, then you are likely to favour **representative democracy**, as it allows a small group of people to dedicate themselves full-time to making the decisions, and also licenses them to make those decisions swiftly, without the need for further consultation. If you favour **fairness** – maximising citizens' involvement in decision-making – both **direct democracy** and **plebiscitary democracy** provide more immediate information about voters' preferences.

If you favour **decisiveness** in government, then **representative democracy** is better for allowing those in power to get on with the job uninterrupted. **Plebiscitary democracy** also provides for a definite decision on an issue (although, as the Brexit example shows, this only works when the consequences of the outcome of the vote are made very clear beforehand). If you favour building the maximum amount of **consensus,** then **direct democrac**y is the ideal, though it will only work in small groups. If it is well managed, then **deliberative democracy** is likely to generate decisions that reflect the thinking of society as a whole. Those decisions are also more likely to be based on evidence and reason than emotion and tribal loyalties.

Neither of these last two models of democracy are good at taking swift and urgent decisions: if a hijacked plane is flying over central London on its way to Wembley Stadium on the day of the Cup Final, it's not going to work to convene a Citizens' Assembly to debate whether or not we should shoot it down. Even the most democratic societies have to delegate authority to one person at some point.

4. THE ARGUMENTS

Lowering the voting age

Keeping it at 18	Lowering it to 16 / 11 / 6
Only adults pay taxes, so only adults should be able to select the government that levies taxes.	Children are impacted by how taxes are spent, e.g. on their schools.
Voting requires maturity of judgement.	Being given the right to vote encourages maturity and teaches good judgement.
Voting requires knowledge about the issues.	Children can (and should) be taught about the issues in schools; having the right to vote will make them more interested.
Adults have a greater stake in society.	Children are greatly affected by government decisions: immediately by how their schools are run, indirectly by how the health of the economy affects their parents. Those aged 14+ are likely to be adults before the next election.
Children are likely to be swayed by their parents' views.	Adults can also be heavily influenced by their social group / social media, etc. Older children in particular have no difficulty in disagreeing with their parents.
Children are not good at taking the long view.	Policies that favour children's interests are more likely to take the long view, as they are likely to be alive the longest.
Politicians will pick policies that please children.	Why shouldn't they? All voters deserve equal respect.

FPTP vs PR

FPTP	PR
Simple and easy to understand.	Voters are capable of dealing with complexity.
Provides a clear outcome.	Better reflects what people want; better reflects the complexity of the decision.
Outcomes provide strong, decisive government.	Outcomes provide collaborative, consensual government.
Gives one known person to represent an area.	Those who did not vote for that person feel alienated from them.
Makes government more efficient by allowing the ruling party to make decisions without negotiation.	Makes government more democratic by involving more parties in decision-making.
PR gives too much power to party managers.	FPTP gives too much power to the ruling party.
Gives a clear outcome.	Gives a fair outcome.

Direct democracy

For direct democracy	Against direct democracy
Involves everyone.	Unmanageable and chaotic.
Gives everyone a voice.	Only those with the loudest voice / biggest ego will be heard.
Allows for the free and honest exchange of views.	Can cause division and resentment in a community or make people too afraid to speak their minds for fear of alienating others.
Decisions will be considered and thoughtful, taking into account everyone's views.	Unsatisfactory, messy compromise is likely.
Decisions will be tested against the expertise and experience of everyone involved.	'Groupthink' is likely; controversial and unpopular decisions will be avoided.

Representative democracy

For representative democracy	Against representative democracy
Elected representatives can make decisions in a thoughtful, measured way.	Elected representatives become detached from the people they represent.
By devoting themselves to the business of governing full-time, elected representatives become e xpert in governing.	By devoting themselves to the business of governing full-time, elected representatives become detached from ordinary people.
Party membership for elected representatives means we know what they stand for.	Party membership for elected representatives means they don't think for themselves.
Elected representatives in a four- or five-year parliament are more likely to take the long view.	Elected representatives in a four- or five-year parliament are more likely to lose touch with the people.
Elected representatives remain accountable to the people.	Elected representatives will tell people what they want to hear to get re-elected.
It means we don't have to think about politics.	We ought to think about politics – it matters!

Referendums

For using referendums	Against using referendums
Keeps voters directly involved in decision-making.	Decisions may be ill-informed.
People feel listened to.	The losing side are not listened to, and, unlike in an election, they have no comeback.
Provides a final resolution.	Situations change and opinions change.
Directly represents the will of the people.	Causes division and animosity.
Provides a clear-cut decision.	Most issues are not binary; does not allow for nuance and complexity.

Deliberative democracy

For deliberative democracy	Against deliberative democracy
Allows for careful consideration of the issues.	Too slow and cumbersome.
Involves all sectors of society.	Who chooses who will be on the panel? Having everyone vote is more truly representative.
Ensures expert guidance is considered.	Who chooses the experts? Having everyone vote is more truly representative.
Avoids the divisive conflict of a binary decision.	Avoids honest, open debate.
Likely to produce a nuanced, balanced decision.	Likely to produce an unsatisfactory, messy compromise.
Mature and responsible way to take decisions.	Too detached from ordinary people.

5. THE MOTIONS

1. This house would make voting in general elections compulsory.
2. This house would reduce the voting age to 16 / 14 / 11 / 6.
3. This house would introduce proportional representation.
4. This house would set up a Citizens' Assembly to respond to the climate emergency / [insert another issue].
5. This house would ban referendums.
6. This house would delegate democratic decisions to the lowest level.
7. This house would make it compulsory for 50% of MPs to be female.
8. This house would hold annual elections to Parliament.
9. This house would introduce a written constitution.
10. This house would abolish all political parties.
11. This house would fund political parties from taxation.
12. This house believes democracy has failed.

Keep thinking...

A selection of further reading to help you think more deeply about the issues around democracy.

The Vote: How It Was Won and How It Was Undermined, Paul Foot (Viking, 2005)

Paul Foot was unapologetically a revolutionary socialist, so didn't really believe in democracy; he thought the radical change needed for a fairer society could never be achieved via elections and parliaments. However, his survey of how British people throughout history have fought from the bottom up for the right to be listened to and represented is both meticulously researched and inspiring in its passion for equality and justice.

***Politically Homeles**s*, Matt Forde (Quercus, 2020)

Matt Forde describes himself as a 'political obsessive', but as obsessives go, he is unusually funny and engaging – not many political commentators are also stand-up comedians. It's also refreshing that, unlike most people at the top of politics, he comes from a provincial working-class background. He describes how democracy works from the inside, having served as a Labour Party aide for many years, but he is far from partisan. He makes a strong and admirable case for open-mindedness, courtesy and respect in debate. The chicken katsu curry metaphor will stay with you for a long time.

Liberalism and Its Discontents, Francis Fukuyama (Profile, 2022)

Francis Fukuyama wrote a famous (and much misunderstood) essay called 'The End of History' in 1993, in which he argued that following the collapse of communism, liberal democracy was the way of the future. The war on terror, the failure of the 'Arab Spring', and the rise of populist dictators or semi-dictators have all threatened this confidence. In this book, he carefully considers where democracy has gone wrong, and how it can be helped to recover.

The Shortest History of Democracy, John Keane (Old Street, 2022)

This is a concise but informative history of democracy from Ancient Athens to the present day. It is also both a thought-provoking analysis of the problems that democracy throws up and an inspirational celebration of democratic ideals.

The Good State: On the Principles of Democracy, A.C. Grayling (OneWorld, 2020)

Grayling is a distinguished philosopher, and brings his analytical powers to bear on how UK democracy in particular could be better. He argues for PR, lowering the voting age, and introducing a written constitution. Carefully and intelligently argued, this book will make you think harder about democracy.

How Democracies Die: What History Reveals About Our Future, Steven Levitsky and Daniel Ziblatt (Penguin, 2019)

Written largely in response to Donald Trump's assault on democratic values in the US, this book by two Harvard professors looks back into history to see how democracy has been threatened and how it can be defended. The writers make clear that democracy cannot be taken for granted; it is a fragile thing which needs a lot of care and attention.

Of the People, By the People: A New History of Democracy, Roger Osborne (Bodley Head, 2011)

This is a very well-researched, readable account of the evolution of democracy across the world from Ancient Athens to the twenty-first century, though it stops short of the recent rise of populism.

The Age of the Strongman: How the Cult of the Leader Threatens Democracy around the World, Gideon Rachman (Bodley Head, 2022)

Rachman looks at the growing number of leaders around the world who win democratic elections, but then behave like dictators (controversially, Boris Johnson features among them). He asks how this has happened, and what can be done to protect democracy.

Politics, David Runciman (Profile, 2014)

David Runciman is one of the most interesting and thoughtful commentators on politics. Although a Cambridge professor, he writes in a very accessible, easy style. This book will introduce you to some of the basic concepts of politics and democracy, and should convince you that, as Professor Runciman says, 'politics matters'.

Julius Caesar, William Shakespeare (1599)

Ancient Rome, like Shakespeare's England, was very far from being a democracy. Nonetheless, Shakespeare's play provides food for thought on many democratic issues. Which is more important, principles or power? When is it justified to use violence to overthrow a government? Can some uses of rhetoric to persuade be irresponsible? Should we always listen to 'the people'? How far should we take into account the character of leaders when electing them? Do revolutions make societies worse or better?

CHAPTER 6

Education

In this chapter we're thinking about...

- **Should private schools continue to exist?**
- **Should faith schools continue to exist?**
- **Should schools be allowed to select on grounds of ability?**
- **What should be taught in schools?**
- **What place should public exams have in education?**

This chapter focuses on education up to the age of 18. It is currently compulsory in the UK for almost all young people to be in education or training until that age. It also focuses mostly on the education system in England and Wales. Scotland and Northern Ireland have separate education systems, controlled by their devolved governments, which differ in some significant ways from England and Wales.

1. THE FACTS

Why bother learning to read?

When most people couldn't read and write

Until about 180 years ago, no one saw much point in teaching most people to read and write, still less to have any kind of broader education. Why bother? They didn't need to know how to write essays to dig a field or steer a plough or hew coal or (later) work in a factory. The great engineer and pioneer of the Industrial Revolution, Isambard Kingdom Brunel (1806–1859), once said that he would never hire a man who could read. Presumably it might distract him from his work. There was even less reason to educate girls. Their role was to look after their husbands and their (many) children, as well as often having to work. How could they do that with a book in their hand?

Priests needed an education, to study theology and read the Bible, preferably in the original, so that they could instruct the faithful. Those in positions of power needed an education in order to run the country. Everyone else did some kind of manual labour, and you didn't need book learning for that. Given that your position in society was almost entirely determined by the family you were born into, education tended to be restricted to the sons (and occasionally the daughters) of the upper classes, and was mostly conducted by private tutors in private homes. A very small selection of clever poor boys were picked out for education in the 'public schools' (see below), and the church offered others a way of advancement (Cardinal Wolsey, the most powerful cleric in Henry VIII's England, was a butcher's son), but these were very much the exception. Reading, writing, learning and thinking about anything that wasn't in front of your nose – that was for the top people only.

A brief history of state education

It wasn't until the early nineteenth century that education began to be paid for by the state. Sunday schools and elementary schools existed, tending to focus mostly on religious instruction; these were usually sponsored by church-based charities. In 1833, Parliament passed legislation to limit the hours that children could work in factories, and, in the same year, approved a grant of £20,000 to two major educational charities. A moral and religious education

Most people left school at 14

was seen as necessary to helping adult citizens better understand their responsibilities in society. It was the first time that the state had given any financial support to education (though they were still spending less on schools than they did on looking after Queen Victoria's horses). This injection of cash was followed by the first attempt at quality control by the state, when school inspections were introduced in 1839, although the government still did not think it was necessary to give any direction to schools on what they should teach.

In 1870, the Elementary Education Act was passed. This allowed (though did not require) school boards to be set up in areas where there was a clear need for elementary education. These boards could then set up schools, run by the state rather than the church, funded by a mix of government grants and local taxes. Education remained optional until 1880, when it became compulsory for all five to ten year olds. The Education Act of 1902 merged local school boards into larger local education authorities, and allowed them to open secondary schools, though attendance remained voluntary after the age of ten, and some schools still charged fees. In 1918, fees for state schools were abolished and education became compulsory for all children up to the age of 14, with the national government and local education authorities sharing the cost. A small number of poorer children won scholarships or government grants to 'direct grant schools', which tended to offer a more academic curriculum, and were obliged to admit at least 25% of non-fee-paying students. This system was abolished in 1975, when direct grant schools had to choose between becoming non-fee-paying, non-selective state schools or turning into independent private schools.

These reforms were not entirely motivated by an altruistic desire to help poor people better themselves. They were also a pragmatic response to the need for a more educated workforce as the economy began to require skills beyond the purely physical. And there were limits. Up until the start of the Second World War in 1939, the great majority of state-educated children left school at fourteen. Only a minority stayed on at school after the age of 14, most of them leaving at age 16. Even fewer went on to higher education. Barely one in 150 of university students had been entirely educated by the state. Education beyond the most basic level was not for children whose parents couldn't pay fees.

After the war, education for all

More chances for more children

And then along came the Second World War. The social upheaval it brought, along with the sense of a shared struggle against a common enemy, brought a major shift in the way people thought about the role of government in their lives. In 1944, one year before the end of the war, an Education Act was passed with support from the Conservative, Labour and Liberal parties (who were sharing power in a wartime coalition), establishing a new settlement for education.

The government would now pay for education for all until the age of 15, along with medical inspections, travel to and from school, lunch, and milk at break time. All through schools from ages 5–14 were replaced with primary schools for ages 5–10 and secondary schools from ages 11–15. Local education authorities would provide grants for university, increasing the number of poor children who could aspire to a degree. Women teachers would now be paid the same as men teachers, and, daringly, women would no longer have to resign their teaching jobs when they got married (a requirement which had of course never applied to men).

All of the above measures helped to create a more egalitarian and inclusive atmosphere around education in the postwar years, and greatly improved the educational opportunities of poorer children. However, we were still a long way from being a society in which every child attended the same sort of school and had more or less the same experience (we still are). This was partly because of the continued existence of private schools (see below), but also because of the way that state schools were structured under the provisions of the 1944 Education Act. These new structures raised issues and debates which continue to this day.

God in the classroom

The first complication was the involvement of the two main churches: the Church of England and the Roman Catholic Church. Pre-war, a huge number of schools were run by these churches, on a partly charitable basis. While the influence of Christianity in British society had begun to wane in the twentieth century, it was still a significant force, both culturally and institutionally. It proved impossible for the government to persuade the churches to hand over all their schools to the state. A compromise was reached, whereby church schools could opt to be either 'voluntary aided', in which case the state paid, but the church kept control

Why did you go to church in Year 5?

of the buildings, the governors and the appointment of the staff, or 'voluntary controlled', in which case the state met the cost and appointed the governors and staff, but the school could maintain its Christian ethos. Children who attended a church school would take part in regular worship in the tradition of the church running it while they were at school, and would receive religious education lessons informed by the doctrines of that church. There would also be an expectation that they would attend church with their families on Sundays (though the school could not enforce this).

Approximately 50% of state schools in the immediate postwar period were church schools. To a degree, these schools reinforced class divisions. Anglican families were, on the whole, likely to be higher on the social scale, while Catholics were more likely to be first- or second-generation immigrants, often from Ireland or Southern Europe, and therefore less socially established. While there was never the kind of tribal division between Protestants and Catholics which existed in Northern Ireland (and which led to a virtual civil war in the province from 1969 to 1998), church schools didn't exactly encourage mutual understanding between different faiths, or indeed between believers and non-believers. There were no state schools for Nonconformist Christians (whose churches tend to be run more democratically, by their congregations), or for non-Christian faiths.

Faith schools, paid for by taxes, continue to form a significant part of the state education system to this day. They now include Jewish, Muslim, Hindu and Sikh schools. In 2010, in a bid to make them more inclusive, the government introduced the '50% Rule' for newly established faith schools, which meant that they could only admit half of their students on the basis of their religion (though in 2018, it was decided to allow faith schools to admit 100% intake of faith adherents in the case of oversubscription of places). The percentage of faith schools has dropped since 1945, but they still make up approximately one third of state schools in England.

Faith schools tend to achieve better GCSE and A Level results than non-faith state schools, and also tend to have fewer students who qualify for free school meals (a key metric for poverty). They are frequently popular and oversubscribed, allowing churches to use them as recruitment tools. Did you suddenly get dragged along to church by your parents when you were in Year 5? You won't have been the only one. Some faith schools apply very stringent criteria for entrance, insisting for example on evidence of baptism (the ceremony that inducts a child into the Christian church) within three months of birth, along with a record of more or less continuous church attendance. They may also require teachers to toe the church's line on moral issues, making life difficult for teachers who are openly gay, divorced or have children outside marriage. Other faith schools interpret their remit more broadly, only insisting on a general sympathy with Christian values, and adopting an inclusive approach to different lifestyles. Some church schools, reflecting the make-up of their local area, actually have a majority Muslim intake.

Grammar schools for winners, secondary moderns for losers

Faith schools are one of the many aspects of our educational system which baffle foreigners. Some countries, such as the United States and France, make an absolute separation between church and state, insisting that religion is an entirely private matter and should have no role in any state-funded institution. In France, you cannot even wear a headscarf or a necklace with a crucifix on at a state school. Here, despite the fact that in the 2021 census fewer than half of British people identified themselves as Christian, state education continues to be heavily influenced by the churches (Christian schools still make up the great majority of faith schools).

Sheep and goats

The other major change in the postwar education settlement was the introduction of selection. While all children educated by the state would attend the same kinds of school until the age of 11, the 1944 act provided for three different types of school post-11: grammar, technical and secondary modern. Grammar schools were for the more intellectually gifted children, capable of abstract thought; technical schools were for the more practically inclined; and secondary moderns were for … well, for anyone left over. Church schools were also expected to adhere to this structure.

How would it be decided which children should attend which school? All children would take an exam in English and Maths, popularly known as the eleven-plus. The theory behind this division of schools was that different institutions would meet the needs of different kinds of children, to everyone's benefit.

Technical schools never really got off the ground, comprising only 2% of schools, so that in practice, there were only two types of school: grammars and secondary moderns. In practice, too, a clear hierarchy emerged: grammars were good schools, secondary moderns weren't. The eleven-plus was not a helpful and informative diagnosis of each child's personal educational profile. It was a brutal competition, with a binary outcome. Fail the eleven-plus, and you could say goodbye to any hope of higher

Were grammar schools fair?

education or a professional career before you'd even reached puberty. It wasn't just expectations that were unequal: grammar schools received three times the funding of secondary moderns, tended to hire more highly qualified teachers, and were dominated by middle-class children, partly because their parents could afford tutors to coach them for the eleven-plus. Poorer areas tended to have fewer grammar schools than more prosperous ones. Grammar schools were for a minority, serving approximately 25% of children. Almost all the rest found themselves in secondary moderns, with little hope or expectation that their education would allow them to rise above the circumstances into which they had been born.

The role of grammar schools has been much mythologised. Some people argue that they provided a way for clever working-class girls and boys to fulfil their potential and to achieve a level of educational and professional success that would have been unimaginable for their parents and grandparents. There are indeed very many examples from the postwar generation of people who rose from humble backgrounds to the top of their professions, who were and are deeply grateful for the opportunities a grammar school education gave them. But it can also be argued that a booming economy and an increase in the number of professional and managerial jobs in the postwar years had as much to do with increased social mobility as the existence of grammar schools. And there were a lot of people left behind.

Doubts about both the efficiency and fairness of selection at eleven grew through the 1950s and 1960s. The eleven-plus didn't seem that accurate at diagnosing ability. Some grammar school students struggled academically, while students at secondary moderns turned out to be brighter than expected. Middle-class parents whose children ended up in secondary moderns were not happy with the system. More and more local education authorities quietly moved to a **comprehensive** system, in which schools took children of all abilities, without any selection. In 1964, after thirteen years of Conservative government, Labour returned to power, with a mission to make Britain a more equal society. The new education minister, Anthony Crosland, sent out a directive 'requesting' all local education authorities to make plans to move to a comprehensive system. 'Requesting', not 'requiring'. Nonetheless it (almost) did the job. Grammar schools were on the way out. Labour were out of power from 1970 to 1974, but the Conservative government in those years did nothing to stop the abolition of selection (the future Conservative prime minister, Margaret Thatcher, was education secretary, and authorised the creation of a huge number of comprehensives). Labour were back in power in 1974, and by the time they made way for the Conservatives under Thatcher in 1979, only a small minority of education authorities were still holding on to selection at eleven, sometimes alongside comprehensives. While there have been frequent calls for the return of grammar schools, at the time of writing only 5% of such schools remain in England and Wales. Northern Ireland retains its grammar schools, although most of these no longer take students purely on grounds of ability. Scotland has had no selective state schools since the mid-1960s; its remaining 'grammar schools' retain the name for historical reasons, are fee-paying and similar to private schools in England. There are examples of ambitious middle-class parents moving to the few remaining areas which still have grammar schools in the hope of bagging what they see as a private education for free. There are almost certainly no examples of anyone moving to an area in order to send their child to a secondary modern.

Who's in charge of schools?

Schools are doing it for themselves

In 1987, schools in England and Wales underwent another great upheaval. This time it was not to do with which children went to which schools, but with who should be in charge of schools.

For forty or so years after the Second World War, state schools were run by local education authorities (LEAs), which were themselves run by local councils. LEAs would cover a particular town, or wider rural area, or part of a large city. All the state schools in that area would be under the control of the LEA. The LEA determined which children went to which school; normally (as is still the case in most countries), you went to the school nearest to your house, whether you liked it or not. The LEA would oversee and control school budgets, direct long-term policy, and offer training and support to teachers. New school buildings, along with services like catering, cleaning and routine maintenance and repairs, were paid for and administered by the LEA. School staff, teaching and non-teaching, worked not for their school, but for the LEA. The LEA might also organise and direct shared endeavours between schools such as sports competitions and musical concerts. Schools were funded by a combination of local and national taxes.

If you were the headteacher of a state school, you still had the authority to run your school on a day-to-day basis. You could appoint your own staff – although they were technically hired by the LEA, in practice the LEA delegated most hiring decisions to headteachers. You could decide what was taught in the school,

Who are you going to call? The LEA

how the school day was structured, and who in the school should be in charge of what. But if you wanted a new sports hall, you had to go cap in hand to the LEA. If the school lunches kept being served cold, you took it up with the LEA. The cleaners were slacking off? You got the LEA to have a word with them. Needed a new roof for the science block? You called the LEA. The Head of Maths told you that the syllabus had changed and she urgently needed new textbooks for next year? Well, that depended on how much the LEA let you have for books.

Defenders of the LEA system argued that it promoted economies of scale, and cooperation between schools. Services like cleaning, catering and maintenance could be more efficiently and economically organised when they were spread over a wider area. Teachers, rather than operating in isolation in their schools, could seek mutual support from across the town or borough. LEA subject advisers could facilitate training and discussion, getting English teachers together to swap tips on Shakespeare, putting Maths teachers in one room to quiz each other on quadratic equations. An LEA provided a shared identity for an area, catering for its particular character; schools in the Lake District have very different needs from schools in inner London, and LEAs could reflect this. Moreover, it was democratic. LEAs were accountable to the council, which was accountable to local voters. If parents didn't like the way schools were run in their area, they could put pressure on the council to do better; if the council didn't improve, they could be voted out.

Kenneth Baker, the Conservative education minister from the mid-1980s, had other ideas. He believed that the LEA system was over-centralised, over-bureaucratic, and in danger of being captured by politically motivated councils. He wanted to give back control to headteachers and parents, school by school.

First, he created a number of **City Technology Colleges** (CTCs), which were funded directly by the national government on a *per capita* basis – that is, the amount of funding they received depended on how many students they had on their books. The national government also decided their curriculum (what should be taught in schools). CTCs were run not by the LEA, but by educational trusts supported by local businesses. More widely, he announced the creation of **grant-maintained schools**. Provided a majority of current parents approved the move in a ballot, any school could 'opt out' of local education authority control. The school would then, as with CTCs, receive direct funding from the national government. Opting out was accompanied by 'local management of schools', which delegated almost all decisions to

Goodbye LEAs...

the headteacher. Now the headteacher could call up a local builder to come in and fix the leaking roof in the science block; negotiate their own contract with a catering company for school lunches, shopping around for quality and value; sack the cleaners if they didn't dust; and tell the Head of Maths that she'd have to wait for her textbooks, because all the money was going on a new sports hall. Crucially, headteachers had more freedom to decide who came to their school, even using some limited forms of selection, and parents had more freedom to decide which school to send their children to. Opting out was a significant change, but it didn't sweep through the entire school system. It was more popular in the secondary sector, where 19% of schools chose it; only 3% of primary schools opted out. It did, however, pave the way for a fundamental shift in the way schools were run in the early twenty-first century.

In 1997, Labour came to power under Tony Blair. CTCs and grant-maintained schools were abolished by the new government in 1998 (the schools remained, but were administered differently). That didn't mean that Labour wanted to go back to the old days of LEAs – quite the reverse. Just two years later, in 2000, the government introduced **academies**. Academies can best be described as grant-maintained schools on steroids. Headteachers can set their own budgets, hire their own staff and decide how much to pay them, and have a great deal of control over what is taught. Many academies choose a particular focus, e.g. prioritising science or the creative arts. In 2006, LEAs were abolished for good.

Academies were greatly expanded in the 2010s under the Conservative–Liberal Democrat coalition, with schools being given financial incentives to switch to academy status, and in some cases (if they were judged to be failing) effectively being forced to convert. **Free schools**, introduced in 2011 by the same coalition, were a further extension of the academy concept. They can be set up by local groups such as charities or faith communities, or just by groups of parents. The national government provides the funding, but the headteacher and governors have a huge amount of freedom to decide how the school is run, and diverse approaches are encouraged.

At the time of writing, most state schools in England and Wales are now academies or free schools: 80% of secondary schools and 39% of primary schools. This change in how schools are run – more diverse, more atomised, less centralised – reflects a wider change in society. Schools, which were once public institutions run by local government, are nowadays more like businesses, competing for customers (and thus funding), the good ones

Schools are like businesses

expanding, the bad ones declining. Parents are no longer passive recipients of education for their children from a government that is there to look after them; they are more like consumers, looking around for the best deal. The introduction of league tables for exam results in 1992 under Ken Clarke, successor to Kenneth Baker, further encouraged this competition between schools, as parents could see exactly how schools measured up against each other in their outcomes. (Exam league tables were abolished in Wales in 2001, and in Scotland and Northern Ireland in 2003.) Also in 1992, regular inspections of schools by OFSTED (the Office for Standards in Education) were instituted. These inspections award grades ranging from 'Outstanding', through 'Good' to 'Requires Improvement', down to 'Inadequate'. OFSTED inspections can be immensely stressful for teachers, with the fate of a school hanging on the verdict of inspectors who never spend longer than a week on the premises. In March 2023 one headteacher took her own life after her school was graded 'Inadequate', leading to calls for reform of the system. The grading of a school by a single word or phrase has been much criticised as failing to do justice to the complex and varied judgements involved in assessing a school's performance, and it has been argued that inspectors should take on a more supportive role. Advocates of the OFSTED regime say that it provides valuable information for parents, and that it is right that schools should be held accountable.

Defenders of a 'market-based' approach to education say that allowing schools to act in a more individual way, pitting them in competition against each other, incentivises them to raise their game, making them meet the needs of pupils better. It also gives parents more freedom to make decisions about their children's education, in the way that those parents who can afford to pay school fees have always been able to do.

There is no doubt that schools do work harder now to attract and retain students, demanding more of teachers (and indeed of students). It was much easier in the LEA days for schools and teachers (and sometimes students) to get away with complacency and laziness, and some of them did. However, as in any competitive system, there are winners and losers. The disparity in the quality of schools between more prosperous and less prosperous areas within a town or city is more marked than it was in the days of the 'one size fits all' LEAs. Parents now have more choice and more control, and are encouraged to take greater responsibility for their children's education. Ambitious and well-connected parents can get more out of the state system. However, less confident and assertive parents – who are already more likely to be socially and economically disadvantaged – may get left behind. On the one hand, choice brings freedom; on the other, it favours those whose circumstances mean that they are better at using that freedom. The question of how schools should be run comes back, like so many issues do, to a central point of clash. Which works better: **collaboration** or **competition**? And which is fairer?

Working together or competing?

A brief history of private education

Here's another thing that baffles foreigners about our education system: why are private schools called 'public schools'?

Well, once upon a time they actually were public, in the sense of being free and open to people from all levels of society. The very oldest and longest established English private schools started life as non-fee-paying schools. In 1382, William of Wykeham, who had himself risen from a modest background, set up Winchester College 'for such poor and needy scholars, clerks, present and to come, in order that they may be able to stay or be busy at school … to hold out helping hands and give the assistance of charity.' The key focus of the school was to train up clever poor boys to become priests, because so many had been lost in the years of the Black Death. To get them into the swing of it, they were expected to speak nothing but Latin while they were at school.

Winchester College was followed by Eton College, founded by Henry VI in 1440. After the Dissolution of the Monasteries in 1541, Henry VIII founded Westminster School on the site of a charity school set up by Benedictine monks before the Norman Conquest. Westminster was then refounded in its current form by his daughter Elizabeth I in 1560. All three monarchs intended their foundations to educate mostly poor scholars. Many more schools were established in the sixteenth and seventeenth centuries. All of these institutions were originally aimed at poor boys; almost all of them survive today as expensive and exclusive private boarding schools.

During the eighteenth and nineteenth centuries, a combination of economic necessity and greed led the public schools to scale down their commitment to educating the poor. By the mid-nineteenth century, only about 10% of boys at the top schools paid no fees. The ethos of the schools had changed, too, in response to changes in society. The Protestant Reformation and the subsequent break with the Roman Catholic Church meant that there was less focus on nurturing priests. The expansion of the British Empire brought different training needs for the sons of the upper classes. The men who went out to run the newly acquired

Schools were like badly run prisons

colonies needed certain qualities of character to succeed in their role: an absolute certainty of their innate superiority, the ability to repress their emotions, and a ruthless drive to dominate over other people. Nineteenth-century private schools did the job perfectly. They were brutal places. Nowadays, top boarding schools tend to resemble boutique hotels; then, they were more like badly run prisons. Private schools took boys away from their mothers at a vulnerable age, put them in cold, overcrowded, unhygienic buildings, starved them, beat them, encouraged other boys (and some of the teachers) to abuse them physically, emotionally and sexually, and made them play ruthlessly competitive sport from dawn to dusk. All this while repeatedly telling them that they were the best in the world and that God had chosen them to rule over people with differently coloured skins. By the time they were done, former pupils were ready to crack the whip in Africa, India or the Far East without pity or conscience.

Pastoral care wasn't really a thing in nineteenth-century private schools. Nor, it must be said, was broad-based academic study that prepared you for the modern world. The curriculum focused almost entirely on Latin and Greek. This continued for a long time; in the mid-1930s, Eton College still had three times as many classics teachers as science teachers. The focus on classical education was part of a more generalised aristocratic disdain for anything that might be considered useful. Families who had made their money through commercial activity were considered inferior to those who had inherited their wealth and had never had to work for it.

Despite this snobbery, the rising commercial class which had been spawned by the Industrial Revolution was determined not to miss out on education for its children. Successful industrial entrepreneurs were frequently 'Dissenters' – that is, members of Protestant churches other than the Church of England – and were therefore excluded from the established Anglican schools. A number of 'Academies' were set up in the eighteenth and nineteenth centuries to provide for the sons of Dissenters, often with lower fees. Other marginalised groups were catching up too. As discriminatory laws against Catholics were relaxed, private schools for their children were set up, usually run by priests, monks or nuns. Girls' private schools started to appear from the mid-nineteenth century, although their focus tended to be more on preparing girls for suitable marriages than for academic or professional achievement. Only a very few women attended university, and they were not awarded full degrees at Oxford and Cambridge until 1920 (Oxford) and 1948 (Cambridge).

Private schools have a near-death experience

By the beginning of the twentieth century, the status and role of private schools was well established. They educated the elite who would go on to rule at home and abroad. They provided pretty much the only pathway to university study. State schools were never in competition with them; they were there to provide the lower classes with the minimum level of education necessary to enable them to do their menial work.

The financial crisis of the 1930s and then the upheaval of the Second World War from 1939 to 1945 shook the certainty and security of private schools. Numbers declined and budgets were tightened. Some of the smaller ones went to the wall. The wartime spirit of solidarity and collective endeavour, and the postwar reforms this engendered, threatened the private schools' sense of elitism and entitlement. There was a very brief window towards the end of the war and in its immediate aftermath when it might even have been possible for the government to abolish private education altogether, forcing all schools into the state education system. But it didn't happen. The postwar Labour government focused instead on reshaping the state system (see above), In the vague hope that an improved state sector might somehow put the likes of Eton College out of business.

Private schools survived. They still tended to prioritise social status and sporting success over academic achievement (a third of the boys at Marlborough College in the early 1960s had failed the eleven-plus, and would have gone to secondary moderns if their parents hadn't been able to pay the fees). Grammar schools presented them with significant competition. From the 1970s on, though, they began to sharpen up their act. More attention was paid to the quality of teaching and to academic standards; boys' schools opened their doors to girls, in the hope of making their ethos gentler and more diligent (as well as doubling their potential customer base); facilities were upgraded and made more comfortable and better suited to the modern world. In 1980, the Conservative government introduced the Assisted Places Scheme, which, in an attempt to return to the original 'public school' ideal, paid for academically able children whose parents could not afford the fees to attend private schools. The scheme did open up opportunities for many poorer children, and also broadened the social base of private schools, though it was also exploited by better-off families who worked out how to beat the system via clever accounting. Assisted places were abolished by the Labour government in 1997, the money saved being redirected to reducing class sizes in state primary schools for children aged five to seven years.

Private schools are reborn

The reshaping of the landscape of state education in the late twentieth and early twenty-first century (see above), making state schools more competitive and dynamic, had a significant impact on private schools. They could no longer rest on their historical laurels – they, too, would have to compete in the marketplace, making sure their exam results saw them topping the tables. Schools applied their considerable financial muscle to the task. They were helped by the fact that most of them continued to be registered as charities, a legacy of their founding purpose and a significant tax benefit. Teachers, helped by smaller class sizes, better resources and more time for preparation than state school teachers, now focused ruthlessly on achieving the highest grades at GCSE and A Level. Schools hired people specifically to help get students into the top universities. Olympic-sized swimming pools, state-of-the-art theatres, acres of rugby and cricket pitches, en-suite facilities in the bedrooms and haute cuisine in the dining rooms all helped persuade parents to stump up for the fees, which were now rising steeply, well ahead of inflation. As globalisation kicked in, bringing many of the world's super-rich to London, and economic inequality rose in the UK and around the world, private schools became less of a training ground for the English ruling classes, and more of a luxury product for the global elite. Their international reach led many to expand abroad, setting up franchised subsidiaries in the Far East and America.

Many private schools offer bursary schemes, meeting the cost of part or all of the fees for children who could not otherwise afford to attend. Some schools have formed partnerships with state schools, supporting them with expertise and access to their facilities. There are modestly earning middle-class families who make considerable sacrifices to educate their children privately. But it is still the case that private schools are economically and socially exclusive institutions, which do not introduce the children who attend them to people from a wide range of backgrounds.

What advantages does a private education give you?

Private schools cost a lot of money. As of 2023, the median annual income for the UK was **£34,000** before tax. The annual fees for St Paul's Girls' School (a day school) were **£28,872** (and more in the sixth form). The annual fees for Eton College (a boarding school) were **£46,296**.

What do parents get for all that money?

What do you get for your fees?

Here are some facts.

- Private schools educate 7% of British children, rising to 18% in Years 12 and 13 (the proportion is higher in London and the South East, and lower elsewhere).
- 70% of students at private schools come from families in the top 25% of incomes; just 7% come from families in the bottom 25% of incomes.
- The student / teacher ratio (the number of students per teacher) in the private sector is approximately 9:1; in the state sector it is approximately 18:1.
- Private schools spend, on average, twice as much per student as state schools do. Their assets (premises, facilities, etc.) are worth three times more than those of state schools.
- Private school students get almost twice as many A Levels at A* and A grades as state-educated students, and more than three times as many GCSEs at grade 7 and above. (The top grade for GCSE is 9.)
- 36% of private school students are granted extra time in public exams because of special educational needs. For non-selective secondary state schools, it's 23%.
- Private schools make twice as many appeals against public exam results at A Level as state schools.
- 30% of students at Oxford and Cambridge have been educated privately. (This percentage has considerably decreased in recent years as Oxford and Cambridge have taken steps to recruit more state-educated students.)
- Privately educated students can expect, on average, to earn 12% more than state-educated students.

Here is how former private school students are represented in some of the most powerful and influential sectors of British society, as of 2023:

- 29% of MPs
- 54% of journalists
- 61% of government ministers
- 71% of senior officers in the armed forces
- 74% of judges

Britain has had 58 prime ministers. Twenty of them – more than a third – were educated at one private school, Eton College.

More than a third of PMs went to Eton

A brief history of the curriculum

Up until the mid-1980s, there were only two curriculum requirements for state schools. They had to have at least one lesson of religious instruction a week, and they had to begin every day with an act of collective worship of broadly Christian character.

That was it. Tick the religion and worship box and you could do what you wanted. In theory, a school could have forty lessons a week of origami or face-painting or making radio-controlled cars. In practice, most schools followed a reasonably balanced timetable, with a variety of lessons in different subjects, not that different from what you might see today. What happened in those lessons, however, was very much up to individual teachers.

Some teachers were brilliant, inspirational mavericks, re-enacting the Battle of Agincourt with rulers for swords and exercise books for shields, making the class pretend to be lizards in Biology lessons, marching round the rugby pitch declaiming Shakespeare. Others were just really boring, or couldn't keep order, so nobody learnt anything. If you were lucky, you got a good teacher; if you weren't, you didn't. There was very little quality control, not least because there were no shared expectations about what teachers should be teaching.

The energetic Mr Baker (him again) thought that wasn't right. There needed to be a standardised curriculum, specifying what was learnt in schools, to ensure that all children were properly prepared for life. The Education Reform Act of 1988 mandated, in great detail, the content of teaching over ten subject areas, including a requirement for children to study science, technology and a foreign language to the age of 16. Their knowledge would be assessed with tests at ages 7, 11 and 14, in standardised assessment tests (SATs).

From then on, teachers were no longer their own bosses. Since 1988, there have been many changes to the national curriculum. Each education minister (and they change about once every five years) wants to make his or her mark by tugging the curriculum this way or that. It is now widely recognised that Baker's curriculum was overloaded, and the tendency over the years has been to simplify it. SATs are now based less on tests, and more on teacher assessments, and in 2008, SATs for 14 year olds were scrapped entirely. Academies are not bound to follow the national curriculum, and nor are private schools. Governments tend nowadays to exercise control over the curriculum more through the syllabuses for public exams (see below). However, the principle has remained the same. What children learn in schools is decided not by teachers, but by governments. It is somewhat paradoxical that the more control schools have been given over how they can run themselves, the less control they have over what they can teach.

The government decides what you learn

A brief history of public exams

The first public exams were commissioned by schools from universities, as a way of checking up on what their students were learning. Exam papers were set and marked by university lecturers, and were physically brought to schools in a locked case by examiners, wearing academic gowns, who also invigilated the exams. The first exams took place in 1858 (for boys only; girls were not allowed to take public exams until 1867). The questions mostly rewarded memory, with little scope for analysis, still less original thought. A few sample questions for 14 year olds from 1858:

- Obtain the sum of forty-six times seven thousand and twenty, seventeen times one million and one, and thirty-three times thirty-three.
- Name in order the Queens and the children of Henry VIII. On what grounds was he divorced from his first wife?
- In what three ways was our Lord tempted in the wilderness?

There was no government supervision or quality control of exams. The qualifications gained by successful students were awarded by the university exam boards, not the government.

In 1918, the first national qualifications were introduced: the School Certificate, taken at age 16 by those wishing to matriculate from (leave) school, and the Higher School Certificate, taken at age 18 by those wishing to enter university. The existing exam boards dropped their own qualifications and began awarding these. In 1951, the General Certificate of Education (GCE), was introduced. The School Certificate was replaced by Ordinary Level examinations (popularly known as O Level exams), and the Higher School Certificate by Advanced Level exams (popularly known as A Levels). O Levels and A Levels were taken almost entirely by the minority of students who attended grammar schools; approximately 80% of students left school with no qualifications at all. Like the Higher School Certificate, A Levels were used as a gateway qualification for the tiny minority of students who went on to university (just 3.4% in 1950, as opposed to 37.5% in 2022–23). In 1965, the Certificate of Secondary Education (CSE) was created, to provide a (less academically demanding) qualification for students at secondary moderns.

Ten times more people go to uni now than in 1950

In 1988, the education minister Kenneth Baker (yes, him again – he wasn't one to let the grass grow under his feet) merged O Levels and CSEs into one exam, to be taken by all 16 year olds: the General Certificate of Secondary Education, (GCSEs). The first GCSEs relied heavily on coursework, completed by students in their own time. Coursework was almost entirely removed from GCSEs by the Conservative government in 2010. At the time of writing, GCSEs are based entirely on exams taken at the end of the course. Some A Levels had an element of coursework, but this has been greatly reduced since 2010. GCSEs moved away from the need to memorise huge amounts of content that O Levels had called for, testing more creative and analytical skills. A Levels have developed in the same way. GCSE and A Level exams are set and marked by exam boards which are private companies, competing with each other for business from schools. They devise their own syllabuses, but these have to be modelled closely on guidelines set by the government.

The introduction of exam league tables in 1992, ranking schools according to their GCSE and A Level results, hugely raised the stakes attached to public exams, for schools as well as students. State schools as much as private schools were encouraged to compete against each other. Exam results were now the key metric (statistics used to assess and compare) for the success or failure of schools; headteachers could lose their jobs and schools be closed down if grades weren't good enough.

As a result, public exams began to resemble professional sport, with intensive coaching, training plans, ruthless focus on achievement, rewards for successful managers and the sack for failures. This focus on results, along with greater transparency from the exam boards on the criteria for success in public exams, led to a significant inflation of the number of top grades, particularly at A Level, leading to monotonously identical complaints every summer that exams were getting easier. (These complaints were deftly parodied by the satirical magazine *Private Eye* with their headline: *Are the Olympics getting easier? Concern at falling standards as Britain wins more gold medals.*) The reality was that schools and students were getting better at preparing for exams, because they mattered more. Improved results, though, made it harder for universities to discriminate between candidates.

A Levels remain one of the longest-lasting public exam systems in the world. They have not been without rivals though. In 1984, the Business and Technology Education Council introduced qualifications for 18 year olds (popularly known as 'BTECs'). These focussed on more practical subjects, such as Childcare, Tourism, Plumbing or Hospitality. National Vocational Qualifications (NVQs, launched in 1987) had a similarly practical focus. Technical Levels (T Levels) replaced BTECs from 2020.

Public exams are like profes- sional sport

Many private schools (and a few state schools) now offer the International Baccalaureate (IB), an exam with a broader-based syllabus and a more international focus, as an alternative to or even a replacement for A Level. In 2008, the Pre-University Qualification (popularly known as the Pre-U) was launched, targeted at private schools who felt that A Levels were not academically rigorous enough.

Like everything else, public exams were disrupted by the Covid-19 pandemic. In 2020, they were cancelled and replaced by teacher-assessed grades, adjusted by an algorithm which took into account a school's past results and the demographic of its students. This algorithm produced catastrophically inaccurate and unfair outcomes, hugely favouring more advantaged schools. Following a public outcry, the government abandoned the scheme and announced that teacher assessments would be accepted without any moderation or qualification. In 2021, public exams were once again cancelled and replaced by teacher assessments, but this time a more nuanced and carefully thought-through system was used. In both years, grades were significantly higher than usual, creating pressure on university places.

No one forgets a good teacher

2. THE ISSUES

Why education matters

Education matters. How children and young people are educated makes an immense difference both to them as individuals, and to society as a whole.

For individuals, a good education can set them up for life, while a bad one can hold them back for life. In 1997, a teacher recruitment campaign used the slogan 'No one forgets a good teacher.' This is true. The best teachers can be life-changing. Unfortunately, it is also the case that bad teachers can be hard to forget. And what applies to teachers applies to schools and education in general. They shape people, determine what they will become, for better or for worse.

Schools also shape society. A well-educated workforce will greatly increase the productivity and efficiency of the economy, increasing the prosperity of a country; a badly educated workforce will hold everybody back. What children learn at school makes a difference, too. If the curriculum encourages children to think for themselves and come to their own conclusions rather than looking for the 'right' answer (as tends to be the case in the US and most European countries), they are likely to grow up as self-confident, assertive adults, though perhaps sometimes with too much self-confidence and not enough discipline. If, on the other hand, the curriculum prioritises rote learning and the acquisition of knowledge (as tends to be the case in most Asian countries), it is likely to produce adults who are highly disciplined and focused, though perhaps less assured at problem-solving and original thinking.

Then there's how children learn. If they are encouraged to work collaboratively, they are more likely to become good team workers, though perhaps with a mistrust of ambition and excellence. If they (and their schools) are set against each other in competition, they may acquire more drive, but at the cost of empathy for their less successful colleagues.

Schools also form a society's view of itself. Are children taught to be proud of their country, or are they encouraged to take a more critical view of their history? Do the novels, plays and poems they study reflect the lives they lead themselves in the here and now, or do they hold up an ideal of timeless truths? Schools give us the stories we tell ourselves about our society. There's a reason dictators always rewrite textbooks.

How are the benefits of education distributed? A society where schools are more or less the same, educating all the children in their area, will be likely to have a strong sense of solidarity and equality, but may perhaps lack an entrepreneurial spirit. If, on the other hand, schools are encouraged to compete with each other, establishing a hierarchy of good and less good schools, society will become more divided and unequal, though it may also produce more driven high achievers at the top.

Everyone has a view on education

Everyone has a view on education. That's because everyone has experienced it. If you're debating the regulation of the media, you may have to admit that you've never been a journalist; argue about the ethics of warfare, and it may be necessary to concede that you've never been in a war. But everyone has spent (or is still spending) many, many hours in a classroom. If you're reading this book, there's a high likelihood that you are directly involved in education right now, as either a student or a teacher.

This universal experience is both a blessing and a curse when it comes to debating education. On the one hand, it means that everyone can filter the issues through their lived experience. On the other hand, it can lead to a narrowness of vision, in which everyone sees education through what has happened (or is happening) to them. The history of education policy is littered with politicians who initiated wide-ranging reforms based on what it was like when they were at school (a long time ago, and they only went to one kind of school) and / or what works / doesn't work for their own children (not all children are the same). So it's very important when debating education to step back from your experience, whether current or past, and consider the wider issues. Don't focus on why Mrs Gupta is an amazing Maths teacher, or how boring Mr O'Flaherty's lessons are, or how unfair your Geography grade was. Think broad and long, about the whole picture, the whole country, and what sort of future can and should be created in schools; think about young people who are not like you are (or were).

Should private schools be abolished?

Is private education fair?

'Private education is not fair. Those who provide it know it. Those who pay for it know it. Those who have to sacrifice in order to purchase it know it. And those who receive it know it, or should.'

So said the playwright Alan Bennett (himself a grammar school boy) in a lecture at Cambridge University in 2014. Was he right?

Every parent wants the best for their children

There is no doubt that receiving a private education gives you a great many advantages (go back and reread the section above on **What advantages does a private education give you?**). But is it fair that some people should receive these advantages just because of how much money their parents have?

Every parent wants the best for their children. This is a normal healthy instinct which ensures children are brought up with love and care. A good parent will do all they can to see that their children are well nourished, are kept in good health, live in a comfortable house, have adequate clothing, toys to play with, access to activities they enjoy, family holidays. Most of these things cost money. You wouldn't think much of a parent who starved their child, or left them in rags, or made them sleep in the street, to save money. Of course parents spend money on improving their children's well-being. So why shouldn't they do the same for their education, one of the most important benefits you can give a child? How is it fair to prevent people from spending their own money on their own children?

Why shouldn't people be able to choose which schools to send their children to? Why should they have to attend schools run by the state? It's unfair to restrict people's choice – they should be free to educate their children as they see fit. Making everyone do the same thing is what dictators do. Preventing people from paying for education would be almost impossible to enforce without an unacceptable level of control over people's lives.

Private schools promote academic excellence. Moreover, the greater freedom that private schools have means they can be at the forefront of developments in educational thinking, which may influence and inspire state schools. This is fair to everyone as it raises standards overall.

On the other hand …

Buying a child a private education is not like buying them a coat or a computer game or even a holiday in the Caribbean. Private education is a **positional** good. That is, it gives someone an advantage over other people by providing them with higher status; as they rise, someone else must fall. I can have a nice new coat, and you can have a nice new coat. My having a nice new coat doesn't stop you having a nice new coat. If a country is prosperous enough, everyone can have a nice new coat. But not everyone can have the distinction on their CV of having been to a top school (or they wouldn't be top schools); not everyone can have a place at a top university (or they wouldn't be top universities); not everyone can have access to the country's elite (or they wouldn't be the elite). If you achieve these advantages through your own hard work and talent, that's fair. If you achieve these things because of who your parents are, that's not fair.

No one chooses their parents

Giving people choice over their children's education isn't really fair. Most people don't have the money to send their children to private school. So freedom of choice is restricted to a small number of parents who already have a great many advantages. How did they get to be so wealthy anyway? Very likely, they too had a private education, thanks to who their own parents were, giving them access to high-earning jobs. Privilege is very often handed down the generations. And even if they come from a humble background and have earned all their money through their own hard work and talent, that doesn't apply to their children. No one gets to choose their parents. It's unfair that the children of less successful people should be punished for their parents' failings.

Private schools take resources away from state schools, to their disadvantage. The best teachers and the best students are concentrated in a small minority of schools, leaving the rest behind. If resources were distributed more equitably, standards would rise all round. Moreover, state schools would get much more attention and support if the children of wealthy and powerful people were educated in them. This would be both fairer and more effective; it would result in a much better-educated population overall.

Is private education socially divisive?

Some of the advantages of private education are tangible, like class sizes, facilities, exam results. Others are harder to put your finger on, but nonetheless real: confidence; polish; an expectation that you will be successful and respected; a network of well-placed friends who can help you out in later life. Clever state-educated people who make their way to top universities or high-status jobs often report feeling profoundly alienated from their privately educated colleagues, who seem to be speaking a different language, one that they were never taught. Private school students don't quite have a secret handshake, but they might as well have. This means that they are more likely to give jobs and promotions to people who are like them, and to exclude people who aren't. Private schools embed inequality in subtle and therefore more dangerous ways.

The domination of the most influential professions by privately educated people means that those in power have little in common with, or understanding of, the majority of the population. How

Attacking the elite means attacking excellence

can a prime minister who went to Eton understand what it is like for someone who was brought up by a single mother living on benefits? If he had been to a comprehensive, he would have come across people like that. The narrowness of experience of privately educated people means they are more likely to protect their privileges and the privileges of those like them at the expense of everyone else.

On the other hand …

People aren't all the same, and they never will be. Total equality is unenforceable and inhuman. There's nothing wrong with having an elite of people who are better educated than others. It encourages excellence. You say privately educated people exude confidence? Well, maybe they have more to be confident about. If they get all the top jobs, that's a good thing, because their education will make them better at those jobs, to everybody's benefit. And if they then hand out jobs to other privately educated people, maybe that's because those people are better qualified for them.

If you destroy elite education, you destroy excellence. Dragging people down to the same level is bad for everyone. You don't make the weak strong by making the strong weak. A society with a well-educated elite will thrive and prosper; a society where people are made to feel ashamed of doing better than others will fail.

By the way … don't, in a debate on private education, use the argument that anyone who goes to or went to a private school / sends or sent their children to one cannot argue for their abolition. This is the **ad hominem** fallacy, when you attack the person rather than the argument. A system or measure is right or wrong regardless of what the person who is talking about it has done or is doing in their own lives. What's more, most people have very little control over which school they are sent to as children, and, once they are parents, cannot be expected not to do the best they can for their own children within the existing system, whatever its flaws. As Clement Attlee, Labour prime minister from 1945 to 1951, said when his daughter asked him why he, as a socialist, had sent her to a private school: 'My dear, we must live in the world as it is, and not as it ought to be.'

Should state-funded faith schools be abolished?

Pray how you like but not on our taxes

Faith schools are an anachronism (out of date). The 2021 census showed that Britain is no longer a majority Christian country, still less a Jewish, Muslim, Hindu or Sikh country. The majority of British people have no religion.

Even if Britain was more religious, it would make no sense for the government to support faith schools through taxes. The government doesn't sponsor churches or mosques or synagogues or temples – why should they sponsor faith schools? Religion is a private matter. People should be free to worship how they like, and to bring up their children in the faith of their choice, but not on taxpayers' money, and not on state-owned property.

Faith schools are divisive. They prevent children from becoming fully integrated members of society, by surrounding them only with people of their faith group. Church schools tend to be dominated by the children of pushy middle-class parents who know how to game the system, bagging a positional good for their kids by feigning a non-existent faith. This encourages parental hypocrisy, setting a terrible example for children. Non-faith schools suffer through the loss of these families' support. They then turn into 'worse' schools, creating social division. Some faith schools with a more fundamentalist tendency may promote homophobic and misogynistic values.

State-sponsored faith schools have no place in a democracy; public institutions should be neutral on issues of belief.

On the other hand ...

Faith schools have a unique and precious character. They promote values such as kindness, altruism, the common good, and solidarity with those less fortunate than ourselves. You don't have to be a believer to want those values to thrive. Non-faith schools, both state and private, are less likely to promote these values, driven as they are by the ruthlessly competitive ethos of contemporary education.

Even though Britain may no longer be a majority Christian country, its culture and history are still fundamentally Christian. One of the most unifying national events of recent years, the funeral of Queen Elizabeth II in 2022, was a thoroughly Christian affair. Preserving church schools preserves a crucial part of our national identity, and therefore our national unity.

Not all children are the same

Faith schools provide children brought up in non-Christian faiths with a strong sense of their own identity which may protect them against discrimination. People of minority faiths have, throughout history, been forced to either defend or stifle their identity in order to fit in with the majority: Muslims have had to defend themselves against false accusations of holding terrorist views; Jews have had to change their names. Schools for minority faiths protect children from these pressures, allowing them to grow up in a safe, secure environment.

Closing down faith schools would be a discriminatory assault on people on grounds of their beliefs. It would be the act of a dictatorship, not a democracy.

Should state schools be allowed to select on the grounds of ability?

Children are not all the same; they need to be taught according to their particular educational needs. Anyone who has taught (or been in) an all-ability class knows how hard it is to meet the needs of the whole class, and how the strongest students tend to be held back by the weakest. Selective schools recognise this basic fact about human nature.

Creating schools that cater for the very brightest allows those students to thrive in an atmosphere where academic achievement is celebrated. These schools will create the leaders of tomorrow, who will be better educated to everyone's benefit. They will also be places where excellence and ambition are celebrated. Making everyone go to the same identikit schools only encourages mediocrity.

Many private schools select on grounds of ability, and thereby create institutions that achieve excellent results and give bright children a very strong start in life. Why should these opportunities be restricted to children whose parents can afford school fees? State-funded selective schools enable clever children from poorer backgrounds to achieve success and fulfil their potential. They promote social mobility.

On the other hand ...

It is a fallacy that children have a fixed, finite level of ability that can be measured. The sorting hat works in *Harry Potter*, but nowhere else. Environmental factors such as their socio-economic background and the way in which they are taught at school all impact on children's academic achievement. Much better than dividing them up into different groups at a particular age is for teachers to be constantly responsive to their particular needs as they develop. Some children develop later than others; some may have family issues which hold them back at certain stages.

Less able children need more help

Comprehensive schools do not need to be identikit and mediocre. They can use setting for subjects to ensure children are taught at the right level, while still keeping them all in the same institution. This respects diversity while still ensuring social solidarity.

Of course selective schools get better results. That's not because they are better schools; it's because they exclude children who are less likely to get good results. Having to teach only clever children can make teachers lazy and complacent, as they know that their students are going to do well even if they teach them badly.

Why should more able children get better treatment? They are already advantaged by being more able. All children are equally worthy of respect and care. Teaching the less able is more difficult but more worthwhile, as they are the ones who need more support.

Telling the majority of children at a certain age that they are failures is not only cruel, it is also ineffective. The blow to their self-confidence can be lifelong, and will diminish their ambition and drive. It makes for a more divided society, breeding resentment and discontent.

Wealthy parents can afford to pay for tutors to help their children pass whatever test is set up. This creates an unfair advantage for families that already have more advantages. Selective schools tend therefore to be socially as well as academically exclusive.

What should be taught in schools?

This might seem obvious. All children should learn the basic skills they need for life. But what sort of life? Children should be taught to understand the world as it is (and was). But what if we disagree about the way the world is (or was)? And who should make these decisions?

What skills?

At a certain level, this is uncontroversial. No one would argue with the need for children to be literate and numerate, being able to read and write and use numbers. Beyond that, it gets more complicated. Should children be learning skills to equip them for the workforce? Or skills that enable them to live a more fulfilling life? Should they be trained to follow orders? Or to think for

Learn how to work or learn how to live?

themselves? What if this means they challenge those in authority over them? Is that a good thing or a bad thing?

Which is more important, knowledge or skills? Are there certain facts all children should know? Or is it more important to focus on what they can do?

Which is more important, creativity or discipline? Are subjects like Music and Drama (or even English Literature) dispensable luxuries which will distract children from the hard work of making a living? Or are they part of what makes us more fully human?

How can children be truly prepared for the future when we don't yet know what the future will look like? Given that it is likely that most of the jobs taken by children currently at school don't yet exist, what is the point of preparing them for the workforce? Wouldn't it be better to cultivate their character rather than increase their knowledge? Artificial intelligence might mean they don't have to work at all. Should we be preparing them for leisure, not work?

What content?

Should history teaching be used to create and sustain our national identity by celebrating British successes and creating pride in our nation? Or should children be encouraged to be more critical of their heritage? Should the focus be only on Britain, or should they learn about the history of other countries, too?

Should the books children study in English be chosen because they are recognised as being great works of literature, or because their writers and what they write about reflect the social, cultural and ethnic make-up of the student body? Who gets to decide which works of literature are great? Why do some writers make the cut and others not? Why are so many of them (still) dead white men? Does selecting writers on the basis of their ethnicity promote diversity and broaden minds, or is it tokenistic box-ticking? Does it matter that writers from earlier periods express attitudes towards gender and race that we now find offensive, or should we just see them in the context of their times? Should we ban books with discriminatory language, or engage with them? Are there any 'timeless truths', or is what is called the truth just what the people who happen to be in power say is true?

Should children study Latin and Ancient Greek? Are they dead languages which have no relevance in the modern world, or the gateway to civilisations which help us to understand our own times? Is Mandarin more important than French because China is more economically powerful than France, or is French more important than Mandarin because France is closer to our own culture?

Are humanities subjects more important, because they teach empathy and understanding of people who are not like us? Or should STEM (Science, Technology, Engineering and Mathematics) subjects be prioritised because they are more economically valuable? Should girls and members of ethnic minorities be pushed towards studying STEM subjects because they have historically been excluded from them?

Timetables are powerful

Who decides what gets learnt?

Should it be teachers, because they are the experts in education? Or parents, because they are entitled to decide what their children should learn? Or governments, because they are democratically elected and accountable to the people? Or even children, who should be trusted to make their own choices?

As you can see, the curriculum raises a lot of questions. The key point is that it is not simply an administrative matter of making sure that you have this many lessons of English and that many lessons of Maths each week. It is profoundly contentious and debatable. What children are taught in school, and how they are taught it, has a huge impact both on how they see the world and on how they operate in the world, and therefore on the sort of world they will make as adults. It really matters what is on the curriculum, and who controls it. That timetable you have stuck on the front of your planner didn't just fall from the sky – someone decided what you should learn, and that someone (or those people) have a lot of power over you, and over the society you live in.

Are public exams fit for purpose?

There is no doubt that the use of assessment is an essential part of teaching and learning, whether it's a quick informal response to a student's oral contribution, or detailed feedback on a long piece of written work. Assessment provides teachers and students with information about what students have or have not learnt, and guides them in what they need to do next.

However, this kind of 'formative' assessment, which is part of all effective teaching, and is a collaborative affair between teachers and students, is very different from public exams, such as GCSEs and A Levels, set and marked by external authorities. These exams tend to be very focused on outcomes, measured in grades, with huge consequences hanging on them for both students and teachers. Fail to get the grades as a student, and you don't get into university / get the job you wanted; fail to get the grades as a teacher / school and you slip down the league tables, have fewer students wanting to come to your school, and may even be heading towards losing your job / closure.

Have public exams had their day? Or should we keep them?

There is much that is anachronistic about public exams in the UK. Producing an extended piece of writing with no collaboration with anyone else and with no opportunity to consult any external sources (in the expectation that all the necessary information will be – temporarily – stored in the student's head) is a very ineffective way to produce quality work, and one which is highly unlikely to be replicated in anyone's working life in the twenty-first century. The requirement (unless you have a special exemption) to write by hand is also decidedly last century, and does not allow for the constant back and forth of editing on the go which composing on a keyboard allows, and which every writer knows hugely improves the quality of any piece of work. Mass public exams at 16 made sense when the majority of students left at that age; now that some form of education or training is compulsory till 18, they simply interrupt that education. The stress that public exams cause is another significant argument against them. For some students, this is a minor and short-lived inconvenience; for others, it has a major impact. Students who already have fragile mental health are particularly at risk.

Exams also distort teaching, and arguably prevent learning. Here is a personal example. When I was an English teacher, my Year Eleven classes effectively stopped learning in November. The rest of the year was devoted to preparing for mock exams, taking mock exams, returning mock exams, revising material, working through past papers, analysing mark schemes and model answers in the hope of bagging a few extra marks here or there, going on study leave, taking exams, waiting for results. Students got very good at doing English exams, but they didn't learn anything new about literature or reading or writing. My impression was that this was their experience across all subjects. Finally, in September of Year Twelve, they started learning something again. Year Eleven had to be that way (and I suspect is that way in most schools) because of the high stakes of GCSE exams for the students (and the school), but nine months of learning nothing new is an awfully long time in the life of a young person at their most receptive and open. Not to mention that it was incredibly boring and stressful.

There was one exception to this routine. The Year Eleven group I taught in 2019–20 had their GCSEs cancelled because of Covid, so we spent March onwards studying (remotely) a wide range of literature in a much freer way, without any need to worry about exams. It was salutary to note that those of that cohort who went on to take English in Year Twelve were (in my view, and that of my colleagues) far ahead of where previous cohorts had been when they had started sixth form, because they had spent the summer term learning, not being assessed.

This account does not, I am aware, form any kind of conclusive evidence. It is the subjective experience of one person with a very small sample. However, the massive controlled experiment that the cancellation of public exams in 2020 and 2021 provided can help us to think differently about the role of exams.

Exams are tough but so is life

The strongest argument for public exams is the information that the grades provide. This information helps employers to pick employees, universities to pick students, parents to pick schools. It is objective information, because all students have to take the same exams, which are marked according to objective criteria by people who have no stake in the outcome. The teacher assessments that replaced GCSEs and A Levels in 2020 and 2021 produced greatly inflated grades, suggesting that teachers cannot be trusted to assess objectively.

In response to the concerns about the impact on students' mental health, it can be argued that working life is going to be stressful, competitive and full of deadlines, so why should school not be like that too? Protecting students from these stresses is not going to help them in later life. Exams give focus and purpose to learning, and provide objective recognition of hard work and success.

Data about public exam results gives parents valuable information to help them to choose schools for their children, information which should not be kept from them, and this incentivises schools to raise their standards.

Who is education for?

3. THE POINT OF CLASH

On private schools

Which is more important? **Freedom for** parents to choose their child's education? Or **freedom from** the inequality and division that private education creates? Which should we prioritise: **excellence** for a few, or **equal treatment** for all? **Individual freedom** or the **common good**?

On state-sponsored faith schools

Is religion a valuable part of society and culture which deserves to be preserved, whatever our beliefs? Or is it a reactionary anachronism? Is faith something **embedded in culture**, or a purely **private** matter? Do people of faith need to have their culture protected by the state, or should they be expected to look after it themselves?

On selective schools

Which is more important, excellence for the **few** or equal treatment for the **many**? Should we prioritise nurturing the **strong** or supporting the **weak**? Should schools promote **academic achievement** or **social solidarity**? Does the existence of an elite make for a **successful** society? Or a **divided** society?

On the curriculum

Should schools **transmit** the values of the culture they find themselves in, or should they encourage children to **question** those values? Is their purpose to turn out **economically productive** adults, or **happy** people? Should the curriculum be determined by those in **power**, or those on the **receiving** end of it?

On public exams

Do exams promote **rigour** and **discipline**? Or do they just teach children **how to pass exams**, at the expense of real knowledge and understanding? Does the competition inherent in exams bring out the best in children, or does it cause them damaging **stress**? Do exam results provide parents, employers and universities with valuable **information**, or are they too easily manipulated by cunning tactics? Would children **learn more** if they didn't have to take exams?

Do public exams and the publication of results ensure academic **rigour** for students and **accountability** for schools? Or do they turn schools into joyless exam factories, and young people into nervous wrecks?

4. THE ARGUMENTS

For private schools	Against private schools
Parents should be allowed to spend their money on their children's education as they see fit.	It is unfair for parents to be able to buy their children advantages over other children.
Parents should be allowed to choose their children's school.	Choice creates inequality and division.
Private schools promote excellence.	Private schools promote social division.
Private schools provide an excellent education for future leaders.	Private schools produce leaders who have no idea of how most people live.
Private schools ensure a diverse educational system.	Private schools ensure a fragmented and unequal educational system.
Private schools bring out the best in teachers and students.	Private schools take the best teachers and students away from the state system, making it less well resourced and supported.
Freedom to choose is more important than freedom from inequality.	Freedom from inequality is more important than freedom to choose.

For state-sponsored faith schools	Against state-sponsored faith schools
Faith schools embody admirable values which need to be protected.	Faith schools embody outmoded and backward-looking values.
Christianity is part of our national heritage and should be celebrated as such, regardless of our beliefs.	Britain is no longer a Christian country.
Faith schools reflect and promote the diversity of our multicultural society.	Faith schools promote division and undermine integration.
Parents should be entitled to have their children educated in their own faith.	Parents can bring up their children in the faith of their choice, but not on taxpayers' money.
Religions represent cultural communities, and faith schools reflect this.	Religion is a private matter, and the state should have no role in it.
Faith schools help protect minorities from discrimination.	By undermining integration, faith schools make discrimination more likely.
It is discriminatory to stop children from attending a school which reflects their faith group.	It is discriminatory to stop children from attending a school because they do not belong to a particular faith group.

For selective state schools	Against selective state schools
Children are not all the same. Schools should reflect this.	Different kinds of children's needs can be met within a well-run comprehensive school.
Selective schools produce better outcomes for more able children.	Selective schools produce poorer outcomes for those who are not selected.
More able children's needs should be prioritised because they will be the leaders of the future.	Less able children's needs should be prioritised because they need more help.
Selection by exam is objective and fair.	Whatever selection system you set up will be manipulated by wealthier parents who can afford private tutors.
Selective schools promote social mobility by enabling clever poor children to achieve their potential.	Selective schools promote social division as they end up being dominated by children from wealthier families.
Selective schools encourage the most able to achieve their potential.	Selective schools cause the majority who are not selected to feel and act as failures.
You don't make the weak strong by making the strong weak.	You make society weaker overall by only helping the strong.

For public exams	Against public exams
Public exams motivate students to learn.	Public exams turn students off learning by making it boring and stressful.
Public exams raise standards by encouraging rigour and focus.	Public exams lower standards by encouraging students to spend more time on exam technique than actual learning.
Public exams are fair because they provide an objective assessment of learning and ability.	Public exams are unfair because privately educated students and those with access to tutors will be better prepared for them.
Public exams prepare students for the stresses and challenges of working life.	Public exams are artificial and outdated and bear no relation to working life.
The discipline of preparing for and sitting exams is good for young people.	The stress of preparing for and sitting exams is bad for young people.
Public exam results provide valuable data for parents, employers and universities.	Public exam results only tell you how good students are at passing exams; qualities of character are more important.

5. THE MOTIONS

1. This house would abolish private schools.
2. This house would make it illegal to charge for education.
3. This house would make it compulsory for Oxford and Cambridge to admit 90% of their students from state schools.
4. This house would allow Oxford and Cambridge to admit only one student per year from each school.
5. This house would require all private schools to admit 25% of non-fee-paying students.
6. This house would require 90% of government ministers to be state-educated.
7. This house would abolish state-funded faith schools.
8. This house would ban schools from selecting students on the grounds of their membership of a particular faith group.
9. This house would abolish GCSEs.
10. This house would replace public exams with teacher assessments.
11. This house would abolish exam league tables.
12. This house would require 50% of the history curriculum to cover non-British history.
13. This house would require 25% of texts studied for GCSE English Literature to be by non-white authors.
14. This house would ban books containing discriminatory language or attitudes from school libraries and syllabuses.
15. This house would make the study of Maths compulsory for all students till age 18.
16. This house would make the study of Economics compulsory for all students till age 16.
17. This house would make the study of Mandarin compulsory for all students till age 16.
18. This house would reintroduce grammar schools.
19. This house would make it illegal for any school (state or private) to select students on the grounds of ability.

Keep thinking…

A selection of further reading to help you think more deeply about the issues around online life.

The Secret Teacher: Dispatches from the Classroom, Anon (Guardian Faber, 2017)

This book tells it like it is. The (anonymous) author reveals the day-to-day reality of teaching in a tough state school in a witty, entertaining and sometimes moving way. (Spoiler alert: teaching is hard work.) Students will learn what it is like being a teacher, and teachers will recognise themselves. Along the way, you will be prompted to much reflection on what works and what doesn't in real schools.

School Wars: The Battle for Britain's Education, Melissa Benn (Verso, 2011)

Benn is a passionate advocate of a properly funded, state-run, non-selective education system, to be used by all children. She argues that good state schools are good for everyone, and will make for a society that is both fairer and more effective. She is particularly adept at exposing the weaknesses in the arguments of those who maintain that comprehensive schools lower standards. Benn reminds us that the British people are famously supportive of universal free healthcare in the form of the NHS – why shouldn't they be equally supportive of universal free education? Some of her examples have become a little out of date in the fast-moving world of education, but her arguments are still thought-provoking and valuable.

The Making of Her: Why School Matters, Clarissa Farr (William Collins, 2019)

From 2006 to 2017, Farr was High Mistress (headteacher) of St Paul's Girls' School in London, one of the most academically and socially exclusive schools in the country. Here she considers what this experience taught her about education: what should schools be doing? It soon becomes clear that her position at St Paul's was one of great privilege (which, to be fair to her, she freely acknowledges), but that doesn't stop her from offering some very thoughtful and intelligent reflections on education. She makes a strong case for the benefits of both single-sex and private schools, and also reminds us that a private education brings its own pressures. Her observant account of the day-to-day life of St Paul's from the point of view of its head will be enlightening to anyone who has not experienced a private school, or who wonders what headteachers do all day.

Engines of Privilege: Britain's Private School Problem, David Kynaston and Francis Green (Bloomsbury, 2019)

If you are debating private education, read this book. Kynaston and Green provide a meticulously researched and rigorously argued critique of private education and its damaging influence on British society. Almost any argument in favour of the continuance of private education is rebutted here. The authors do, however, acknowledge that it is very hard to come up with a practical strategy for the abolition of private schools.

The Old Boys: The Decline and Rise of the Public School, David Turner (Yale University Press, 2015)

This history of English private schools gives valuable background on how they have developed over the centuries, and their central role in British life. Turner is a firm supporter of private schools as centres of excellence and achievement which add much to public life.

Posh Boys: How the English Public Schools Ruin Britain, Robert Verkaik (Oneworld, 2018)

This is not the most subtle critique of the power of private schools in British society that you will ever read. Some of its arguments are little more than personal attacks, consisting of a list of bad things done by people of whom the author does not approve who happened to attend a private school, followed by the school's name in brackets, as if it was all the school's fault. However, it does uncover some shocking facts, and will provide anyone debating private schools with much valuable information.

CHAPTER 7

Immigration

In this chapter we're thinking about...

- **What are the costs and benefits of immigration?**
- **Who should be let into the UK, and who shouldn't?**
- **Why people do feel the way they do about immigration?**

1. THE FACTS

All British people are immigrants

How did we get here?

All British people are immigrants, if you go back far enough. There has been immigration to what is now known as the UK since the first humans walked out of Africa 50,000 years ago; if there hadn't been, there wouldn't be any people here now. Some of the legionaries who occupied Britain following the Roman invasions that began with Julius Caesar in 55 BCE were black. Colonisation by Saxon farmers, and later invasions by the Vikings and then their Norman descendants in 1066 brought more foreigners to England, and all helped to shape the language we speak today. There were black people living in Shakespeare's England (the character of Othello is said to be based on a Moroccan diplomat living in London). However, for the purposes of understanding current issues around immigration, it is probably most helpful to start from the end of the Second World War in 1945. This is a good place to start as it coincides with two significant events: the **dismantling of the British Empire** (see Chapter 9, **Colonialism**) and the **establishment of the welfare state** (see Chapter 13, **The Welfare State**). Both of these have had a major impact on **how the UK has responded to immigration**.

The dismantling of the British Empire

In the 20 years after the end of the war in 1945, Britain granted independence to almost all of its former colonies. The British had had some sort of empire for over 300 years, and its legacy left a residual sense in popular culture that we were superior to (particularly non-white) former members of the empire, while at the same time having a (rather condescending) obligation to them.

Former residents of the empire had a no less conflicted mix of responses. Many of them had received an education heavily influenced by British values, and often saw the UK as 'home' and a country full of opportunity. At the same time, many carried a justifiable resentment at how Britain had plundered the resources of their native countries (not least through kidnapping people for the slave trade). When they arrived in the UK, they were often shocked and bewildered at how much racism and rejection they met with from the native population.

Obviously, not all immigrants to the UK are from former colonies, but the above does apply to a significant number.

Who does the welfare state belong to?

The establishment of the welfare state

The setting up of the welfare state following the Second World War created institutions such as the NHS, state education, state-subsidised housing, and social security, which were available to all UK residents, including recent immigrants. Some native British people resented (and still resent) immigrants for putting a strain on these much valued national institutions; others acknowledged (and still acknowledge) the way in which these institutions are supported by being staffed and funded (through taxation) by immigrants. You might say that the split is between those who emphasise the 'National' in 'National Health Service', and those who emphasise the 'Service'. Who the welfare state belongs to, and who is therefore entitled to benefit from it, has been one of the key issues around immigration.

How the UK has responded to immigration

There are four principal ways in which the UK has responded to immigration since the end of the Second World War.

1. **Need.** The UK has always needed immigrants to do the difficult, dirty and dangerous jobs native Britons do not want to do.
2. **Fear.** There has been a constant refrain in the media and popular discourse of immigrants as being something to fear: they are taking our jobs; they are taking our culture; they are more likely to be criminals.
3. **Welcome.** Immigrants have added to the diversity, energy and prosperity of the UK, and have been welcomed as such. Also, those fleeing war and oppression have often been welcomed in a spirit of compassion and solidarity.
4. **Change.** There is no doubt that immigration has changed Britain, culturally and economically. Whether this is for the better or the worse is a matter for debate.

1. Need

Britain immediately after the Second World War needed immigrants. Large parts of many cities had been reduced to rubble by German bombing; tens of thousands of men of working age had been killed in the war; there were shortages of everything; the country was on its knees and needed to get back up.

In 1947, the government's Foreign Labour Committee estimated that a million workers needed to be found; 350,000 of these were recruited from mainland Europe (itself even more heavily ravaged by war than the UK). In the 1950s, London Transport actively recruited West Indians, while factory owners in Lancashire targeted Pakistanis. With the expansion of the European Union in the early 21st century, workers from Eastern Europe provided the UK with plumbers, builders, nannies and cleaners willing to provide reliable and cheap services for the more prosperous classes. The agricultural sector also came to depend on the casual labour of Eastern Europeans to pick fruit and harvest crops. Today, you only need walk into a hospital or healthcare centre to see how many immigrants have been hired by the NHS. The UK economy would look very different if there had been no immigration.

Britain needed immigrants

2. Fear

Despite Britain's need for immigrants, a pattern soon emerged of anxiety about and resistance to immigration, particularly expressed (sometimes covertly, sometimes less so) towards people with differently coloured skins.

In 1962, the UK government passed the Commonwealth Immigration Act. This restricted immigration to those citizens of Commonwealth (former British Empire) countries with job offers and / or relevant qualifications. A strict quota was imposed on other migrants. In practice these other migrants were almost all black or brown, and everyone knew it. There was much talk of the 'colour problem'. In the 1964 election, Peter Griffiths, a Conservative MP representing a West Midlands constituency, saw off his opponent with the slogan 'If you want a n****r for a neighbour, vote Liberal or Labour'. Numbers of immigrants entering the country fell substantially as the quotas were progressively tightened. The Race Relations Act, passed in 1965, outlawed discrimination on grounds of race, but was only weakly enforced. The Commonwealth Immigrants Act, passed in 1968, restricted immigration still further; now only Commonwealth citizens who had a parent or grandparent born, adopted or naturalised in the UK could come here. Almost all of these people were white.

The stage was set for a notorious speech by the leading Conservative politician Enoch Powell in April 1968, in which he called for an end to 'coloured' immigration. He referred to 'the River Tiber flowing with much blood'; though this was an erudite reference to Virgil's *Aeneid* (Powell had been a professor of Classics), it was widely seen as a provocation to interracial violence. He also expressed his sympathy for a constituent who feared that 'In this country in 15 or 20 years' time the black man will have the whip hand

Refugees have been greeted with horror, alarm and kindness

over the white man.' Powell was sacked from his front-bench job by Edward Heath, the then Conservative leader, but had a huge amount of popular support; London dockers went on strike in support of him, and one poll suggested that 75% of people agreed with him. In 1971, yet another immigration act restricted Commonwealth immigration to Australia, Canada and New Zealand, all overwhelmingly white countries. Heath's successor as Conservative leader, Margaret Thatcher, was only a little more temperate than Powell when she said, 'some people have felt swamped by immigrants ... they've seen the whole character of their neighbourhood change.' Her carefully calculated intervention helped her to win the 1979 election and become the UK's first woman Prime Minister.

With wars, instability and climate change ravaging many poorer countries in the late twentieth and early twenty-first century, many more refugees and asylum seekers have since come to Britain. People traffickers, often working for criminal gangs, have taken advantage of the plight of people fleeing war and disaster, charging them extortionate sums for dangerous crossings of the English Channel, which have often ended in tragedy. Images of tattered inflatable boats washed up on beaches and people cowering in the backs of lorries bring these migrants into the public eye. Their arrival has been greeted with horror and alarm by some, with kindness by others. In 2023, 67,000 people claimed asylum in the UK, of whom just over a third came illegally on small boats. Almost all of them were granted asylum. Asylum seekers and refugees make up 11% of immigrants to the UK.

Public resentment at supposed high levels of immigration was a significant factor in the vote to leave the EU in the referendum of 2016. The Leave campaign made much play of the millions of Turkish immigrants they said would come to the UK once Turkey joined the EU. Nigel Farage, then leader of UKIP (the United Kingdom Independence Party, specifically set up to campaign for the UK's exit from the European Union), unveiled a poster purporting to show a long queue of potential immigrants with the slogan 'Breaking Point'.

3. Welcome

Despite the shameful, and often shameless, history of racism described above, there have been times when Britain has opened its doors to those in distress, particularly in response to wars and natural disasters. Refugees from Hungary and Czechoslovakia were made welcome following the invasion of those countries by the Soviet Union in 1956 and 1968 respectively. Bengalis escaping floods, famine and warfare in their country settled in the East End of

London. In 1971, the then leader of Uganda, Idi Amin, expelled all people of Asian heritage from the country, confiscating their homes and businesses and allowing them to take only £50 out of the country. Uganda being a Commonwealth country, the British government decided to take them in. Many Ugandan Asians were successful business people or highly qualified professionals, but now had to start from the bottom. They established a new British tradition: the open-all-hours corner shop, a business which could be set up with minimal capital, staffed on a rota by family members. Customers loved the convenience offered (previously, all shops shut at 5 pm and on Sundays and often on Wednesday afternoons as well), and the incomers prospered, with many of their children finding their way into the business and political elites.

Britain has welcomed those in distress

The recent influx of immigrants from the EU has also been welcomed by many. Small businesses run by Eastern European immigrants often offered a higher level of service than those run by native British people because, as has been the case for immigrants throughout history, they had more to prove.

In March 2022, following the Russian invasion of Ukraine, over 150,000 people responded to a UK government scheme inviting them to open up their homes to Ukrainian refugees. The UK government has been similarly generous to refugees fleeing the Taliban takeover of Afghanistan in 2021, and to immigrants from Hong Kong, a former British colony.

4. Change

Whether immigrants were welcomed or not, Britain did undergo significant change. In 1991, 5.5% of the population came from ethnic minorities; in 2001, it was 10%; by 2011, it was 14%. (Not all members of ethnic minorities are immigrants, of course, but the majority are descended from relatively recent immigrants.) In the same year, 2011, more than one third of Londoners had been born abroad. In May 2016, Sadiq Khan, whose father emigrated from Pakistan to work as a bus driver in the UK, was elected Mayor of London - the first Muslim mayor of a capital city in the western world. In October 2022, Rishi Sunak became the first UK prime minister of South Asian heritage. His first appointments as foreign secretary and home secretary were both people of colour, and he himself had previously been chancellor of the exchequer. To have so many non-white people in positions of power in the UK would have been unthinkable in 1945.

Towns, and still more so cities, have changed beyond recognition since the war. The drab, grey, monocultural world of postwar

Immigration has changed Britain beyond recognition

Britain was brightened by new styles of food, music, clothing and worship, as immigrants established themselves in solid and lasting communities. Some native Britons had their lives enriched by eating Bengali curries, drinking Italian coffee and dancing to reggae music at the Notting Hill Carnival; others felt threatened by change.

In the twenty-first century, the expansion of the European Union changed the face of immigration. Britain joined the Common Market in 1973. In due course, the Common Market became the European Community, and then the European Union (the EU). Following the Maastricht Treaty of 1992, free movement of people within the EU was established. This meant that anyone from any country within the EU could travel to any other country, not only for tourism but also to work, at any time and without any need for a visa giving them permission to enter. In 2004, the EU significantly increased in size, admitting ten more countries, most of them from Eastern Europe; this was followed in 2007 by the addition of Bulgaria and Romania. In consequence, huge numbers of EU citizens, particularly from Eastern Europe, came to work in the UK, drawn by the prospect of better work opportunities and higher wages than they could expect to find back home. As so often in the past, many of the jobs taken by these immigrants were difficult, unpleasant and poorly paid.

When the UK finally left the EU on January 30th, 2020, the rules changed around immigration and the right of people from EU countries to live and work in the UK. As a result, many EU nationals left the UK, resulting in labour shortages in many sectors of the economy.

Who's allowed to live, work or study in the UK?

- Anyone with British nationality has the right to live, work or study in the UK.
- Commonwealth citizens (from a collection of 54 countries, most of them former territories of the British Empire) can apply for a '**right of abode**', allowing them to live, work or study in the UK. They need to prove a connection to the UK through their parents or marriage.
- Citizens of non-Commonwealth countries (including, since the UK's departure from the EU in January 2020, EU citizens) must apply for a **visa**, giving them the right to live, work or study in the UK. To be successful, they must meet certain criteria. To study, they must have been accepted onto a

recognised course. To work, they must have educational qualifications equivalent to A-Level standard, an offer of a job paid at least £25,600 (the median income for the UK in 2022 was £29,900), and a good level of English.

- Anyone who has a '**well-founded fear of persecution or serious harm in their own country**' can apply for asylum. This applies to anyone, even if they have arrived in the UK with no visa or other travel document, off a dinghy on a beach in Dover or out of the back of a lorry. These rules on asylum are part of international law, and are supposed to apply to every country in the world.
- The application process for asylum (protection in a new country) is supposed to be completed within six months but often takes longer. During the application process, asylum seekers may not work. They are given a very basic subsistence payment, and may be obliged to live in detention centres. If successful, they are awarded refugee status, and are allowed to stay in the UK to live and work for an initial five years.
- In April 2022, the UK government announced that asylum seekers arriving in the UK 'illegally' (nearly all of them, as there are very few safe legal routes) would be deported to the African country of Rwanda and told to apply for asylum there. This measure was designed to make the UK a less attractive prospect, thus undermining criminal gangs shipping people across the English Channel. The policy was widely seen to contravene international law, and no immigrants were ever sent to Rwanda. When Labour came to power in July 2024, it cancelled the Rwanda scheme.

Not everyone can live, work or study in the UK

How many immigrants are there in the UK?

Approximately 15% of the UK population were born abroad. This figure is for the UK as a whole, though. In large cities like London, Birmingham and Manchester, the proportion of immigrants will be much higher; in rural areas and small towns it will be far lower. In 2023, net migration to the UK was 685,000; this means that 685,000 more people arrived in the UK than left it. The proportion of immigrants in the UK significantly increased between 2000 and 2020, largely due to free movement from the EU, particularly from the newly joined Eastern European countries. Since the UK left the EU in 2020, the number of immigrants from the EU has significantly fallen.

Immigrants don't take jobs from natives

2. THE ISSUES

Arguments about immigration have three main points of focus: **economic**, **cultural** and **moral**.

Economic

Does immigration make us richer or poorer?

It is sometimes said that immigrants take jobs from natives (people who were born in a country). This is a **fallacy** (a popular but misguided idea) because it assumes that there is a fixed number of jobs in the economy. In fact, the number of jobs available goes up and down depending on the state of the economy; an increase in labour supply leads to an increase in labour demand. The more people are working, the more goods and services they can afford to buy, and thus the more jobs are created. Immigrants don't just work, they also consume. They need to eat, to live somewhere, to travel to work, to have their medical needs met, their children educated. They might even want to go out once in a while. All of this creates work for shelf stackers, builders, bus drivers, doctors, teachers, baristas, waiters and snack sellers in cinemas. If all the immigrants in the UK left tomorrow, a lot of the people left behind would be out of a job, with little prospect of finding a new one.

It is also sometimes said that immigrants put a strain on the welfare system, the education system and the NHS. This too is a fallacy. The great majority of immigrants tend to be young, healthy and in work. They are therefore likely to be contributing to the welfare and education systems through their taxes, and taking out less than the native population, who are likely to include higher numbers of people who do not pay tax and are dependent on the welfare system. Immigrants are more likely to be working for the NHS than using it.

On the other hand, there is evidence that immigration can bring down wages, particularly in low-paid jobs in sectors such as agriculture. Wages that seem impossibly low to someone brought up in the UK might seem wonderfully generous to someone from a country where living standards are lower. This is bad news if you are a UK worker competing for work in one of these sectors.

Overall, it can reasonably be asserted that immigration is a net economic benefit for the UK. This means that, across the whole economy, immigrants add more than they take. There are two problems with this assertion, however. Firstly, it is of little comfort that the economy as a whole is benefiting from immigration if you personally are not. To give a concrete example: a middle-class woman who finds a Polish cleaner willing to work harder for less money will experience immigration as an economic benefit; a native English working-class woman who might otherwise have taken that cleaning job for more money will not. Immigration is good news if you need a cleaner, and bad news if you are a cleaner. Secondly, there are reasons apart from economic ones why people might object to immigration. These are discussed below.

Immigration is good news if you need a cleaner, bad news if you are a cleaner

Cultural

Does immigration change our society for the better or the worse?

Life is not just about money. It is also about how you feel, not least how you feel about yourself, your sense of identity, and this is closely connected to how you feel about the society in which you live.

People in favour of liberal policies on immigration are likely to think of themselves as open-minded and tolerant, willing to accept a diversity of cultures and lifestyles, excited by the multiplicity of people. They are likely to have a university degree, and to have left their home town to study, perhaps not returning there once they start work. They may be well travelled, and want their children to have similar opportunities for travel. They are more likely to live in large cities, places which favour autonomy and anonymity over community. (The biggest votes for Remain in the 2016 EU referendum came in the most diverse areas of London, itself one of the most diverse cities in the world.) Such people find the sheer variety of cities exciting rather than threatening. They may think of themselves not so much as British, but as 'citizens of the world'. It is often said that Londoners have more in common with people from New York than people from Newcastle, with Parisians more than Prestonians. When the UK voted in 2016 to leave the EU, many Remainers felt they had lost something important from their country.

Those who want limits on immigration also have a strong sense of their own identity. They are more likely to value stability over diversity, security over openness, solidarity over individualism. Many of them live in towns with very low levels of racial and cultural diversity; they may still live in or very near to the place where they grew up. They are less likely to have a university degree. They have been described as 'citizens of somewhere'. They might say that they don't recognise where they live any more and that it isn't the place they grew up in, because immigration has changed it so much. If they voted Leave in the Brexit referendum, it may have been because they felt they had already lost much of their identity due to the way in which immigration had changed their community. When the UK left the EU, they felt as if they had got something back for their country.

Neither way of seeing the world is right or wrong, but both are strongly felt. Concerns about identity can be more significant than financial considerations. Many people voted Leave despite knowing this would leave them economically worse off because they felt that controlling immigration would help them 'get their country back'.

Moral

Is encouraging immigration the right thing to do?

Leaving your own country to come to another one is a hard thing to do. It calls for considerable sacrifices. You have to leave behind your family and friends. You may have to pay someone a lot of money to get you into the UK, and may not get what you thought you paid for. You may risk your life crossing the English Channel in a leaky dinghy. You may not be guaranteed a job when you come to the UK, and may experience a good deal of financial insecurity. Added to that, newly arrived immigrants are likely to experience culture shock as they adjust to a new way of life (Why is it so cold all the time? Why is the food so horrible? Why does no one say what they really mean?) They will have to negotiate a fiendishly complicated bureaucracy to gain the right to remain in the UK, made even harder if English is not their first language. They may face hostility, resentment and both covert and overt racism. In the worst cases, immigrants may fall victim to people traffickers, who keep them as virtual slaves, taking away their passports, effectively imprisoning them, forcing them to work in dangerous and unhealthy environments for little or no pay. Women may be forced into sex work by criminal gangs.

Why does anyone do it? The situation must be very bad in your own country to put up with all that. Many immigrants are fleeing appalling poverty; devastation caused by climate change; utter destruction of their homes and livelihoods as the result of war; brutal, often life-threatening, persecution on account of their race, religion, gender or sexuality.

All of the above means that we have a moral responsibility to give immigrants as much support as we can, and to welcome them with generosity and kindness. We in the UK are fortunate to have so much; we we should help those less fortunate than ourselves.

Why do people leave their countries?

Or, to look at it another way ...

Just as a parent has a moral responsibility to look after their own children, and to prioritise them over other people's children, we have a moral responsibility as a nation to look after and protect our own people first. It is simply unfair to share our resources with people who come from outside our community. Institutions like the welfare system and the NHS depend on a sense of national solidarity; that sense will be undermined if we share them too freely with immigrants from outside.

It is immoral for governments to impose the significant economic and cultural disruption caused by immigration on a population without their consent. Those in power do not feel the true effects of immigration (they are more likely to have cleaners than to be cleaners). The benefits of immigration (cheaper labour, greater profits for businesses) tend to go disproportionately to those who are already prosperous, while the harms (lower wages, job losses) are more likely to be felt by the less well-off.

Moreover, by encouraging often very well qualified immigrants to come to the UK, we are depriving their own countries of their skills. Every doctor originally from India working for the NHS is one less doctor working for the Indian health service, which is in much greater need of them, and has paid for their training. It is immoral to deprive poorer countries of these people. They, too, need to protect their own communities.

Flexibility or security? Openness or community? Local or universal?

3. THE POINT OF CLASH

Economically, the clash comes down to this question.

Which is more important: the **flexibility** of businesses to hire who they want and pay them what they want, with the resultant prosperity for the economy and the more ready availability of cheaper goods and services? Or the **security** for British workers of having their jobs and conditions protected, even if that means higher prices and less variety of goods and services?

Culturally, the clash comes down to this question.

Which do you value more: **variety** and **openness**, even if that means having to tolerate people who are not like you? Or **security** and **community**, even if that means excluding people who are not like you? When you walk into your local pub or café, do you want to see people like you who understand you, or people who don't know you and will let you be whoever you want to be?

Moral

Do we have a duty to care for the whole of humanity, regardless of where they come from? Or is our first responsibility to those closest to us, our own family, town and nation? Is solidarity best expressed **locally** or **universally**?

Do we best help people in countries suffering from poverty, war and tyranny by helping them **escape** those societies? Or should we encourage them to **stay** to make those societies better?

4. THE ARGUMENTS

For immigration	Against immigration
Immigrants fill necessary but unpleasant jobs that native people don't want to take.	Using cheap migrant labour for these jobs allows employers to exploit workers; the answer is to improve working conditions for all.
Immigrants make a net contribution to the economy in taxes.	Immigrants increase the need for public expenditure because of the increased level of infrastructure they require.
Immigrants enrich our country culturally by bringing a greater variety of people.	Immigrants undermine the cohesiveness and unity of society.
We have a moral duty to welcome people who are less fortunate than us.	We have a moral duty to look after our own people first.
The idea of a homogenous national identity is a myth; all societies are hybrid and mixed, and are richer for it.	A homogenous national identity helps hold society together.
Immigration brings skilled, ambitious, educated people from other countries to our benefit.	Immigration takes skilled, ambitious, educated people from other countries which need those people more than we do.
Immigration makes us more prosperous.	The economic benefits of immigration go disproportionately to the already prosperous.
We have a moral duty to help people escape from countries affected by tyranny, war and poverty.	We have a moral duty to encourage people to stay and fix countries affected by tyranny, war and poverty.

5. THE MOTIONS

1. This house would reinstate the right for EU citizens to work in the UK.
2. This house would remove all controls on immigration.
3. This house would only admit skilled workers to the UK.
4. This house would only admit workers with degree-level qualifications to the UK.
5. This house would not recognise qualifications obtained outside the UK.
6. This house believes that immigration is good for the UK.
7. This house would rather be a citizen of somewhere than a citizen of the world.

Keep thinking…

A selection of further reading to help you think more deeply about immigration.

The Windrush Betrayal, Amelia Gentleman (Guardian Faber, 2019)

Gentleman led *The Guardian*'s exposure of the so-called 'Windrush' scandal, when hundreds of people who had lived in the UK almost all of their lives and considered it home were abruptly denied healthcare, falsely accused of breaking the law, and, in some cases, deported. This shocking injustice stemmed directly from the then government's policy of creating a 'hostile environment' for illegal immigrants. Gentleman recounts the human stories in harrowing detail, but also analyses how the actions of those in power led to so much unnecessary suffering. The book is a chilling reminder of the moral and human cost of being 'tough on immigration'.

The Road to Somewhere: The New Tribes Shaping British Politics, David Goodhart (C. Hurst and Co, 2017)

Goodhart argues powerfully in favour of the need for cultural cohesion, and against the damage that immigration causes to social solidarity. He distinguishes between 'anywheres', who are flexible and mobile in their cultural identity, and 'somewheres', who identify strongly with one place and culture. He makes the troubling point that 'anywheres' tend to have more education, privilege and power than 'somewheres', and often view the latter with contempt, imposing their world view on 'somewheres' without negotiation, and with little consideration of their real needs. His argument does much to explain the appeal of Trump in the US and Brexit in the UK.

This is London: Life and Death in the World City, Ben Judah (Picador, 2016)

This is journalism as it should be: brave, honest and based on direct experience. Driven by a passionate desire to know what the lives of immigrants in London are really like, Judah works, eats and sleeps with some of the poorest and most marginal people, often putting himself in no little personal danger. Out of this courageous exploration, he brings us a completely honest and unvarnished account of life amongst the various national communities which make up our capital city. The results may surprise and shock you. This book is certainly an antidote to the notion that immigrants are without exception hard-working, honest, exemplary citizens.

Small Island, Andrea Levy (Headline, 2005)

This wonderful novel (adapted into a successful play by the National Theatre in 2019) interweaves the experiences of a West Indian family and a white London family in the years just after the Second World War. The conflicts and discoveries, the misunderstandings and revelations which this encounter brings say much about the British experience of postwar immigration. It is also a great read. Levy, the author, herself came from a mixed-race background.

The Next Great Migration: The Story of Movement on a Changing Planet, Sonia Shah (Bloomsbury, 2020)

Shah's argument is that stability is a myth, and that borders are against nature. All animals move in search of safety and resources; they always have, they always will and they always should. She starts with examples from the animal kingdom, and then applies what she learns from animals to human behaviour, ending with an account of what it is like to be an immigrant in today's world.

White Teeth, Zadie Smith (Hamish Hamilton, 2000)

An infectiously enthusiastic celebration of multicultural London, this novel brims over with hope. Written on an epic scale and with a large and generous cast of characters from a multiplicity of backgrounds, it makes you feel that diversity works, and is right. Published in 2000, its optimism is untempered by the fear that followed the terrorist attacks on America of September 11, 2001, or the rancour caused by the Brexit referendum and its aftermath.

Lovers and Strangers: An Immigrant History of Post-War Britain, Claire Wills (Allen Lane 2017)

A rich and fascinating account of the lived experience, for both immigrants and natives, of postwar immigration to the UK. Divided into sections such as 'Voters', 'Teachers', 'Broadcasters', 'Lovers', 'Scroungers', etc., it highlights the way in which immigrants have shaped and changed British society since the war.

Bloody Foreigners: The Story of Immigration to Britain, Robert Winder (Little Brown, 2004)

A meticulously researched and highly entertaining history of immigration to the UK from the Ancient Romans to the 21st century. Winder is firmly pro-immigration, and celebrates the cultural and economic richness it has brought to Britain, while arguing that most of the 'problems' that immigration is said to bring arise not from immigrants themselves but from the ignorance and prejudice of native Britons. Published in 2004, it does not cover the uptick in immigration from Eastern Europe, nor the Brexit referendum and its consequences.

3

PART THREE

Justice

How to think about justice

Justice is about treating people as they should be treated; about giving people what they deserve.

So, in this section, we think about **race**. How can we best combat racism? Through quotas, or through treating everyone the same? By celebrating cultural difference, or by creating a shared national identity?

We think about **colonialism**. Britain once had the world's largest empire. How should we respond to its legacy? Should we pay reparations for slavery? Should we apologise for the slave trade? Should we take down statues that celebrate colonialists? Should we return objects displayed in museums to the countries we took them from?

We think about **crime and punishment**. Why do people commit crimes? Should criminals be punished, or helped to change their ways? What is the best way to prevent crime? Is it ever all right to break the law?

We think about **war and violence**. What is war good for? When is it justified? What rules should it follow? When is it valid to use violence?

CHAPTER 8

Race

In this chapter we're thinking about...

- **Is racism best dealt with at an individual level or at a systemic level?**
- **Are quotas the most effective and fairest way to deal with racism?**
- **Is encouraging people to celebrate their racial and cultural identity an effective way of dealing with racism?**

Although this chapter focuses on how best to respond to racism, many of its ideas and arguments can be adapted to debates on how best to respond to sexism, homophobia, transphobia and other forms of discrimination.

1. THE FACTS

We were all the same race once

What race is and what race isn't

We were all the same race once. The species *Homo sapiens* – our species – evolved in the east of Africa. About 70,000 years ago, people started to move out of Africa, spreading across the world. As they arrived in new areas, they made evolutionary adjustments to new climatic conditions. People who ended up in northern Europe evolved over many generations to have paler skin as an adjustment to the lower levels of sunlight; arrivals in the tropical regions of South and East Asia made similar adjustments to cope with higher levels of humidity. This slowly led to variations in appearance and skin colour between people living in different parts of the world.

Walking out of Africa wasn't the last time humanity went in search of new homes. Populations have always been and always will be in constant flux. Wherever people have gone – wherever they go – they have always mixed and melded, adapting to local conditions, changing local societies, having children with people who don't look like them. Migration, and the inconstancy and instability it creates, is one of the very few constants throughout history. There have never been and never will be fixed racial groups staying in one fixed place. There is no such thing as 'racial purity'.

While what we know as racial differences may have evolved in particular parts of the world, they are no longer inherently connected with them. There are black people in Belgium, white people in Wuhan, South Asian people in Southport, and people of multiple ethnicities everywhere. You could say that it makes no sense to call some people 'mixed race', because in the long run we are all mixed race. If we were able to trace back far enough, we could all find African, Asian, Chinese and Indian ancestors. Hitler may well have had Jewish ancestors somewhere in his family line.

Of course, people are not all the same. The diversity of humanity is one of the glories of life. Some differences between people are genetic, that is, inherited from their parents. Skin colour is one of the things we may inherit from our parents. A person with two black parents is likely to look different from someone with two white parents; they will almost certainly have darker coloured skin. But that will be the only significant difference between those two

Racism = prejudice plus power

people: skin pigmentation. The differences between races are, quite literally, skin deep. On a visit to South Africa, then under the rule of the racist apartheid regime, the (white) cricket commentator John Arlott was required to state his race on an official form. He replied with one word: 'human'. He was right. There is only one race – the human race – and we all belong to it. We all look different; we all are different. But we're all human.

So race doesn't exist then? Well, not quite. Race does exist. It exists as a **social construct**: that is, although there are no inherent differences between groups of people based on their skin colour or other physical characteristics, people have very often been categorised according to race, and have been treated differently (often worse) on the basis of these categories. Sometimes these categories have been determined by obvious physical characteristics such as skin colour, as in anti-black racism. At other times the categories have been based on religious, cultural or even geographic origin, as, for example, in the case of anti-Jewish racism (commonly known as antisemitism), anti-Irish racism in nineteenth- and early twentieth-century England, or the prejudice expressed in much of the tabloid press against immigrants from Eastern Europe in recent years.

So race does exist in people's minds. This categorisation by perceived difference has given rise to **racism**, which in turn has given rise to hatred, injustice and some of the most monstrous crimes in history.

What is racism?

There is a simple formula to define racism: **prejudice plus power**. **Prejudice** means perceiving a particular group of people as inferior and / or a threat, without any rational justification for this belief. **Power** gives people the means to act on this prejudice. So, an enslaved black woman working on a cotton plantation in nineteenth-century America who believed that all white people were inherently evil (perhaps understandably, given the way she would have been treated by them) would not, strictly speaking, be a racist, because she would not have the power to act on this prejudice. The white overseer who beat her for not working hard enough and justified his actions by his belief that black people were little better than animals and could only be motivated to work by the threat of violence, was a racist. This distinction is important to remember when talking about racism. It is not just an attitude of mind; it also depends on social context.

Why are people racist?

Racism is stupid and immoral

Racism is **stupid**. It has no basis in scientific fact. It's stupid in another way, too. It leads to a colossal waste of human potential by excluding huge numbers of people from important areas of society (in the worst cases by killing them) on a completely irrational basis. Think of all the millions of bright, talented but enslaved African-Americans who might have been doctors, lawyers or teachers but wasted their lives in menial labour because their white owners thought that was all they were fit for. Think of what the six million Jews murdered in the Holocaust might have added to Europe if they had lived.

Racism is also fundamentally **immoral**. It is wrong, unfair and evil to treat someone worse because of their skin colour or cultural background.

Given that racism is stupid, immoral and wasteful of human potential, why has there been (and why is there) so much of it? Why are people racist?

There are two broad answers to this question: **individual** and **social**.

Individual

Be honest. Look into yourself. Have you never, ever succumbed to the temptation to put someone else down, either in your head or out loud, to make yourself feel better? We've all done it. We all do it. It's human, when you're feeling threatened or insecure or inadequate, to cheer yourself up by reminding yourself that there's someone somewhere worse than you. You might have got a bad mark for your Maths test, but you did better than Ahmed. You might not have been invited to sit at the cool kids' table at lunch, but at least you have more friends than Bridget, who has none. Charlie's mum might (as Charlie never tires of reminding you) drive a bigger car than your mum does, but at least your mum has got a car, unlike Dilip's mum. From there it's a short step to reassuring yourself that Ahmed did worse at Maths because he's not as smart as you, which must mean that you're smart, that Bridget has no friends because she's not very likeable, which must mean that you're likeable, that Dilip's mum can't afford a car because she doesn't work hard enough, which must mean that your mum works hard. Making Ahmed stupid and Bridget unpopular and Dilip's mum lazy is all the more tempting if you are secretly afraid that you might be stupid or unpopular or have a lazy mum. So

Racism: individual or social?

you get rid of your fears by projecting them on to someone else. You're not the worst, because someone else is worse than you.

Essentially, the individual view sees racism as a personal moral failing, often prompted by psychological insecurity. The human tendency to put other people down as a form of self-protection gets scaled up from individuals to whole groups and morphs into racism. So someone ends up saying to themselves, 'Don't give that job to a black person, because they're all lazy; give it to me because I'm white and therefore hard-working,' or, 'It's not my fault I can't get a better job; it's because the Jews keep all the best jobs for themselves.' And so on. This kind of racism often thrives when people are feeling under social or economic pressure. Which leads us to the second reason people are racist.

Social

Racism is not just something done by individuals. It is also – more importantly and more powerfully – something embedded in societies. How and why it becomes embedded in a society has much to do with the particular history and circumstances of that society.

Let's look at some examples of how and why societies become racist.

1. Divide and rule

Racism is a very convenient, and very effective, way for people at the top to hold onto wealth and power. If a small minority at the top have almost all the wealth and power, the majority without wealth and power are going to get resentful, perhaps even rebellious. If you can divide that majority into different groups, one supposedly superior to the other, and then set them against each other, you can divert their anger away from you and short-circuit any threat to your authority.

To take an example: in the early days of the United States, many of the white people in the southern states were desperately poor, while other white people were very wealthy. The arrival of enslaved people from Africa to work on plantations not only gave white people an economic uplift by providing them with free labour, it also gave them a psychological uplift. They might be badly off, but there was someone else worse off than them, and that made them feel better. Developing a racist ideology that 'proved' they were inherently superior on account of their skin colouring made them feel even better. It meant they had no need to challenge the system that made them poor. What's more, they had motivation and justification to keep the black people in their place and stop them rebelling against the system. All this was very convenient for the wealthiest class, who now had no need to share their wealth. America is still dealing with the legacy of the racial division which began with slavery.

Why are people racist?

2. Justifying exploitation

If you've taken something from somebody that's rightly theirs, you should feel bad about it. One way of not feeling bad about it is to tell yourself that they didn't deserve to have it in the first place. An even better way is to tell yourself that you're actually doing them a favour by taking it away from them.

This is the basic strategy of **imperialism**, when one country invades another and takes over its assets and people. The British Empire, which lasted for hundreds of years and ruled over many millions of people (see Chapter 9, **Colonialism**), justified itself at least partly through racism. British people were encouraged to think that Africans / Indians / Aborigines, etc., were inferior. They couldn't look after themselves. They needed us to civilise them and bring them Christianity, tarmac roads and flush toilets. We were actually doing them a favour by taking over their countries and exploiting their assets and labour. We could therefore not only feel entitled to all the wealth this brought us, but be proud of our noble civilising work.

3. Justifying humiliation or failure

Germany lost the First World War in 1918. The Allies, who had defeated them, then proceeded to kick them when they were down by imposing humiliating and economically disastrous surrender terms. As a result, Germany slid into economic chaos in the 1920s, with runaway inflation which ruined millions of people. They wanted someone to blame. Step forward the Nazis, who weaponised the German people's anger and frustration and turned it towards the Jewish community, ultimately leading to the horror of the Holocaust. Antisemitism shows us how racism can kick up as well as down. The Nazis, like many antisemites, believed that Jewish people had an unjust hold on wealth and power which needed to be taken away from them.

4. Self-protection

When a vulnerable group is threatened, one way of protecting itself from threats is either to exclude or to exploit another group. So, in Bristol in the 1950s, bus drivers and conductors, supported by their union, initially refused to work with recent immigrants from

What does the UK look like?

the West Indies on the grounds that they would take their jobs, until a city-wide boycott of buses forced them to back down. Similarly, the establishment in 1948 of the apartheid regime in South Africa, which systematically excluded the black majority from wealth and power, was in large part motivated by the fears of white workers and farmers that their fragile economic status might be threatened by the black majority.

What is the racial make-up of the UK?

Here is the data from the 2021 census for England and Wales:

- White 81.7%
- Asian 8.6%
- Black 4%
- Chinese 0.7%
- Mixed race 2.9%
- Other ethnic groups 2.1%

For Scotland, the latest data available at the time of writing is from the 2011 census, as follows:

- White 96%
- Asian 2.1%
- Black 0.6%
- Chinese 0.6%
- Mixed race 0.4%
- Other ethnic groups 0.3%

For Northern Ireland in the 2021 census, the figures were:

- White 96.8%
- Asian 1.1%
- Black 0.6%
- Chinese 0.5%
- Mixed race 0.8%
- Other ethnic groups 0.2%

Across the UK, large cities tend to have an above average level of racial diversity, while small towns and rural areas tend to be less diverse. London is by a long way the most diverse city in the UK, at 46.2% non-white. Some London boroughs are majority non-white.

In 1951, the UK was 99.9% white.

Is the UK a racist society?

Let's get the numbers

In order to understand fully the racial politics of the UK, you need to understand both the history of the British Empire, and the history of immigration to the UK since the Second World War. You can learn about the first in Chapter 7, **Immigration**, and the second in Chapter 9, **Colonialism**. Read (or reread) those chapters now.

In this chapter, we will concentrate on the situation in the UK at the time of writing. Because racism is an injustice crying to the heavens for vengeance, and because people's response to it is often coloured by their own, often very painful, experience, it can be hard to be objective and accurate about how far a society is racist or not. So let's get some cold, hard data.

Education

The figures below, and in the following lists, show the percentage out of each ethnic group, rather than out of the total (with the exception of the data on the prison population).

Students achieving GCSE English and Maths grade 5 or above (2021)

- All students 51.5%
- White 50.9%
- Asian 60.6%
- Black 49.5%
- Chinese 83.8%
- Mixed race 51.5%
- Other ethnic groups 53.1%

Students getting 3 A grades or more at A-Level (2021)

- All 28.9%
- White 26%
- Asian 25.2%
- Black 16.5%
- Chinese 42.2%
- Mixed race 25.8%
- Other ethnic groups 23.2%

Students aged 18 entering higher education in 2021

- All 38%
- White 33.3%

… and more numbers

- Asian 54.9%
- Black 48.6%
- Chinese 72.1%
- Mixed race 40.8%
- Other ethnic groups 48.1%

Oxbridge

In 2021, 23.6% of the intake of Oxford University was from ethnic minorities.

For Cambridge University in the same year, it was 34.6%.

Crime

Number of people per 1,000 arrested (2020–2021)

- All 10.8
- White 8.7
- Asian 8
- Black 22.5
- Chinese or other ethnic group 7.9
- Mixed race 11.9

Percentage breakdown of the prison population (as of June 2023)

- White 72%
- Asian 8%
- Black 12%
- Chinese or other ethnic group 2%
- Mixed race 5%
- Not recorded 1%

Income

People living in low-income households, defined as receiving less than 60% of the national median income (a 2-year average up to 2022)

- All 17%
- White 16%
- Black 26%
- Asian 27%
- Chinese 18%

- Mixed race 17%
- Other ethnic groups 23%

... and yet more numbers

Business

As of March 2023, according to the FTSE 100 (a list of the top companies in the UK):

- 96% of companies had at least one ethnic minority director on their board, and almost half had more than one non-white director.
- 10% of the top positions of chief executive officer, chief financial officer and chair of the board were held by ethnic minorities.

Health

Percentage of people compulsorily detained in mental hospitals because they are considered to be a risk to themselves or others (2021–22)

- White 0.07%
- Asian 0.1%
- Black 0.3%
- Mixed race 0.1%
- Other ethnic groups 0.2%

Percentage of adults who are overweight or obese (2020–21)

- All 63.5%
- White 64.5%
- Asian 57%
- Black 72%
- Chinese 37.5%
- Mixed race 59.5%
- Other ethnic groups 66.2%

Covid

Government research revealed that black and Asian people were approximately twice as likely as white people to die of Covid during the pandemic. The reasons for this cannot be definitively proven, but are likely to include having to work in more exposed occupations, having to live in more crowded accommodation, and lack of trust in government leading to low vaccine uptake.

Does racism still happen?

Experience of discrimination

A survey conducted between February and November 2021 by the Evidence for Equality Social Survey revealed that:

- Almost 17% of ethnic minorities had experienced a race-based physical assault.
- Nearly 33% had experienced racial discrimination in education and employment.
- Nearly 20% had experienced racial discrimination when seeking housing.
- Over 40% of black people had experienced racial discrimination from the police.

Politics

Representation of ethnic minorities at the highest reaches of UK politics has significantly increased in recent years. In the summer of 2023, the prime minister, the home secretary, the foreign secretary, the first minister of Scotland and the mayor of London were all from ethnic minorities, as were (in line with the national percentage for ethnic minorities in England and Wales) 18% of cabinet ministers. However, only 10% of MPs elected at the 2019 general election were from ethnic minorities. Following the 2024 general election, this rose to 14%.

Institutions

A number of important institutions in British society have in recent years been found to be systemically racist.

- In October 2020, a report by the Equality and Human Rights Commission found that the Labour Party had failed to deal adequately with antisemitism in the party.
- In January 2023, a report commissioned by the United Nations found that the UK justice system was institutionally racist.
- In March 2023, a report into the Metropolitan police (the police force for London) concluded that it was guilty of institutional racism.
- In May 2023, the Chief Constable of Police Scotland acknowledged that the Scottish police were institutionally racist.
- In June 2023, a report into English cricket concluded that the game suffered from 'widespread and deep-rooted' racism.

Good news or bad news?

This selection of data suggests a mixed picture. On the positive side, there is evidence of above average achievement in education and the highest reaches of politics for (some) ethnic minorities, and some progress in business. On the negative side, people from ethnic minorities are still more likely to be arrested, to be poor and to die from Covid. Black people are more likely to be overweight or obese, and are three times more likely than white people to end up in prison and also three times more likely to be compulsorily detained in a mental hospital than people of other races. A very large number of people from ethnic minorities regularly experience racial discrimination, both individually and from powerful institutions. Above all, they are not yet **equal**. In a truly egalitarian, colour-blind society, the differences between ethnic groups in the data listed above would be barely noticeable. So race still matters in Britain.

Racism in Britain is not as bad as it was. When I was at school in the 1970s, racism was overt and shameless. Racist 'jokes' abounded in the classroom (some of them came from teachers), and on TV night after night. There was a popular (and very unfunny) sitcom called *Love Thy Neighbour* about a black family living next door to a white family which essentially consisted of a string of racial stereotypes and insults. A weekly programme called *The Black and White Minstrel Show* showed mostly white actors in black make-up singing 'black' songs. Black footballers were greeted with monkey noises whenever they got the ball, and had bananas thrown at them. With a few exceptions, all that seems unimaginable now. But that doesn't mean racism has gone away.

Sport is often a kind of barometer for measuring the national mood. Let's take one recent sporting event which says a lot about the current state of race relations in the UK: the European Men's Football Championships, held in the summer of 2021.

The England team had a number of high-profile and highly regarded black players. Their manager, Gareth Southgate, who for a few weeks assumed a status as a national icon second only to the Queen, wrote a notably gracious letter to the English people on the eve of the tournament inviting them to come together in unity and mutual respect. 'Why would you choose to insult somebody for something as ridiculous as the colour of their skin?' he asked. The England team 'took the knee' before the start of each match in support of the Black Lives Matter movement. Some England fans booed them. The then Home Secretary Priti Patel (herself the daughter of immigrants) defended the booers and criticised the team for engaging in 'gesture politics'.

What football tells us about us

Then England started to do rather well. The Home Secretary found it in her heart to forgive the team for their stand against racism, and was photographed wearing an England shirt (with the tell-tale creases that revealed she had just got it out of the packet). In July, England got to the final against Italy (held at Wembley Stadium in London). The score was 1–1 after extra time, and it went to penalties. England lost.

Someone – in fact, a lot of people – chose to draw attention to the fact that the players who had missed the penalties were all black. That night, and the next day, social media was swamped with racial abuse of those players. Condemnation of the abuse was widespread and came from the top of British society: the prime minister, the leader of the opposition and Prince William all spoke out. Many people were subsequently prosecuted for hate speech. Nonetheless, it happened; there were still a lot of people out there who thought it was all right to attack players for the national team because of the colour of their skin. And, earlier in the tournament, a high-profile politician had tried to use race as a dividing issue when she condemned 'taking the knee'.

In December 2022, England went out of another international tournament, the FIFA World Cup, when they were beaten by France. Harry Kane, the England captain, missed a crucial penalty which could have kept the team in the tournament. This time there was no social media storm, just sympathy for Kane and disappointment. But Harry Kane was white.

Racism in Britain: a lot done; a lot still to do.

So what should we do? That's what we're going to be thinking about in the next section.

2. THE ISSUES

A word before we start. I've already said that the stupidity and wrongness of racism are beyond debate. However, what can be debated is exactly how we should best combat racism. It's important to remember, with such an emotive subject, that while racism is self-evidently wrong, there is not one self-evidently right response to it. In debates about racism, engage with and criticise the other side's arguments as vigorously as you can, but at the same time assume that they are as anti-racist as you are; you just have different views about the best way to be anti-racist. Above all, don't accuse them of being racist just because they disagree with you.

Is racism best tackled at an individual level or at a systemic level?

A lot done; a lot still to do

Where you stand on this question is likely to depend on whether you put more emphasis on the **individual** or the **social** explanation of racism. Which of these explanations you favour is likely to depend on how you respond to broader questions about society. Is society nothing more than a collection of individuals, each of whom has complete control over whether they behave well or badly? Or is our behaviour, to a greater or lesser extent, determined by the structures in which we live, which can only be changed at a systemic level? Do we need to fix ourselves or the system?

If you see racism primarily as a personal failing of character, then it needs to be tackled at an individual level, by denouncing racist behaviour when it happens, and by passing laws preventing people from discriminating against other people on the grounds of their race. If you see it primarily as something embedded in society, then it needs to be tackled at a systemic level, by proactively educating people against racism, passing laws obliging institutions to be representative of the community they serve, and actively favouring ethnic minorities over the majority in order to compensate for their inherent disadvantage.

To take an example. In 1993, Stephen Lawrence, a black teenager, was murdered in South London by a group of white youths. They were motivated by racial hatred. Although six men were arrested on suspicion of murder, none of them were charged, and Lawrence's family were denied justice. The government commissioned an inquiry into the case, chaired by Sir William Macpherson. The Macpherson Report, published in 1999, concluded that the investigation had failed not because of incompetence, but because the Metropolitan Police was guilty of **institutional racism**. If Sir William had favoured an individual response to racism, he might have singled out police officers who had been negligent because of their racist views, and called for them to be disciplined, dismissed or even prosecuted. Instead, he called out the whole institution of the Metropolitan Police as racist, because the way in which it was set up tended to make it treat people from ethnic minorities worse than white people. To be clear, he wasn't saying, 'All police officers are racist.' He was saying that the way that the police force was run led to racist outcomes, even though individual police officers may not have wanted this.

What is institutional racism?

The measures he proposed to remedy the Met's institutional racism reflected this approach. They included:

- Performance indicators to measure how well racist incidents were investigated by the police.
- Performance indicators to measure how satisfied members of ethnic minority communities were with how they were policed.
- Compulsory training of police officers in racial awareness.
- Targeted recruitment of members of ethnic minorities to the Metropolitan Police, in order to ensure that it better reflected the cultural and ethnic composition of the communities they served.

All of these measures involved intervening in the police force to make it less racist as a whole. They were **proactive** measures, preventing a problem before it happens. An individual response to racism would be more **reactive**. While it would respond swiftly and decisively to any racist behaviour by individual officers, disciplining or dismissing them as necessary, it would take no action unless and until there was evidence of such behaviour. Moreover, the reactive approach squarely places the responsibility for racist behaviour on the individuals found guilty, rather than implicating the institution of which they are a part.

The individual response is sometimes known as the 'bad apple' theory. Racists are like rotten apples in a barrel. If they are left in the barrel, they will turn the other apples rotten. Remove them from the barrel and you remove the problem. For those who favour an institutional approach to racism, the reason the apples are rotting is because they're stored in the wrong way; it's the barrel that needs looking at.

The example of the Stephen Lawrence case and the Macpherson Report on it can help us to think about different responses to racism.

Are quotas the most effective and fairest way to deal with racism?

This is another question which hinges on whether you favour the **individual** or the **social** approach to racism.

If you take the **individual** approach, quotas are neither effective nor fair. Selection for jobs or educational programmes should be entirely merit-based. Consider someone's relevant experience

Rotten apples? Or rotten barrels?

or their A-Level results; ignore their ethnicity. If you can provide evidence that someone has been discriminated against because of their race – if a black person has been turned down in favour of a less qualified white person, and if it is clear that this was because of their race – the person or people making that decision is or are acting in a racist way, and action must be taken against them. You can prosecute them under the 2010 Equality Act, which makes such discriminatory behaviour illegal; you can discipline them or dismiss them. Deal with the guilty individuals. But leave the institution alone to continue to make its selections on the grounds of merit.

This is what is known as the **colour-blind** approach. The colour of someone's skin is irrelevant to their fitness for a job or a course of study, and it should be ignored. On the face of it, this looks like natural justice. However, critics of the colour-blind approach point out that it acts as if race does not exist. Unfortunately, say these critics, it does. Not as an objective fact determining people's abilities, but as a **social construct** which affects the way people are treated. People from ethnic minorities are systematically and unfairly disadvantaged by their race. White people are systematically and unfairly advantaged by their race, a phenomenon sometimes known as **white privilege**. We need to recognise our own unconscious bias and intervene to correct this imbalance. Quotas are a very effective, and therefore very fair, way of doing this. It is naive to think that we live in a world where everyone is treated the same, and that quotas interrupt natural justice. Unofficially, informally, but powerfully, quotas have always existed, making sure that positions of influence and advantage have overwhelmingly been occupied by white men. How else did they get all the top jobs? Are they really all inherently smarter and more capable? Race-based (and gender-based) quotas are simply acting to remove the effects of existing discrimination to everyone's benefit; they make institutions both fairer and more effective, by widening the talent pool.

If people really were appointed to jobs and awarded places on courses of study entirely on merit, with race playing no part, the proportion of people from ethnic minorities in influential positions would match very closely their proportion in society; that hasn't been the case for most of history. You may point to the high level (as of 2023) of representation of ethnic minorities at the top of government and business. But that didn't just happen. It happened because of two significant programmes of intervention.

When David Cameron became leader of the Conservative Party in 2005, he thought the party was not diverse enough. He set up

How intervention works

an 'A-List' of people who would be top of the list when selecting candidates to become Conservative MPs, with a specific priority for women and members of ethnic minorities. As a result, eighteen years later, there were a lot of women and black and brown people at the top of the Conservative Party, and therefore at the top of government. The A-List wasn't strictly speaking a quota system, as it steered constituencies towards selecting women and members of ethnic minorities rather than requiring them to appoint a certain number, but it definitely wasn't colour-blind (or gender-blind); it was making an intervention into the selection process in favour of women and members of ethnic minorities. If David Cameron hadn't taken this action, the British government might well have remained overwhelmingly white and male (as it has been throughout history).

Similarly, business leaders, supported by the government, set up the Parker Review in 2015, with a specific brief to encourage an increase in ethnic minority representation at the top of business. Like David Cameron's initiative in the Conservative Party, it did not set specific quotas, but it did give a very strong steer to businesses to go out of their way to recruit people from ethnic minorities. As a result, representation significantly increased over the following eight years.

Supporters of quotas would argue that the examples of Cameron's A-List and the Parker Review above show that intervention to make institutions more representative is both necessary (without it, government and business would still be overwhelmingly white) and that it works (it has brought in many talented people who would otherwise have been excluded). The change in representation these interventions have created has also changed people's perceptions about race, and what people from ethnic minorities can do. When, in October 2022, Rishi Sunak became the first Asian British prime minister, his appointment was not only a rebuke to any racists who thought Britain should only be led by white people, it could also be seen as an inspiration for young Asians who might want to go into politics. As they say, 'If you can't see it, you can't be it.' Once you can see it, there's more chance you'll be it.

Opponents of quotas would argue that they are not, actually, in the interests of people from ethnic minorities. If you feel, or the people around you feel, that you have only been appointed to a position or offered a place on a course of study because of your race, then this could cost you much respect (and self-respect). Nobody wants to be labelled as a 'diversity hire'. Without quotas, you can be confident that any success you achieve is thanks to your own efforts and abilities. To be given something simply because of the colour of your skin is patronising and demeaning.

Moreover, quotas can be an imprecise tool that could inadvertently benefit the wrong individuals. Not all people from ethnic minorities are the same, and they should not be treated as one amorphous mass. Some are underprivileged; some are not. Should the black daughter of a hedge-fund manager living in South Kensington and attending an expensive private school really be given a university place over the white son of an unemployed single mother living in Sunderland and attending an underfunded state school? In June 2023, the US Supreme Court ruled that the 'affirmative action' programmes run by many American universities, whereby quotas were used to increase recruitment of black and Hispanic students, were illegal. Those who welcomed this ruling pointed out that many of the students offered places under these schemes in fact came from wealthy and privileged backgrounds. They also claimed that many students of East Asian heritage (Chinese, Japanese, Korean) were effectively discriminated against for not being the 'right sort' of minority.

Supporters of quotas argue that they are **necessary** because of existing institutional and societal prejudice, **fair** because they address this prejudice, and **effective** because they recruit more talented people. Opponents of quotas argue that they are **unnecessary** because prejudice is better confronted on a personal than an institutional level, **unfair** because they exclude people unreasonably, and **ineffective** because they select people on the wrong grounds.

Is encouraging people to celebrate their racial and cultural identity an effective way of dealing with racism?

How you approach this question will depend on what you believe about identity. Here are three ways of thinking about **identity**.

1. **Racial, cultural or religious identity as a member of a group**

   Our identity is determined by the ethnic group, culture or religion we are born into. We should accept, embrace and celebrate this identity, and defend it against anyone who tries to marginalise or diminish it.

What is identity?

2. **National identity**

   Our identity is determined by the national group into which we were born, or which we have adopted by choosing to live in a particular country. We should accept, embrace and celebrate this identity, even if that means abandoning parts of our cultural identity or our personal preferences.

3. **Personal identity**

   Everyone is entitled to develop and express their own identity. There are as many different identities as there are people, and even individual people's identities can change and develop over time. No one has the right to tell another person what sort of person they should be. The only rule is that you should not prevent other people from being who they want to be.

Let's look in more detail at each of these ways of thinking about identity, and how each approach might impact on the way we think about race.

1. Racial, cultural or religious identity as a member of a group

Throughout history, people have been (and still are) prevented by prejudice from expressing their racial, cultural and religious identity. Reggae music has been denounced as decadent; there have been protests against the building of mosques (as once there were protests against the building of Catholic churches); Hindu children have been forced to take part in Christian nativity plays and carol services during Diwali; school canteens have failed to serve kosher or halal food.

Multiculturalism – the active assertion and promotion of different cultures within society – is an attempt to address and overcome this prejudice. It recognises that Britain is not a monocultural society where everyone is the same. It is highly diverse, and this should be celebrated. Keep the nativity plays, but also celebrate Eid, Diwali, Hannukkah and Chinese New Year in schools. This should be the case even in schools with a majority white student population; it will teach students about their nation's diversity. Dish up fish and chips on Friday, but have vegetarian, kosher and halal options too. A longer menu not only makes people from different traditions feel more welcome, it also makes lunch (and life) more interesting. Local and national governments should support, both morally and financially, cultural events like the Notting Hill Carnival, Holi celebrations and dragon parades at Chinese New Year. They should encourage white people to come, not only for education, but also for fun. This doesn't mean that you have to stop singing 'Land of Hope and Glory' at the Last Night of the Proms – you can have that too. It's all part of the glorious diversity and variety of contemporary Britain.

Make lunch more interesting

Opponents of multiculturalism argue that, far from creating a society which is tolerant and accepting of difference, it leads to fragmentation and division. It encourages people to live in ghettos, cut off from wider society, where they only associate with people like them for fear of diluting their cultural identity. It undermines national unity, as people prioritise their own cultures over their national identity. Rather than decreasing racism, it increases it, because it separates people, and encourages us to see them as defined by their racial, cultural or religious identity, rather than judging them as individuals.

Just because someone is born into a particular identity, it does not mean they necessarily want to embrace its values. Someone of Jamaican heritage might actually prefer Debussy to drum and bass; some people born Hindu convert to Christianity; there are Muslims and Jewish people who love pork pies. Defining people by their culture stops them from expressing their personal identity and preferences. Moreover, not all cultural practices should be celebrated. Should we be prevented from denouncing female genital mutilation, forced marriages and homophobia just because they form part of a cultural tradition?

2. National identity

To understand the concept of national identity, you first need to decide what a **nation** is. Here are two possible definitions:

1. A nation is an area of land with borders, a head of state and a government.
2. A nation is a way of knowing who you are and where you belong.

If you favour the first definition of a nation, you are likely to see your country as nothing more than an administrative unit. There is no reason for people within that unit to adhere to a particular way of being, other than keeping the laws passed by the government of the day. If you favour the second definition of a nation, you are likely to have a strong sense of your own national identity.

Those who defend the idea of national identity argue that belonging to a nation brings certain rights, such as the right to be protected by the state; the right to access benefits such as health services

You can love Debussy and drum and bass

and education; the right to live and work freely. In return, they say, people need to show that they belong to the nation by embracing its identity; they need to **assimilate** that identity, even if it means abandoning or denying parts of their own cultural identity. This is no more than keeping the rules of the club. Moreover, it ensures that the nation is united by common values, giving everyone a shared sense of who they are, preventing division and tension.

According to the political theorist Benedict Anderson, a nation is an 'imagined community'. That is, it exists only in people's minds. But what exists in our minds changes the way we see the world, and is therefore real. And there are things which people of a shared nationality do have in common. Language; food; landscape; climate; how society is structured; how people behave; a system of government. Someone brought up in Britain will see the world differently from someone brought up in Burundi or Bahrain.

So what does it mean to be British? Being British in Southall (a predominantly Indian area of London) is a different experience from being British in South Shields (a predominantly white area in the north-east of England). What unites us? Is there more to being British than just owning a British passport?

An attempt to answer this question was behind the introduction in 2014 of the requirement on schools to promote 'British Values' (namely, 'democracy, the rule of law, individual liberty, mutual respect and tolerance of those with different faiths and beliefs'). The hope was that teaching these values to children would encourage national unity and prevent fragmentation. Critics of this requirement have complained that it is more than a little arrogant (and inaccurate) to assume that these values somehow belong to Britain, and not to other countries and cultures. They also pointed out that British society does not always live up to them.

Supporters of the promotion of national identity accept that nations do not always live up to their ideals. However, it is still important to have those ideals to aspire to. Above all, it is important to **share** them; without shared ideals and values, and a shared culture, society becomes either a random collection of disparate groups with nothing in common, tending towards mutual suspicion and prejudice, or a mass of lonely, unconnected individuals, neither of which is conducive to tolerance and harmony. A strong sense of national identity is a powerful force against racism, because it unites rather than divides us. If our primary identity is to be British rather than black, white, Asian or Chinese, then the colour of our skin becomes irrelevant. We all belong, equally.

What does it mean to be British?

Opponents of the promotion of national identity argue that, however hard you try, it ends up excluding people. What makes someone British? Eating fish and chips? Respect for the monarchy? Supporting the England football team? If you make fish and chips your national food, you exclude people who grew up eating aloo gobi; if you require (as is the case for all new British citizens) an expression of allegiance to the monarchy, you exclude people whose ancestors, as citizens of former colonies, suffered under the ancestors of the king; make everyone support England at football, and you cut out people who want to support a team connected with their own heritage (and also Scots, Welsh and Northern Irish people). This sense of exclusivity can then slide into racism. Aloo gobi isn't British, so the people who eat it aren't 'one of us'; criticising the British Empire means you hate Britain, so you don't belong here; those black players who missed their penalties don't really belong in the England team, and therefore don't belong in England. And so on.

The question comes down to this. Does having a strong sense of national identity, and expecting all citizens to adhere to this identity, **unite** us or **divide** us?

3. Personal identity

Racism, like other forms of discrimination, stems from people's inability to accept diversity: the fact that there are multiple ways of being in the world. It is just one of many examples of people being discriminated against because of their personal identity. It happens also to women, gay people, trans people and disabled people, even young people and old people – anyone who may be seen as 'other'. We need to resist all forms of discrimination by passing laws to prevent it, and by proactively promoting diversity through education and quotas. We need to protect everyone's right to express their own identity, provided they do so in a way that respects other people's identity. A diverse society is a healthy society.

Critics of this approach – sometimes known as **identity politics** – argue that it leads to disunity and fragmentation of society, and leads to a selfish, individualist outlook. Everyone ends up promoting their own identity over their duties to society as a whole. It can encourage a victim mentality, in which people no longer take responsibility for their own success or failure. I didn't fail to get that university place / job because I didn't work hard enough;

it's someone else's fault because I was discriminated against. It risks creating an inverted hierarchy, a kind of Top Trumps of victimhood. You might be discriminated against for being black, but I'm black and gay, so I win! It is a luxury for prosperous, well-educated people that does not deal with the real problems facing economically disadvantaged people. A black person who can't pay their gas bill doesn't need their identity celebrated. They need lower gas prices.

3. THE POINT OF CLASH

Is racism something done by **individuals**? Or is it embedded in the structures of **society**? Can it be dealt with by either educating or punishing people who are guilty of it? Or do we need to actively intervene to change the structures of society?

Are race-based quotas **fair**, or do they go against **natural justice**? Do they widen the talent pool, or encourage the promotion of incompetent people? Are they necessary because of systemic racism, or do they breed resentment and injustice? Are they **empowering** for people from ethnic minorities, or are they **patronising** and demeaning?

Should racial, cultural and religious groups be encouraged to **celebrate** their identities, or should they **assimilate** to the culture of the country to which they belong? Does **multiculturalism** make society more tolerant, diverse and exciting, or does it promote division and ghettoes? Is it empowering for people from ethnic minorities, or does it demean them by sticking a label on them?

Is there such a thing as a national identity? Should we conform to it? Does it create **harmony** and unity, or does it **exclude** people who are different?

Should everyone be allowed to create their own **identity**, or should they conform to the wider norms of society? Should we encourage people to be aware of and call out discrimination, or should we encourage them to take responsibility for their own success or failure?

4. THE ARGUMENTS

Racism is an individual problem	Racism is a systemic problem
Racist acts are committed by individuals.	Individuals' behaviour is shaped by the society or institution to which they belong.
Blaming institutions or society for racism takes responsibility away from individuals.	Blaming individuals for racism takes responsibility away from institutions or society.
Most racism stems from people's psychological insecurities.	Most racism is part of a strategy for those who have power to hold on to that power.
Making people take responsibility for their behaviour is the best way to get them to change it.	Changing structures is the best way to change the way people behave.

For race-based quotas	Against race-based quotas
Quotas are fair because the existing system is unfair.	Quotas are unfair because they go against natural justice.
Quotas ensure people from ethnic minorities have role models.	Role models created by quotas are not genuine role models.
Quotas ensure institutions reflect the society they serve.	Quotas give a distorted picture of society.
Quotas empower people from ethnic minorities by giving them access to positions of influence.	Quotas patronise and demean people from ethnic minorities by giving them positions based only on the colour of their skin.
Quotas are a necessary response to discriminatory practices.	Quotas end up discriminating against other minorities, e.g. poor white people, or people from the 'wrong' minority.
Quotas widen the talent pool.	Quotas promote unqualified people.

For celebrating racial, cultural and religious identity	Against celebrating racial, cultural and religious identity
Racial, cultural and religious identity is a vital part of who we are and needs to be defended.	Defining someone by their racial, cultural and religious identity denies their individuality.
A multicultural society is culturally richer.	A multicultural society is fragmented and divided.
Promoting different cultures combats racism by increasing awareness and tolerance.	Promoting different cultures encourages racism by separating people from each other.
Celebrating national identity is restrictive and excludes people.	Celebrating national identity is inclusive and creates harmony because it means we have more in common.
People have a right to develop and express their own identity.	People's first responsibility is to society as a whole.
Diversity is part of life and should be celebrated.	Shared values keep society together.

5. THE MOTIONS

1. This house would oblige schools to appoint teachers who reflect the ethnic profile of the student body.
2. This house would oblige all universities to ensure that the ethnic profile of their student body reflects the ethnic profile of the UK as a whole.
3. This house would oblige all businesses with more than 100 employees to ensure that the ethnic profile of their workforce reflects the ethnic profile of the UK as a whole.
4. This house would reserve some constituencies for ethnic minority MPs only.
5. This house would make the teaching of black history compulsory.
6. This house would make it compulsory for 20% of texts studied for English Literature GCSE and A-Level to be by writers from ethnic minorities.
7. This house would make it compulsory for all businesses employing more than 10 people to provide anti-racism training for their staff.
8. This house would make it compulsory for all schools to celebrate non-Christian religious festivals.
9. This house would scrap the requirement for schools to teach British values.
10. This house believes promoting a shared national identity is the best way to defeat racism.
11. This house believes that the UK is a racist society.

Keep thinking...

A selection of further reading and viewing to help you think more deeply about the issues around race.

Natives: Race and Class in the Ruins of Empire, Akala (Two Roads, 2018)

Akala is much more than a rapper. Here he reflects thoughtfully on both his own experience as a black man in Britain, and on the wider currents that have brought us to where we are now. He has become wealthy and influential, but he is aware of, and eloquent about, the barriers he has had to overcome.

Jews Don't Count, David Baddiel (TLS, 2021)

The comedian, writer and avid football fan (he co-wrote and co-performed the England football anthem, *Football's Coming Home*) opens our eyes to the continuing, and shockingly widespread, existence of antisemitism in British society. Much of it is expressed quite shamelessly by people who should know better. Baddiel sees antisemitism as the 'forgotten racism', frequently overlooked. He writes with wit and humour, but also with an angry passion.

Why I'm No Longer Talking to White People About Race, Renni Eddo-Lodge (Bloomsbury, 2017)

Eddo-Lodge is one of the most powerful advocates you will find for the case that British society is systemically racist. She argues that white people are unable to see racism because it does not affect them. They ignore the way systemic racism benefits them and dismiss calls for reform because 'to the privileged, equality feels like oppression.' This phenomenally successful and influential book did much to guide people's responses to the Black Lives Matter movement. It also has one of the most ingeniously designed covers I have ever seen.

Identity: Contemporary Identity Politics and the Struggle for Recognition, Francis Fukuyama (Profile, 2018)

In this book, Fukuyama argues that contemporary identity politics, which encourages people to celebrate their own racial and / or cultural identity above all else, is a threat to liberal democracy.

It undermines the shared values which are necessary to keep society together, and sets people against each other.

Admissions, Joshua Harmon (Samuel French, 2019)

Sherri is head of admissions at a progressive private school in America. She has just hit a career high by achieving a record number of entrants from ethnic minorities to her school through a programme of active recruitment. Meanwhile, her son Charlie is applying for Yale, one of the top universities in the US, as is his best friend Perri. Perri is mixed race. Charlie is white. Perri gets a place at Yale. Charlie doesn't. Everyone knows Perri got his place because of his race. Suddenly Sherri is less keen on quotas.

This short play is brutally honest and savagely funny. It dramatises with great skill and even-handedness the debate around race-based quotas; reading or watching it will make you question many of your assumptions.

Brit(ish): On Race, Identity and Belonging, Afua Hirsch (Jonathan Cape, 2018)

Hirsch reflects thoughtfully and intelligently on what it means to be black in Britain today, based both on her own experience and on wider research. As a mixed-race person who is also socio-economically privileged (privately educated, growing up in a prosperous London suburb), she has a foot in both camps.

Not So Black and White: A History of Race from White Supremacy to Identity Politics, Kenan Malik (C. Hurst & Co., 2023)

Malik makes a deep dive into the history of racism, taking us right back to its origins in the beginnings of the British Empire. He shows how racism is frequently used by those with wealth and power to keep control by dividing those beneath them. The contemporary tendency to define people by their racial identity, however much it intends to celebrate and recognise their experience, is in danger of mimicking the racist mindset and perpetuating this division. You will learn a lot from this thoroughly researched and tightly argued book.

This Is Not America: Why Black Lives in Britain Matter, Tomiwa Owolade (Atlantic Books, 2023)

This is one of the most intelligent and original books about race in Britain that you will ever read. Owolade, the son of Nigerian immigrants, argues that thinking about race in Britain has been too much influenced by reaction to issues of race in America, above all in the wake of the Black Lives Matter movement. He points out that while most black people in America are descended from enslaved people, most black people in Britain are descended from people who came to the country voluntarily, and this makes a great difference. He decries the tendency to lump all black people in Britain together as one undivided whole: West African culture is very different from Caribbean culture. He also makes a strong case for the value of a distinctive British identity, and shows how it might be possible to be both proudly black and proudly British. Even if you disagree with him, he will make you think deeply. Read this book next to *Why I'm Not Talking to White People About Race Any More* and see who wins the debate.

How To Argue With A Racist: History, Science, Race and Reality, Adam Rutherford (Weidenfeld & Nicolson, 2020)

You might think the title of this book is overly optimistic. Anyone who can believe the lies of racism is surely beyond persuasion? In fact, it will change the way you think about race. Rutherford is a biologist by training, and of mixed-race heritage. He calmly but unstoppably unveils the science behind the absolute equality of races. Not only is there no scientific foundation for the notion that white people are more intelligent than black people, it also turns out that black people aren't naturally better at sport, and nor are Jews born being good with money. He has a sense of humour, too. On being told on social media to go back to where he came from, he points out that he quite often returns to Ipswich to see his parents.

CHAPTER 9

Colonialism

In this chapter we're thinking about...

- **Should we apologise for the slave trade?**
- **Should we pay reparations for the slave trade?**
- **Should we take down statues which celebrate colonialists?**
- **Should we return artefacts from museums to the countries they were taken from?**

The past isn't past

This chapter focuses primarily on the **British Empire** as a way of thinking about colonialism and its consequences. This is partly because this book is aimed primarily at British readers, and partly because, although there have been (and are) many other empires, the British Empire was one of the most significant and wide-ranging in history.

One question we're **not** thinking about in this chapter is whether the British Empire was a good thing. This is not because this is not an important question: rather, because it is too big a question. The British Empire was (as we shall see below) very big indeed, and went on for a very long time across very many countries. Historians of the British Empire who have devoted decades of their lives to writing multiple books based on their reading of tens of thousands of sources still have significant gaps in their knowledge of the topic. There is simply too much evidence for even the most talented and committed debater to consider in a five-minute speech after fifteen minutes' prep. We focus instead in this chapter on how we should manage the legacy of the British Empire in the present. That doesn't mean, though, that we don't need to think about the history of the British Empire. Understanding the past is essential if we want to understand the present.

1. THE FACTS

What is colonialism?

Colonialism is when one country takes over another country. As people don't normally want to have their country taken over by another one, this takeover is often (though not always) accompanied by violence, and is often (though not always) sustained by violence.

If your country has been colonised, you no longer have control over it. All the important decisions about your country are taken by people from another country. They may be present in your country, giving you orders directly, or they may be hundreds or even thousands of miles away, ruling over you through local proxies. They may rule your country wisely, kindly and effectively, or they may be brutal and exploitative. They may bring prosperity to your country by trading with you, or they may steal your resources, enslave your people, or even sell your people to other

Colonised people lose control

countries. They may respect your culture, your traditions, your religion, your way of seeing the world and acting in it, or they may try to eradicate your way of life, either by persuasion or through violence.

There is no one experience of being colonised. It may be beneficial for the colonised people, or it may be utterly disastrous. It may be a bit of both, and all points in between. The colonised people may become more prosperous through the opportunities provided by the colonisers; they may be subjected to daily humiliation as they see their culture and their race denigrated as being inferior; they may have to watch as their homes are destroyed and their children are sold into slavery; or they may just quietly get on with their lives, barely noticing that they have been colonised. However, what all colonised people have in common is that they have lost control. Their country is no longer theirs.

Why do countries colonise other countries?

The most common motive is **economic**. If you have control over another country, you have control over its resources and its people. You can buy what the country has at greatly reduced prices, and get its people to work for you for low or even no wages, thereby making your country much more prosperous (almost always at the expense of the colonised country). However, colonising countries can also be motivated by a wish to spread a particular religion, way of life or style of government which the colonising power thinks is superior, and from which the colonised people will benefit, e.g. Christianity, democracy, etc. If a colonising country has a higher level of economic and technological development than the colonised country, it may believe it is doing the colonised country a favour by helping them to develop more quickly.

Is colonialism racist?

Not necessarily. It is possible for colonisers and colonised to be of the same race. However, colonialism very often leads to racism. Here's how.

When you are ruling over another people, taking away their power, telling them what to do, it is very hard not to feel that you must be better than them. This feeling is understandable, but it has no basis in reality. The people you are colonising are human beings like you with exactly the same range of attributes and talents. Your culture may be more technologically advanced, but this is likely to be because of historical accident rather than because you are smarter. Their culture may actually be more advanced than yours in many ways. So why then should you rule over them? If you can tell yourself (and them) that you are inherently superior to them, it will be much easier to rule over them. Once you embrace this belief, you can tell them what to do and exploit them, with confidence in your own rightness and with no guilt. If you can get them to embrace this belief, they will be more likely to accept your power over them. If they have a different coloured skin from you, then that can quickly become the rationale for your superiority. And so you end up with racism.

To give one example. The suffering of the millions of people enslaved and taken from Africa to plantations in British colonies was compounded by racism, as their white masters treated them as an inferior species on account of their skin colour. But the barbarity of the slave trade wasn't caused by racism; the added barbarity of racism was caused by the slave trade. Telling themselves, and the world, that black people were inherently inferior to white people made it much easier for slave traders to justify kidnapping and torturing black people, and buying and selling them like cattle. It also made it easier for them, and for the millions of other people who prospered directly or indirectly from the slave trade, to get rich without guilt. Though the slave trade is over, the racism it created lives on: an example of how what happened then matters now.

What is an empire?

An **empire** is a collection of countries ruled over by one country. It is the practice of colonialism on a large scale.

There have always been empires, and perhaps there always will be. There has never (yet) been a world where every country and every people has had complete control over their own destiny.

A (very) brief history of the British Empire

The British Empire was an accident

Nobody decided Britain should have an empire. There was no memo from the king or the prime minister; no meeting with 'establish an empire' entered in the minutes as the key action point. As John Seeley, a Cambridge history professor, famously remarked in 1881 (at the height of imperial expansion), 'We seem … to have conquered … half the world in a fit of absence of mind.' This was an exaggeration, but it conveyed a truth: that the British Empire emerged from a succession of events rather than from a grand plan. However, this succession of events led ultimately

America was British once

to the establishment of a vast, and vastly influential, historical phenomenon, the effects of which continue to be felt to this day in Britain and around the world. Although the (many) countries around the world which were once British colonies are now almost all independent, they have all been profoundly influenced by their experience of British imperialism.

Given that the British Empire extended to almost every corner of the world, a helpful way to understand its history is to consider it region by region. Note that 'Britain' as we understand it today did not exist until the Act of Union in 1707, which formally united England, Wales and Scotland and created a 'United Kingdom', also known as 'Great Britain'. So in the account of the empire below, early colonisers are referred to as English and representing the English state.

North America

English-speaking settlement in North America began in 1607, when the first English colony of Jamestown was established by Captain John Smith and his fellow adventurers. Naming the place after their King, James I, the settlers hoped to find treasures as well as a sea route through to the Pacific on behalf of the Virginia Company. In 1624, the Crown (representing the English state) took over the failing settlement, but within fifty years it had been long abandoned. Even so, the present-day region surrounding the original site remains known as Virginia, in memory of Queen Elizabeth I, the 'Virgin Queen'.

In 1620, a group of Puritans (members of a Christian religious sect), sometimes known as the Pilgrim Fathers, left England for America on a ship called the *Mayflower*, escaping persecution for their faith. They founded a colony called Plymouth, after the city in Devon, England, in what is now Massachusetts. They were soon followed by other refugees from religious persecution. In 1634, Roman Catholics founded Maryland, and in 1639, Congregationalists founded Rhode Island. It wasn't long before the itch to expand led to military conflict; the Dutch colony of New Netherlands was seized, and New Amsterdam was renamed New York.

In due course the number of American colonies expanded to thirteen. Far from home and proudly self-sufficient, the colonists became more and more detached both economically and culturally from England. This detachment grew into resentment as they found themselves forced to pay tax to a government they had played no part in electing. Taking the slogan 'no taxation without representation', the colonists announced they were breaking free from Britain in 1775. The British government tried to repress this rebellion through military intervention, sparking the American War of Independence. In 1776, the United States of America was formally founded with the signing of the Declaration of Independence, a document which continues to be enormously influential on the way in which Americans see themselves. In 1783, the British conceded defeat and granted independence to the United States. This new-found freedom was not, however, extended to the millions of enslaved people who had been brought to America by British slave traders, nor to the Native Americans, the original inhabitants of America.

No freedom for slaves

English involvement in what is now Canada began in 1670, when King Charles II gave a royal charter to the Hudson's Bay Company to trade in fur. Gradually English settlers took over more and more of the country, though there was frequent conflict with French colonists for territory and resources. The population was greatly increased by the arrival of refugees from the clearances of the Scottish Highlands and the Irish famines in the early and mid-nineteenth century. Colonists rebelled against British rule in 1837, and in 1867 Canadians were effectively granted self-government, though the British monarch remained (and remains) the head of state. Tensions in Canada between English speakers and French speakers in Canada persist to this day, expressed in particular by a powerful movement for independence in French-speaking Quebec, an example of the continuing effects of colonialism.

The expansion of both the United States and Canada came at the cost of the lives and culture of millions of Native Americans, who were driven from their lands, often with great brutality.

The Caribbean

As well as territory in North America, England (as it was then) also gradually took control of most of the Caribbean islands from the early seventeenth century onwards. Bermuda became a colony in 1612, St Kitts in 1623, Barbados in 1627, Nevis in 1628, Jamaica in 1655, and the Bahamas in 1666. As part of a complicated history, Tobago was first claimed as an English colony in 1582; Roman Catholic settlers from England and some other European nations arrived in Trinidad in 1784; by 1889, Trinidad and Tobago were together under British rule.

The economy of the West Indies took off spectacularly with the establishment of sugar plantations, which met the immense demand for the sweet stuff in Britain and the rest of Europe. Originally the sugar plantations were worked by white labourers

Slave owners got compen-sation

brought over from England, but these workers were then replaced by enslaved people from Africa, who came to form the majority population of the West Indies. There were numerous rebellions by enslaved people on the islands in the late seventeenth and early eighteenth centuries.

In 1807, the buying and selling of slaves was outlawed in the British Empire, but not slavery itself. It was not until 1838 that slaves were freed (although not in areas ruled by the East India Company, mainly in modern-day India or Pakistan; nor in America, where slaves had to wait till 1863 and the defeat of the Confederates in the civil war to be freed.) Slave owners, but not the former enslaved people, were compensated by the British government to the tune of £20 million. This amounted to 5% of Britain's Gross Domestic Product (GDP) at the time, equivalent to about £28.5 billion today. The debts incurred by the British government to make this payment were still being paid off by the British taxpayer well into the twenty-first century.

Africa

Britain's involvement in Africa began in 1815 when it acquired what was then known as the 'Cape Colony' on the southern tip of Africa (part of modern South Africa). This part of Africa was originally colonised by Dutch settlers known as 'Boers'. Conflict continued between the Boers and the British, culminating in the Second Boer War of 1899–1902, after which the British finally took full control of the area. During the so-called 'Scramble for Africa' in the late nineteenth century, in which European countries fought to take over African countries, Britain bagged an impressive haul, acquiring Nigeria, Sierra Leone, Southern Cameroon, Gambia, the Gold Coast (now Ghana), Tanganyika and Zanzibar (now Tanzania), Egypt, North Rhodesia (now Zimbabwe), Southern Rhodesia (now Zambia), Orange Free State and the Transvaal (now in South Africa), Bechuanaland (now Botswana), Basutoland (now Lesotho), British East Africa (now Kenya and Uganda), the Sudan, British Somaliland (now northern Somalia), and Nyasaland (now Malawi).

Asia

British involvement in Asia began as a private enterprise. The East India Company took over large parts of the area purely with an eye to commercial exploitation. They acquired Penang in 1786 and Malacca in 1825 (both now in Malaysia), Java (now in Indonesia) in 1811, Singapore in 1819, and Burma (now Myanmar) in 1826, while also spreading their influence across the whole of India and what is now Pakistan. In 1839, Britain went to war with China in an attempt to defend its trade in opium (an addictive drug). In the 1842 treaty to settle hostilities, Britain was granted Hong Kong, at that time a small port, as well as special concessions in the much larger port of Shanghai, along with a handful of others.

Australia began as a big prison

In 1857, there was a major rebellion in India against British rule, which was brutally suppressed. In 1858, the British government officially took control. India was regarded as the 'jewel in the crown' of Britain's empire, and Queen Victoria was named 'Empress of India'. The Indian people continued to struggle for independence for many years. In 1919, nearly 1,500 people taking part in a peaceful protest were killed by British troops at Amritsar, in what became known as the Jallianwala Bagh massacre. In the first half of the twentieth century, a non-violent movement for Indian independence was led by Mahatma Gandhi.

Australasia

In 1770, Captain James Cook landed in Botany Bay in what is now Sydney, New South Wales, on the eastern coast of Australia, and claimed it for Britain. Britain had been in the habit of 'transporting' people who had been convicted of (often quite minor) crimes to America. With the loss of the American colonies, Australia became the new dumping ground for convicts. The first batch arrived in 1788. Transportation of criminals continued until 1868. Freed convicts and their descendants established their own independent culture and livelihoods, though they remained under British rule. There was a less happy outcome for the indigenous people of Australia, who had their land seized, their culture destroyed, and their population decimated through disease and violence.

Captain Cook also claimed the North and South Islands of New Zealand for Britain in 1769 and 1770 respectively. Initial contacts between the indigenous Maori people and the British were largely confined to trading. In 1840, the British and the Maoris signed the Treaty of Waitangi, effectively establishing New Zealand as a British colony. Relations between the white settlers and the indigenous people were generally more peaceful than those in Australia, but they were very far from equal and there was much exploitation of the Maoris.

Europe

Two islands in the Mediterranean joined the British Empire in the nineteenth century. Malta was taken over in 1814 as part of Britain's bounty from the Napoleonic wars; in 1878 Britain acquired Cyprus

The empire helped win the war

in exchange for military support for the Ottoman Empire in their war against Russia.

Middle East

After the First World War, Britain was given a mandate to govern Palestine, Mesopotamia (now Iraq) and Transjordan in 1922, but not full colonial control. Britain also occupied Turkey in 1918–1923.

The end of empire

Millions of imperial subjects fought for Britain in the Second World War; arguably Britain might not have won the war without them. Even as the Nazi occupation of Europe from 1940 to 1944 left Britain isolated and in existential peril, it still managed to hold on to most of its empire (though Singapore, Hong Kong and Burma – now known as Myanmar – were all occupied by the Japanese). The process of decolonisation really took off after the end of the war, partly due to a shift in the way Britain saw itself, and partly because Britain was nearly bankrupted by the conflict and could no longer afford to defend its more distant territories. In 1945, 700 million people outside the UK were under direct British rule; by 1965, it was 5 million, 3 million of them in Hong Kong.

Here's how Britain let go.

1921 Southern Ireland (then the Irish Free State, now Eire) gains independence. The six counties of Northern Ireland remain part of the United Kingdom.

1922 Egypt gains independence.

1926 The Balfour Declaration strengthens the independence of the dominions of Canada, Newfoundland (now part of Canada), Australia, New Zealand, South Africa and the Irish Free State; they can now pass their own laws, though the British monarch remains their head of state. The fact that these countries all have a majority white population (apart from South Africa, which has a dominant white minority) is a significant factor in their being granted independence.

1932 Iraq gains independence.

1946 Jordan gains independence (previously part of Transjordan).

Britain lets go

1947 India gains independence. The new state of Pakistan, in the western part of India, is created. The intention is that India will be a Hindu state and Pakistan a Muslim state. However, both countries have large minorities from the other religion, and the partition of India sparks a brutal civil war in which up to a million people die.

1948 Ceylon (now Sri Lanka) and Burma gain independence. Britain withdraws from Palestine. The Arab–Israeli war breaks out as the new state of Israel is declared on territory which used to be part of Palestine.

1956 Sudan gains independence.

1957 Ghana gains independence.

1960 Cyprus and Nigeria gain independence.

1961 Tanzania gains independence.

1962 Uganda, Jamaica, and Trinidad and Tobago gain independence.

1963 Malaysia and Kenya gain independence. In Kenya this follows the Mau Mau Uprising of 1952–1960 in which thousands of people are executed by the British, many are held in detention, and a million are left homeless and destitute.

1964 Nyasaland (now Malawi) and Zambia gain independence.

1965 Singapore separates from Malaysia to become an independent country. Gambia and the Maldives gain independence.

1966 Barbados and Lesotho gain independence.

1968 Mauritius gains independence.

1970 Fiji gains independence.

1973 The Bahamas gain independence.

1978 The Solomon Islands gain independence.

1980 Zimbabwe gains independence.

1997 Hong Kong reverts to Chinese rule.

The British Empire is over …

How big did the British Empire get?

Very big.

It reached its highest point in the early 1920s. Here's how big it was then:

- Including territories under formal British protection, it covered over 13 million square miles, or 25% of the world's land surface.
- It ruled over 500 million people, a quarter of the world's population at the time.
- Of the 195 nation states in the world today, 94 – nearly half – were once ruled at least in part by the British. It is literally true that the sun never set on the British Empire, in the sense that it covered so many time zones that it was always daytime somewhere in the empire. (Some said this was because you couldn't trust the British in the dark.)

Does the British Empire still exist?

Not really. All that is left of it are the British Overseas Territories, a collection of fourteen states, mostly small islands with very few people; the total population of these territories is about 300,000 (about 0.0037% of the world's population). Each of them has the British monarch (currently King Charles III) as their head of state, but they all run their own affairs.

The empire lingers on in other ways. In addition to the British Overseas Territories, King Charles is head of state in fourteen countries outside the UK (including Australia, Canada and New Zealand). These countries form the 'Commonwealth Realm'. In theory, their governments are appointed by King Charles through his local representative, the governor-general; in practice, all these countries are fully independent democracies.

The Commonwealth is a much larger group of 56 countries, almost all of them formerly part of the British Empire. It is a voluntary association of independent states, headed by King Charles. Commonwealth heads of government meet regularly to discuss matters of shared interest. The Commonwealth Games – a kind of pared-down Olympics – take place every four years. Citizens of Commonwealth countries resident in the UK are allowed to vote in general elections, a privilege not extended to other non-British residents.

Essentially, though, the British Empire is over, and it's not coming back.

So why does the British Empire still matter?

... but it hasn't gone away

The empire might be over, but it hasn't gone away. Its legacy is still hugely influential, both in contemporary Britain and around the world. It has shaped the world we live in, and continues to shape it. Here are some ways in which the British Empire continues to influence Britain in particular.

Cultural

You've got a *cushy* job which allows you to take Friday afternoon off to go clothes shopping. You spend the time browsing a selection of *dungarees*, *bandanas*, *bangles*, and *khaki* trousers. Then you go home to take a shower and wash your hair with *shampoo*. For dinner you have *curry* with *naan* bread and *chutney* on the *verandah* of your *bungalow*. Then you get into your *pyjamas* and go to bed. All the words in italics come from the Urdu, Hindi or Tamil languages; British rule over India brought them into the English language.

No work next day, as it's a Saturday. You live in London and think you should make the most of the museums. Strolling round the British Museum and the Victoria and Albert, you gaze on dozens of artefacts which were taken – some would say stolen – from former British colonies (an 'artefact' is an object made by humans which has particular cultural or historical interest). Walking through London between the two museums, you pass on almost every street corner statues of men (they are all men) who are celebrated for their role in either expanding or defending the British Empire. You decide you don't fancy going home yet, so you call up a friend. What shall we do? Watch the stars arriving at a premiere at the Empire cinema? (One of the lead actors has just been awarded an OBE, which stands for 'Order of the British Empire'.) Have a drink at one of the fifteen or so pubs in London named after Queen Victoria, the former Empress of India? (Not to mention the fictional 'Queen Vic' pub in *EastEnders*.) Your friend tells you she's got tickets for a cricket match: England are playing India at Lord's. When you get there, the ground is half full of British Indians, eager to see India triumph over their former colonial masters. This seems rather ungrateful, as it was the British who introduced cricket to India, where it is now a national obsession. Looking through the record of past England matches, you realise that cricket is played almost entirely by countries which were once British colonies. England lose. Never mind, let's go out for a curry (introduced from India). You wash it down with a nice cup of tea (also from India). Your friend has coffee (from the West Indies) with a couple of spoonfuls of sugar (also from the West Indies). You take the Tube home on the Victoria line (that Empress again).

The slave trade made us rich

The empire lives on in our language, our culture, our cuisine, our public spaces and our leisure activities.

Economic

Britain's status as a successful, prosperous country does not just derive from the hard work and ingenuity of its people. Much of its wealth was derived from the exploitation of colonised peoples in its empire, and in particular from the slave trade. The cotton trade, which depended on cotton imported from slave plantations, was one of the foundations of the industrial revolution, which itself established the modern British economy. London, Liverpool, Bristol and Hull would not be the cities they are today without the vast sums brought in by their status as major slave ports. We may disagree about how we should respond to this legacy, but we cannot deny its reality.

Demographic

One of the most significant, and most visible, legacies of the British Empire is in the population of contemporary Britain. The end of the empire after the Second World War was accompanied by a huge increase in immigration from former member countries, changing Britain from an overwhelmingly white country to an increasingly diverse and multicultural society. You can learn more about this process in Chapter 7, **Immigration**, and Chapter 8, **Race**. The key issue here is that it would not have happened if the British Empire had not existed. As Ambalavner Sivandan, the director of the Institute of Race Relations, said in 2008, 'We are here because you were there.' But we / they have not always been – are still not always – made welcome. Much of the racism experienced by ethnic minorities in Britain derives from attitudes developed in the imperial period. If you're a black or brown British person, the empire hasn't gone away.

Psychological

The widespread sense that many British people have of Britain as being somehow unique, exceptional, inherently superior and able to go it alone without other countries derives to a significant degree from the imperial legacy. So, too, does the sense which many British people have of resentful inferiority and regret that we are no longer as powerful as we once were. Both these feelings played a huge part in the debates around Brexit (the decision to leave the European Union following a referendum in 2016). Obviously not all British people think this way, but enough for it to be fair to say that the legacy of the British Empire continues to influence the way that many British people think and act.

So the British Empire and its legacy still matters. There's more to it than chicken tikka masala and cricket. It matters for the way we see ourselves, the way we act in the world, and the way we act towards each other. We need to think – like debaters – about what the British Empire means and how we should respond to it.

2. THE ISSUES

Should we apologise, or pay reparations for, slavery?

Apology or reparation?

What should you do if you have treated someone **unjustly**: if you have taken or damaged something that belongs to them, or inflicted suffering on them that they do not deserve?

The first step is to admit that you have been unjust. This is what an **apology** is; an admission that you are in the wrong. It marks a shift in the relationship between you and the person you have wronged. You accept that there has been injustice, and you take responsibility for that injustice.

The second step is **reparation**. You make right the injustice in some way. If you have taken something, you give it back. If you have damaged something, you fix it or pay someone else to fix it. If you have made them suffer, you do whatever you can to take away the suffering. It may not always be possible to make full reparation, but you should do as much as you can.

This pattern of recognition of wrong, apology and reparation in the face of injustice is part of the fabric of any family, friendship or relationship. There are two cakes left in the fridge, one for you, one for your sister. You eat both. This is an act of injustice, because one of them belonged to your sister. Your sister is upset; she was looking forward to the cake. You say sorry, and go out to the local baker's to buy her a new cake. You get a slightly bigger one to make up for the upset. Your sister eats it. You and your sister are friends again. Job done.

It works too in wider society, in a more impersonal way. A man murders another man. The victim's wife is (very, very) upset. Murder is unjust; the murderer took the man's life, and deeply hurt the person who loved him more than anyone in the world. The murderer may accept responsibility for his crime by pleading guilty; he may apologise to his victim's widow; or he may not be sorry at all. Even if he does apologise, he can never provide full reparation, because he cannot give back his victim's life, and nor can he go out and buy her another husband in the way you could buy your sister another cake. However, the state can give the man's widow a form of reparation. They can impose a **punishment** on the murderer which recognises the gravity of the crime. This might take the form of a very long prison sentence, perhaps for the rest of his life, or, in countries which have the death penalty, it might mean taking the life of the murderer, just as he took the life of his victim. To do nothing – to allow the murderer to face no consequences for his crime – would be to fail to acknowledge to the widow the injustice of the taking of her husband's life, and so would be a further injustice.

It looks like there is a simple solution to the problem of injustice. The person responsible for the injustice admits they have behaved unjustly and makes reparation for the injustice (you say sorry to your sister and buy her a new cake). If the person responsible for the injustice will not admit they have been unjust (the unrepentant murderer), or if it is impossible for them to make reparation (the murdered person can't be brought back to life), the state makes reparation to whoever has suffered the injustice (the victim's widow) by imposing an appropriate punishment on the person who has wronged them (the murderer is either executed or sent to prison for a very long time).

You can buy your sister a cake (and maybe give her a hug with it) because you are both alive, and live in the same house. The murder victim's widow can see justice done because both she and the murderer are still alive, and live in the same country under the same laws. But what if the injustice was done not to one person by one person, but by many, many people to many, many people? What if the perpetrators and the victims came from different countries? And what if it happened a long time ago and all the people involved are dead? How can justice be done then?

The Atlantic slave trade, which lasted from the mid-sixteenth century to the early nineteenth century, involved millions of people being kidnapped from Africa and forcibly transported to work on cotton and sugar plantations in the West Indies and the southern states of America. Approximately one third of those transported in this way – over 3 million people – were taken by British traders. Enslaved people suffered appalling conditions on the sea journey from Africa, locked up in the holds of ships with little or no sanitation, half-starved and subject to fatal diseases. Many of them were thrown overboard when they got sick so that their owners could claim insurance on them as 'damaged property'.

What should we do about slavery?

Once they arrived in the West Indies or America, they continued to be treated like animals. They were forced to work long hours in blazing heat, and were beaten if they didn't work hard enough, answered back or tried to escape. They had no independence or freedom; they were bought and sold as their owners' property; the women were often raped by their owners, and any children they had were also the property of their owners.

The Atlantic slave trade was a monstrous, revolting, spectacular injustice done to millions of people over hundreds of years, with consequences which continue to be felt to this day. It was theft, kidnapping, rape, torture and murder on an industrial scale. I've said above that to do nothing in the face of injustice is a further injustice. But what, actually, can we do about the slave trade? Can we – should we – apologise? Can we – should we – pay reparations?

For an apology

Making an apology for the damage done by the slave trade is nothing more than stating the truth. This happened. It shouldn't have happened. We did it. It was wrong. We regret it.

Even though no living British person was directly involved in the slave trade, all British people, to a greater or lesser extent, have profited from it. The Industrial Revolution in the late eighteenth and early nineteenth century was the foundation of the prosperity we enjoy today; the cotton industry, which was powered by slave labour, was a major component of that economic success. We would not be where we are now without the slave trade. While we – living British people – may not be directly **responsible** for the suffering inflicted by the slave trade, we are **liable** for it, because we have prospered from it. Say someone steals a phone from someone else at knifepoint, and then gives it to you. You may not have been the one who actually held the knife, but if you use that phone, knowing it was stolen, you are profiting from the injustice of the original theft.

We need to take responsibility for the evil actions on which our prosperity was founded. A formal apology by the British people – represented by the king or prime minister – would be a way of accepting that responsibility. As well as being an act of justice, it would be good for us as a nation. It would give us a more honest view of our past, and thus of our present. It would stop us deluding ourselves that Britain is somehow inherently superior and entitled to special treatment, and so might help us to make better decisions about our future.

Words are easy

Against an apology

We can – and certainly should – acknowledge that the slave trade was a monstrous injustice. But it would be absurd to apologise for it. An apology is an acceptance of responsibility for a wrong action. You cannot apologise for something you did not do. If the king or prime minister were to apologise for the slave trade, that would debase the language of apology. They, along with the rest of us, were not alive when it happened.

If they say they are apologising on behalf of the British people who were involved in the slave trade, that too is meaningless. Those people are dead, so cannot give their consent for an apology in their name. In any case, even if they could be magically brought back to life, the overwhelming majority would probably be completely unapologetic about what they did then, just as they were when they first did it.

Apologising for something that happened two hundred years ago keeps us stuck in the past. What was done to those millions of enslaved people was shameful, but it cannot be undone. It is pointless to focus on something which cannot be changed. In many ways, apologising for the past is the easy way out: sorry that we exploited your ancestors, but don't expect us to do anything for you now. Much better to focus on what needs doing in the present. There are any number of injustices happening in our time, which we can acknowledge through an apology, but can then go on to fix.

An apology is just words. Words are easy. Words do not put right the wrong. They do not address the continuing injustices caused by the slave trade. It costs very little for the king or prime minister to have their speechwriter craft a few well-shaped sentences, and for them to deliver them in a solemn voice. It would cost a lot more to deliver a proper level of aid to countries impacted by the consequences of the slave trade, or to address the effects of the systemic racism that the slave trade gave rise to. But it would do far more to make up for the harm done. Stop saying sorry for eating my cake. Go out and buy me a new one.

For reparations

Although the practice of slavery was ended nearly two hundred years ago, British people today continue to profit from it. The prosperity of Britain's major cities, the wealth of many long-established British companies, and the creation of many of the great houses, monuments and institutions which we celebrate as part of our heritage were all originally funded by profits from slavery. To take one example: we might feel proud of the magnificent art collections in Tate Britain and Tate Modern in London, but Tate is a sugar company, and the sugar trade depended on the exploitation of enslaved people. Behind the beautiful art there lies an ugly truth of exploitation.

We acquired this wealth unjustly, through the kidnapping and abuse of millions of people. We should put right this injustice by repaying some of that wealth to those countries whose development was damaged by the slave trade: the West Indies, whose economic development was held back by our exploitation of them; countries in Africa, whose political, cultural and social development was distorted by their people being taken as slaves. We may not be guilty of the crimes of our ancestors but we do need to take responsibility for what they did, because we live in the world they created.

Even after slavery was ended in the United States in the mid-nineteenth century, the black descendants of slaves continued to suffer horrific levels of racist discrimination and abuse, particularly in the southern states. Black people were segregated from white people, and were systematically denied the right to vote or to participate in public life. Marriage between people of different races was against the law. Lynchings (public murders by a white mob) of black people were routine events throughout the late nineteenth and early twentieth centuries. Even today, black people in the United States are more likely to have a lower income, to live in a poorer area, and to end up in prison. The practice of slavery which gave rise to this systemic racism began under the British Empire. The racism suffered by many black British people may be less extreme, but it still has its origins in the attitudes generated by the slave trade. Contemporary racism is an ongoing injustice, caused in large part by the slave trade; those who have indirectly profited from the slave trade should make financial amends for it to those who are directly affected by the racism it has created.

Against reparations

It is fundamentally unjust to hold someone responsible for actions taken by someone else. Imagine you buy a house. The previous owner added a garden extension. The man you bought it from dies soon after the sale. Then one day the builder who did the extension knocks on your door. The previous owner never paid him for his work, he tells you. You're living in the house now, you're enjoying the extension I built, so you owe me for my work.

Am I responsible for my ancestors?

Should you pay him? Of course not. The builder would have no grounds in law to sue you for non-payment, because you did not commission the work. Nor would it be fair to pay him, because you have done nothing wrong. You may feel guilty sitting in the extension on a sunny day, knowing that your comfort is based on the fact that someone else was cheated, but that is not a rational feeling; the true guilt lies with the man you bought the house from. Similarly, although it may be true that people living in Britain today continue to profit from the slave trade, it is not fair that they should pay reparations for crimes they did not commit.

Paying reparations immediately after the end of the slave trade would have made sense. Doing so now, nearly two hundred years later, does not. Britain, Africa and the West Indies are all completely different places from what they were in the early nineteenth century. Say my great-great-great-grandfather stole your great-great-great-grandfather's horse. At the time, that was a disaster for your ancestor. He was a milkman who depended on the horse to pull the cart that delivered milk and cheese to the area. When he lost his horse, he lost his livelihood, and his children starved. But you're a merchant banker living in a big house and I'm a cleaner living in a rented room, surviving on benefits. What am I supposed to do? Buy you a horse? What would you even do with it? However great the injustice, it cannot meaningfully be put right once the original circumstances have irrevocably changed.

Putting people into groups as oppressors and victims is both unjust and inaccurate. Some countries in the global south still suffer from the long-term effects of the slave trade; some don't. Some black people suffer from the effects of racism; some don't. Why should British taxpayers' money be given to governments which may be corrupt and tyrannical, just because of what our country did to their country two hundred years ago? Why should a white bus driver give money to a black billionaire just because the bus driver's ancestor mistreated the billionaire's ancestor?

As well as being unfair, this arbitrary division is bad for the people involved. Treating people as victims because of the country they come from or the colour of their skin takes away their dignity and their agency, making them passive; treating people as oppressors on the same grounds creates either crippling guilt or bitter resentment. Judging people as groups in this way prevents us from treating people as they are. It recreates the racist practice of attributing characteristics to racial identity: saying all white people are oppressors makes no more sense and is no more just than saying all black people are lazy. It keeps alive the damaging dynamic of oppressor and victim, when we could be moving on to a more equal relationship.

Statues matter

Should we take down statues which celebrate colonialists?

Why do statues matter?

They're only lumps of stone. They can't talk, they can't think, they can't do anything. But you could say something similar about photos. They're only a collection of pixels, or ink on paper. And yet these collations of light and colour can be a significant part of our identity. They say important things about who we are. We're unlikely to have photos on our phones or in our houses of people we hate. We keep photos of people we love, as a memory of happy times with them, and as a way of telling other people and reminding ourselves of how much they mean to us.

Public statues of famous people are a kind of national photo album. When a city or a country goes to the trouble and expense of commissioning, paying for and putting up a statue of someone in a prominent public space, it is a very definite way of saying that this person is both important and admirable. It is a powerful statement of the identity of the civic or national community. Statues define the space we live in. They are big, public and permanent. We walk past them every day. On a sunny day, we eat our lunch in their shade. Statues say who we are.

Why do statues get taken down?

The destruction of a statue may be an act of rebellion against tyrannical rule, as when, in 1956, a monument to the Soviet leader Stalin was torn down in Budapest as part of the Hungarian uprising against the Russian-backed communist government (the uprising was swiftly crushed by a Russian invasion). Or a statue may be a casualty of war: in 2003, a statue of the Iraqi dictator Saddam Hussein was toppled in Baghdad following the American-led invasion of Iraq. Or statues may be taken down as part of a peaceful transition of power. In 2014, Ukraine marked the independence from the former Soviet Union it had won in 1991 by removing from public view an estimated 1,320 statues of the communist leader Lenin (many were replaced in occupied parts of Ukraine following the Russian invasion in 2022).

More recently, statues have been threatened not because of their association with present or recent regimes, but because of the actions and attitudes of the individuals they commemorate.

Statues aren't safe

From late May to June 2020, as part of the Black Lives Matter movement that took off in response to the murder of George Floyd by a policeman in the US, there were demonstrations across the UK. In Bristol, a statue of Edward Colston, a seventeenth-century merchant whose philanthropic donations to the city had been largely fuelled by money he had made from the slave trade, was pulled down by an angry crowd and thrown into the harbour. In London, a statue of Winston Churchill, who was prime minister during the Second World War, was daubed with the words 'was a racist'. In Oxford, thousands of people gathered to demand the removal from the front of Oriel College of the statue of Cecil Rhodes, a leader of the British takeover of large parts of southern Africa. There were similar demonstrations in southern states of the US against statues commemorating leaders of the Confederate cause (the losing side in the American Civil War of 1861–65, which fought to retain the practice of slavery).

In response to these protests, the British government passed a law forbidding the removal of any historical statue or monument with 'contested heritage' without advance planning permission from the local authority. They also made the destruction of statues and other memorials punishable by up to ten years in prison – three years more than the maximum sentence for sexual assault. So, in the eyes of the law, attacking a statue is worse than attacking a woman. Statues, it seems, matter a lot.

But what happens when we change our minds about the person commemorated by a statue? If you find out your partner's been cheating on you for years, you can take down their photo from your mantlepiece or remove it from your phone. That's a simple action involving one person. Removing a statue from a public place, though, impacts far more people. It changes a place that belongs to a whole community. And not everyone in the community will have the same view of the person commemorated. Some may hate them; some may love them; some may be indifferent. And even some who condemn everything the person did and said may argue for the retention of their statue.

For taking down statues

Edward Colston made a fortune from the kidnapping and enslavement of thousands of people. Winston Churchill defended the expulsion of Native Americans and First Nations people from their native lands by saying that they had been replaced by 'a stronger race, a higher-grade race' (i.e. white people); he described Hindu Indians as a 'beastly people with a beastly religion'; during the Second World War, he was widely blamed for diverting grain

Don't celebrate racism

shipments to Britain rather than using them to relieve the Bengal famine, in which an estimated three million people died. Cecil Rhodes, when prime minister of South Africa, was responsible for driving black people off their land, denying them the vote and excluding them from all but the most menial jobs. He justified this policy by comparing black people to children and saying they were fit only for manual labour. These were repugnant opinions and repulsive actions. Maintaining statues of men like this in a public not only endorses, but actively celebrates their behaviour and attitudes.

Take the example of Jimmy Savile (1926–2011). In his lifetime, he was a successful DJ and media personality, who raised millions of pounds for charity. He counted prime ministers and members of the royal family amongst his friends, and was regarded as a national hero. Statues of him and plaques to him were put up in public places, and streets and hospital wings were named after him. Then, after his death, he was revealed to have been a predatory paedophile, who had used his status to systematically abuse hundreds of children. As soon as these revelations were made public, the statues and plaques came down and the streets and hospital wings were renamed.

No one would dream of defending a statue of Jimmy Savile. We don't want to celebrate a serial child abuser by commemorating him in a public place. And yet we continue to celebrate men who profited from the exploitation and mass murder of thousands of enslaved people. Why?

Can you imagine a statue of Hitler in a public square in Israel? Of course not. Thousands of Israelis are descended from victims of the Holocaust. To make them walk past a statue of the man who oversaw the murder of their family members every day would be deeply cruel. And yet the many British people of colour who are descended from victims of the slave trade and of colonialism are daily confronted with statues celebrating the men and women who became rich and powerful through the plunder, kidnapping and murder of their ancestors.

You say these statues are part of our history, and we cannot change history. Sending children down coal mines is part of our history; we don't do that any more. Preventing women from voting or owning property is part of our history; we don't do that any more. Sending men to prison for being in a consensual same-sex relationship is part of our history; we don't do that any more. Signs outside boarding houses that said 'No blacks, no Irish, no dogs' are part of our history; we don't do that any more. Similarly,

Retain and explain

celebrating men whose power and prosperity was built on theft, kidnap and murder is something we used to do, but we don't – or at least we shouldn't – do that any more. And that means taking down those celebratory statues. That's not changing history; it's changing the way we think about it in the light of what we now know and value.

For keeping statues

These statues were erected in a different time, and need to be understood as such. Our cities and public spaces have evolved organically over the centuries; they are a living record of our past. To tear them down and rebuild them in the light of our current beliefs will prevent us from understanding our heritage, both the good and the bad. Stonehenge may well have been the site of human sacrifice; should we take it down? The Christian Church inspired the Crusades, a brutal war against Muslims for belonging to the 'wrong' religion; do we demolish Westminster Abbey? Shakespeare's play *The Merchant of Venice* contains vile anti-semitic language, reflective of the attitudes of his time; should we ban it from our classrooms and our theatres? Better by far to look at these monuments of our culture in the context of their times. Try to understand why pagans sacrificed humans, what prompted the Crusades, the history of anti-Jewish persecution in early modern England. So too with statues. Keep Colston's statue up, but with a well-researched, well-designed plaque making clear how he made the money he gave to Bristol and what the consequences of his line of business were. Don't eradicate: understand. Retain and explain.

Dividing people of the past into heroes and villains is naive and dangerous. It stops us understanding the complexities of history. Very few people are all bad or all good. Yes, Colston (like many people of his time) made money from the slave trade; he also established schools and other public institutions which have benefitted thousands of Bristolians and other British people down the years. Yes, Churchill (like many people of his time) held racist beliefs; he also ensured Britain did not capitulate to the Nazis in 1940, thereby saving the lives of hundreds of thousands of British Jewish people. Yes, Rhodes laid the foundations for racist regimes in southern Africa; he also established scholarships which have helped thousands of students. Rather than reacting in fury to what these people did wrong, we should try to understand them fully and accurately. Having their statues in our cities does not mean that we approve of everything they did or said. Rather, it reminds us that they were important people in our history. Taking down the statues prevents us from understanding that history.

Don't destroy, build. Rather than attacking the bad in the past, celebrate the good in the present (and the past). Joining Winston Churchill in Parliament Square are statues of Millicent Fawcett, who campaigned to give women the vote (originally opposed by Churchill, though he did change his mind), and Nelson Mandela, leader of the struggle against the racist apartheid regime in South Africa (Churchill backed the white rulers of South Africa who went on to establish apartheid). So Parliament Square is, like parliament itself, a place of dialogue and debate. Make all our public spaces like that. Let the present talk to the past. Put up monuments to people whose values we celebrate today. Don't tear down monuments to racists; put up monuments to anti-racists.

Don't destroy, build

Should we return artefacts from museums to the countries they were taken from?

The British Museum in London is somewhat misnamed. True, it's in Britain; true, it is one of the most iconic sites for visitors to Britain from overseas. But it is emphatically not a museum of Britain. It is a museum of the world. Anyone can go there, and entry is free. Once inside, you can wander not only through time, but also around the world, drifting from Europe to Africa to India to China to Australasia to North and South America and back again. All periods of history and all cultures are represented through the artefacts collected in one building in Bloomsbury. But how did they get there?

It would take too long to work through every non-British artefact displayed in the British Museum, not to mention the many more kept in storage, or the even more kept in many other museums across Britain (the British Museum is not the only museum in Britain, nor is London the only place in Britain). Let's look at just a couple of the most high-profile artefacts from this most high-profile of museums, as a way of thinking through the issues.

The Benin Bronzes

What are the Benin Bronzes?

The Benin Bronzes are a series of sculptures and related artefacts created from the sixteenth century onwards for the royal court of what was then the Kingdom of Benin in West Africa. The British Museum owns over 900 of them. Over 100 are displayed at any one time in the museum, on a constantly changing basis.

Hand back the Benin Bronzes?

The Kingdom of Benin still exists, but it is now part of Nigeria, neighbouring the independent Republic of Benin. Nigeria was a British colony, but became an independent country in 1960.

How did they get to Britain?

In the late nineteenth century, as part of the 'Scramble for Africa' (see p202), Britain was aggressively expanding its power in West Africa. In February 1897, British forces launched an attack on Benin City, the capital of Benin. The city was captured and a brutal occupation followed, costing many lives. Hundreds of artworks and artefacts were taken as 'spoils of war' and were brought back to Britain. Some were given to the British Museum; others were sold to private collectors. Over the years, the British Museum bought up most of the bronzes that were in private hands, ensuring that almost all of the bronzes now belong to the museum.

Who wants them back?

In 2018, in a meeting with the then director of the British Museum, the current King of Benin formally requested that the bronzes should be returned to Benin City. In 2021, the Nigerian Ministry of Information and Culture made the same request.

Why do they want them back?

Because they were stolen.

Because they belong in Benin.

Because they can best be understood if seen in Benin.

Are they going to get them back?

Discussions are continuing. The most likely outcome is that the sculptures will be loaned to Nigeria to be displayed there, but will continue to be the property of the British Museum.

The Elgin Marbles

The Elgin Marbles, also known as the Parthenon Sculptures, are ancient Greek sculptures dating from the fifth century BCE. They were originally on the walls of the Parthenon in Athens, Greece.

How did they get to Britain?

In 1812 the Earl of Elgin, a British aristocrat, was based in Athens as Britain's ambassador to the ruling Ottoman government. At the time, Greece was part of the Ottoman Empire, which was centred on what is now Turkey. Greece did not become an independent country until 1830. Elgin removed the marbles from the Parthenon and brought them back to Britain, claiming that he did so with official agreement; this claim has been widely disputed. In 1816, he sold them to the British government, who put them in the British Museum.

Who wants them back?

In 1983, the Greek government formally requested the return of the Elgin Marbles to Greece.

Why do they want them back?

Because (they claim) they were stolen.

Because half the collection remains in Athens, and splitting it makes the collection incomplete.

Because they can best be understood in the place they come from.

Are they going to get them back?

In November 2023, the marbles caused a major diplomatic incident. The Greek prime minister, Kyriakos Mitsotakis, was on an official visit to the UK. During a TV interview, he reiterated his government's position that the marbles should be returned to Greece, likening their being kept in Britain to 'cutting the Mona Lisa in half'. The British prime minister, Rishi Sunak, promptly cancelled his meeting with Mr Mitsotakis.

The position of the British Museum is less confrontational. At the time of writing, they are discussing the possibility of loaning the marbles to Athens on a long-term basis.

Those are two examples on which we can base a more general discussion about whether artefacts should be returned to their country of origin.

For returning artefacts

Many artefacts in British and other western museums were stolen, with the theft often accompanied either by the threat of violence or actual violence. Even when they were 'legitimately' acquired, negotiations were conducted on a far from equal basis because of the vastly greater economic and military power of the colonialists. Keeping property that has been stolen or acquired in an unjust way is simply wrong.

Are museums racist?

The British Museum and other museums like it are not just neutral collections of artefacts; they are political statements. Assembling artefacts from former colonies all round the world in one building, in the city that was once the capital of the British Empire, reproduces the structures of colonialism. It says to the people of former colonies, 'Your stuff is ours. We are going to keep it because we are more important than you, and we can look after it better than you because we are at a higher level of development.' It is an inherently racist institution.

It makes no sense to look at West African bronzes or ancient Greek sculptures in London; they don't belong there, as they are from a completely different culture. Imagine if Stonehenge was dismantled and reassembled in the middle of Singapore, or if Westminster Abbey was moved to the Saudi Arabian desert. Either structure would look completely out of place. What is more, it would be impossible to understand them. Stonehenge was built to capture the rising sun on the longest day of the English summer; Singapore is on the equator. Westminster Abbey is a building for Christian worship, and the site of the coronation of British monarchs over centuries; Saudi Arabia is an Arab Muslim country. Historical artefacts need to be understood in the context in which they were created and in which their creators lived.

Against returning artefacts

Artefacts may have been originally stolen, but the people who stole them are long dead, as are the people they were stolen from. It is unfair both to punish living people for the crimes of the dead, and to return property to people who have never owned it. If, when researching the history of your house, you discover that the last owner but five got hold of the house by cheating the last owner but six out of it, you are under no obligation to track down the descendants of the last owner but six and hand over the title deeds to them. They have no right to the house because they never owned it. You, on the other hand, have paid for it, live in it, and look after it.

The point of museums is to allow the maximum number of people to see and learn from historic artefacts. Artefacts should therefore be in the best run and best situated museums. The British Museum and other museums like it have hundreds of years of experience of looking after valuable historic artefacts. Six million people come to the British Museum every year; only 1.5 million people visit the Parthenon every year.

Another function of museums is to bring together objects from different cultures and times so they can be understood in their wider context. Museums help people to understand other cultures and to see the universal value of every culture. It is a wonderful thing that the whole world is under one roof in the British Museum; it unites people and cultures. As the former Director of the British Museum, Neil McGregor, put it, 'Where else can the world see so clearly that it is one?' The logical extension of returning all artefacts to their original countries would be that you could only see British artefacts in Britain, Greek artefacts in Greece, Nigerian artefacts in Nigeria, and so on. The world would become more divided, and everyone would live in their own cultural ghettoes, with no mutual understanding.

Museums show the world as one

Times change, countries change. Britain is no longer an imperial power. Benin is not the same in the early twenty-first century as it was in 1897. Greece is not the same country as the one the Elgin Marbles were taken from. Assuming that countries and cultures have a fixed, unchanging identity borders on racism. You wouldn't say to someone who was born in Greece but came to London forty years ago, got a job, learned English, married an Englishwoman, brought up children in London and became a British citizen, 'You're not really British – go back to Greece!' In the same way, the Elgin Marbles, and many artefacts like them, have been in Britain for so long that they are fully integrated into British culture.

3. THE POINT OF CLASH

Should countries which have founded their prosperity on the slave trade acknowledge their **liability** for it, by making an apology and / or by paying reparations? Or can we only meaningfully demand apology or reparation from people who are directly **responsible** for wrong actions? Is acknowledging historic wrongs a healthy **recognition of reality**, or is it a dangerous **distraction from the present**? If we have **profited** from the wrongdoings of our ancestors, are we **responsible** for them, even though we did not commit them?

What is the point of public statues? Is it to **celebrate** people whose actions and beliefs we admire? In that case, we should take down statues which celebrate racists and slave traders. Or are public statues a **historical record**, marking people who have been significant in our national story, even if we no longer agree with everything they did and said? In that case, we should keep

Are we responsible for the past?

existing statues, but with a better understanding of the people they represent. Should we **remove the racists**, or **retain and explain**?

What is the point of museums? Is it to bring together artefacts from all times and all cultures under one roof, to enhance our **understanding**? In that case, artefacts should be kept where they can be best preserved and seen by the most people. Or are museums an expression of **power**, a kind of cultural colonialism, where artefacts have been taken as trophies of conquest? In that case we should return artefacts to the countries they were taken from. Can we best understand and appreciate artefacts in the setting of the cultures from which they **originated**? Then send them back to their places of origin. Or are they best understood when set against artefacts from **other cultures**? Then keep them in the museum. Who do artefacts belong to? The **world** or their **country of origin**?

4. THE ARGUMENTS

For an apology for slavery	Against an apology for slavery
An apology is a way of recognising the fact of the evil of slavery.	An apology is only meaningful if given by the person or people who committed the action.
An apology would help us to a better understanding of our place in the world.	An apology keeps us stuck in the past, rather than dealing with the problems of the present.
Though we may not have been active participants in the slave trade, we have profited from it, and wΩe should acknowledge responsibility for it.	We cannot acknowledge responsibility for actions we did not commit.
The slave trade may have ended, but its consequences live on.	The world today is completely different from the world of the slave trade.
Contemporary racism began with the slave trade; an apology is a way of addressing the causes of racism and thus of tackling it.	An apology is only words, and is a way of avoiding meaningful action against racism.

For reparations for slavery	Against reparations for slavery
Our current prosperity is based on slavery; reparations are a way of paying back what we stole from enslaved people.	It is fundamentally unjust to make people pay for actions they did not commit.
Reparations will correct the unequal and unfair balance of economic power that has arisen because of the slave trade.	Reparations may go to governments which are corrupt and incompetent.
Reparations are a way of acknowledging the immoral foundations of our prosperity.	Dividing people into exploiters and victims on account of their race is as immoral and stupid as racism.
Reparations are a way of putting right a historic injustice.	Reparations distract us from addressing contemporary injustices.

For taking down statues of colonialists	Against taking down statues of colonialists
Public statues are a celebration of their subjects; we should not be celebrating slave traders and racists.	Public statues are a historical record; we should not edit out historical fact just because we do not like it.
It is immoral to celebrate people who are guilty of such crimes.	History is complex; almost all public figures did some good and some bad.
We need to make a public statement of our abhorrence of racism and slavery.	We should not impose our values on historical figures from different times.
Statues of racists and slave traders in public places are offensive to people of colour.	Statues are just bits of stone. Save the campaigning energy to combat actual examples of racism in education, employment, policing, etc.
Our public spaces should reflect the sort of society we want to live in.	There should be room for diversity and debate in public spaces; respond to statues of racists by erecting statues of anti-racists. Let Nelson Mandela answer back to Churchill.

For returning artefacts to their country of origin	Against returning artefacts to their country of origin
Most artefacts in western museums were either stolen, or acquired under duress. It is immoral to keep objects taken in this way.	It is unfair to penalise museums and the people who visit them for the actions of people long dead.
Museums are monuments to colonial power and exploitation.	Museums are celebrations of the diversity of the world's culture.
Artefacts can best be appreciated and understood in the place they came from.	Artefacts can best be appreciated and understood within a museum which can preserve them effectively and display them to as many people as possible.
Taking artefacts away from the culture which created them destroys their meaning; imagine Stonehenge in Singapore.	It is healthy and natural for cultures to mix and blend with each other. Cultures are enriched by being more diverse. Singaporeans add to the diversity of Britain, and British people add to the diversity of Singapore; the same goes for artefacts.
Museums concentrate cultural power in already rich and powerful places, e.g. the British Museum in London.	Museums unite the world under one roof, promoting mutual understanding. Sending all artefacts back to their country of origin will divide the world into mutually ignorant ghettoes.

5. THE MOTIONS

1. This house would oblige King Charles III / the British prime minister to make a public apology for the slave trade.
2. This house would oblige any institutions which have profited from the slave trade to make a public apology.
3. This house would oblige any institutions which have profited from the slave trade to pay reparations.
4. This house would pay reparations for slavery.
5. This house would take down public statues of people who have expressed racist views.
6. This house would take down public statues of people who were involved in the slave trade.
7. This house would return to their country of origin any artefacts displayed in museums which were either stolen or taken under duress.
8. This house would return the Elgin Marbles to Greece.
9. This house believes artefacts should only be displayed in their country of origin.
10. This house believes colonialism is immoral.

Keep thinking...

A selection of further reading, listening and viewing to help you think more deeply about the issues around colonialism.

Colonialism: A Moral Reckoning, Nigel Biggar (William Collins, 2023)

Biggar does not deny that the British Empire has been guilty, like any long-lasting state, of both criminal and incompetent actions. However, he argues that these are more than outweighed by many good actions: the abolition of slavery; the opening up of trade; the imposition of the rule of law; and the fight against German and Japanese fascism in the Second World War. His challenging but thoughtful arguments about the morality of colonialism will help you to clarify your own views.

Legacy of Violence: A History of the British Empire, Caroline Elkins (Bodley Head, 2022)

In meticulously researched detail, Elkins catalogues the ways in which Britain used violence to maintain its grip on its empire. Many of her examples are deeply shocking and harrowing to read. Her argument is that colonialism is inherently violent.

Empire: How Britain Made the Modern World, Niall Ferguson (Allen Lane, 2003)

Ferguson mounts a robust defence of the British Empire, arguing that it helped modernise the world to everyone's benefit by spreading technology and free trade, and suppressing many barbaric practices. You may not agree with his conclusions, but you will learn a lot from his examples.

The British Empire: A Very Short Introduction, Ashley Jackson (Oxford University Press, 2013)

This short book does just what it says on the tin. Concise, clear and easy to read, it gives a brief but accurate summary of how the British Empire came to be, what it was, and how it ended. It is packed full of useful facts for debaters.

Keeping Their Marbles: How the Treasures of the Past Ended Up in Museums … and Why They Should Stay There,
Tiffany Jenkins (Oxford University Press, 2016)

Although this book takes a very clear position on artefacts in museums (keep them there), it is remarkably and admirably even-handed. Jenkins gives a very full and fair exposition of the arguments for return of artefacts before making her own case for the value of a museum as a celebration of world culture. This book, more than any other, will help you understand both sides of the artefact debate.

Learning From the Germans: Race and the Memory of Evil,
Susan Neiman (Allen and Lane, 2019)

Neiman is a Jewish American, brought up in the Deep South of America, now living in Germany. Despite Germany's past, she feels safer being a Jew in Berlin than she does in Mississippi. She shows how the Germans have come to terms with their horrific history by facing up to the evil of Nazism full on. Meanwhile, many Americans are not only in denial about the place of slavery in their history, but actively celebrate the Confederate regime which supported it and mourn its passing. The result of this misreading of history is that American society is still shot through with racism. Meanwhile, anti-semitism, once rife in Germany (even before the Nazis came to power) has all but vanished from that country. Although not explicitly about the British Empire (except to the extent that the American slave trade was founded by the British), this book will make you think deeply about how a country's past lives on in its present, for better or for worse.

The Whole Picture: The colonial story of the art in our museums & why we need to talk about it, Alice Procter (Cassell, 2020)

Procter argues vigorously and uncompromisingly that, far from being neutral spaces conserving objects of interest and beauty, museums and art galleries support a hidden and dangerous agenda of cultural domination and appropriation. You will never walk round a museum in quite the same way after reading this thought-provoking book.

Blood Legacy: Reckoning With a Family's Story of Slavery, Alex Renton (Canongate, 2021)

Renton's family owned slave plantations in Jamaica and Tobago. In this book he tells the story of his ancestors' lives, and then visits the countries they worked in to learn how the legacy of the slave trade lives on today. He faces up to the advantages the legacy of the slave trade has given him as a white man, and comes down firmly on the side of apology and reparation for slavery.

Empireland: How Imperialism Has Shaped Modern Britain, Sathnam Sanghera (Viking, 2020)

Sanghera has researched deeply into the history of the empire. He shows how it has made modern Britain what it is, both economically and culturally. He has a personal connection with the imperial story as the child of Indian immigrants. Describing the racism he experienced growing up in the West Midlands, he connects today's racism very clearly to the imperial past. You will find no better explanation of how the British Empire continues to be important in contemporary Britain. A sequel, *Empireworld,* was published in 2024.

Empire (Goalhanger Podcasts)

Anita Anand and William Dalrymple discuss all aspects of imperial history with each other and with well-informed guests in an engaging and accessible way.

12 Years A Slave, dir. Steve McQueen (Fox Searchlight Pictures, 2013)

Chiwetel Ejiofor stars as Solomon Northrup, an African–American man who is living freely in Washington, D.C., in 1841 before he is drugged, kidnapped and sold into slavery. Based on the real Northrup's memoir of his enslavement, this film is brutal and uncompromising in its depiction of the reality of slavery. Some scenes are hard to watch, but none of them are exaggerated.

CHAPTER 10

Crime, Punishment and the Law

In this chapter we're thinking about...

- **Why do people commit crimes?**
- **How should society respond to crime?**
- **Is breaking the law ever justified?**

1. THE FACTS

Different times, different crimes

What is crime?

A crime is any action that is **against the law**.

Does calling an action a crime mean that the action itself is always wrong?

Not necessarily.

An action might not be inherently wrong in itself, but it might become a crime because of the circumstances in which it takes place. Driving at 70 miles an hour is not a crime on a motorway, but it is in a built-up area. Being drunk is not a crime in a pub, but it is if you leave the pub and drive home in your car while still drunk. Smoking a cigarette in your house is not a crime; smoking a cigarette in your workplace is. Shooting someone in the head because you don't like them is a crime. Shooting someone in the head because they are about to detonate a suicide bomb in a crowded place and you are an armed police officer is not.

Are certain actions crimes everywhere and always?

Some actions are crimes in some countries, or even parts of countries, and not in others. Helping someone suffering from a terminal illness to die is a crime in the UK, but not (subject to certain conditions) in the Netherlands, Canada, and many other countries around the world (see Chapter 17, **Assisted Dying**). Denying that the Holocaust (the murder of six million Jews by the Nazis) happened is not a crime in the UK, but it is in Germany and Israel (see Chapter 4, **Free Speech**).

What is and is not a crime changes over time, as laws are changed. Having an abortion was a crime in the UK until the law was changed in 1967 (see Chapter 16, **Abortion**). Once, you could refuse to give someone a job simply because they were black; with the passing of the Race Relations Act in 1976, racial discrimination became a crime in the UK (see Chapter 8, **Race**). Some actions go in and out of being crimes as the law ebbs and flows. In 1920 it became a crime in the US to make or sell alcohol; with the repeal of Prohibition in 1933 it was legal again. Abortion was a crime in most of the US until the 'Roe v. Wade' ruling by the Supreme Court in 1973; when this ruling was overturned in 2022, it once again became a crime in many (though not all) states in the US.

Why create crimes?

There have been – are – some laws which can seem like crimes in themselves, because of their self-evident immorality. Until 1967, consensual gay relationships between men were criminalised in the UK; hundreds of men were sent to prison as a result. In South Africa under apartheid, and in many states in the US until quite recently, sexual relationships between people of different races were against the law. Barack Obama (US president from 2008 to 2016) was the son of a black father and a white mother. If he had been born in Alabama rather than Hawaii, his existence would have been evidence of a crime; Alabama only repealed its law against interracial marriage in 2000.

Some laws are controversial. Some people regard abortion and assisted dying as murder; others believe they should be freely available (see Chapter ? Abortion, and Chapter ? Euthanasia).

Usually, though, when people talk about crime, they mean actions which are universally accepted as being wrong, such as theft, physical assault and murder. This is how we will understand crime in this chapter.

Why do we need to define some actions as crimes?

The justification for making an action a crime by passing a law against it is usually the need to protect society from the harm caused by that action.

What is punishment?

Punishment (in the context of a debate about crime and punishment) is any action taken by the state against someone who has broken the law. The most common forms of punishment currently used against people found guilty of crimes in the UK are:

- **Deprivation of liberty**: sending someone to prison for a certain time.
- **Financial penalty**: a fine.
- **Community service**: doing menial but important work in the community.

Corporal punishment (beating or flogging someone) and **capital punishment** (killing someone) are no longer used in the UK, and there is very little support for bringing either of them back.

What the **purpose** of punishment should be is very much a matter for debate, and is discussed below, in section 2, 'The Issues'.

What happens in court?

Who decides who gets punished?

If the police suspect someone of having committed a crime, and have enough evidence to prove it, they have the right to **arrest** them. They then refer the case to the Crown Prosecution Service (CPS). The CPS makes the decision on whether or not someone should be **prosecuted**. Usually, they will base this decision on whether or not there is enough evidence to convict them (find them guilty). Very occasionally, they may decide that, even though there is enough **evidence** to **convict** someone, it is not in the public interest to prosecute them. If they decide that a prosecution should go ahead, it is mounted in the name of the king (in his role as head of state), and a **trial** is held.

Lesser crimes are tried before **magistrates**, who are trained but unpaid volunteers; more serious crimes are tried before a **jury**, with the trial presided over by a **judge**. A jury is a group of twelve people selected at random, with no legal training. At the start of the trial, the person accused of a crime – the **defendant** – can plead either **guilty** or **not guilty**. If they plead guilty, the magistrate or the judge will pass a sentence, enforcing a certain punishment. The punishment may be reduced if the defendant pleads guilty. The magistrates or judge can choose to give a **suspended sentence**, meaning that the defendant does not have to go to jail; so, for example, a sentence of six months suspended for a year means that you do not have to go to prison provided you do not break the law for a year. If you break the law during that time, you automatically go to prison for six months, in addition to any other sentence you receive.

If the defendant pleads not guilty, a full trial follows. The defendant is innocent in the eyes of the law until they are proved guilty. Both the **prosecution** (acting for the victim) and the **defence** (acting for the defendant) are represented by lawyers, called barristers. They call **witnesses**, whom they question about the case. Witnesses have to take an oath before they give evidence; it is a crime to knowingly lie under oath. Witnesses cannot report anything they have not seen or heard for themselves. At the end of the trial, the magistrates or the jury discuss the evidence among themselves in private and determine if the defendant is guilty or not. If they find them guilty, the magistrates or the judge decide a **sentence**, taking into account how serious the crime is, if the defendant has a history of criminal actions, and if there are any mitigating circumstances that might explain their crime and reduce their sentence.

If the defendant is found not guilty, they are free to go.

When did we start locking people up?

How has society responded to crime?

In the beginning, there was no state, there were only tribes. If someone killed or hurt someone from your tribe, or stole your cattle, you killed or hurt one of their people in return or took some of their cattle. You would most likely do it back worse to deter them from doing anything more to you. This didn't normally work; it just meant something even worse was done back to you. And so the cycle of revenge and counter-revenge escalated, sometimes into full-scale war, often carried out by people long removed from the original offence.

Later, there were recognisable states: large bodies of people with a clearly defined ruler, usually a king or queen. When someone committed a crime, the monarch – in the person of his or her representatives – would administer punishment. Sometimes this would be a fine, especially if the crime was theft. Most punishments, though, were physical: flogging, castration, being locked up in stocks in a public place, mutilation, enslavement or (very commonly) death. Prisons were only used to hold people temporarily until punishment could be enforced. Disease was rife in prisons, and prisoners had to depend on friends and family to feed them.

In the early eighteenth century in England, the range of punishments began to broaden. Now criminals could simply be removed from the country. Initially they were sent to the American colonies, where they were put to work as forced labourers; once America gained independence, they were dispatched to the newly established colonies in Australia. Other criminals were kept on 'hulks', ships anchored in harbours. They were taken off the ships to do brutally hard physical work each day, and were locked up on the ships in chains by night. Prisons moved from being holding pens to being instruments of punishment in themselves.

The late eighteenth century saw the first moves towards making the prison system both more humane and more efficient. In 1777, the campaigner John Howard condemned prisons as chaotic, vicious and corrupt. He called for the professionalisation of the prison service: paid prison officers would be expected to maintain certain standards, monitored by regular inspections. Prisoners should be given an adequate diet and kept in clean, hygienic conditions. In 1791, the philosopher Jeremy Bentham invented the **panopticon**, a prison building in which all the cells radiated around one central point, allowing one man to supervise all the inmates at once, removing privacy from prisoners and strengthening control. Over the next few decades, dozens of prisons were built on this model.

How prisons became kinder

In the first half of the nineteenth century, prison became the most common form of state punishment. Prisons were seen as a way to reform criminals by providing them with an opportunity to reflect on their crimes (often by being kept in solitary confinement), and to learn the virtues of hard work (though the work on offer was largely pointless, such as walking on treadmills or lifting heavy weights). Local prisons became part of a national system when they came under central government control in 1877. The death penalty – once handed out for trivial offences like stealing a rabbit – was now used only for major crimes like murder or treason.

In the late nineteenth and early twentieth century, the focus moved away from punishment and towards rehabilitation. Campaigners and prison leaders, many of them inspired by their Christian faith, sought to help criminals to change their ways and lead better lives, by making prisons into more humane institutions which provided educational opportunities. In 1907, the Probation Service was set up. Probation officers offered newly released prisoners active support in re-establishing themselves as honest members of society, by helping them find work and accommodation. They also supervised 'community sentences', an alternative to prison in which offenders did unpaid work in the community but were not locked up at night. In 1908, the Borstal system was established. Previously children and young people found guilty of crimes had been imprisoned with adults; now they had their own dedicated institutions. Borstals set high standards of discipline and demanded hard physical work from their inmates, but in return offered them a technical and vocational education, along with skills in reading, writing and numeracy, which would prepare them to make an honest living on their release. In 1933, the first 'open prison' was established, offering greater freedoms for offenders judged to pose little risk to the public. The philosophy behind open prisons was summed up by the reformer Sir Alex Paterson: 'You cannot train a man for freedom under conditions of captivity.' Hard labour and flogging in prisons were abolished in 1948, and whipping and birching from 1962. Capital punishment was suspended in 1965 and formally abolished in 1969, apart from for crimes of treason, spying and piracy with violence. These crimes ceased to be capital offences in 1998. It was still no fun being in prison (it wasn't meant to be), but there was an intention to use prisons to help their inmates prepare for a more honest and productive life on their release.

From the second half of the twentieth century onwards, however, just as British society was becoming more liberal on issues around race, gender and sexuality, it became increasingly illiberal in its

The return of punishment

attitudes towards law and order. Egged on by sensational coverage of crime in the tabloid press along with (often inaccurate) stories about 'soft' prison regimes, and responding to mounting public anxiety about the issue, politicians vied with each other to be 'tough on crime'. In 1989, the then Home Secretary Douglas Hurd said that 'prison is a very expensive way of making bad people worse'. This view was less common, however, than that of Michael Howard, Home Secretary from 1993 to 1997, that 'prison works'. Sentences lengthened. Numbers of people in prison soared.

This drift away from seeing prison as an opportunity for reform, and towards seeing it as punishment, has continued into the twenty-first century. At the same time as prison numbers have risen, spending has slumped. Following the financial crisis of 2008, the prisons budget was reduced by 25%. There were major cuts in staffing and pay for prison officers leading to a drop of morale among prisoners as well as those set to guard them. Rehabilitation and education programmes for prisoners were drastically reduced because of budgetary limitations, and were further hit by the Covid pandemic.

Prisons now are dirty, overcrowded places, plagued by drug abuse and violence. Cells built to house one prisoner in the nineteenth century routinely hold up to three. In July 2024, the government was obliged to announce that it was releasing many prisoners early because there was simply no more room in existing prisons.

So what are the numbers on British prisons at the moment?

Prison population

- In 1900, there were 86 prisoners for every 100,000 people in England and Wales; in 2022, there were 159 for every 100,000.
- The prison population in England and Wales had risen by 80% between 1993 and 2023.
- In 2022, 43,000 people were sent to prison in England and Wales, of whom 61% had committed non-violent offences.
- 27% of prisoners are from ethnic minorities, as against 13% of the population as a whole.
- 96% of prisoners are male.
- England and Wales have the highest imprisonment rate in Western Europe.

Prisons aren't working

Sentence lengths

- The average sentence is now two years longer than in 2008.
- Three times as many people were given sentences of 10 years or more in 2022 than in 2008.
- The average minimum sentence for murder rose from 13 years in 2000 to 21 years in 2021.
- England and Wales have more people serving life sentences than Austria, Belgium, France, Germany, Italy, the Netherlands, Russia and Sweden combined – the highest rate in Europe by some way.

Overcrowding

- 99% of prisons were classed as overcrowded by 2024.

Mental health

- 70% of prisoners have at least one mental health condition.
- 10% of prisoners are receiving treatment for their mental health.

Staffing

- The number of frontline prison officers was cut by 26% between 2010 and 2017.
- In 2022, 15% of prison officers left the service, 47% of them after less than three years, 25% of them after less than a year.
- Of serving prison officers, 35% have been in the service for less than three years.

Cost

- The average cost of keeping someone in prison for a year is **£47,434**. By way of comparison, the cost of sending a boy to Eton College – one of the most prestigious and most expensive boarding schools in the country – for a year is **£49,998**.

Reoffending

- 55% of prisoners serving less than 12 months are convicted of a crime within one year of their release. In the year up to December 2022, prisoners sentenced to short-term detention represented 59% of all prisoners.

Why do people do bad things?

It is pretty much beyond debate that Britain's prisons are in a bad way. However, that doesn't in itself prove that prison is not the answer to crime. It is still perfectly possible to argue that imprisoning criminals is the best way to respond to crime; we just need to make prisons work better.

To think about the best way to respond to crime, we need to step back from the detail and look at the principles: to consider each of the issues.

2. THE ISSUES

The aim of any policy connected to crime must be to **reduce** it; to **prevent** people from committing crimes. If you want to stop someone from doing something, it is a great help to understand **why** they are doing it. Once you know this, it will be much easier to persuade and / or make them stop. So the following question is a really important one when thinking about crime.

Why do people commit crimes?

One way of thinking about this issue is by comparing the relative weight of two words separated by a single letter: **deprived** (that is, lacking in social, economic and emotional advantage) and **depraved** (that is, naturally tending towards bad actions).

In essence, the question is:

Are people depraved because they are deprived?

or

Are people deprived because they are depraved?

Do people commit crimes because of circumstances beyond their control, such as upbringing, economic status, social status, the structures of society, the attitude of people around them? (**Depraved because deprived**.)

or

Do people commit crimes because of a failing in their own character and / or choices, over which they have full control? (**Deprived because depraved**.)

Let's look at those two perspectives in more detail.

Is it society's fault?

Depraved because deprived

People are essentially good, until something stops them being good. These things might be:

- Poverty: their own or that of their parents.
- Inadequate support from the state, e.g. poor education, healthcare, housing.
- Racism, or other forms of discrimination.
- Untreated mental illness, which itself may be triggered or made worse by socio-economic conditions.
- An unjustly structured society, which means that they have no hope of improving their lot honestly.

At the most extreme level, it is wrong to condemn a starving person for stealing a loaf of bread to keep themselves or those dependent on them alive. Even when a person or their family is not close to death, they might still be led into crime because of the way society has treated them. Would you want to be hardworking and honest if you and everyone around you had no prospect of anything better than poverty, hatred and contempt? Locking criminals up in prison with many more people from similar backgrounds (prison populations are overwhelmingly composed of people from the lowest socio-economic backgrounds, many with mental health issues) is unlikely to make them into better people.

The answer then is first to engage more positively with people who have committed crimes, trying to understand what led them into crime, offering them assistance and training to turn their lives around, making them feel that society is on their side and wants them to be better people. Community service, in which they do something useful with their time that teaches them new skills, will be much more constructive than locking them in a cell for 23 hours a day. Prison should be reserved only for those people who present a genuine threat to public safety. At the same time, we should work to change the social conditions which drive people into crime.

Deprived because depraved

People can be good or bad; it is within their control to choose which path they take. To blame society, upbringing, discrimination, etc., for bad behaviour is to take away from human dignity by

Or is it their fault?

assuming that people have no responsibility for who they are or how they live. It is patronising to assume that all people who live in deprived conditions will inevitably be depraved.

When people commit crimes, they need to be punished to show them, and the rest of society, that what they did was wrong. If it costs a lot, that is money well spent. If people face no consequences for bad behaviour, they will simply behave worse, to their own detriment and that of those around them. Once we accept the notion that criminals must find someone or something else (poverty, racism, society) to blame for their actions, we undermine the moral basis of society. As Michael Howard put it when he was Home Secretary, 'If you don't want to do the time, don't do the crime.'

These two positions were brought together in a neat piece of **triangulation** (finding a middle way between two apparently opposite positions) by Tony Blair when, as Shadow Home Secretary, he promised a future Labour government would be 'Tough on crime, tough on the causes of crime':

'Tough on crime' = deprived because depraved.

'Tough on the causes of crime' = depraved because deprived.

How should we respond to crime?

Pragmatic or principled?

Responses to crime can be either **pragmatic** or **principled** (or a bit of both). A pragmatic approach prioritises what **works**. A principled approach prioritises what is **right**. We need to find a response to crime that will work, by reducing crime as much as possible (**pragmatic**). We also need to find a way to respond to crime that creates a society that is as **fair** and **moral** as possible (**principled**).

The most skilful debaters will use arguments based on both pragmatism and principles. Both come into play in debates around crime and punishment, sometimes in tension, sometimes supporting each other. Of the different responses to crime below, some lean more towards pragmatism, some more towards principle.

Responses to crime

Criminals need to suffer

1. Retribution

Retribution means punishing someone in proportion to their crime. It is the most immediate and obvious – you could say the most instinctive – response to crime. If someone hurts you or someone you love, or damages or steals something that is yours, you want them to be hurt back. It seems right and fair that they should suffer for having made you suffer. In the earliest societies, making them suffer was your responsibility, or the responsibility of your family or tribe. Nowadays we get the state to exact retribution on our behalf. Sending someone who has killed another person to a state-run prison after a properly conducted trial is different from (and a good deal more civilised than) the victim's brother killing the murderer, burning down his house and taking his wife and children into slavery, but the essential principle is the same: people who have done bad things must suffer for what they have done. Sentences for crimes should be based on the crime committed, not on the criminal. A first-time offender committing the same crime as a hardened criminal should get the same sentence, because the purpose of punishment is to express society's disapproval of the crime.

The retribution approach leans firmly towards **principles** over **pragmatism**. People who commit crimes should be punished simply because it is the right thing to do. Retribution sends a message about the kind of society we are. Allowing people to get away with murder or other crimes is in itself fundamentally immoral. Even if a pragmatist can prove that community service is cheaper than prison and is more likely to prevent people from reoffending, we should still send people to prison. Picking up litter or redecorating community centres, however useful, is not unpleasant enough to register society's disapproval of crime.

Retribution is also kinder to the victims of crime. Someone who has suffered an injustice has a very deep psychological and emotional need to see the perpetrator punished. Families of murder victims often speak of finally being able to move on when a guilty verdict is passed on a murderer. Providing criminals with support rather than punishment may help them to restart their lives, but it can leave their victims' lives stuck. Why should she be walking the streets freely, while my son is in the cemetery? Why should he have a thriving career, while my daughter is stuck at home, physically or mentally damaged by an assault?

Criminals need help

The retribution approach leans very much towards the 'deprived because depraved' interpretation of crime. It assumes that people are responsible for their actions, and that they must therefore take the consequences of those actions.

2. Containment

Containment means doing what is necessary (and only what is necessary) to protect society from someone who poses a threat to public safety. It is a very **pragmatic** approach to crime. It is not concerned with what happened in the past; it is only interested in how to prevent harm in the future. Is someone who has been found guilty of a crime likely to offend again? If so, they should be locked up in order to protect society. Do they show remorse, and are they sincerely committed to changing their way of life? Then there is no point in wasting taxpayers' money, and the criminal's time and talents, by sending them to prison for years. Better to offer them retraining and re-education so they can lead a more productive life. It might feel wrong to be teaching someone convicted of stabbing how to chop vegetables so they can work in a restaurant on their release, but provided it is clear they can now be trusted with a knife, it is a much more effective use of resources. Save prison for the small minority of criminals who are beyond redemption.

The containment approach could even extend to imprisoning people for crimes they have not yet committed, but are very likely to commit. So, for example, if a terrorist organisation calls for the killing of one particular ethnic or religious group, you might imprison someone simply for being a member of that group, on the grounds that they are highly likely to commit murder, even if they have not done so yet.

Containment leans more towards 'depraved because deprived'; it recognises that the majority of criminals may be led into crime against their will, and need help to leave crime behind. It does, however, also recognise that some people may be irredeemably bad, and need to have their liberty taken away for the greater good of society.

3. Deterrence

Deterrence means setting the penalty for a crime at a harsh enough level to discourage people from committing the crime. It is a determinedly **pragmatic** approach. It sees punishment purely as a mechanism for preventing crime. If people know that certain actions will result in unpleasant consequences for them, they will avoid taking those actions. The more unpleasant the consequences, the more likely they are to avoid the action. If being caught stealing a car means you only have to spend a couple of weekends weeding in the local park, you might conclude that it is worth the risk, and carry on helping yourself to a few Hondas; if it means ten years in prison, you're more likely to stop. If crime is rising, increasing sentences will bring it down

Criminals need scaring

There are two problems with deterrence as an approach. The first is that it depends on the certainty of detection. If police resources are so overstretched that car crime is never pursued, then it doesn't matter how severe the sentences are; car thieves know they can get away with it. The second is that it assumes that criminals are rational, clear-thinking people, who conduct a careful cost–benefit analysis before each significant choice. In fact, a very large number of people in prison are suffering from mental health issues that make it hard for them to take responsibility for their actions. Others, because of the way they have been brought up, have never learnt to consider consequences before acting. So you can make an argument against deterrence on a pragmatic basis; it doesn't actually work with most of the people who commit crimes.

Deterrence depends on the 'deprived because depraved' view. People are responsible for their actions, and can avoid doing the wrong thing if given suitable disincentives.

4. Restoration

Restoration means making a criminal put right the harm they have done, by restoring what they have taken or repairing what they have damaged. It is a sibling of retribution and appeals on a very basic emotional level. Remember when (siblings again) your brother stole your favourite toy? The first thing you wanted was for him to give it back. Restoration is easy for some crimes. If someone has damaged your property, they pay for it to be repaired or, even better, they repair it themselves. If they have stolen your money, they return it. It gets harder for crimes against the person. A murderer can't give back a life he has taken; a rapist can't 'make up' to a woman he has raped.

Some restorative justice involves a straightforward reimbursement, either by paying damages for harm done, or by paying a fine. It can also, though, offer a kind of emotional or psychological restoration. A murderer is made to meet his victim's family (with a third person present to mediate). Seeing what he has done to them may be punishment in itself, and may also encourage him to abandon violence now he knows what it does to people. The family may in

Criminals need improving

turn be healed by being able to express their anger and grief to the person who has caused it. Some may even choose to forgive the person who has harmed them, which in itself can bring both sides comfort and resolution.

Using community service rather than prison is a kind of restorative justice. Someone who vandalised the toilets in the park made the local area worse; now they're scrubbing graffiti off walls, they're making the area better.

Restorative justice is mostly about **principles**. It believes that it is the right thing for people to take responsibility for their actions by taking concrete action to redress the wrong. However, it can also be **pragmatic**. If someone has to face up to the consequences of their actions in this very direct way, they are more likely to be reformed. Having to look the mother of a man you murdered in the eye will make you stop and think before killing again. It leans more towards 'deprived because depraved', believing that people are responsible for their actions.

5. Reform

Reform means focusing on helping the criminal to live a better and more productive life in the future. In some ways, it is the ultimate **pragmatic** response to crime. The crime has been committed and it can't be undone; what matters is making sure the criminal doesn't do it again. Retribution, deterrence and restoration all look to the past; reform looks to the future. Containment also looks to the future, but it is a very high-cost solution. Someone who is in prison contributes nothing to society, and costs us a lot (almost as much as sending a boy to Eton). Far better to help them to change their ways, so that they can become a constructive member of society. You can do this in two ways. First, by understanding what in their background led them into crime, and helping them to overcome it, through therapy, counselling, etc. Second, by offering them training and education which will give them useful skills, so they can earn a living in an honest and productive way.

There are **principles** involved in the reform approach. It implies a belief that people are basically good – depraved only because they are deprived – and that everyone deserves to be treated with respect and kindness, whatever they have done. It also believes that people are capable of change for the better. It is about hating the sin, but loving the sinner. When it works, it is much the most cost-effective approach. When it doesn't, it can be the cause of injustice and danger.

Why follow the rules?

Is breaking the law ever justified?

To consider this question, we first need to understand what the law is for. This means understanding the **rule of law.**

The rule of law means that, in order to function properly, a society has to have rules. We may not like the rules, but until they are changed, we have to play by them.

To take an analogy from sport: football, like all sports, has rules. The game would make no sense otherwise. The rules are enforced by the referee. If the referee says you were offside when you scored a goal, it's not a goal, even if everyone on your team and more than half the fans disagree. And if your response as a player is to abuse and threaten the referee, you get sent off the pitch. So you should be. If referees were to lose their authority, and all decisions were made by majority vote amongst the players and fans, then play would become impossible, and football would be over.

The rules of football are like the laws of a country; the referee is a combination of the judiciary, the body of judges and magistrates who interpret the law, and the police, who enforce the law. So when you hear people angrily denouncing 'unelected judges' or 'biased police', remember the football match. In a democracy, laws can be **changed**, but they shouldn't be **broken**.

Referees aren't elected; they're appointed. Their job is not to reflect what fans or players want to happen. Their job is to decide if the rules have been broken or not. So too with judges and magistrates; they are there to interpret the law and to decide if it has been broken or not. That decision has nothing to do with what they, or anybody else, want or don't want to happen. It is determined entirely by what the law says.

The rule of law in a democracy keeps us safe. We are all equal before the law. Respect for the rule of law is one of the fundamental bases of a civilised society. Once you start allowing people to break it, there will be no controls on anyone's behaviour, and no one will be safe.

This all seems obvious. But what happens if a certain law is fundamentally immoral? In South Africa under apartheid (1948–94) the black majority were denied the most basic human rights. The government controlled where they could work, live or travel. An important instrument of this control was the 'passbook'. Many black people protested against the pass laws by publicly burning their passbooks. This was against the law.

What if the law is immoral?

Were they right to break the law? You could say that the rule of law must be upheld in all circumstances, however objectionable individual laws may be. If people didn't like the passbook laws, they could campaign to change them.

The problem was that they couldn't. As well as having their work and personal lives controlled, black people in apartheid South Africa were not allowed to vote or take part in any political activity. You could argue that a state like apartheid South Africa which systematically excluded a majority of its population had therefore forfeited its legitimacy, along with any need to respect its laws.

The United States, on the other hand, is one of the great democracies of the world. Surely the rule of law should be respected there? Rosa Parks didn't think so. On December 1st, 1955, she refused to get off a bus to make way for a white passenger who, according to the rules around racial segregation on buses in Alabama at the time, was allowed to take her seat. So she was breaking the law. Her protest helped spark a decade-long campaign of **civil disobedience** (the non-violent breaking of a law which some consider to be unjust) by black people and their allies in the southern states against racial segregation. Campaigners would, for example, enter restaurants, bars and other public places from which black people were excluded by law. Their campaign ultimately achieved significant advances for black Americans.

Again, you could argue that the law is the law, and that there are legal ways to challenge existing laws. The problem in this case is that, while in theory the United States in the 1950s and 1960s, unlike apartheid South Africa, had a universal franchise (that is, everyone was allowed to vote), in practice there were measures in place in many southern states to prevent the vast majority of black people from voting or engaging in political activity. There would have been no point in campaigning lawfully against racial segregation; it would have changed nothing, and the manifest injustice of the laws would have remained.

The Republic of Ireland in 1971 was a fully democratic country. Every adult was allowed to vote. It was also a country in which it was against the law to possess or use any form of contraception, in line with the teaching of the Catholic Church. A group of feminist campaigners thought this was wrong, so in May of that year they took a train from Dublin to Belfast in Northern Ireland, where contraception was legal. They announced they were going to buy contraceptives in Belfast and bring them back to the Republic of Ireland; this would be against the law. On their return to Dublin, they threw handfuls of pills towards a crowd of waiting

Breaking the law for show

supporters. It was a symbolic gesture, designed to draw attention to the absurdity of the law. It was made even more symbolic by the fact that they hadn't realised that, while the use of contraceptive pills was legal in Northern Ireland, it was only possible to buy them with a GP's prescription. So they bought boxes of aspirin instead. The pills with which they showered the crowds in Dublin would have stopped a headache, but not a baby. Still, the intention to break the law was there.

You could say that they should have campaigned within the law to legalise contraception. However, none of the main political parties in Ireland at the time was willing to challenge the power of the Catholic Church by contemplating a change in the law. The campaigners felt that only a high-profile symbolic piece of **direct action** (breaking the law to draw attention to an issue) would spark change.

More recently, in Britain, climate campaigners from organisations such as Extinction Rebellion and Just Stop Oil have taken to breaking the law by blocking the road, glueing themselves to buildings, attacking paintings in art galleries and disrupting major sporting events. They have been doing this to raise awareness of the climate emergency, and to demand that more urgent action is taken to address it.

You could argue that the campaigners should stay within the law. They would argue that climate change is an emergency which poses an existential threat to humanity; it may be necessary for the rule of law to be set aside for a while to bring home the extremity of the situation. Campaigners are willing to accept the consequence of prison sentences or fines in order to focus public attention on the emergency.

With any breaking of the law for a **principled** purpose (to fight racism, sexism or climate change), there is also the **pragmatic** question of whether it works. Will it become counterproductive if the action alienates possible supporters? The racism of apartheid South Africa or 1950s Alabama was so manifestly unjust that few would argue that burning a book or sitting on a bus was a disproportionate response. Women throwing pills into a crowd was a bit of fun in the tight-lipped, puritanical world of 1970s Catholic Ireland, shocking only to those who would have had no sympathy with the women's cause under any circumstance. However, the considerable inconvenience caused to people who find their journey to work delayed – or even an ambulance's journey to a hospital blocked – by an Extinction Rebellion or Just Stop Oil protest may alienate people who would otherwise be sympathetic to the environmental cause.

Does direct action work?

3. THE POINT OF CLASH

What is state-sponsored punishment for? Is it to show society's **disapproval** of crime? Or to prevent people from committing crimes in the first place? Or to keep society **safe**? Or to make criminals **put right** what they have done wrong? Or is it an opportunity to help criminals live **better lives** in the future?

Is the rule of law so important that the law must never be broken? Or should we consider each case on its own merits pragmatically, and decide whether the **benefits** of breaking the law in some circumstances outweigh the **harms**?

4. THE ARGUMENTS

For prison	For community service
Society needs to show its disapproval of crime by locking people up.	Prison is hidden; community service is public, so is a more effective way of showing society's disapproval.
Prison is a better deterrent than community service.	Prison may deter, but it is very bad at preventing reoffending.
It is offensive to victims of crime that criminals should walk free.	It is better for victims of crime to see that criminals are doing something constructive to atone for their crimes.
Society needs to be protected from criminals.	The great majority of criminals are not dangerous.
Community service takes jobs from honest people.	Community service frees up honest workers for more rewarding and better paid jobs.
It is morally wrong to let criminals lead normal lives.	It is morally wrong to waste years of someone's life doing nothing in a prison cell.
Criminals need to be punished.	Criminals need to be helped to lead better lives.

For longer sentences	For shorter sentences
Longer sentences deter people from committing crimes.	Most crime is committed by people whose upbringing or mental state prevent them from thinking about the consequences of their actions.
Prison may be expensive, but the alternative is to tolerate crime.	Prison is an ineffective waste of taxpayers' money.
Victims have a psychological need to see that criminals are being punished.	Restorative justice (mediated meetings between criminals and their victims) is a much better way to meet victims' needs.
Prisons keep us safe.	Nearly half of former prisoners reoffend within a year; prisons are colleges of crime.
Criminals need to be off the streets.	Criminals need to be reintegrated into society as soon as possible, doing something useful.
Long sentences send the message that we are a moral society.	Long sentences send the message that we are a vindictive society.

For direct action (breaking the law to draw attention to an issue)	Against direct action
Legal protest on racism / climate change has not achieved anything.	Do legal protest better.
Racism / climate change is such an urgent issue, it justifies breaking the law.	Once you undermine the rule of law, you make us all unsafe. What if racists or climate change deniers start taking direct action?
Direct action works in getting people's attention.	Direct action alienates people who might otherwise have been sympathetic.
Direct action can be non-violent.	Non-violent direct action still has many negative consequences.
Campaigners for votes for women in the UK used direct action; no one would now argue that women should not have the vote.	The cause was right, but the means of protest were wrong.
Justice is more important than the law.	The rule of law is our only sure protection against injustice.

5. THE MOTIONS

1. This house would replace prison with community service for non-violent offenders.
2. This house would release all prisoners serving sentences of less than five years.
3. This house would offer education and retraining programmes to all prisoners.
4. This house believes that prison does not work.
5. This house would introduce mandatory life sentences for murder.
6. This house would introduce life sentences for anyone found guilty of three successive crimes.
7. This house would oblige all convicted criminals to take part in mediated meetings with their victims.
8. This house would give prisoners the vote.
9. This house believes crime is the fault of society, not criminals.
10. This house would never break the law.
11. This house supports direct action to tackle climate change.
12. This house supports direct action to fight racism.
13. This house believes unjust laws should be broken.
14. This house supports Just Stop Oil / Extinction Rebellion.

Keep thinking…

A selection of further reading and viewing to help you think more deeply about the issues around crime and punishment.

A Bit of a Stretch: The Diaries of a Prisoner, Chris Atkins (Atlantic Books, 2020)

Chris Atkins was not a typical prisoner. A successful and highly educated documentary maker, he was sent to prison for tax fraud. This candid diary of his time in HMP Wandsworth, one of the most overcrowded and dysfunctional prisons in Britain, is both hilarious and horrifying, exposing the absurdities and inadequacies of the prison system with wit and anger. Why is it easier to get hold of controlled drugs than paracetamol in prison? Why can't his three-year-old son visit him without proving he does not have a criminal record? Why are open prisons full of white people from private schools?

Crime and Punishment, Fyodor Dostoevsky (Penguin Classics, 1866)

Raskolnikov, a destitute law student in nineteenth-century St Petersburg, decides the world would be better off without his landlady, so he kills her with an axe. His crime plunges him into inner torment as he grapples with his guilt. One of the great psychological and moral novels of all time, *Crime and Punishment* will make you think deeply about the most fundamental questions. What makes people commit crimes? Are they responsible, or is society to blame? Are people basically good or basically evil? Can a murderer ever be redeemed?

King: A Life, Jonathan Eig (Simon and Schuster UK, 2023)

Martin Luther King is one of the most famous campaigners for racial justice. His fight for equality for African–Americans was brutally curtailed when he was assassinated in 1968, aged just 39. But though he and many of his followers were victims of violence, he preached and practised non-violent resistance. This sometimes involved breaking the law when the law was unjust.

This thorough, gripping and authoritative biography raises many issues that are still relevant in the era of Black Lives Matter. When is it right to break the law? Does direct action work? Is non-violent resistance to injustice enough?

Shades of the Prison House: A History of Incarceration in the British Isles, Harry Potter (The Boydell Press, 2019)

Despite the author's name, there is nothing about Hogwarts in this book. Instead, the author gives us a thorough, detailed and informative history of prisons in the UK from the early Middle Ages to the present day. The history of prisons is also the history of attitudes to crime and criminals. Should we punish them or reform them? The pendulum has swung back and forth over the years; right now we are living through a period which favours punishment over reform. Potter has direct personal experience of prisons, having worked as a prison chaplain for many years.

Fake Law: The Truth About Justice in an Age of Lies, The Secret Barrister (Picador, 2020)

The Secret Barrister takes on all aspects of the British legal system, explaining how it works, and how it doesn't. He (or she) looks at the way issues around the law are represented – and often misrepresented – in the media. This book will leave you much better informed about the British legal system, but also much more concerned.

Suffragette, written by Abi Morgan, directed by Sarah Gavron (Pathé/Film4/BFI, 2015)

The women who campaigned to be given the vote regularly broke the law. They smashed windows, blew up postboxes and cut telegraph wires in an attempt to raise awareness of their cause. Many were sent to prison. Some went on hunger strike and were subjected to brutal force-feeding. No one would argue with the justice of their cause. But were they right to break the law? Would women ever have got the vote in Britain if they hadn't? *Suffragette* is a sympathetic dramatisation of their struggle, showing us both their sacrifices and their successes.

Time, written by Jimmy McGovern, directed by Lewis Arnold (BBC, 2021)

Mark Cobden is an English teacher who knocks down a cyclist and kills him while driving drunk. He pleads guilty, accepting the full punishment for his crime. His time inside opens his eyes to the failings of the prison system: the violence, the cruelty, the abandonment of people who need help. However, the decency of a conscientious prison officer, the unsentimental compassion of a female chaplain, and Cobden's own efforts to help other prisoners offer some hope. Most moving of all are Cobden's attempts to find forgiveness from the widow of the man he killed.

Twelve Angry Men, written by Reginald Rose, directed by Sidney Lumet (1957)

A teenage boy is accused of murdering his abusive father. Eleven of the twelve jurors deciding his fate are convinced he is guilty. Only one, Davis, holds out for his innocence. The judge demands a unanimous verdict. With patience and determination, Davis wins over his fellow jurors one by one until the boy is finally acquitted. This film (also a play) vividly dramatises the way in which personal experience and prejudice can get in the way of rational responses to crime. It also offers a hopeful message about the power of persuasion and perseverance in the pursuit of justice.

CHAPTER 11

War and Violence

In this chapter we're thinking about...

- **When is war justified?**
- **What makes some wars just and others not?**
- **What rules should there be for war?**
- **Is violence ever justified outside war?**

1. THE FACTS

What is war?

What is war?

War is **organised, sustained violence on a large scale** between **states** or **large groups**.

Let's break that definition down a bit.

Organised. War is normally conducted by armed forces, that is, large bodies of soldiers, sailors and airmen and women formed into disciplined, structured units with a clear chain of command. Typically, members of the armed forces will be given ranks and will wear uniforms. Armed forces have been throughout history (and still are) overwhelmingly male, though women also fight in many countries, including Britain since 2018. In some countries, such as Britain, the armed forces are fully professional, that is, they are made up entirely of people who have volunteered to serve. In other countries, such as Switzerland, all male citizens have to undergo military training (unless they are medically exempt), and may be called up for service in case of war. In a very small number of countries this applies also to women. Many countries resort to **forced conscription** (that is, making it compulsory for men between certain ages to join the armed forces) in time of war. Britain did this in both the First and the Second World Wars. In wartime, many more women also choose to serve in the armed forces, if their country allows it. Exemptions may be granted, for example on the grounds of health, disability, profession or caring duties. People called conscientious objectors can also refuse to fight because of their personal beliefs and may then be given other duties (see **pacifism** below).

Sustained. A war that goes on for some time in many different locations. How long? The record for the shortest war in history probably goes to the Six-Day War between Israel and a coalition of Arab countries in 1967, which began when Israel attacked Egypt. Israel won swiftly and conclusively, gaining control over a significant amount of new territory and placing approximately a million Arabs under their control. At the other end of the scale, the so-called Hundred Years' War actually lasted for 116 years between 1337 and 1453, though it was interrupted by a number of truces. It was initially fought between England and France over who had the right to rule France. It soon spread into a wider conflict

War will always be with us

between various factions in western Europe. France is generally considered to have won. England was never invaded, but lost its territories in France.

On a large scale. One person being shot, one bomb being detonated or dropped, or one missile being fired does not constitute a war (though any of these might be the starting point for a war). Nor does one confrontation between two units from different states or groups make a war; this sort of confrontation is usually described as a **battle**, a subsection of a war. As a very rough rule of thumb, you could probably say that the number of violent encounters between armies need to get into double figures before you can reasonably describe a conflict as a war. **Total war** is when violence is used on civilians as well as on military targets, often resulting in mass casualties.

Violence. Violence is the defining characteristic of war. All wars involve violence against property and people. This can range from one man strangling another with his bare hands, to killing in close combat with knives, swords or guns, up through bombardment from artillery on the ground or from planes or drones in the air, all the way to wiping out whole cities and their populations with an atom bomb.

States. Most wars take place between nation states. Armies, navies and air forces representing these nation states are ultimately commanded by the leaders of those states, who may (especially in a democracy) be civilians with no previous military experience.

Large groups. Some wars take place between different factions within a nation state (see **civil wars** below), or between the official government of a state and a rebel group within it (see **terrorism** below).

War has a very long history. Ever since our species evolved into tribes competing for territory and resources, groups of humans have engaged in organised violence against each other. War is likely to have a long future, too. The First World War, which ended in 1918 following the death of 17 million people, was initially described as 'the war to end all wars'. If only. A little over twenty years later, the Second World War broke out; it cost the lives of 73 million people. Several wars are going on around the world at the time of writing. Sadly, it is highly likely that this last sentence will continue to be accurate more or less forever.

Why do wars start?

War has many reasons

The most common motivation for starting a war is **economic**, when one state wants to accumulate territory and resources by taking them by force from another state. They may do this from a position of strength, by invading another country, or they may be trying to regain what has been taken from them in a previous war.

Wars may also be fought for **ideological** reasons, when one state wants to impose a particular way of living on another state or states. This might be in favour of a certain religion, as when European countries invaded Muslim countries during the Crusades from the eleventh to thirteenth centuries in the hope of converting those countries to Christianity, or it might be in favour of a political system, as when Soviet Russia invaded Hungary in 1956 and Czechoslovakia in 1968 in order to impose their version of communism on those countries.

Another common motive for war which is not directly connected with economics is **national identity**. Most countries have a sense of shared identity, rather like most families. A country may fight a **defensive war** if that identity feels threatened by invasion from another country, or it may attack another country to strengthen that sense of identity. Wars of national identity can be purely defensive, as when Britain, in imminent danger of invasion by Nazi Germany, took the decision in 1940 to fight in order to protect itself. However, national identity can also be used to justify the most horrific atrocities, as when, following the collapse of communism in the early 1990s, the country formerly known as Yugoslavia split into Serbia, Croatia and Bosnia. Each of these new countries was strongly defined by its religious identity: Serbia was Orthodox Christian; Croatia was Catholic Christian; Bosnia was Muslim. The region soon descended into a vicious war, in which hundreds of thousands of people were driven from their homes and tens of thousands were brutally murdered, simply for belonging to the wrong religion. Such actions are known by the grotesque euphemism of 'ethnic cleansing', when people from different national or religious identities are seen as dirty, diseased or somehow less than human (see **genocide** below).

Wars are nearly always framed by those who run them as being about ideology or national identity, not economics. It is much easier to persuade young men to risk their lives for God or England or democracy than for a few more oilfields or easier access to a trade route. This does not mean that these justifications for war are always a cynical sham; most wars are in fact based on a mixture of economics, ideology and identity.

Starting wars, ending wars

How do wars start?

There may be a formal **declaration of war** by one state against another, which is later followed by armed hostilities. This is what happened on September 3rd, 1939, when the British prime minister, Neville Chamberlain, made a solemn broadcast from Downing Street, announcing that '... this country is at war with Germany.' Or there may be a concerted but unannounced assault on one country by another, as when Russian forces invaded Ukraine on February 24th, 2022. Or small-scale skirmishes may gradually escalate until one day it is clear that two countries are at war, as when American support for South Vietnam in its fight against communist North Vietnam gradually morphed into a full-blown war between America and North Vietnam in the mid-1960s.

How do wars end?

Sometimes there is a clear **victory** by one side over another, as when British, American and Russian forces invaded and occupied Nazi Germany in 1945, leading to Germany's **unconditional surrender**. Or there may be a **ceasefire** and an agreement to end the fighting without a clear-cut sense that one side has won, as when North Korea and South Korea ceased fighting in 1951 and divided Korea in two.

What kinds of war are there?

Wars of aggression and defence

This is the most common and simplest kind of war. One country attacks another. The attacked country fights back. A recent example is the invasion of Ukraine by Russia in February 2022.

Wars of collective self-defence

This is when a country which is attacked has allies, who have pledged to come to its defence. In September 1939, Germany invaded Poland. Britain and France had an agreement with Poland to defend it if it was attacked, so they declared war on Germany even though, at that stage, German armies were nowhere near either Britain or France.

The North Atlantic Treaty Organisation (NATO) is one of the biggest pacts of collective self-defence in history. NATO was formed in 1949, initially in order to protect western democracies against the threat of Soviet communism. It is made up of the USA, Canada, and the great majority of European countries. Its charter states

Different kinds of war

that 'an attack on one is an attack on all'. Following the attacks on New York and Washington on September 11th, 2001, commonly known as 9/11, NATO countries jointly launched an invasion of Afghanistan, which was seen as harbouring Al-Qaeda, the group responsible for 9/11. Following Russia's invasion of Ukraine in 2022, Finland and Sweden, fearing they might be next, joined NATO in 2023 and 2024 respectively. Ukraine has been working closely with NATO since 2008, but has not yet been approved to join. Belonging to a self-defence pact like NATO imposes an obligation on your country to fight for other countries if they are attacked, but also means your country is much safer as it is under the protection of many other countries.

Civil wars

Civil wars happen within states. There may be factions with different ideologies, as in Spain between 1936 and 1939 when the left-wing Republicans (an alliance of communists, socialists and liberals) fought against the right-wing Nationalists (an alliance of conservatives, monarchists and fascists). The Nationalists won, and established a dictatorship under General Franco which lasted until his death in 1975. Or they may be between different ethnic or religious groups or tribes, as in Rwanda in 1994 when the majority Hutu tribe murdered up to a million members of the minority Tutsi tribe. The 'Troubles' in Northern Ireland (1969–1998), in which more than 3,000 people died, were in many ways a kind of tribal civil war between the majority Protestants and the minority Catholics.

Pre-emptive wars

A pre-emptive war is one in which a country attacks another country to prevent itself from being attacked. In 2003, US forces, with British support, invaded Iraq, having received intelligence that Iraq had 'weapons of mass destruction' which it might use against western countries, even though Iraq had not launched any attacks. No such weapons were ever found, and Iraq descended into violent chaos, greatly destabilising the wider region.

Interventionist wars

The late twentieth and early twenty-first centuries saw a flurry of interventionist wars, in which countries went to war with other countries that posed no immediate threat to them, claiming to act entirely from motivations of morality, often a wish to protect vulnerable minorities. These wars were sometimes described as 'humanitarian wars'. So, for example, in 1999 NATO went to war with Serbia in an attempt to stop the Serbs persecuting the

Kosovar Albanian minority in Serbia, who wished to establish their own country in Kosovo. To emphasise the moral basis of this war, the then British prime minister, Tony Blair, ended his broadcast to the nation announcing the action by saying it was 'simply the right thing to do'.

Asymmetric wars

In an **asymmetric war**, a smaller force attacks a larger one in a way which allows it to have an impact out of proportion to its size. Often this is through **terrorism**, in which attacks are launched unannounced on civilians, for example by detonating bombs in public places. This kind of action may cause relatively little damage compared to the effects of a full-blown war, but it has a profound psychological impact on a country, making people feel very insecure. The Irish Republican Army (IRA), who wanted the British out of Northern Ireland, detonated a series of bombs in England during the Troubles (1969–1998) in the hope that this would make English people put pressure on their government to withdraw from Northern Ireland. Another motivation for terrorism is to provoke the state or government which is under attack to respond with greater force, with the aim of winning support for the terrorists' cause. The British Army's often brutal response to IRA attacks in Northern Ireland did much to encourage many in the minority Catholic community to support the IRA.

Could war threaten the survival of humanity?

Nuclear weapons are so powerful, and there are so many of them, that if enough were used, they could threaten the survival of humanity. They are currently owned by the US, the UK, China, Russia, France, India, Pakistan, North Korea and Israel.

Nuclear weapons have (so far) only been used once in warfare. In August 1945, nuclear bombs were dropped by the US on the Japanese cities of Hiroshima and Nagasaki. It is estimated that up to 140,000 people (nearly 40% of the population) were killed in Hiroshima, and up to 80,000 people (over 30% of its population) were killed in Nagasaki. Almost all of them were non-combatants (people not directly involved in fighting). Japan surrendered very soon afterwards.

Russia acquired its first nuclear weapon in 1949. During the Cold War, which lasted from the end of the Second World War in 1945 until the fall of communism in 1989–1991, there was much anxiety that a nuclear war between Russia and America could break out at any moment. The closest this came to happening was during the Cuban Missile Crisis in October 1962. Russia stationed nuclear missiles in communist Cuba, 90 miles from the US coast. America felt directly threatened by these missiles. The US president, John F. Kennedy, demanded that Russia remove the missiles. Russia refused. For a few days an apocalyptic nuclear war looked like a real possibility. Finally, much to everyone's relief, the Russians withdrew their missiles from Cuba in return for America withdrawing their missiles from Turkey at a later date, and war was averted.

What are the rules of war?

Are there any rules for war?

If you play football – anywhere from the World Cup Final to an under-10s match in your local park – you know what the rules are. You expect the players to abide by the rules. You know that the rules will be enforced by the referee, and you expect all the players to accept the referee's decisions.

But war is not a football game. It is a life and death struggle, in which the objective is to kill your enemy and / or destroy large parts of their territory. There are no rules, and there is no referee.

Except that there are. There have been a number of attempts to establish rules for war, and to create bodies which can act as a referee to enforce these rules. Here are some of the most important ones.

The rules of war

First Geneva Convention

In 1863, Henry Dunant of Switzerland set up the Red Cross as a strictly neutral agency providing humanitarian aid to all victims of war. (The Red Cross continues to perform this role; in Muslim majority countries it is known as the Red Crescent.) He also summoned representatives of all the leading powers to Switzerland for the first Geneva Convention in 1864. The convention focused particularly on **care of the wounded**, and established the following principles:

- Wounded soldiers should always be offered **treatment**, regardless of which side they are on.
- **Hospitals** and other places where sick and wounded soldiers are being treated should not be attacked.
- **Non-combatants** treating the wounded should not be attacked.

How to fight fair

Hague Convention

There were two conferences held in The Hague, in the Netherlands, in 1899 and 1907. They agreed the following rules for the conduct of war:

- **Poison gas** must not be used.
- Soldiers who have **surrendered** must not be killed.
- **Looting** (stealing property from occupied territories) is not allowed.
- **Undefended** places should not be bombarded.

Later Geneva Conventions

In 1949, in the aftermath of the Second World War, three more Geneva Conventions were assembled, each dealing with different aspects of the conduct of war.

The Second Geneva Convention established rules around **war at sea**:

- **Shipwrecked** and wounded sailors must be cared for, whatever side they are on.
- **Neutral** ships (those from countries not directly involved in a war) and **hospital** ships must not be attacked.

The Third Geneva Convention dealt with prisoners of war (POWs).

- POWs must be properly **fed and housed**.
- POWs must receive any necessary **medical treatment**.
- POWs must not be **tortured** or **executed**.
- If POWs are accused of crimes, they must receive a **fair trial**.

The Fourth Geneva Convention covered treatment of **non-combatants in an occupied or enemy area**, seen as **crimes against humanity**:

- There must be no **collective punishment**. Collective punishment is when a whole group of people is targeted because of the actions of a few of them, as for example when a whole village is burnt to the ground and all the people in it are killed because a few enemy soldiers took refuge in the village.
- There must be no **forced deportation**: non-combatants must not be made to leave their homes.

- There must be no **forced recruitment**: non-combatants must not be made to join an enemy army.
- If an army occupies the territory of another country, the occupying power must take all reasonable steps to ensure the maintenance of **public health and hygiene**.
- There must be no **intentional harm to civilians** or civilian possessions beyond what is necessary during a military operation.
- Special care must be taken of families with children under 7, of pregnant mothers and of children up to 15.

What is genocide?

United Nations Genocide Convention

In 1949, the United Nations defined **genocide** as any act 'committed with the intent to destroy, in whole or in part, a national, ethnical, racial or religious group'. Genocide happens when a war changes from being a conflict with another state's army into an attempt to wipe out an entire race or religion or people. The most notorious example of genocide in history is the Holocaust, the murder of six million Jews by the Nazis for no other reason than their race. Sadly, the Holocaust is by no means the only example of genocide. The wars in Rwanda and in the former Yugoslavia in the 1990s (see above) both had elements of genocide.

The breaking of any of the above **rules of war** are commonly seen as **war crimes** – 'grave breaches' of the Geneva Convention. States or individual leaders who are believed to be guilty of these crimes may be referred to either the **International Court of Justice** (ICJ) or the **International Criminal Court** (ICC), both of them based in The Hague in the Netherlands. The ICJ deals with states, while the ICC deals with the most serious international war crimes, such as genocide, crimes against humanity and the crime of aggression (killing without justification). Member states of the **United Nations** (see below) are expected to abide by the rulings of both courts. However, the courts' rulings are frequently ignored, and are very difficult to enforce.

International bodies and agreements

Along with the establishment of the rules of war, a number of international bodies and agreements have been created to prevent wars happening, and to police their conduct when they do.

Who's the referee?

In 1919, in the aftermath of the First World War (1914–1918), the **League of Nations** was established. It sought to prevent war through the use of **collective security**. This meant that all members of the League would come to the assistance of any member who was attacked. The hope was that this would prevent any country from launching a war of aggression. Although it had some minor successes, it proved powerless in the face of the rise of fascist regimes in Italy, Germany and Spain, and failed completely to prevent the outbreak of the Second World War. As the Italian dictator Benito Mussolini said, 'the League is very well when sparrows shout, but no good at all when eagles fall out'.

In 1928, the **Kellogg–Briand pact** was signed by all the major powers. This declared simply and solemnly that the signatories renounced war 'as an instrument of national policy in their relations with one another'. Despite these fine words, the pact did not stop the Second World War breaking out in 1939, and nor did it prevent a number of smaller conflicts in the run-up to that war.

In 1945, in the aftermath of the Second World War, the **United Nations** (UN) was created with the intention of protecting human rights and preventing war. It continues to this day, working out of its headquarters in New York. Every nation in the world is a member. The main ruling body is the Security Council. The Security Council has five permanent members – Britain, China, France, Russia and the USA – and ten non-permanent members. The permanent members were chosen because their countries were victorious in the Second World War; this method of selection is widely seen as out of date, though there are no plans to change it. Permanent members have a veto on any significant decisions taken.

The UN Charter does not outlaw war. It accepts the right to self-defence. The UN can pass resolutions condemning what it sees as **illegitimate use of force**, but it does not have the means to enforce these resolutions. It sometimes sends **peacekeeping forces**, composed of soldiers from several different member nations, into war zones with a mission to protect non-combatants. They are only allowed to use their weapons in self-defence.

The **pessimistic** view of all these conventions and institutions is that they are well intentioned but fundamentally pointless. If you see one man on the street attacking another, you can call the police; they have the physical and legal power to stop the attack. But if one country attacks another, there is realistically nothing that can be done to stop them, other than fighting on the side of the country under attack. If you know someone on your street is kidnapping and torturing people, the police can come and arrest them, and they can be prosecuted and sent to prison. When nations kidnap and torture people on an industrial scale, there is no police force to call out to stop them; all you can do is go to war against them.

The **optimistic** view is that at least these conventions and institutions offer some hope of preventing war, and some resistance to the practice of war crimes. They may not have stopped war and war crimes from happening, but they do provide a very public statement of moral values in the conduct of war, and this may influence states and individuals to act with a little more humanity.

Are you ever allowed to be violent?

Apart from the armed forces, who else is allowed to use violence?

You are allowed to use **reasonable force** to defend yourself or another person, protect your property, prevent crime or apprehend a suspect. The force used should be in proportion to the threat. If a man snatches your handbag on a crowded train platform, it is reasonable to trip him up to get it back; it is not reasonable to deliberately push him under an incoming train. If a man starts punching you, it is reasonable to punch him back to make him stop; it is not reasonable to pick up a nearby knife and stab him until he is dead. If a suspected criminal is avoiding arrest, a police officer can run after them, force them to the ground and handcuff them; they can't shoot them in the back. A police officer can shoot someone dead if they suspect they are about to detonate a suicide bomb in a crowded place, but not if they suspect them of shoplifting.

What is the law on guns?

It is against UK law for anyone other than trained police officers and members of the armed forces to carry a weapon in public. Otherwise, guns may only be used in certain very controlled circumstances: for sports such as target shooting or clay pigeon shooting; for hunting certain wild animals, in clearly defined areas; by farmers to keep down pests such as foxes and rabbits. In all these cases, a licence is required to own a gun. Applicants for gun licences are subject to rigorous checks.

In some countries, all police officers carry guns. This is not the case in the UK, where fewer than 5% of police officers are armed. The only time you will see armed police on the streets is outside certain high-profile public buildings, such as 10 Downing Street (the residence of the prime minister) or the Houses of Parliament.

There are armed police units on standby 24 hours a day who can be called out to respond to incidents in which the use of weapons is the only way to protect the public.

2. THE ISSUES

How can war ever be justified?

War is humanity at its worst. War brings death, destruction and misery. It ends young lives far too soon. It creates heartbroken mothers and fathers, widows and widowers, orphaned children, survivors who have to spend the rest of their lives with disfigured bodies and shattered minds. It destroys in seconds homes and neighbourhoods that were built with years of love. It brings famine and disease in its wake. It poisons people's souls, sowing hatred and bitterness. Turn on any news bulletin covering any war; read any account written by someone with first-hand experience of war; above all, experience war yourself – and you will turn away from war with revulsion and disgust.

And yet … what is the alternative?

An absolute rejection of war and violence in all its forms is called **pacifism**. It was very popular during and immediately after the First World War, in reaction to the horrors experienced in that war. But it brings problems. Here are a few scenarios to illustrate those problems, and to consider situations in which war and / or the use of violence might be justified.

When might war and / or violence be justified?

A man takes out a gun. He shoots another man in the head, killing him. What do you think about that? Simple – it's wrong. Isn't it?

Let's look again.

The man who is shot is on a crowded train and has a suicide bomb strapped round his waist which he is about to detonate, killing everyone on the train. The man who fires the shot is a police officer.

Is it still wrong? Or look again.

The man who is shot is a soldier in an army representing a government which is responsible for the genocidal murder of thousands of people, and the kidnap and rape of many more. If the army is not stopped, they will continue to murder, kidnap and rape. The man who fires the shot is part of an opposing army, trying to stop the first one.

When is violence the lesser evil?

Is that wrong? Or look again.

The man who is shot is part of an army invading your country, threatening to take it over, take away your freedom, and run it for the benefit of another country. The man who fires the shot is part of your country's army and is trying to stop him.

Is that wrong? Or look again.

The man who is shot is part of an army already occupying your country, running it for the benefit of another country. The man who fires the shot is part of an army trying to get that army out of your country.

Is that wrong?

All of the above examples can be used to support the case for saying that the use of violence may be justified if it prevents a greater evil. If you're a pacifist, you leave yourself – and, more importantly, all the people you are responsible for, from your immediate family all the way up to your national community – defenceless. Refusing ever to use violence means that suicide bombers can murder at will, and armies acting under the orders of brutal dictators can terrorise whole nations. Violence is an evil, but it may sometimes be the lesser evil.

However, this approach brings its own problems. Actions which started out with the intention of preventing an evil can themselves end up just as great, if not an even greater evil. You don't have to look very far into history to see this happening: revolutions which end up imposing a tyranny even worse than the one they were trying to overthrow; wars which go on long past the point when their original cause has been resolved; police who act with brutality out of proportion to the need to control crime.

How can we stop this happening? How can we keep violence within limits? How can we reconcile the use of violence with living in a civilised society? One definition of a civilised society is one in which the state has a **monopoly of violence**, so only police and armed forces are allowed to use violence, in protection of their citizens. Most people would find this preferable to a society in which anyone can use violence to get their way. But what if the instruments of the state misuse the powers given them? What if the police unfairly target a particular minority group? What if the government launches a war you think is unjust? Should you resist the state's use of violence in these cases, even though it is, in the state's terms, legitimate?

What makes a war just?

Just war theory

Let's say we accept that war is sometimes necessary to prevent a greater evil. The next question is: how can we tell if *this* particular war is justified or not? Time for **just war theory**. The concept of a just war was built on ideas developed across the ancient world – in Egypt, Greece, the Roman Empire and China, and later still by Hindu and Sikh thinkers.

In the European Christian world, St Augustine of Hippo in Roman North Africa (354–430), Isidore of Seville (c. 560–636), and St Thomas Aquinas of Sicily (1225-1274) all confronted the inconvenient fact that the founder of Christianity, Jesus Christ, appeared to be a pacifist: he told his followers to 'resist not evil', and to 'turn the other cheek'. How could Christians therefore engage in war? What could make a war 'just'?

Over the centuries just war theory has developed into a set of principles which are generally accepted by people of all faiths and none, and are used as the basis of international law on war. For a war to be 'just', that is, ethically acceptable, all the criteria below must be met.

1. War is the last resort

Problems: Who decides when it becomes the last resort? The other side may not be ready to talk now, but they might be in the future, when circumstances change. Even if there is no other solution to the problem that the war intends to resolve, might not living with the problem be a lesser evil than war?

2. War is initiated by a legitimate authority

Problems: Who decides which authority is legitimate? What if the legitimate authority cannot, or should not, be trusted? What happens when a corrupt dictator is in charge of an army? What if the legitimate authority is clearly on the side of evil? Under the apartheid system in South Africa (1948–1991) the 'legitimate' authority was an openly racist government that systematically discriminated against the majority black population; the African National Congress, which fought against the apartheid system, was seen as 'illegitimate'. Whose side would you have been on, the 'terrorists' fighting against apartheid, or the 'legitimate' racist government?

3. The war is fought in a just cause

Problems: Who decides what is a just cause? Look into history and you will see that in almost every war both sides have believed

The problems of just wars

that justice (or God or democracy or human rights) is on their side, even though they can't both have been right. What if there is some justice on both sides? It is very rare in a conflict or disagreement that one side is 100% right and the other side 100% wrong. When does a war become justified? When the balance between just / unjust stands at 51 / 49? 60 / 40? 75 / 25? Who decides?

4. There is a reasonable chance of success

Problems: No one can see into the future. How can you tell? No one ever went into a war expecting to lose it, but one side usually does. How confident of success do you have to be to start a war? 50%? 75%? 90%? Might it actually be better not to take the risk, given the terrible consequences of war? To look at it another way, might there actually be times when your cause is so just that it is right to carry on fighting even when there is no chance of success?

5. The end result intended by the war is a good one

Problems: Who decides what is a good result? Even if it is a good result, will it justify the evil unleashed by the war? You may have good intentions, but war is such a messy and unpredictable business, it is highly likely that you will not fulfil them all. You may have to make compromises along the way which cancel out the goodness of the intention. Britain and the US fought the Second World War with the good intention of ridding Europe from Nazi dictatorship, but to do so they had to ally themselves with the Soviet Union, which ended up occupying half of Europe and imposing communist dictatorships that were little better than the Nazi dictatorships they replaced. They also wrecked or flattened a good many cities, destroyed essential infrastructure and killed many civilians before they were done.

6. The use of force is proportionate

Problems: Who decides what is proportionate? In the heat of battle and under the threat of death and destruction, how do you stop soldiers from overreacting? Can the taking of life really be reduced to this kind of cold analysis, as if you were making investment decisions for a business?

7. Non-combatants are protected

Problems: Is this always possible? What if an airstrip from which bombers are taking off to attack your country is in the middle of a city, and you cannot attack it without killing non-combatants? What if enemy fighters deliberately hide in civilian areas, or even schools or hospitals? Can you attack those places? Is it all right

Philosophers to the rescue

to bomb an armaments factory, even if the people working in it are not soldiers? Do they count as combatants because they are assisting the war? Are all citizens of a country you are at war with combatants if they do not resist their government?

You can see that questions about war are complex and difficult; there is much to think about. Time to turn to those experts in thinking – philosophers.

Philosophical ideas

Philosophy can help us to think about issues to do with war and violence. Here are some philosophical ideas which we can use in debates.

- **Deontology**
- **Consequentialism**
- **Double effect**

1. Deontology

Deontology essentially means playing by the rules. It is a way of thinking that assumes that there are certain absolute rules which must always be followed. Our choices should be determined by those rules, even if following the rules brings consequences we may not like.

How might we apply a deontological approach to thinking about war and violence?

For war or the use of violence

If your cause is just, you should fight for it, whether that is defending your own freedom, or protecting others who cannot protect themselves. War may bring terrible consequences, but failing to confront injustice or tyranny or genocide or other kinds of evil would be worse. Once you compromise on your principles, your life, either as an individual or as a society, is no longer worth living. Better to die on your feet than live on your knees. Better to die right than live wrong.

Against war or the use of violence

There is no justification for taking another person's life, or for deliberately using violence against them. It doesn't matter how good or right your cause is – violence and killing are simply wrong.

Once you concede this principle, you open the door to barbarism. Even if refusing to use violence to resist aggression leads to the triumph of injustice, that is still better than becoming unjust ourselves by resorting to violence. Better to put your hands up than to put your hands round another man's throat. Better to die innocent than live guilty.

Where to start: the beginning or the end?

2. Consequentialism

Consequentialism is pretty much the opposite of deontology. Whereas deontology starts at the beginning, with rules to live by, consequentialism looks to the end: where will our actions lead us? Don't ask: is this action right? Ask: what will the **consequences** of this action be? If the consequences of an action are good, the action is good.

How might we apply a consequentialist approach to thinking about war and violence?

For war and violence

War and violence may be unpleasant, but there will be times when they are necessary, when the good consequences outweigh the bad actions. Tripping someone up who has stolen your handbag may give them a broken nose, but it is better than letting them get away with theft. Seeing a suicide bomber shot in the head on a crowded train is shocking for the passengers, but it is better than them all being blown up. The death of millions of soldiers and the destruction of thousands of buildings in the Allied invasion of Europe in 1944–45 was terrible, but less so than allowing the Nazis to continue to rule Europe.

Against war and violence

Violence breeds violence. Look at how much lower the murder rate is in the UK, where gun ownership is strictly controlled and the police are hardly ever armed, than in the US, where there are more guns than people and the police are routinely armed to an almost military degree. Violence may be necessary sometimes, but only as a last resort; the less of it we use, the less there will be.

War is untidy, unpredictable, chaotic. Wars nearly always go on for longer than expected, and cost more lives and more money than anyone expects. Once you destabilise a country by invading it, you cannot control what happens next. Look at how the brutal terrorist organisation Islamic State took over large parts of Iraq after the American and British invasion of 2003. You may start a war with a good intention, but it nearly always brings more harm than good.

Even when there is a clear moral case for war, there are situations in which the harms of war outweigh the benefits. To give an example from the Second World War: when Nazi Germany invaded the Netherlands in 1940, the Dutch government and royal family escaped to England and the Dutch army surrendered almost immediately. That wasn't because they liked having the Nazis rule over them. It was because they knew they were hopelessly outnumbered and were bound to lose; fighting on would lead to unnecessary death and suffering. As a result there was much more left when the Netherlands were liberated by the Allies in 1945 than in other occupied territories. (Though liberation came too late for the thousands of Dutch Jews who had been murdered by the Nazis, or for the many victims of the Hunger Winter of 1944–1945, an artificial famine caused by the occupiers.)

For a consequentialist, decisions around war come down in the end to a cost–benefit analysis.

3. Double effect

The principle of **double effect** is a way of thinking that can be used to justify doing bad things for a good end, and so is very relevant for thinking about war and violence. For believers in double effect, it can be right to do something that has a bad consequence, provided that:

1. You **intend** to achieve a good consequence by the action (and have a reasonable chance of achieving it).
2. You **do not intend** any of the bad consequences of the action.
3. You do everything you can to **minimise** the bad consequences of the action.

So the **intention** of your action is the most important thing, more important than the consequences. In this respect, double effect leans much more towards the **deontological** approach: as long as you are acting from the right principles, it doesn't matter if some bad things happen as a result of your action.

Let's take a scenario to which we can apply the principle of double effect.

Can you do wrong to do right?

You are the president of a country under attack by another country. Every night, enemy planes are bombing your capital city. Hundreds of homes have been destroyed and thousands of people have been killed. You want to stop the enemy planes. Your intelligence people tell you they have located the airfield from which they are taking off, and to which they return every night. You know that if you bomb this airfield during the day when all the planes are there, you can stop the raids on your city and save thousands of lives. But you also know that right next to the airfield is a school. If you bomb the airfield there is a very high probability that the school will also be hit and children will be killed. You can't tell the school to evacuate the children, as that would alert the enemy air force to move the planes.

You don't want to kill children. But nor do you want to see thousands of people killed in your capital every night. What should you do? Should you order the raid on the airfield, knowing that children will almost certainly die?

For a believer in double effect, ordering the raid is the right thing to do, provided that:

1. Your **intention** in ordering the raid is the **good** one of protecting the people who are being bombed in your city every night.
2. Your **intention** is **not** the **bad** one of killing schoolchildren, even though you recognise that this is a likely consequence of your action.
3. You instruct your commanders to take all possible steps to **minimise the harm** done to the schoolchildren during the raid.

That's one example. Double effect can be applied in all sorts of other ways to situations associated with war and violence.

Now we have established some of the broad principles for thinking about war and violence, let's apply them when thinking about some specific issues (and possible debate topics). When reading the scenarios below, think about which of the arguments used are deontological, and which are consequentialist. Also look out for use of the double effect argument.

Does intention matter?

Is the use of drones justified?

Drones are remotely operated planes which can fire missiles or drop bombs without the need for a human crew on board.

For

It is the duty of any government pursuing a war to minimise its own casualties. Drones ensure that no lives are put in danger, other than enemy lives. Modern technology means that attacks can be very precisely targeted, minimising non-combatant casualties. When targeting is carried out by human pilots, who may be distracted by the need to avoid enemy fire, it is harder for them to be precise. Someone sitting safely in a bunker in their own country will make better decisions than a pilot under pressure over enemy territory.

Against

It is cowardly to engage in fighting in which you put yourself at no risk. Part of the morality of warfare is that you give your enemy a fair chance to fight back; drones remove that possibility. Yes, they can be shot down, but shooting them down will cost money, not lives. Because of the very small risk involved in using drones, they are likely to be used more widely and more indiscriminately. Even the most sophisticated technology cannot tell you everything that is going on on the ground; how do you know that what looks like a barracks may not in fact be a refugee centre? Drones are also bad for the people controlling them. Killing people without putting yourself at risk is what psychopaths do. Drones dehumanise their targets, and make war feel like a computer game. It isn't. It is about real men, women and children. Engaging in face-to-face combat makes you realise the consequences of your actions; using drones creates the false notion that actions in war have no consequences.

Should we have nuclear weapons?

For

It would be better if nuclear weapons didn't exist, but they do. Some of them are owned by countries and regimes who might attack our security and our freedoms. If we don't have them, those countries could effectively do what they wanted, because they could threaten to use nuclear weapons on our cities without fearing that they might be used in return against their cities. Having our own nuclear weapons deters other countries from using them. It actually helps to keep the peace and stops wars breaking out, because no one wants to risk nuclear weapons being used.

During the Cold War (the period from the end of the Second World War in 1945 until the fall of communism in 1989) both Russia and America had nuclear weapons, but they did not use them; nor did they start a direct, more conventional war against each other. This was because the risk of **mutual destruction** dissuaded both sides from starting a war. Although the loss of life in Hiroshima and Nagasaki in 1945 was horrific, dropping nuclear bombs on those cities may actually have saved lives in the long run by bringing the war between America and Japan to an end more quickly.

Do nuclear weapons keep us safe?

Against

Nuclear weapons are fundamentally immoral, and we should have nothing to do with them. They are not in any true sense weapons of defence against enemy soldiers. They can only be used to kill whole populations of cities, almost all of them non-combatants. Far from keeping us safe, they make us more of a target for attack. It was just luck that there was no nuclear confrontation during the Cold War. Their very existence is a danger to humanity, and we should do all we can to rid the world of them. The more of them there are in the world, the greater the risk that they may fall into the hands of terrorists or psychopaths, with horrific consequences. We may trust our current government not to use them irresponsibly, but we cannot guarantee that with future governments. A nuclear war could lead to the destruction of humanity itself.

Should we intervene in other people's wars?

For

If you saw one man beating up another man on the street and you could stop him, it would be immoral not to intervene. Similarly, when we see one country unjustly attacking a smaller and weaker country, we have a duty to intervene. Not to do so only encourages unjust aggression. This makes the world less safe and, in the end, makes us less safe. Intervening in wars on the right side establishes a principle that unjust actions will not be tolerated; this makes the world more humane and secure. Intervening in this way improves our own reputation and respect around the world.

Against

Going to war is not a humanitarian action, like sending medicine or food. It is inherently destructive. We should only go to war when our security is directly threatened and we need to defend ourselves. It is immoral for leaders to put the lives of their soldiers at risk just to make them and their followers feel better about 'doing the right thing'. War is messy and chaotic, and nearly always has unintended consequences. Even if you start with good intentions, you may end up destabilising a country or countries, making the situation worse. Once you are in a war, it is very hard to get out of it. Very few wars are simple matters of right and wrong; there is nearly always good and bad on both sides. It might look and feel good to say you are fighting on the side of right, but the reality is nearly always more complex.

Should the police be armed?

For

The police are there to keep us safe. If they are armed, potential criminals and other disturbers of the peace will respect them and their authority more. They will be deterred from behaving in a dangerous or anti-social way. Terrorist outrages can be stopped immediately, by an ordinary police officer shooting the terrorist, rather than having to wait for armed back-up. Provided police are properly trained, the use of armed force will remain very rare, but we will all be safer for knowing that it is there, immediately available, when we need it.

Against

Arming the police is solving a problem that doesn't exist. Thanks to Britain's strict gun laws, weapons are not routinely carried on the streets. In the rare cases where there is an armed criminal or terrorist on the loose, we have well-trained squads of armed police ready to deploy at a moment's notice. Police carrying guns would actually make criminals more likely to acquire and use guns, as they might see it as their only way of protecting themselves. Armed police on the streets would send a message that we are an inherently violent society. The more guns there are, the more violence there will be. Police are routinely armed in the US, and yet the US has one of the highest murder rates in the world. Giving police access to guns may attract the wrong sort of people to the force, who may use their weapons to commit crimes themselves.

Is it ever right to be a pacifist?

For

Deliberately killing or injuring another person is fundamentally wrong. The fact that other people might do it to us does not mean we should do it back to them. We may not be able to stop wars from happening, but we can at least take responsibility for our own actions. Far from being cowardly, pacifism is in fact a courageous option: men and women who refuse to serve in wars may be jailed, and are likely to be snubbed by the people around them. The actions of one individual may not change the world, but the actions of many individuals will. Opposing racism, homophobia and sexism was once seen as a minority, outlier position; now it is mainstream, largely because of the courage of early campaigners. Opposing war could go the same way.

Are pacifists cowards?

Against

Refusing to fight under any circumstances simply allows injustice to flourish. If we are not prepared to defend ourselves, bullies and tyrants will be able to do what they want. Pacifism may actually lead to greater violence and suffering, because aggressors will not be deterred or stopped. We have a duty to our wider community to protect vulnerable people from attack; sometimes the use of violence is the only way to do this. Pacifism is selfish. The pacifist gets to feel good about themselves (even if it is from a prison cell), while other people are risking their lives to protect them.

3. THE POINT OF CLASH

Is war such a terrible thing that it should **never be used**? Or is it sometimes the **lesser evil**?

Can we make war less bad by having certain **rules for warfare**? If so, which ones?

Is it always wrong to kill **non-combatants** in war? Or is this sometimes inevitable?

Should we ever fight wars on **moral** grounds? Or only for **self-defence**?

Is the use of violence **outside of war** ever justified? Or should we leave guns for the battlefield?

Is **pacifism** ever justifiable? Is it cowardly or courageous? Visionary or naive?

4. THE ARGUMENTS

For using drones	Against using drones
Drones save lives by not putting our soldiers at risk.	Drones are a cowardly form of warfare.
Drone operators will make better decisions because they are not in personal danger.	Drone operators may make reckless decisions because they are not in personal danger.
Drones can be used in a very precise and targeted way to minimise non-combatant casualties.	It is impossible for even the most sophisticated drone to tell us who may be in a building and what they are doing.
Drones are a more efficient and scientific form of warfare.	Drones make war look like a computer game. War isn't a game.

For keeping nuclear weapons	Against keeping nuclear weapons
We need nuclear weapons to protect ourselves against other countries which have them.	Having nuclear weapons makes it more likely that they will be used against us.
The consequences of starting a nuclear war are so serious that having them deters other countries from attacking us.	The consequences of a nuclear war are so serious that no one should have nuclear weapons.
Nuclear weapons are highly unlikely to be used.	If they are not going to be used, why have them?
If we don't have nuclear weapons, worse people will get hold of them and we will be unprotected.	Having nuclear weapons of our own makes them more available to bad leaders, including in future governments.
Nuclear weapons kept the peace during the Cold War.	It was simply luck that nuclear war never broke out during the Cold War.

For interventionist wars	Against interventionist wars
We have a moral duty to intervene when we can see a country being unjustly attacked.	War can never be 'humanitarian'; it is only justified in self-defence.
Intervening makes us safer by deterring potential aggressors.	Intervening makes us less safe by creating more enemies.
A targeted intervention can make a country safer.	Wars almost always create instability.
Intervening on the side of right is good for our international reputation.	There is almost never a 'right' and a 'wrong' side in a war.

For arming the police	Against arming the police
Armed police will be treated with more respect and this will lead to less crime and antisocial behaviour.	Armed police will create a more violent atmosphere on our streets and this will lead to more crime and antisocial behaviour.
Armed police will deter criminals and terrorists from using weapons.	Armed police will make criminals and terrorists more likely to use weapons to defend themselves.
Armed police can provide an instant response to a terrorist incident.	The existing system of armed police on standby works well enough.
Providing guns will incentivise people to join the police as they will feel safer.	Giving police guns will attract the wrong sort of people to the force.

For pacifism	Against pacifism
Killing and violence are always wrong.	Killing and violence may sometimes be necessary to stop something worse happening.
Pacifism is a courageous choice, as it stands out against social norms.	Pacifism is a cowardly choice, as it depends on other people to protect you.
Pacifism encourages people to think about peace as an option.	Pacifism is futile and will not stop war.
Pacifism may one day end war.	War is part of human nature and will never end.

5. THE MOTIONS

1. This house would ban the use of drones in warfare.
2. This house would scrap Britain's nuclear weapons.
3. This house would ban British troops from being deployed outside British territory.
4. This house would arm the police.
5. This house would forbid any military operations in which non-combatants might be killed.
6. This house would introduce one year's compulsory military service for all 18-year-olds in the UK.
7. This house would create an international police force to arrest and prosecute people guilty of war crimes.
8. This house would hold national leaders legally responsible for the actions of their armed forces.
9. This house believes war is inevitable.
10. This house believes war is always wrong.
11. This house would be pacifist.
12. This house believes there is no such thing as a just war.

Keep thinking...

A selection of further reading and viewing to help you think more deeply about the issues around war and violence.

In Defence of War, Nigel Biggar (Oxford University Press, 2013)

Professor Biggar is no stranger to controversy: he has also written in defence of colonialism (see Chapter 9, **Colonialism**). In this book, he makes a reasoned case for an ethical justification for war. He also argues, as a theologian, that the practice of war is compatible with Christian faith.

Testament of Youth, Vera Brittain (Victor Gollancz, 1933)

This memoir gives another perspective on war: that of the women left behind. Vera Brittain lost her brother, her fiance, and two close friends in the First World War; the experience marked her for life.

Arguing About War, Michael Walzer (Yale University Press, 2004)

Michael Glazer is one of the leading philosophers of 'just war theory', and this collection of essays explores many different aspects of the ethics of war.

War: An Enquiry (Vices and Virtues), A.C. Grayling (Yale University Press, 2017)

Written by a philosopher, this book provides an excellent short history of war down the ages, and considers the ethical issues around war in a very lucid way.

All Quiet on the Western Front, dir. Edward Berger (Netflix, 2022)

Based on the classic novel of the same name first published in 1929, this is one of the most impressive war movies ever made. It brings to life the lived experience of warfare for a group of young German men fighting in the First World War, tracing their journey from idealism to disillusionment.

Thirteen Days, dir. Roger Donaldson (Beacon Pictures, 2000)

In October 1962, the Soviet Union placed nuclear missiles in Cuba, 90 miles from the US coast. The resulting crisis brought the world closer to nuclear war than before or since. Based on transcripts of meetings in the White House, this film dramatises many questions around the existence and use of nuclear weapons.

4

PART FOUR

Money

How to think about money

Money may not be everything, but you can't do much without it.

So, in this section, we think about **economic inequality**. Is it right that some people have more money than others? How much more should they be allowed to have? Does inequality reward people for hard work and talent, or does it drive people apart?

We think about the **welfare state**. Who should look after us when we are sick or out of work or too old to work? Should the state pay for us or should we pay for ourselves? Do we spend too much on benefits or not enough? How can we make the NHS work?

CHAPTER 12

Economic inequality

In this chapter we're thinking about...

- **How much economic inequality should there be?**
- **What are the costs and benefits of economic inequality?**
- **How might economic inequality be reduced?**
- **Which societies work better: equal ones or unequal ones?**
- **Which is more important: freedom or fairness?**

1. THE FACTS

Some people have always had more than other people

A brief history of economic inequality

Some people have always had more than other people. There has never been a society in which everyone has exactly the same and there almost certainly never will be. However, the degree of **economic inequality** – the difference between how much **income** (how much people earn), **wealth** (how much money people have) and **possessions** (how much stuff people own, all the way from big things like houses and cars down to shoes and spoons) – has varied across societies and over time.

To go right back to the beginning: the first humans were hunter-gatherers, living in tribes. The men went out to hunt animals to provide meat and skins, while the women stayed home to nurture the children, tend the fire, make clothes and gather roots and berries. When the men returned from their quest, they would share their spoils with the whole tribe. Nobody owned anything beyond a few weapons or tools and the clothes they stood up in. People lived in makeshift accommodation, moving from place to place as they tracked their animal prey, so no one had time to acquire property in the form of land or permanent housing. It was necessary for their survival to live and work cooperatively, so, while there doubtless were leaders and followers, it is unlikely that there were significant differences in **wealth**, or perhaps even a concept of ownership. It was possibly the period of the greatest human solidarity in history, tainted only by hunter-gatherers' tendency to murder sick babies, old people and anyone they didn't recognise, and by the unlikelihood of living beyond the age of thirty-five.

Then people discovered agriculture. Finding out that if you put some stuff into the ground in spring, you could take out a whole lot more in the autumn changed everything. It meant that the cycle was broken of getting food, eating it, then having to get some more, day after day after day, with no time or leisure to do anything but survive. It also meant you had to stay in one place, leading to the rise of permanent villages. Agriculture still meant a lot of hard manual work, digging, planting, harvesting, storing, transporting, but once you'd planted stuff you couldn't do much else for a few months. Best of all, you often ended up with a surplus of food.

Who got the surplus? Those who were best at growing their crops or raising their animals ended up with more than others in the tribe

Some people owned other people

– the start of the class system. Over time, this group traded their surplus for better food, finer clothes and slaves to do their work. They marked themselves out as the **nobility** with grand titles, to show their superiority. They married their sons and daughters to those of other noble families to acquire more land, goods and animals, and to continue their bloodline. What did these nobles do with their spare time? They created cities, developed high culture and complex religious practices. Many of the most beautiful works of art we have, the most magnificent buildings, the greatest works of literature, have their origin in the spare wealth and time that this economic inequality gifted to the nobility. They also established belief systems which conveniently proved that their hold on the surplus was all part of a plan ordained by God or the gods.

In due course, this new social set-up became a **feudal** society. This meant that part of the stuff which some people had more of than other people was, in fact, people. The nobility owned not only buildings and money (once this had been invented for trading, originally as a system of weights), but also the people who worked for them – sometimes they were known as slaves, sometimes as serfs. Nobles held absolute power over their slaves or serfs: they could beat them if they didn't do what they were told; they could rape their women; they could take their children away from them; they could buy and sell them like animals; they could even kill them. It was a pretty extreme form of economic inequality. A tiny number of people had everything. The rest didn't even own their own bodies.

In due course, a new class emerged, in between nobility and slaves, of merchants. They made money by buying stuff from people, and then selling it to other people for more money, thereby making a **profit** (the surplus on their transactions). There had always necessarily been people buying and selling things, usually in the market squares of towns and cities, but this new merchant class – sometimes known as the **bourgeoisie** – engaged in these transactions on a different scale. They operated at a national or even international level. Their business meant that there was far greater interaction between different countries and regions. This led not only to the merchant classes enriching themselves financially, but to their societies becoming culturally richer. Cities like London, Amsterdam and Venice became more dynamic and cosmopolitan as a result. Many members of the bourgeoisie spent their spare cash on commissioning and acquiring remarkable works of art. They began to challenge the nobility (who didn't after all do that much) for dominance.

Capital creates more capital

The next big shift came in the late eighteenth and early nineteenth centuries with the Industrial Revolution, which began in Britain. New technology now allowed the production of goods on a vastly greater scale than had ever been possible before. Small quiet towns were transformed into great industrial cities, dominated by vast factories belching smoke into the air. The factories were staffed mostly by people who had once lived and worked in small agricultural communities. Now they worked long hours in tedious and dangerous jobs and lived in cramped and dirty conditions. The factory owners did not literally own them in the way that the nobility once owned serfs or slaves, but they might as well have. The workers had little or no power over their lives, and had lost much of the sense of community they might once have had in the villages they came from.

The raw materials they worked on in these factories were often taken from poorer countries where they had been extracted by actual slaves. Poor women in Lancashire made clothes out of cotton which had been picked in the West Indies or the southern states of America by people who had been kidnapped and forcibly transported to the plantations, and were kept there as possessions of the plantation owners. The wealthy bourgeois minority were arguably at least doing something to earn their riches – they were churning out products, inventing machines and providing jobs for workers – but they still held on to a huge amount of wealth, while the great majority had little or nothing and virtually no prospect of ever having any more.

Around this time, society moved from feudalism to **capitalism**. The world was now divided between those who had **capital** – money, factories, property – and those who offered **labour** – what they could do with their bodies to transform raw materials into more valuable stuff. Those with capital used the labour of those without capital to increase their own capital. Because capital tends to create more capital, while labour just gets used up and can't create any more of itself, the capitalist class inevitably continued to have far more than the labouring class. After a bit, though, the labouring class noticed something. There were a lot more of them than there were of the capitalist class. What was more, the capitalist class would be lost without them. If they got together and collectively demanded better pay and conditions, the capitalist class would have to treat them better. **Trade unions** – organisations of workers in a particular industry who acted as one – became more powerful. If they threatened to withdraw their labour collectively by going on strike, they could get concessions – better pay or conditions – from the capitalist class.

Communism meant equality of poverty

Trade union action gradually led to improvements for workers in the nineteenth and early twentieth centuries. As **democracy** (see Chapter 5, **Democracy**) spread, political parties were created to represent workers' interests (the British Labour Party, for example, takes its name from its original purpose – to represent the 'labour interest', that is, working people). Concessions were won such as paid holidays and sick leave, shorter hours and state support for those in need (see Chapter 13, **The Welfare State**).

This gradual approach to reducing economic inequality wasn't enough for some, though. In Russia in 1917 a revolution broke out, which after a horrifically violent struggle ushered in the world's first communist state. **Communism**, in theory, was dedicated to bringing about a perfectly equal society. In *theory*. In practice, the communist regime in Russia, and in other countries which tried to implement the communist system (Eastern Europe from the late 1940s; China from 1949; North Korea from 1951; Cuba from 1959; Vietnam, Cambodia and Laos from the mid-1970s), ended up replicating many of the old inequalities. A tiny group of party officials at the top hogged almost all the wealth and power in the name of protecting the revolution. There was also less to go round. The fact that nobody could keep any of the wealth they created meant there was no incentive to work hard, so most people didn't. As the Russian saying put it: 'We pretend to work, and they pretend to pay us.' The consequence was economic stagnation at best, devastating famine at worst. Although there was undoubtedly more equality between people than under capitalism, it was often an equality of poverty.

In the non-communist world, there was a more sustainable movement towards greater equality. The Second World War cost millions of lives. It also destroyed a lot of the accumulated wealth of the richest people, and through the experience of shared suffering created a greater sense of social solidarity. In the thirty years after the war, most western democracies set up state support for people who needed it (see Chapter 13, **The Welfare State**), expanded free education (see Chapter 6, Education), and introduced **progressive taxation**, whereby those who earned more paid higher rates, as a way of redistributing wealth. Societies became more equal. Many people from poorer families progressed up the social scale, often thanks to education, and achieved a level of prosperity unimaginable to their parents or grandparents.

Peak economic equality across the western world was probably reached around the mid-1970s. Then a steep rise in the price of oil following a war in the Middle East hit western economies badly. Generous state provision was beginning to look like an unaffordable luxury. At the start of the 1980s, governments across the western world took a turn to the right. Leaders like Ronald Reagan in the US and Margaret Thatcher in the UK cut taxes and regulations, allowing capitalism to break free of restraint. They argued that this freedom would create greater prosperity to everyone's benefit. This trend towards greater economic freedom spread further as communism collapsed in Russia and Eastern Europe in the late 1980s and early 1990s, to be replaced by an even more extreme form of unbridled capitalism. Even China, while remaining nominally communist, embraced a form of state-directed capitalism. At the start of the twenty-first century, developments in information technology ushered in the era of **globalisation** – the world as one big marketplace, where stuff is made in countries with the lowest wages and sold in countries with the highest wages.

> **The gap between the rich and the rest is vast**

The last forty years have undoubtedly seen a significant increase in the overall prosperity of the world. That prosperity has not, however, been equally shared, either between countries or within countries. In almost every society there is more economic inequality now than there was forty years ago. To give just one example: in the early 1980s, Chief Executive Officers (CEOs) of the top 100 UK companies earned on average 20 times the median UK income (the **median** is the midpoint in a list of all the incomes in the UK); in the early twenty-first century, it was 50 times; in 2021, the ratio had risen to 120 times the median income.

Across the world, a tiny minority – the so-called 'one per cent', or even 'nought point one per cent' or 'nought point nought one per cent' – are extremely wealthy, some of them staggeringly so. The gap between the very rich and the rest is vast, and is getting wider. Whether this is a good thing for society is what we are now going to consider.

People are not all the same

2. THE ISSUES

People are not all the same. Some are stronger, smarter, more hardworking than others. In that sense, inequality is inherent in human nature. But should these differences be reflected in economic outcomes?

Here are a couple of stories to help us to think about the issues. The first story will help us think about whether economic inequality makes society fairer or less **fair**, and also whether it makes it more or less **efficient**. It is about two pairs of people who share the same workplace, but have very different lives: a surgeon and a hospital porter, and a CEO (the boss of a company) and his office cleaner. The second will help us think about arguments given for economic inequality, and the strengths and weaknesses of each argument. It is about sausages. (They can be vegan sausages if you want. This is an inclusive book.)

To start with: the surgeon and the porter, and the CEO and the cleaner.

1. Differences in income

The surgeon earns a lot more than the porter; the CEO earns a lot more than the cleaner. It is only **fair** that people who do more demanding or more responsible jobs should be paid more. Being a surgeon takes a lot more training and requires a lot more brain power than pushing patients on trolleys. The head of a company with 1,000 employees has a lot more responsibility than the woman who cleans his office.

What's more, it **works better**. Without the incentive of higher pay, why would anyone put in the years of training and hard work to become a surgeon, or put in the long hours and endure the stress of being a CEO? It means we get better people to do these important jobs. And that's better for society as a whole. The lives saved by a skilful surgeon, and the jobs and wealth created and supported by a successful CEO, give back benefits to society that are worth far more than the extra money they are paid.

On the other hand ...

Is a surgeon really more important than a porter? If the patients aren't brought to the operating theatre, the surgeon can't do any operations. Aren't they both important?

Is having responsibility really harder than not having it? The CEO certainly has more responsibility, but he also has more power, and more autonomy over his life. He can fire the cleaner; the cleaner can't fire him.

Harder jobs may also be more interesting jobs. Both the CEO and the surgeon deal with interesting complex problems every day, and are highly esteemed by society; the porter and the cleaner have to do boring and repetitive tasks, and have little social status. The CEO and the surgeon are unlikely to spend much time comparing the price of different tins of tomatoes to make sure they can feed their children; the porter and the cleaner probably do. Who has the easier life really? Why should the person with the easier life also have more money?

Who has the easier life? A CEO or a cleaner?

2. Differences in possessions

The money the surgeon and the CEO earn helps them to buy stuff. If the surgeon lives in a bigger house in a nicer part of town, she and her family are likely to have a nicer life than if they live somewhere else. If the CEO gets to drive (or is driven) to work in a nice car, life is easier and more pleasant for him than if he has to take the bus – and he may get some extra work done. This is fair, as having this stuff is part of the reward for the surgeon and the CEO's greater levels of expertise and responsibility.

The hospital porter and his family live in a small cramped flat in a less pleasant part of town, but the existence of nicer houses will motivate his children to work harder at school so that one day they too can live in a nice house. (Maybe they will even be able to buy a nicer house for their dad when he retires.) The cleaner has to come into work on the bus, but when she tells her children about her boss's Bentley, they will be motivated to start their own businesses in the hope that one day they too will be able to afford a nice car, and will make their mum proud.

On the other hand ...

Houses and cars are not just objects for use. They are also symbols of status. Living in a certain part of town, driving a certain kind of car, tells people you are successful. When the hospital porter's children look up the surgeon's house on Google Maps and compare it with where they live, they feel inferior. When the cleaner's children think about their mum having to travel into work on a dirty and unreliable bus at five in the morning to clean her boss's office while he sits in the back of a comfortable car reading the paper, they feel angry and resentful. Large visible differences of wealth like this breed division in society. The surgeon and the porter, the CEO and the cleaner may live in the same city, but they have nothing in common. They have such different life experiences that they might as well be from different countries. Inequality undermines social solidarity.

The surgeon and the hospital porter have nothing in common

3. Differences in educational opportunity

The surgeon is ambitious for her children. She spends quite a lot of her income on school fees for them. At their well-appointed private school, they receive high-quality teaching from the best in the profession in small classes which mean they get lots of attention. The school's wide range of extracurricular activities extends their skills and confidence even further. Expectations for them are high, and they meet these expectations by securing places at elite universities. At school and university they meet other young people from similar backgrounds who reinforce their parents' values of ambition and hard work, and who will also provide a useful network of contacts in later life. When they enter the working world, they have a great deal to offer, thanks to their excellent education and the focus and motivation they have acquired from it, meaning that they add much value to the economy and society. They have been given a great deal of **educational** and **social capital**, and they use it well.

The CEO is also ambitious for his children. On weekends, he takes them to concerts, the theatre, the opera. Every school holiday, he and his wife take them to a different foreign country. As a result, they experience a wide range of cultures, and become more open-minded and more confident in dealing with the world. When they grow up, they will work in businesses that connect the UK to the rest of the world, greatly adding to the UK's economic and political clout. The children of the CEO have acquired a great deal of **cultural capital**, and they use it well.

The porter's children attend a state school with large classes and poorer facilities, with fewer students going on to university, but they can still find work when they leave school. They are more likely to end up working in menial and low-paid jobs, stacking shelves or driving delivery vans, but these jobs are important too, and no less essential to society.

The cleaner's children will not set foot in a theatre or an opera house, partly because they cannot afford the tickets, and partly because their mother does not feel confident in these environments. Their holidays (when they can afford them) will be spent in a cheap hotel in a crowded resort. But they will still be loved and happy, and will get as much (maybe more) pleasure from watching *Love Island* as the CEO's children will from sitting through *The Nutcracker* for the fifth time.

Most importantly, the porter's and the cleaner's children will benefit when they grow up from living in an economy and a society in which excellence is cultivated by the educational and cultural resources which the surgeon and the CEO can provide to their children. Forcing equality on everyone out of a dislike of **elitism** would undermine this excellence to nobody's benefit. It would also be unfair – why shouldn't parents be free to give their children the best experience they can?

Equality undermines excellence

On the other hand ...

The surgeon's children may not actually like their private school very much. It may make them feel stressed and inadequate. Everyone else seems to get better grades than they do; everyone else goes on nicer holidays. However hard they try, they will never be good enough. They don't really want to study History at Oxford. They'd rather be a gardener or a carpenter, but that's simply not possible for someone from their social class. The pressure to achieve, to get ahead, causes them to develop mental health problems and eating disorders.

The CEO's children may think they have a broad cultural background, but while they might know a lot about Puccini and Tuscan hill towns, they have little understanding of their own fellow citizens who do not go to the opera, and whose idea of foreign travel is a week in Benidorm. When they come across such people, they look down on them and dismiss their opinions and way of life with contempt. When they grow up and become powerful members of society, the decisions they make will show little respect for people who are not like them. Those people will become angry and resentful at being treated with such disrespect, with potentially dangerous consequences for society.

The porter's children might actually be very suited to studying History at Oxford. The cleaner's children might fall in love with Shakespeare and relish the chance to learn about other cultures. But they never get the chance because of the families they were born into and the cultural and educational opportunities they lack, and as a result much talent is wasted, to the detriment of society.

4. Differences in health outcomes

The surgeon may work for the NHS, but her extra income means she can afford to pay for private healthcare for herself and her children. This saves the NHS a lot of money. The CEO knows that it is important for him to keep in good shape to do his important job well, so he goes to an expensive gym three times a week and eats a healthy diet. He makes sure his children eat healthily too, spending extra on organic food. He also spends a lot on sports activities for his children which keep them fit. He teaches his children self-control with their food, and the self-discipline to exercise regularly.

Being poor makes you sick

The porter and the cleaner can't afford gym membership for themselves or rowing-club membership for their children. But they still get exercise pushing trolleys and hoovers around. As neither of them own a car, their children get lots of exercise walking everywhere. They can keep their weight down by not eating too much and eating a good diet with fresh fruit and vegetables. All these things are entirely in their control.

On the other hand ...

Every hour the private doctors spend with the surgeon and her family is an hour lost to the NHS, where they could be helping people who can't afford their fees. The CEO's children are so bombarded with messages about maintaining the perfect diet and the perfect body that his son spends three hours in the gym every day and makes himself ill taking steroids, while his daughter becomes anorexic. Health is another status symbol, like houses, cars and exam grades – no matter how much you have, it is never enough.

Meanwhile the porter's children become overweight, not because they are greedy and lazy, but because the only food the porter can afford is junk food. Broccoli is expensive and fried chicken is cheap. The cleaner smokes and eats lots of Mars bars because her life is boring and stressful, and these are the only pleasures she can afford. Her children see no prospect of ever having a better life, so they drift into taking drugs to help them escape their misery.

Now for the story about sausages.

Harry and Helena are having dinner with their dad. They're having sausages. Both children like sausages. There are five sausages left. Dad gives Harry three sausages and Helena two sausages.

Helena says, 'That's not fair!'

Is Helena right? It depends on the reason for the unequal allocation of sausages. Let's look at some possible reasons for Dad's decision.

1. Helena is three, and Harry is thirteen.
2. Dad thinks boys are more important than girls.
3. Helena is fourteen, and Harry is thirteen, but Harry emptied the dishwasher, swept the kitchen floor, peeled the potatoes and took out the rubbish before dinner, while Helena lay on the sofa watching Netflix.
4. If Harry doesn't get more sausages than his sister, Dad knows from long experience that he will pick up his plate and throw it on the floor, shout and swear all evening, and generally make everyone's lives a misery.

5. Both children have just got their school exam results. Harry got all As, and Helena got all Cs.

The most essential jobs are the worst paid

1. Helena is three, and Harry is thirteen.

In this case, Harry simply needs more food than his sister, because he has the body of a teenage boy, and she has the body of a toddler. Similarly, in wider society, some people have greater needs than others.

Let's imagine two women, Anna and Bella. They work in a call centre for a bank. They sit next to each other. They do the same job, for the same pay. They like a nice chat during breaks, and come to realise that they have very different lives. Anna has six children. The father of those children (having forced Anna into having them) now has nothing to do with them or with her, and cannot be found. Anna also has a recently widowed father, who is disabled, lives with her, and for whom she cares. Bella, on the other hand, is single (and happy to be so) and has no dependants.

Although Anna and Bella earn the same amount, Anna needs more money than Bella. She needs a big house for her children and her father to live in, and she has to buy food for them all to eat. She could work extra hours to generate more income, but then she would not have time to look after her family. Her life is hard. Meanwhile, Bella has money and time to spare. Her life is easy.

Is it fair that Anna's life is harder than Bella's? How is their situation going to affect their relationship? Are they more or less likely to be friends? What if the state gave people an income in proportion to the number of children they had? Would this be a good idea? Or would it just encourage people to have more children? People can to a degree control how many children they have – nonetheless, once the children are there, they need support. Is it right that some children, who have not chosen their family situation, should grow up with less? Isn't it fair that people should be given what they need? Or should people take responsibility for themselves and their families?

2. Dad thinks boys are more important than girls.

Dad is wrong, of course. But there are many examples throughout history and across the world of people being economically excluded, earning and having less, for reasons beyond their control which have nothing to do with their inherent merit. It might be because of their skin colour, their gender, their religion. Sometimes this discrimination is openly enshrined in law, as in the legislation banning black people from certain jobs in apartheid South Africa, or in the requirement for women to resign from certain jobs on marriage in early twentieth-century Britain. Sometimes it is not codified in law but is nonetheless present in the structures of society, as in Northern Ireland in the twentieth century, where the best-paying jobs and the best housing were only available to Protestants. In theory Catholics could apply for a better job or or put in an offer for a better house, but everyone knew their application would go straight in the bin. Sometimes the discrimination is so subtle and deeply embedded that even those practising it are not aware that they are doing so, as in the unconscious bias that leads black people in the UK to be more likely to be excluded from school, more likely to end up in prison, less likely to be appointed or promoted to well-paying jobs.

We all know that treating people unequally on the grounds of their race, gender or religion is wrong – that's beyond debate. What's more, in the UK it's against the law. The Equality Act of 2010 makes it illegal to discriminate against people on the grounds of age, disability, gender reassignment, race, religion or belief, sex, sexual orientation, marriage, civil partnership, pregnancy or maternity. Is having that law enough? Or do we need to impose quotas to ensure that the representation of different types of people in different professions reflects their representation in society as a whole? Or will that be counter-productive, causing women and people of colour to be seen as only having got their jobs because they are the 'diversity hire'? Will it undermine the achievements of those who have got to the top through their own efforts?

3. Helena is fourteen, and Harry is thirteen, but Harry emptied the dishwasher, swept the kitchen floor, peeled the potatoes and took out the rubbish before dinner, while Helena lay on the sofa watching Netflix.

Now this looks fair. Harry works harder and does more for the family than Helena (at least today), so of course he deserves more. This is one of the most fundamental arguments in favour of economic inequality. People who do more demanding or more worthwhile jobs should be paid more – partly because that's fair, and partly because otherwise no one will want to do them.

But does what people earn really reflect the value of their jobs to society? The Covid-19 pandemic made us all think again about this. When the rest of society was locked down, shelf-stackers, bus drivers, hospital cleaners and rubbish collectors all carried on going out to work, often at great risk to their health. Why? Because, while everything else could come to a stop for the time being, society could not function without these 'key workers'. Every Thursday night we all stood outside our houses applauding them. And yet their jobs – essential jobs without which we could not survive – are amongst the worst paid. Thanks for the applause, many said, but could we also have more money?

The most essential jobs are the worst paid

Or what if it's not Helena's fault that she has had what looks like a lazy day? Maybe she has been lying on the sofa because she is recovering from a serious illness. Maybe she is suffering from depression. Maybe she is disabled and it is physically impossible for her to do what her brother is doing. She might feel intensely frustrated and jealous of her brother for being able to make a contribution to the family and being recognised for it. What do we do about people who are not able to work? Do we let them starve?

4. If Harry doesn't get more sausages than his sister, Dad knows from long experience that he will pick up his plate and throw it on the floor, shout and swear all evening, and generally make everyone's lives a misery.

Often people get more, not because they deserve it, but because they have power. They might be high up in a powerful institution within a society, like the Church in medieval England, or the Communist Party in the Soviet Union – as a result, they get the best of everything. Or they might already be wealthy, and build on that wealth by buying newspapers or TV stations, thus exerting influence through the media; or by making large donations to political parties, to ensure that no policies are enacted that might threaten their wealth. Or, more subtly and perhaps more sneakily, they might exercise influence through cultivating relationships with powerful people they were at school or university with, or who are in their social group, who then enable them to get the highest-paid jobs.

Point out that Jesus wouldn't have lived in a big palace like the bishop while people starved? The bishop will let everyone know you're a heretic who's going to Hell. Suggest that being driven everywhere in a limousine isn't very communist? Off to the gulag with you as a counter-revolutionary. Just won an election and want to raise taxes on the very wealthy? All of a sudden a bestselling newspaper has dug up an embarrassing love affair from your past and is going to splash it on the front page if you don't change your mind. Want that promotion? I know you worked hard for it, but the man who gets it shared a dorm with the boss at prep school, so the boss knows he's a good chap.

How things are is not how they should be

This kind of unfairness is less obvious but in a way more damaging than discrimination on the grounds of race, gender or religion. What makes it harder to tackle is that those with an unfair share of the goodies can use their power to make it seem as if that state of affairs is simply a law of nature that can never be altered. It is God's will that the bishop should live in a palace; the Party is on the right side of history; everyone knows higher taxes will wreck the economy, because all the newspapers and TV stations say so; we always appoint people from that school because they get such a good education. Harry never actually has to throw his plate on the floor to get his extra sausages. He knows by now that he will get his way.

What's more, he gets what he wants so often that his sister grows up believing that it is part of the natural state of affairs for boys to get more than girls. Very likely she will end up marrying a man who pushes her around like her brother did, and she will think this is normal too, and perhaps her daughter will as well, and her granddaughter, and so on, until one of them sees that another way of doing things is possible. Beware of people who tell you, 'That's just the way things are.' The way things are is not necessarily the same as the way they should be.

5. Both children have just got their school exam results. Harry got all As, and Helena got all Cs.

Like example number 3, this looks fair. Harry must have worked harder, so of course he deserves a reward. It's certainly replicated in real life – people's earning capacity is very highly correlated to their level of academic qualification. But it may not be as simple as it looks. What if Harry was always allowed the computer to do his homework? What if Harry and Helena's parents paid for a tutor for Harry, but not for Helena? What if they sent Harry to a better school than Helena? What if Helena has no confidence because her Dad has always let her know that he favours boys over girls? What if Helena is just less academic than Harry, but is much better at lots of other things – fixing bikes, say, or baking cakes or telling jokes, or just being kind to her family and friends – any one of which might be more useful than memorising a lot of stuff for a test? Exams look like a level playing field, but all kinds of other factors come into play in fact, which have little or nothing to do with academic ability.

What can be done about inequality?

Can we do anything about inequality?

If you believe that inequality is just part of the natural order of things, then the answer might be 'not very much'. In fact, there are a number of government policies designed to reduce economic inequality. Whether you support them or not depends partly on whether you believe economic inequality is necessary and / or desirable. It also depends on these questions:

- Are they **practical** (do they work)?
- Are they **moral** (are they right)?

One form of government intervention is via the establishment of a **welfare state**. The arguments for and against different forms of welfare state are covered in detail in the next chapter.

Here are some other forms of government intervention which may reduce economic inequality, with practical and moral arguments for and against them.

1. Confiscation / nationalisation

If some people have a lot more stuff than other people, you can just take it off them, and either give it to people who have less, or have the state keep it in the name of the people.

This was practised in its most extreme form in the various Communist revolutions of the twentieth century: Russian aristocrats were killed and their vast houses and estates divided up and handed over to peasants; American companies who had invested heavily in Cuba had their assets seized by the new government; anyone with an education – anyone who wore glasses even – was driven out of Phnom Penh, the capital of Cambodia, and forced to work in the fields.

A less extreme form of confiscation can come in the form of **nationalisation**. This means taking whole industries under the control of the government, so they are no longer owned for private profit, but are run in the interests of the whole nation. Nationalisation was practised on a large scale by the Labour government elected in the UK in 1945: they took over the railways, electricity, iron and steel production and the coal mines, as well as incorporating private doctors' practices into the NHS. It wasn't confiscation exactly, as owners of these industries were paid compensation – it was more like buying them up. Signs outside coal mines following nationalisation proudly proclaimed 'Owned by the people'. Collective ownership, it was felt, meant that these vital industries were held in common by all the people, rather than being in the hands of a wealthy few.

Should we take stuff off rich people?

Nationalisation was almost entirely reversed by the Conservative government of the 1980s. Railways, electricity, iron and steel were all **privatised**. That is, they were put up for sale by selling shares in them to anyone who wanted to buy. The intention was to move ownership from the government to a wide selection of shareholding citizens. In practice, though, the shares eventually ended up in the hands of a small number of wealthy investors. The coal industry was effectively closed down as the pits ran out of coal. (Coal is now discredited as a source of energy because of the climate crisis.) Only the NHS remains in state ownership, though the private sector has considerably more involvement than it once did (see Chapter 13, **The Welfare State**).

For confiscation / nationalisation

Practical

Wealthy people will never give up their wealth unless they are compelled to do so. It is highly inefficient to have vital resources in the hands of a few. The owners will run their assets for their own interests, not those of the country. The need for profit means a lot of money is wasted in payments to the owners and shareholders, rather than being invested in the industry.

Moral

It is just wrong that vital resources are in the hands of a few people. It gives them too much power. Everyone needs electricity, railways, healthcare, etc. It is immoral to turn a profit out of these basic needs.

Against confiscation / nationalisation

Practical

People are incentivised to look after things better if they own them. Handing them over to the state means that no one has any personal incentive to run the businesses well. Having only one provider removes competition, which is the best way to raise standards, to the benefit of customers. Governments are not good at running things – they are too slow and too centralised.

Moral

For the government to take people's possessions is just stealing. If someone has earned their wealth legitimately, they should be allowed to keep it.

2. Redistributive taxation

Who do we tax – and how much?

Taxation is essential. The government has to raise money to build and maintain roads, pay police and soldiers, run schools and hospitals. However, taxation can also be used as a tool to change the balance of wealth in a society; this is called **redistributive taxation**.

The most common form of redistributive taxation is **progressive taxation**, when people who earn more are taxed at a higher rate. Income tax rates in the UK for the most wealthy have gone steadily down since the Second World War. During the war, the top rate was an eye-watering 99.25%. It fell to 90% in the 1950s; 75% in 1971; 60% in 1979; and 40% in 1988. It went up to 45% in 2010, where, at the time of writing, it remains. The lowest rate of income tax was 33% until 1979. After that it was gradually cut in stages, and at the time of writing is 19%.

Taxing higher earners at a higher rate means that they contribute more to the common good in the form of shared assets such as roads, schools and hospitals, so their wealth is shared more widely amongst the community, and they themselves have less. This does help to reduce inequality. The progressive cutting in the top rate of income tax has helped to increase inequality in the UK.

An alternative approach to taxation is to have a **flat tax**. Under this system, everyone pays the same percentage of income tax, e.g., everyone has to pay 30% of their income to the government. Flat taxes tend to increase inequality, as wealthy people get to keep more of their income. Flat taxes are used in a number of countries around the world, mostly former Communist countries, perhaps as a reaction to the extreme forms of confiscation previously practised under Communism.

For progressive taxation

Practical

Progressive taxation raises more money for the state to spend on valuable projects. It increases social solidarity by reducing extremes of inequality. The very wealthy can afford to pay a higher rate than other people.

Moral

Those who have more should give more. If you are more wealthy, it is more likely to be because you are lucky than because you deserve it. It is right for the more fortunate to help the less fortunate.

Those who have more should give more

Against progressive taxation

Practical

Higher tax rates put people off working harder. They discourage enterprise. They drive talented people out of the country, to everyone's loss. Higher tax rates actually generate less tax income, as people find ways to evade (get out of paying) them.

Moral

People are entitled to be rewarded for their hard work and talent, and to keep what they earn. Higher taxes institutionalise envy and a 'something for nothing' culture.

3. Property and land taxes

As well as taxing what people earn, governments can tax what people have. They can tax assets like property or land. Given that many very wealthy people in effect have no income, but live instead off accumulated capital and / or rents from property, this may be a more effective way to take back some of their wealth.

For property and land taxes

Practical

Wealth and land taxes are much harder to evade. A very wealthy person can choose to be paid in another country, or to be paid in kind, to hide their income and wriggle out of paying income tax. Hiding a house is much harder. Moreover, it can't be moved out of the country.

Moral

Why does anyone need more than one house? People owning more than they need is wrong. Second homes push up property prices for local people, meaning they cannot afford to own their own homes.

Against property and land taxes

Practical

High property and land taxes will drive wealthy and talented people out of the country, with the loss of their skills and investment. Higher taxes will also make houses more expensive to buy.

Moral

Why should someone be punished for having done well? If you have earned the money to buy property legitimately, you should be allowed to keep it.

Who needs more than one house?

4. Inheritance taxes

A major source of inequality is inherited wealth. Being left money or property by your parents or other family members gives you a significant advantage. Moreover, you don't even have to work for it (though your parents may have).

Inequality caused by inheritance can be evened out through inheritance tax. This means that the government can take part of anything that is left you when someone dies. One way round this can be for parents to give money or property to their children before they die, though tax law usually requires these gifts to have been made several years before death.

For inheritance tax

Practical

Inheritance tax provides a valuable source of income for the government. Allowing property and wealth to stay in families means that many people have wealth they have not earned; this makes them lazy and complacent, unwilling to work hard and develop their talents. Making everyone earn their own money makes for a more dynamic economy.

Moral

It is not fair that some people get something for nothing. It means that some people have an unfair advantage in life. It is better for people to know that anything they have, they have earned through their own efforts. The children of highly wealthy people who do not have to work are parasites who contribute nothing to society.

Against inheritance tax

Practical

It is a natural human instinct to want to provide for your children, and this is a major incentive to work hard. If people know they will be unable to pass on their wealth to their children, they will be less incentivised to work hard. Wealthy people contribute more to the economy by spending more, even if their wealth is unearned.

Moral

Being able to provide for your children and give them the best start in life is a basic human right. There is no reason why this should not continue to be the case after death. For a bereaved person, to have what your parents worked for taken away from you is cruel and distressing. The government has no right to take what they have not earned, and what is not theirs.

3. THE POINT OF CLASH

In the pre-modern era, economic inequality derived from birth; the nobility had more because of the families they were born into. The UK in the twenty-first century is (or is supposed to be) a **meritocracy**. A meritocracy is a society in which people are rewarded according to their work and their talent. Meritocracies inevitably lead to quite a high level of economic inequality. Much of the debate around the pros and cons of **economic inequality** comes down to the pros and cons of meritocracy, and this provides a good way to think about the point of clash.

Defenders of meritocracy say that it is the **fairest** possible system, because it allocates rewards to people in return for what they offer to society. They also say it is the **most effective** possible system, because it incentivises people to work hard and develop their talents, to the greater benefit of society. Moreover, it gives people the **freedom** to make what they want of their lives. Unequal societies are **fairer**, **more prosperous** and **freer**.

Critics of meritocracy say that it is not actually that fair a system, as people's level of talent and attitude to work are not as much under their control as they appear to be. They are very largely determined by their upbringing and social context. They also say it is not very effective, as it creates a society in which there are winners and losers. The winners think that they are better people than the losers (when in fact they are just luckier), and as a result they feel both arrogant and insecure, constantly afraid they or their children might lose their superior status. The losers are made to feel that their lower status is their fault, for not being smart enough or more hardworking (when in fact they are just more unlucky), and as a result they feel both depressed and resentful.

Should life be a race or a group hike?

It was no fun being poor in the pre-modern world, but at least you could console yourself with the thought that your being poor was all part of God's plan; now if you're poor, it means there's something wrong with you. These so-called 'losers' could actually achieve much more if they were brought up in a more equal society. The social division and lack of mutual understanding and respect caused by economic inequality undermine levels of trust and social cohesion to everyone's detriment. Unequal societies are **unfair**, **ineffective and divided**.

To boil the point of clash down even further. Which is more important: **equality of opportunity**, where everyone has the same chance to succeed, even though this may mean some will be much more successful than others? Or **equality of outcome**, where differences between people are very small, even though this means preventing some people from getting ahead of others? Should life be like a race, in which everyone runs as fast as they can in the hope of coming first? Or should it be like a group hike, in which everyone walks at more or less the same pace, and the stronger walkers look after the weaker ones? Do you agree more with Karl Marx, who said: 'From each according to their ability, to each according to their needs'? Or with Margaret Thatcher, who said: '... let our children grow tall and some taller than others if they have the ability in them to do so'?

4. THE ARGUMENTS

For economic inequality	Against economic inequality
It is fair that some people earn more than others as a reward for more important jobs.	All jobs are important in different ways. Low-skilled jobs are often the most essential, as we discovered during the Covid pandemic.
Rewarding some people more highly than others incentivises people to work harder.	Higher-paid jobs are not necessarily harder work. Low-paid jobs are often more boring and therefore more stressful.
Rewarding some people more highly than others attracts and encourages talent.	It is a matter of luck whether we are born with talent or not, and it is not fair to reward people for something over which they have no control.
People are entitled to earn and to keep whatever they can legitimately earn.	Society has a responsibility to redistribute wealth to ensure everyone has what they need.
People are entitled to pass on whatever advantages their wealth gives them to their children.	It is unfair that some children have a different start in life from others.
Everyone has an equal chance of success, so it is only fair that people are allowed to keep the rewards that go with their success.	Our chances of success are greatly distorted by factors such as class, race and gender, so rewards are not allocated fairly. This unfairness needs to be corrected.
An unequal society rewards excellence.	A more equal society encourages solidarity and mutual trust and respect.
Unequal societies are more dynamic and productive.	More equal societies are healthier and more harmonious.
People are naturally unequal, and society should reflect that.	People deserve equality of respect and treatment, and society should reflect that.
An unequal society is freer.	A more equal society is fairer.

5. THE MOTIONS

1. This house would introduce a maximum wage.
2. This house would introduce a flat tax.
3. This house would introduce a tax on unearned income.
4. This house would introduce a tax on land.
5. This house would abolish inheritance tax.
6. This house would increase inheritance tax to 100%.
7. This house would not allow anyone to own more than one house.
8. This house believes economic inequality is bad for society.

Keep thinking...

A selection of further reading to help you think more deeply about the issues around democracy.

Do We Need Economic Inequality?, Danny Dorling (Polity, 2017)

Dorling is a professor of Geography at Oxford University. This short, accessible, user-friendly book presents the key moral and practical arguments against inequality with great clarity, thoroughly supported by a wide range of data.

Free to Choose, Milton and Rose Friedman (Harcourt Brace Jovanovich, 1980)

Written by a distinguished Nobel Prize-winning economist and his wife, this is a passionate defence of the benefits of a free and therefore necessarily unequal society. The Friedmans' argument is well summed up when they say, 'Equality of outcome is in clear conflict with liberty.' It was written just as Ronald Reagan was coming to power in the US and Margaret Thatcher was taking over in the UK, and heralded a great change in attitudes to inequality across the world. Interestingly, the (American) authors frequently cite the UK as an example of the damage done by an obsession with equality and social justice. They wouldn't do that now.

The Constitution of Liberty, Friedrich Hayek (University of Chicago, 1960)

Densely written in academic prose, this is not an easy read – best suited perhaps to people studying (or intending to study) philosophy. However, it is worth the effort, as it is a meticulously argued case for the primacy of freedom over equality.

Anarchy, State and Utopia, Robert Nozick (Basic Books, 1974)

Another densely argued philosophical book, but one which richly rewards study. It is a classic defence of **libertarianism**: the belief that government should be stripped back to the absolute minimum. Inequality is an inevitable (but for Nozick, desirable) outcome of this maximally free society.

The Price of Inequality, Joseph E. Stiglitz (Allen Lane, 2012)

Stiglitz is another very distinguished economist; he was a close adviser to President Clinton. He gives a devastating critique of the damage that growing inequality has caused in the US (one of the most unequal societies in the world), arguing that it leads to corruption, inefficiency and worse outcomes for everyone.

A Brief History of Inequality, Thomas Piketty, translated by Steven Rendall (Belknap Press, 2022)

The French economist Thomas Piketty has written some much fatter books on inequality, but this slim volume sums up his thinking very clearly. With a mass of telling data acquired over a lifetime's research, he argues that most wealthy people do not in fact deserve their wealth. They are not producing anything or adding anything to society, they simply use their ownership of assets to make themselves and their descendants steadily richer.

The Tyranny of Merit: What's Become of the Common Good?, Michael J. Sandel (Allen Lane, 2020)

Sandel describes himself as a 'public philosopher', and has devoted his life to helping people to think about important issues. Writing in a very approachable and engaging style, he makes a strong case against meritocracy, which he sees not as a fair and equal contest, but as a mechanism for reinforcing privilege.

The Spirit Level: Why Equal Societies Almost Always Do Better, Richard Wilkinson and Kate Pickett (Allen Lane, 2009)

Wilkinson and Pickett use an impressive array of data and examples to show that economic equality is not only fairer, it also leads to better outcomes for health, education, crime levels and well-being. Most interestingly of all, they argue that unequal societies can be as bad for the people at the top as the ones at the bottom.

CHAPTER 13

The Welfare State

In this chapter we're thinking about...

- **What should the state provide and why?**
- **Whom it should provide for and why?**

1. THE FACTS

Provision and support

What is the welfare state?

The phrase 'the welfare state' was first used by the Archbishop of Canterbury, William Temple, in 1941. He contrasted Britain as a 'welfare state' with Nazi Germany as a 'warfare state'. The fact that this phrase was introduced into the English language at the height of the Second World War is significant, as we shall see.

The **welfare state** has two main elements: **provision** and **support**.

Firstly, it means the **provision** by the state, funded by taxation, of services such as healthcare, education and housing. These services may be free at the point of use (such as NHS healthcare and state education), or they may be partially subsidised (such as state-sponsored housing and university education).

Secondly, it covers financial **support**, through social security (also sometimes known as 'welfare' or 'benefits') for people who are in need or unable to work because of unemployment, illness or poverty. Many people who receive benefits are in fact working; they just aren't paid enough to feed their children or have somewhere to live without extra support from the government.

The protection provided against crime by the police and external attack by the armed forces is something different; it is part of the **security state**, not the welfare state.

Although education is often considered to be part of the welfare state, it is covered more fully in Chapter 6 (**Education**) because it raises so many other issues.

How did we get here?

1. The welfare state is conceived: 1942–45

When was the last time a government report drafted by a civil servant sold over half a million copies and launched its author on a nationwide tour, playing to packed houses the length and breadth of the country? The *Social Insurance and Allied Services* report, originally published in 1942, was written by Sir William Beveridge, and soon became known simply as the Beveridge Report. It captured the imagination of the British people as they engaged in a struggle for survival against Nazi Germany. As well as those remarkable sales figures and gig numbers, its ideas were

Want, disease, ignorance, squalor and idleness

phenomenally popular: an astonishing 86% of the public endorsed its conclusions, with only 6% against. It was backed by all the major parties in the wartime coalition. Never has a government policy commanded such universal support, before or since. Its reach stretched beyond the UK: 50,000 copies were sold in the US and, bizarrely, a copy was discovered in Hitler's bunker after Germany's surrender, annotated in German with approving comments.

So what did the Beveridge Report actually say?

At the time Beveridge was writing, welfare in the UK was random and inconsistent, with a mix of local charities and very limited and targeted government support. In particular, healthcare was almost entirely in private hands; lower-income families would go to the doctor only in dire need, and sometimes not even then, because they simply could not afford it. Beveridge's plan was to take this collection of local and voluntary systems and bring them all together into one universal compulsory system. He proposed an attack on five giants stalking the land, who had been especially powerful during the Great Depression of the 1930s: Want, Disease, Ignorance, Squalor and Idleness. These giants were to be defeated through a programme of social security benefits for those in need (Want), free and universal health care (Disease), free and universal education (Ignorance), good-quality state-subsidised housing (Squalor), and government intervention in the economy to ensure full employment (Idleness). Welfare was not to be given out for free, however. It was to be paid for through a programme of compulsory insurance payments made by all working people, which came to be known as National Insurance. All would pay the same rate (a percentage of their income). The benefits were not particularly generous; they were set at subsistence level, the minimum needed for survival. But they were comprehensive, universal and guaranteed.

Beveridge described his plan as 'a British revolution'. It was. For the first time, every single citizen would be guaranteed free health care, financial support in times of need, free education for their children and decent housing as of right. No one was excluded from the benefits; no one was exempted from the responsibility of supporting those less fortunate than themselves.

Why was this plan so spectacularly popular? Why did Beveridge get rock-star treatment on his tour of the nation's town halls? The Second World War had much to do with it. Huddled together in air-raid shelters, fighting side by side on the front line in Europe, Africa and the Far East, struggling to make the same paltry rations last through the week, the British people found that many of the old barriers of class and status lost their meaning in a shared struggle for survival. We were all in it together against Hitler and the Nazis; why shouldn't we be all in it together against the Five Giants? Moreover, there was a sense that, having made so many sacrifices during the war, we were entitled to a better world after it. Few people wanted to go back to the poverty, unemployment and social division of the 1930s. The devastation of war gave an opportunity to start afresh. None other than Winston Churchill, who was anything but a socialist, promised the British people in a radio broadcast in 1943 'national compulsory insurance for all classes for all purposes from the cradle to the grave.' Finally, people had got used to being both looked after and told what to do by the government, which had taken on extraordinary powers to direct and shepherd them during the war, micro-managing their lives. Why shouldn't those powers be turned to making peoples' lives better in peacetime?

From the cradle to the grave

2. The welfare state is born: 1945–48

In the general election of July 1945, Labour under Clement Attlee won a landslide, gaining an overall majority of 145 seats. On accepting Winston Churchill's resignation as Prime Minister, King George VI told him that he thought the people had been very ungrateful. The King may have misjudged his people; they were grateful to Churchill for winning the war, but they now looked to Labour to win the peace.

The new government soon set to work. The National Health Service (the NHS) was established. Private hospitals were taken into government control. GPs, who had run their practices as competing small businesses run for profit, were now paid by the government according to the number of patients they saw. The establishment of the NHS was fiercely resisted at first by the medical profession, who did not want to give up their privileged and lucrative status. The Health Secretary, the ebullient and determined Nye Bevan, had to make concessions, such as allowing doctors to continue with some private practice. As he said later, 'I stuffed their mouths with gold.' Finally, from July 5th, 1948, for the first time in British history, anyone from anywhere in the country could access whatever medical care they needed without paying a penny. Also from July 1948, anyone who was unemployed, sick, a new mother or past retirement age was entitled to financial support from the state. The government invested intensively in housing (an urgent need, since 25% of housing stock had been damaged by bombing during the war), providing people with good-quality homes either free or at a heavily subsidised rent.

The state should look after people in need

3. The welfare state in its prime: 1948–1976

Labour lost power in the election of 1951, and the Conservatives ruled for the next thirteen years. However, they did very little to change the welfare state that Labour had set up, apart from a little tinkering to make benefits more targeted and less universal. Essentially, there was a very broad and widespread consensus across both main parties and the wider population that it was the duty of the state to look after people in need. This lasted for nearly thirty years, across alternating Labour and Conservative governments, into the mid-1970s.

4. The welfare state in middle age: 1976–2010

Just as a war prompted the birth of the welfare state, so a war first put it in danger. It was a war in which Britain was not directly involved, but which had huge consequences far beyond the countries concerned. In October 1973, Arab countries combined to launch an attack on Israel. Israel succeeded in defending itself, but, as the Middle East was a centre of oil production, one of the consequences of the war was a crippling 400% rise in the price of oil. This had a massive and long-lasting impact on economies around the world. As the British economy struggled and numbers of unemployed rose well above the very low levels seen in the thirty years after the Second World War, the benefits bill rose. It wasn't just the rise in the price of oil, though. There were far more single-parent families needing support than in 1945. A huge increase in the number of university students, who all received both tuition and maintenance grants, put a further strain on the public purse. Beveridge had hoped that as the NHS made people healthier, healthcare would cost less; in fact, universal healthcare raised people's expectations of the health system, and thus the cost. In 1976, the Labour Prime Minister James Callaghan was forced to announce cuts in welfare spending. Meanwhile, his opposite number, Margaret Thatcher, the newly elected leader of the Conservative Party, was demanding a fundamental rethink. Society, she said, 'has concentrated too much attention on distributing the wealth we have and too little on adding to it … the appetite of the education service, and of health and welfare, has proved insatiable … we must try to put responsibility back where it belongs: with the family and with the people themselves.' Attitudes were changing. Stories about 'welfare scroungers' began to appear in the press. In 1979, following the 'winter of discontent', a wave of strikes that left the dead unburied, rubbish piled high in the streets and Callaghan's government looking as if it had lost control, Margaret Thatcher was elected Britain's first woman Prime Minister.

There is no such thing as society

Mrs Thatcher rejected the postwar consensus on the welfare state. She thought it encouraged laziness and lack of initiative by making people dependent on the state rather than on their own efforts and hard work. She didn't like the element of compulsion. She thought people had a moral duty to take responsibility for their own lives. She thought rolling back the welfare state would make British people stronger, freer and richer. Famously, she said, in an interview with *Woman's Own* magazine, 'There is no such thing as society. There are individual men and women, and there are families. And no government can do anything except through people, and people must look after themselves first. It is our duty to look after ourselves and then to look after our neighbour.'

Thatcher did not quite manage to abolish the welfare state, but over eighteen years of Conservative government, first under her leadership from 1979 to 1990, then under her successor John Major from 1990 to 1997, there were significant changes. The NHS remained free at the point of delivery, but moved from being one monolithic organisation run from London to being an 'internal marketplace'. It was split into 'purchasers', such as GPs, and 'providers', such as hospitals. If you went to see your GP with stomach pains, and she thought it might be the early stages of cancer, instead of sending you to the one and only cancer specialist for your area, she could now shop around all the different kinds of treatment available, and choose the one which best combined effectiveness and economy. That hospital or consultant would then receive the funds for your treatment. The intention was to incentivise hospitals and consultants to provide better and cheaper treatment by competing with each other, rewarding the most effective, and driving out the incompetent and the overpriced. Similarly, local councils, rather than running their own services for collecting rubbish, maintaining the roads or cutting the grass in the park, were encouraged to invite applications to run these services from private companies who competed with each other to bring down costs (but also took a profit). Perhaps most significantly of all, people who lived in council houses, which had been provided and maintained for many years at low rents by local authorities, were now allowed to buy them. They could no longer call on the council for repairs and upkeep, etc., but they would own their own homes, and could do what they liked with them. This last policy was hugely popular, and exemplified many of Thatcher's values of independence, responsibility and letting people run their own lives. It did, however, also mean that there was much less housing stock available for people who couldn't afford to buy their own homes.

A hand up, not a handout

In 1997, following a landslide election victory even bigger than that of Attlee in 1945, Labour returned to power under Tony Blair as Prime Minister. It was a very different Labour party to Attlee's, however. Blair had rebranded it as 'New Labour', ditching the party's commitment to state ownership and control of industry. Rather than promising more benefits for those not able to work, New Labour wanted to help people back into work; it promised a 'hand up', not a 'handout'; 'a springboard to success, not a road to dependency.' While state education and the NHS remained free and available to everyone, other benefits became more targeted. People on lower incomes received a tax credit, which meant they had to pay less tax, so took home more pay. It was a discreet way of redistributing wealth for an age that was more suspicious of egalitarianism than the 1940s. Also under New Labour, the introduction of consumer choice into health and education was accelerated. League tables based on performance data were introduced to allow people to compare hospitals and schools for themselves. The Health Secretary Alan Milburn promised 'an irreversible shift from the 1940s take-it-or-leave-it, top-down service. Hospitals will no longer choose patients; patients will choose hospitals.' The state would still provide a wide variety of services, but it would do so in response to consumer needs rather than following the direction of the government. It was a welfare state for a more fragmented, individualistic and fluid society than the one which had so welcomed the Beveridge Report five decades earlier.

5. The welfare state nearly dies: 2010–2020

In 1973, war in the Middle East shook the world economy to its foundations. In 2008, it was people in Middle America buying houses they couldn't afford.

It started when large numbers of Americans found they were unable to keep up the repayments on their mortgages, the loans they had taken out to help them buy houses. Their mortgages were 'sub-prime': a euphemism for lending people money they won't be able to pay back. Banks had taken on these risky loans because they gave such high returns – until, that is, they didn't give any returns at all. The situation was further complicated by the fact that vast numbers of loans were bundled up into highly complex packages that were sold and resold many times, until no one could see how much risk there was in the system. And it wasn't just mortgages: banks around the world had been taking on more risk than they should have, in the pursuit of higher profits, via highly complicated financial instruments that even the brainiest traders didn't fully understand. From the summer of 2008 onwards, the whole system collapsed like a house of cards across multiple countries. The world was in the grip of the so-called 'credit crunch', a terrifying situation in which no one wanted to lend anyone any money, causing the economy to freeze up. When Lehman Brothers, one of the biggest banks in the world, went bankrupt in September 2008, we were hours from a breakdown of the entire global financial system, with cashpoints and credit cards ceasing to work. Something had to be done, and it was. Led by Gordon Brown, Tony Blair's successor as Labour Prime Minister, governments around the world pumped billions of pounds into the banks to stop them going under. Catastrophe was averted by this swift and bold action.

Someone would have to pay

The only problem was, someone would have to pay for it all. That someone turned out to be the poorest and most vulnerable members of society.

Gordon Brown lost the election in 2010 and was replaced as Prime Minister by the Conservative David Cameron, who governed in coalition with the Liberal Democrats. They immediately embarked on a policy of 'austerity', cutting public expenditure to pay off the massive debts incurred by the bailout of the banks. Over the course of the next ten years, £11 billion was slashed from the public budget through 28 separate cuts to benefits and tax credits. Public sector workers had their pay frozen. A new system of benefits was introduced called 'Universal Credit.' It was supposed to simplify welfare by bundling several payments into one, but there were many reports of inefficient and delayed distribution and an excessively punitive approach towards applicants. Numbers accessing food banks to feed their families rocketed across the country. Although the Chancellor of the Exchequer, George Osborne, claimed 'We're all in this together', 80% of the savings were made from welfare, and only 20% in tax rises. And yet popular opinion was remarkably accepting of austerity. If there was anger, it was more likely to be directed at 'benefit cheats', luridly and unrepresentatively depicted in multiple stories in the tabloid press and on TV shows like Channel 4's *Benefits Street*. The public mood was sour, crabby, unforgiving. The vote to leave the European Union in the 2016 Brexit referendum and the subsequent three and a half years of messy, fractious divorce proceedings were seen by many as an expression of displaced anger at austerity. It was all a very long way from the sense of solidarity in shared sacrifice and optimism at the prospect of building a better world that emerged from the ruins of the Second World War.

It felt like 1945 all over again

6. How the welfare state came back to life: 2020 –

And then along came COVID-19.

The virus that sneaked out of a wet market in Wuhan in late 2019 cost millions of lives around the world. One life it arguably saved, however, was that of the UK welfare state.

During the spring and summer of 2020, something extraordinary happened in the UK. The experience of being forced to keep apart from each other during the Covid lockdown paradoxically generated a greater sense of togetherness than had been seen since – well, since the Second World War. The bitterness of austerity and Brexit was forgotten. This time we really were all in it together. People shopped for sick neighbours they had barely exchanged two words with before the pandemic; posters and banners exalting the NHS, that great experiment in sharing and solidarity, appeared everywhere, like a national flag; night after night, 'NHS heroes' were celebrated on the TV news; and every Thursday we 'clapped for carers' in a collective act of worship of the welfare state. Broadcasting to the nation on the seventy-fifth anniversary of VE Day in May 2020, the Queen (who, unlike almost everyone else who invoked the spirit of the Second World War, had actually lived through it herself) told us that the men and women who had fought in the war would be proud of us. It felt like 1945 all over again.

The government took action to match the national mood. Workers whose employers were unable to continue paying them were given 80% of their salary by the government. Self-employed people received a similar level of support. Universal Credit was increased by £20 a week. Large grants were made to the entertainment sector to keep shut-down theatres and concert venues from going bust. In the summer of 2020, as restrictions eased, the Chancellor of the Exchequer, Rishi Sunak, instructed us all to 'Eat Out to Help Out'; the government would pick up 50% of the bill in any restaurant, in the hope of reviving the hospitality sector. It had, once again, become the job of the state to give people money to help them through hard times, in a spirit of national solidarity. Sir William Beveridge must have been grinning in his grave.

In due course, the pandemic receded, and so did the level of government intervention and support. Nonetheless, the events of 2020 showed that the founding ideals of the welfare state could still be rediscovered in a time of crisis comparable to that in which it was first conceived and born.

2. THE ISSUES

We are responsible for each other

Should we look after each other, or just ourselves?

You may have read or seen *An Inspector Calls*, a play by J.B. Priestley. In fact, it's highly likely that you either have read it or will read it, as an astonishing 75% of students taking GCSE English Literature study the play. It dramatises very effectively this fundamental question at the heart of any debate about the welfare state. The two sides are represented by Mr Birling, a wealthy industrialist, who is firmly on the side of self-reliance when he says, 'a man has to mind his own business and look after himself and his own', prefiguring Margaret Thatcher's assertion that, 'There is no such thing as society.' The Inspector rebuts this by saying, 'We are members of one body. We are responsible for each other.'

Priestley's play was first performed in 1945, and very much embodies the mix of anger at past deprivation and injustice and hope for the future that characterised that period of British history. The Inspector's philosophy has won an unchallenged victory by the time the curtain falls, as the arrogant self-confidence of Mr Birling and his family is slowly but inexorably dismantled through revelations of their hypocrisy and cruelty. Here, though, we need to consider both sides of the question.

There are, as is often the case, two ways of approaching the question: **moral** and **practical**. This division could also be expressed as **principles** and **pragmatism**. Which is the right approach to take? Which works better?

Moral (principles)

Should we look after each other?

The moral argument in favour of looking after each other values **solidarity** more highly than **freedom**. It maintains that we have a moral duty to care for anyone in difficulty. It accepts that we will have to sacrifice some of our freedom of choice, and some of our income, in order to support each other. It holds that these are sacrifices worth making in the interest of living in a society which is more caring, compassionate and generous. It regards the fact that some people are more prosperous than others as a matter of luck as much as hard work and talent. Life is much easier if you have rich parents (whom you didn't choose). It is also much easier if you have talents such as intelligence and creativity, or qualities of character such as

The welfare state is love in action

resilience and perseverance (which you didn't earn, but were given to you by your parents and / or God, to be used for the benefit of others). If rich people don't deserve to be rich, then poor people don't deserve to be poor, and we therefore ought to help them.

This way of thinking also proposes that the loss of the **positive freedom** to spend our money how we want, to own our own homes, to seek medical treatment where we want and to have our children educated at a school of our own choice, is more than compensated for by the increase in **negative freedom** that comes from being protected against poverty, homelessness, ill health and poor education. We may not be **free to** spend our own money; but we are **free from** being poor.

Moreover, looking after each other binds people together; if we all attend the same schools and the same hospitals and all have a stake in the same welfare programmes, we will be more united as a nation. It is no coincidence that the welfare state has commanded the most support in times of unifying crises such as the Second World War and the Covid pandemic. The writer Caitlin Moran sums up this moral approach very well when she says (accepting the loss of freedom that state-provided housing implies), '... it seems an awfully big price to pay, the dismantling of an entire caring and efficient system just to have your door a different shade of moss green. In the end, the nanny state is love. For all its faults, it's about looking after and looking out for other people. The invention of the welfare state is love in action.'

Should we look after ourselves?

This approach values **freedom** and **responsibility** above all else.

It argues first that the welfare state is wrong because it attacks our **freedom**, undermining our autonomy as individuals, taking away our right to make our own choices about how we spend our money and how we look after ourselves and our families. Why should the state take away money that I have earned to pay for someone else's healthcare or education, or to support them when they are out of work? Why shouldn't they pay for their own healthcare? Why shouldn't they save money to protect themselves against hardship? If I choose to give money to a charity to help people who are less fortunate, I can; but I should not be obliged to do this by law. Moreover, state-run institutions undermine my freedom of choice. If almost all the hospitals are run by the NHS, I have to accept the NHS's way of doing things, whether I like it or not. What if I want a treatment they won't give? When almost every child attends a school run by the state, the state has control over young minds.

What if I want my child brought up with different values from those of the state?

It also argues that it undermines people's sense of **responsibility** by ensuring that they no longer have to accept the consequences of their actions. If I know that I will get free healthcare, why should I bother to look after my health? Why shouldn't I smoke, drink too much, take no exercise, put on weight? If I know that the state will pay for my children to be educated, why should I work harder or make sacrifices for them? If I know that I can get paid (via unemployment benefit) for doing nothing, why should I bother working? It is an essential part of human dignity that we are responsible for our own lives and our own choices. Having a more minimal welfare state makes life more risky and less safe, but this is a good thing. People thrive when they are presented with challenges; too much safety and they become flabby and weak, less likely to fulfil their potential.

People thrive on challenges

The welfare state undermines the bond within families. Parents no longer need to make sacrifices for their children's education, and children of elderly parents no longer need to take responsibility for looking after them. Furthermore, despite its proponents' rhetoric of it being 'love in action', it actually makes people more selfish. People are less likely to give freely to charities, or to help friends, neighbours and family members in trouble, if responsibility for caring for the less fortunate has been taken over by the state. Look at how many more charitable foundations there are in the US, where there is a much less developed welfare state.

A state that takes responsibility for such vital matters as health, education and support in time of hardship away from individuals and families makes people less free, lazier, weaker and more selfish. The fact that some people may fall into unsupported hardship and poverty is a price worth paying for living in a society that promotes human dignity by respecting people's freedom and responsibility. As the economist Friedrich Hayek puts it, 'freedom can only be had at a price … as individuals we must be prepared to make severe material sacrifices to preserve our liberty.'

Practical

Does the welfare state make us richer or poorer?

Obviously, the welfare state costs money. A lot of money. The NHS is the third largest employer in the world, just after the Chinese army and the Indian railways. The question is, what do we get back for our money?

Investing in people makes us all more prosperous

The welfare state makes us richer

If you never take your car to the garage, you will save money. If you never do any repairs on your house, you will save money. But in the long run, you will end up spending more money, because your car will break down and your house will fall apart, and you will have to buy a new car and a new house for much more than you would have spent on maintenance. Investing in maintenance – in looking after valuable assets – costs money in the short term, but saves money in the long term.

The same argument can be applied to the welfare state. By investing in maintaining a state's most vital asset (its people), it makes the state more prosperous. State healthcare makes for a healthier workforce; state education makes for a better educated workforce; state housing improves the well-being and health of the workforce; and benefits for the unemployed and sick, and women on maternity leave, maintain the well-being of people temporarily out of the workforce, so that when they return to work they will be able to contribute more. The money spent on the welfare state is more than recouped by the increased productivity it brings. Moreover, as every well-run business knows, a workforce that is well looked after will be more motivated to work harder.

The welfare state also promotes prosperity by creating jobs, and jobs create wealth. All those millions of NHS workers have to be paid, not to mention teachers and support staff in state schools and civil servants who administer the welfare state, but once they're paid, they spend money on goods and services, providing more work for other people. And the better they're paid, the more money they will have to spend. If doctors get a pay raise and spend it in fancy restaurants, well, that's good news for the people who work in them (as well as motivating doctors to look after the wine waiter when he gets sick, ensuring he can return to his vital work sooner).

The welfare state also promotes risk-taking and creativity, both of which make for a more dynamic economy. Just as a man on a tightrope in a circus will make more daring moves if he knows there is a safety net below him, so people will take more risks when they know there is the metaphorical safety net of the welfare state waiting for them. They will be more willing to invest time and money in setting up a new business which one day might provide employment to thousands of people if they know that they and their families will not face ruin and starvation if the business fails. The creative industries – music, theatre, film, publishing – generate huge amounts of wealth for the UK, but also depend on people entering them being willing to take on a considerable amount of risk early in their careers. Every musician, actor and writer, no matter how successful they may become later, has to start out with little or no income, often for many years. Many now legendary bands, authors and movie stars lived off benefits at the start of their careers. Or rather, they used to. Since benefits have become less generous, people in the creative industries are far more likely to have been privately educated, and to have wealthy parents who can support them through hard times; this greatly reduces the talent pool. J.K. Rowling wrote the first Harry Potter book in a café in Edinburgh when she was a single parent with a young child, living on benefits. She would find that much harder to do now, when she would be expected to find work or have her benefits cut. The Harry Potter brand has brought hundreds of millions of pounds into the British economy, but Harry, Ron and Hermione might never have existed without the welfare state.

No welfare state, no Harry Potter

The welfare state also provides economy of scale. Go to your GP with a tricky health problem, and she can pick the right person to refer you to out of the entire medical profession of the UK. Go to a private hospital, and you will have a more limited range. Moreover, a private hospital has to divert part of its takings to provide dividends for shareholders.

The welfare state makes us poorer

The welfare state as originally conceived by Beveridge was meant only to cover the most basic needs. It was anticipated that people would return to work promptly after receiving medical care, and that they would only need unemployment benefit (which would be the bare minimum to live on) for a very short time. That's not how it's worked out. As healthcare becomes more sophisticated, and people's expectations of it become higher, the cost increases. The more benefits you provide, the more people will want. The more people are employed by the welfare state, the more powerful will be the voices in favour of maintaining it. The welfare state has a natural tendency to grow larger and larger, making the costs go higher and higher. We simply can't afford it.

Moreover, providing so much for so many people is bad for the economy, because it disincentivises hard work and enterprise. If people know all their needs are going to be met, they will have no motive to work harder or to create new businesses. Taking away or reducing welfare provision and making people responsible for looking after themselves will create a more dynamic and energetic culture, which will result in greater prosperity. The tax cuts which reducing welfare would allow will put more money in peoples' pockets, giving them more money to spend, and making them more inclined to start businesses, as they know they will get to keep more of what they earn. Lower taxes and lower public spending will make the economy leaner and fitter.

The welfare state is a monopoly, and monopolies are inefficient. Because the NHS has no competition of any significance, it has no incentive to improve its provision. If it was privatised, the greater choice available would make hospitals raise their game to attract patients.

As well as these fundamental issues, there are also a couple of further questions to be considered about the welfare state.

Should the welfare state be universal or targeted?

Should we make the benefits of the welfare state available to all citizens, or only to those who need them?

In his report, Beveridge regarded universality as a fundamental principle for his planned welfare state. In part, this was in reaction to the notorious 'means test' applied during the Great Depression of the 1930s, which sent inspectors into people's homes, poking and prying, ordering them to sell all but their most essential possessions before they would be granted even the most meagre unemployment benefit. The cruelty and humiliation of this process built a strong resistance to any kind of targeting of benefits in the postwar period. However, as ever, there are arguments on both sides.

Make the welfare state universal

The case for universality is based on the perception of the welfare state as, among other things, a way of building a sense of national community and identity. If it is something which we all own and have a stake in, this will make the country more united. Witness the rainbow posters invoking 'Our NHS' that appeared everywhere during the Covid pandemic. Scandinavian countries are famous for having both a strong welfare state and a strong sense of community and solidarity. When the hedge fund manager's daughter and the hedge cutter's son work together on a class project at school, class barriers become a little lower.

Universality is both simpler and fairer than targeting. When everyone receives a benefit, no one has to be paid to investigate whether they are entitled to it or not. People are more likely to take up benefits if everyone has them, as there is no stigma attached. The process of targeting can be humiliating and subject to error; witness the many stories of vulnerable people having their Universal Credit stopped because they missed meetings due to illness, family crisis or even attending a funeral.

Finally, universality makes the welfare state stronger. The more people involved in an institution, the more voices there are to protect it. One reason for the enduring popularity of and support for the NHS in Britain (former Chancellor of the Exchequer Nigel Lawson once said it was 'the closest thing the English people have to a religion') is that almost everyone benefits from it. By contrast, in the US, 'welfare' is reserved for people in extreme poverty, thereby carrying a sense of shame. A strong argument made for the abolition of private education is that if all children went to state schools, those schools would immediately get better, partly because confident and articulate middle-class parents would insist on it. While private schools still exist, the wealthiest and most powerful people have no personal interest in improving state schools.

The NHS is our national religion

Make the welfare state targeted

The most obvious argument for targeting the benefits of the welfare state is that the less you give out, the less it costs. This enables the government to reduce the burden of taxation, giving people more money to spend.

This argument can then be extended to make the case that targeting is fairer, because it enables the government to give more to those who need it more, awarding benefits more effectively. It is fairer in another sense too. Why should a millionaire get something for free she can easily pay for? Child benefit used to be universal; following the austerity measures of the coalition government of 2010–15, it became available only to those on lower incomes. It was, arguably, absurd that rich parents should get money from the state to feed their children when they were already treating them out of their own income to private school fees and three skiing holidays a year.

Why not just give everyone enough to live on?

This is often known as the **Universal Basic Income (UBI)**. The government gives every citizen, without exception and regardless of their wealth or income, enough to live on, and leaves it at that. No complicated forms to fill in; no armies of civil servants to process claims. It is simple and straightforward.

UBI has not yet been implemented in full in any country in the world, though it has been trialled in partial form in many places, not least during the Covid pandemic, for example in the form of 'stimulus cheques' given to all US citizens.

Give everyone free money

Supporters of UBI claim that having the means to survive is a basic human right, and that governments should ensure that everyone has these means. They also point out that it is not that revolutionary a move. We already accept that all UK citizens have a basic right to healthcare and education for their children free at the point of use without qualification (not to mention the right to call out the police if their house is being broken into, or the fire brigade if it is burning down, without any expectation of having to pay for the service) – why shouldn't they also have the right to have their other needs met?

The simplicity of UBI is very attractive. So too is the absolute equality of its provision; no more shame attached to 'being on benefits'. It may stimulate the economy (in the way that the 'Eat Out to Help Out' scheme of subsidised restaurant meals did in the summer of 2020); if people have more money to spend, they will spend more, creating more jobs. It also enables people to take more risks with innovative projects, sure in the knowledge that they will always have their basic needs met, thereby encouraging the next generation of Richard Bransons and J.K. Rowlings. Looking to the future, it could help solve the problem that automation and the spread of artificial intelligence may make many jobs redundant. It could improve quality of life, encouraging people to spend more time with their families and on voluntary and community work. If people are paid to do nothing, that doesn't mean they will do nothing. Most people prefer to remain active for the sake of their psychological well-being; with UBI, they will have more choice about what form this activity should take. People who receive pensions get money without having to work, but they often lead active and socially valuable lives, giving back to their communities and caring for family members.

Against UBI is the objection of cost. Obviously if no one does any paid work and everyone claims UBI, there won't be any income to feed it. Unexpected shocks to the economy such as the financial crisis of 2008 or the Covid pandemic of 2020–22 may make it impossible to maintain. It isn't fair to give taxpayers' money to people who don't need it. It is immoral to give people money for nothing, and undermines their personal responsibility and autonomy. If you pay people to do nothing, they will, which is bad both for the economy and for their psychological well-being. UBI will also undermine people's sense of solidarity and generosity; if everyone has enough to live on, why should anyone give time or money to those less fortunate than themselves, or do anything to make society fairer?

3. THE POINT OF CLASH

Freedom to or freedom from

On the **moral** question, the point of clash falls on whether you prioritise **freedom and responsibility** or **solidarity and security**.

If you prioritise **freedom and responsibility**, you argue that the benefits of people having full control over their lives and responsibility for the consequences of their choices outweigh the risks of some people falling into unsupported hardship which come from a diminished or absent welfare state. Freedom and responsibility may be costly, but they are worth paying for.

If you prioritise **solidarity and security**, you argue that the benefits of living in a society in which the virtues of compassion and generosity are universalised and institutionalised, and in which no one need fear poverty or deprivation, outweigh the loss of financial and personal freedom which having a welfare state entails. Security and solidarity may be costly, but they are worth paying for.

To simplify the moral clash even further, you can see it as a choice between two kinds of freedom.

Positive freedom – freedom to do what you want with your income and wealth – gives you the opportunity to make your own choices, but means you must live with the consequences of those choices.

Negative freedom – freedom from the harms of economic deprivation – gives you the security of protection, but at the cost of giving up freedom to do as you see fit with your income and wealth.

On the **practical** clash, the question is whether supporting people via the state makes them more productive by giving them the security to manage the ups and downs of life without incurring significant harm, or whether this level of support makes them less likely to work hard and less effective at taking responsibility for their own lives.

To put the practical clash very simply: do you get more out of people by **looking after them**, or by making them **look after themselves**?

4. THE ARGUMENTS

For the welfare state	Against the welfare state
We have a moral duty to look after those less fortunate than ourselves.	We have a moral duty to look after ourselves and those who depend on us.
Prosperity has more to do with luck than hard work or talent, so those with more should help those with less.	Prosperity is the consequence of hard work and talent, so people s hould be allowed to keep what they have earned.
The welfare state creates a sense of community, solidarity and care for others.	The welfare state creates a culture of dependency, in which people get something for nothing and have no sense of responsibility for their own lives.
The welfare state stimulates the economy by making more people more prosperous.	The welfare state damages the economy by requiring punitively high levels of taxation.
The welfare state encourages people to be more creative and willing to take risks because they know they have a safety net.	The welfare state discourages people from taking risks, because they do not need to.
The welfare state is an investment in the economy, promoting the health, education and well-being of the people.	The welfare state is a burden on the economy, taking up resources that would be better off in private hands.
Public provision is better than private provision, because it can operate on a larger scale, and does not have to make a profit.	Private provision is better than public provision, because it can operate more flexibly, and quality is improved by competition.
The welfare state is a mark of a civilised, caring society.	The welfare state is a mark of a decadent, lazy society.

5. THE MOTIONS

1. This house would privatise the NHS.
2. This house would increase funding for the NHS.
3. This house would provide fertility treatment for all who want it on the NHS.
4. This house would refuse treatment for smoking-related illnesses on the NHS.
5. This house would restrict access to the NHS to people on low incomes.
6. This house would make the private provision of medicine illegal.
7. This house would cut benefits.
8. This house would increase benefits.
9. This house would make it compulsory for all local councils to provide housing at a reduced rent for lower-income families.
10. This house would subsidise food prices.
11. This house would subsidise gas and electricity prices.
12. This house would introduce a universal basic income.

Keep thinking…

A selection of further reading to help you think more deeply about the welfare state.

The Citadel, A.J. Cronin (Picador, 1937)

This classic novel, based on the author's own experience as a doctor in the 1930s, shows the reality of life before the NHS. The hero, Andrew Manson, begins his medical career treating miners and their families in a South Wales valley, before being seduced by the money and status of wealthy, smart patients in London. Its disturbing portrayal of the inequalities of health provision before the Second World War has often been cited as a major inspiration for the creation of the NHS.

The Road to Serfdom, Friedrich Hayek (Routledge Classics, 1944)

Hayek rowed decidedly against the tide of the time when he published this book in 1944. In it, he argues that the level of planning and government intervention seen in wartime is a danger to freedom, and must not continue in peacetime. His is an extreme libertarian position: government, in his view, must do as little as possible. He sets up a stark choice. Either we have a completely free market with no state intervention or support, or we will inevitably slide into a Stalinist dictatorship. History proved him wrong, as the great majority of European countries in the thirty years after the Second World War chose a middle path between the two extremes by preserving the capitalist economic system while at the same time supporting a generous welfare state. However, he is important as a major inspiration to Margaret Thatcher. His ideas powered many of her reforms to the welfare state in the 1980s. She is said at one meeting to have pulled out of her handbag a copy of another of his books, *The Constitution of Liberty* (it must have been a big handbag) and slammed it on the table, declaring defiantly '*This* is what we believe!' It was, and we are still living with the consequences.

A Duty of Care: Britain Before and After Covid, Peter Hennessy (Allen Lane, 2021)

Hennessy, a distinguished historian of postwar Britain, draws an optimistic lesson from the unprecedented upheaval of the Covid pandemic. He sees in the extraordinary events of 2020–22 a spirit of generosity and solidarity similar to that generated by the Second World War. Continuing this analogy, he calls for a 'new Beveridge': a reshaping of society and the economy as radical and visionary as that of the generation which established the NHS. Deeply humane and profoundly hopeful, this book will inspire you.

Austerity Britain: 1945–51, David Kynaston (Bloomsbury, 2007)

Kynaston uses a combination of anecdote and analysis to give an excellent account of the introduction of the welfare state, showing how its hopeful vision for the future grew out of the shattered, exhausted landscape of postwar Britain.

The Nanny State Made Me: A Story of Britain and How to Save It, Stuart Maconie (Ebury Press, 2020)

This is nothing less than a love letter to the welfare state. Maconie draws on his own experience as a working-class boy from Wigan, born at the height of the welfare state in the 1960s. He has been enabled by its provision to have a much fuller, richer life than his parents; he is now a successful broadcaster and writer. He intersperses personal memoir with a wide range of interviews with famous and not so famous people, and visits to iconic locations, to make a passionate argument for the welfare state. He believes that the welfare state has made the UK a much better place, and warns of the dangers of dismantling it. If you ever have to argue for the welfare state, pick up this book – I have never come across a stronger case. Maconie comes across as an immensely warm, big-hearted man, who cares deeply for those less fortunate than himself. He is also very funny; several passages had me laughing out loud.

The Five Giants: A Biography of the Welfare State, Nicholas Timmins (Collins, 2017)

Weighing in at over 700 pages, this exhaustively researched and fully documented account of the welfare state all the way from the heady days of the Beveridge Report in the 1940s to the depredations of austerity in the 2010s will tell you everything you ever need to know about postwar British welfare. All that is missing is an account of the impact of the Covid pandemic. Don't be put off by its length. It is an easy read, entertainingly written, with many engaging stories about the key personalities. And you don't have to read it all – the clear organisation and thorough index mean you can dip into selected chapters and sections to find what you need. Timmins is broadly sympathetic to the welfare state, while recognising it has had to adapt to a changing world.

5

PART FIVE

Science and Technology

How to think about science and technology

In this section we think about **science and technology**. Science gives us the power to understand the world; technology gives us the means to control it. Both can be used for great good or great harm.

We think about **online life**. We all spend hours each day on the internet. Our phones and other devices bring us knowledge (and taxis and takeaways); they can also suck our attention away from the people and the world around us. They help us communicate with the people we love; they also spread hatred and lies. They offer us the world for free, but in return they take and keep every last detail of our lives. Do the benefits of the internet outweigh the harms? Who owns the internet? Who should own it? How far should it be regulated?

We think about **climate change**. The climate crisis threatens our very existence on this planet. How should we tackle climate change? Is it the responsibility of governments or individuals? Should those with more sacrifice more? What is the fairest and most effective way to reduce the carbon emissions that cause climate change?

CHAPTER 14

This Online Life

In this chapter we're thinking about...

- **How has the internet changed our lives?**
- **How has the internet improved our lives?**
- **How has the internet made our lives worse?**
- **What might we need to change about our relationship with the online world, both as individuals and as a society?**

1. THE FACTS

A faraway land from long ago

How it used to be

Let me take you on a journey to a faraway land from long ago.

In this strange land, if you wanted to get in touch with a friend to tell them what was happening in your life, you wrote them a letter. You wrote it on a piece of paper with a pen or a pencil. You could type the letter on a heavy metal machine called a 'typewriter', but this was generally considered rather unfriendly – people usually apologised for typing personal letters. You put your address in the top right hand of the page, so your friend knew where to send a reply. You added the date, so they knew when you had written the letter. When you had finished the letter, you took an envelope and wrote your friend's address on it. You put a small sticker in the top right-hand corner of the envelope. This was called a 'stamp' and had the Queen's head on, and you had to go to a shop called the Post Office to buy one (it was a good idea to buy several in one go to save on trips to the Post Office). You folded up your letter and put it in the envelope, which you then sealed. You left the house to take the envelope with the letter in it and would then push it through a slot in a red metal tube about a metre and a half high called a 'postbox'. If you lived in a town, it would only take you a few minutes to walk to one of these, but if you lived in the country you might have to drive for a while to find one.

If your friend lived in the same country, they would get your letter two or three days later. If the letter was urgent, you could pay for a more expensive stamp, which would mean your friend got the letter the next day. If your friend lived abroad, the stamp would cost much more and the letter could take up to a week to reach them. If you were writing to a friend outside Europe, you were best off using an 'airmail' letter. This meant having to write on a pre-printed flimsy form with not much space to write in. However, the letter got there faster – maybe in under a week – and cost less to post.

At long last, your friend got the letter and read it. If they wanted to write back to continue the conversation, they started the process all over again.

If you wanted or needed to communicate with your friend more urgently, you could use a 'telephone'. This was a bulky instrument

You actually had to leave your house to buy stuff

which had to be plugged in and connected to wires outside your house. Most people had only one of these per family, usually kept in the hall. You had to look up your friend's number in the notebook in which you had written their name, address and phone number, then turn a circular dial to select each digit. If your friend was at home, they could answer; if they weren't, they couldn't. If they picked up, you could have a nice chat, though you might be held back by the thought that the phone company was charging you (a lot!) by the minute, and also, if you lived in a house with other people, by the awareness that everyone could overhear your conversation. If your friend lived abroad, talking to them on the telephone would be phenomenally expensive; the only time you would call them would be in a dire emergency, never just to catch up.

In this land, if you wanted to buy something, you had to leave your house and go to a shop. There you could look at things and try them out or on as appropriate. If you decided to buy something, you handed over paper money and / or coins to the shopkeeper. For large sums of money, you might write something called a 'cheque'. This was a small pre-printed piece of paper torn out of a book of cheques provided by your bank. You wrote the sum of money you wanted to pay on the cheque, signed it and dated it (very important or it wouldn't count), and gave it to the shopkeeper. The shopkeeper would take or post the cheque to their bank. The shopkeeper's bank would contact your bank, and money would be moved from your account to the shopkeeper's account. This took at least three days.

If you couldn't or didn't want to leave the house, you could always buy stuff through 'mail order'. To do this, you had to send a letter to a company requesting one of their catalogues. Catalogues were like little books, usually printed in colour on shiny paper with lots of attractive photos of the stuff for sale. You read through the catalogue and decided what you wanted to buy. Then you filled in a form, which was a piece of paper you had to tear out of the catalogue, with your name and address and what you wanted to buy, and put it in an envelope with a cheque (signed with your name and the date, remember!), addressed the envelope, took it to a postbox and posted it. The stuff you ordered would normally come in the post over a week later.

In this land, if you were making your dinner and realised you were missing a vital ingredient, you had to go out to a shop and buy it. If you realised this after five o'clock on a weekday or on a Sunday, you would have to go without, because the shops would be shut.

If you wanted to get a takeaway meal, you could, but you had to walk or drive to the restaurant to get it. Some restaurants gave out menus, so you could order a takeaway over the phone, but you still had to go and fetch it yourself. Taxis existed, but you had to phone some time in advance to book them, or (if you lived in a city) go out into the street, hope you would see one passing, and wave your arm to make it stop.

A record was a disc made of vinyl

If you liked listening to music, you needed to have a machine called a 'record player', which had to be plugged into the electricity in your house. On this you would play 'records', which were discs made of vinyl. You put a needle into a groove on the disc and released the mechanism so the disc went round and round, sending the sound to a pair of speakers. You could buy records in record shops. Music lovers found that records took up a lot of space in their houses. You could also use something called a 'cassette recorder' on which you could play 'tapes', which were small plastic boxes containing magnetic tape that ran from one spool to the other as the sound played. Cassette recorders worked off batteries and could be taken with you anywhere, though the sound quality was not as good as with record players. If you wanted to compile a selection of your favourite songs by different artists, you could do this by putting a blank tape in your cassette recorder and connecting it to your record player and then playing one song after another, taking records on and off the machine. This was a very long and cumbersome process – a real labour of love. You could also record songs off the radio, though this would include material from the DJ, and the sound quality was even worse.

If you liked watching films, you had to wait till they came out in the cinema, and then go to the cinema and watch them at the same time as everyone else. Sometimes films that had been shown in the cinema a long time ago were shown on television, but you had to be in your house in front of the television at the time they were being shown if you wanted to watch them. In the mid-1980s, something called a 'video recorder' was invented. This was a big bulky machine you had to plug in to your television. You inserted a large tape into the machine and set it to record at the time your favourite film or other programme was being broadcast. You could then play the tape later and watch the programme on your TV whenever you wanted. You could also go to a 'video shop' and rent tapes to watch films on your television at home.

If you were interested in sport and weren't able to watch a match in person, you could watch it on the television or follow it on the

Newsflashes came about once every three years

radio. However, you had to hope that your team was the one chosen to have its match broadcast that week, as only one game was shown at a time. If you wanted to know that day's scores, you had to wait until they were read out in a TV programme called 'Final Score'.

If you wanted to know what was happening in the world, you could go to a shop called a 'newsagents' and buy something called a 'newspaper'. This typically consisted of a number of pages with print and photos on, folded together. Different newspapers catered to different levels of education and political viewpoints. They generally came out in the morning, although some had an evening edition or came out only in the evening. If there was important news breaking, newspapers might offer an extra edition in between. For a more immediate update on world events, you could listen to hourly news bulletins on the radio, or watch the news on television. There were three channels on the television, all from the BBC (four following the launch of Channel Four in 1980); two (then three) of them carried news, read out at lunchtime, early evening and late evening. If something really, really important happened, other programmes might be interrupted with a 'newsflash'. Newsflashes came about once every three years.

If you wanted to express your opinion on what was happening in the news, you could write a letter to the editor of your favourite newspaper (which you would have to put in an envelope, put a stamp on, and post). If you were lucky, they might print it on their letters page two or three days later, so that anyone who read that part of the newspaper would know what you thought. The newspaper would normally insist on printing your name and where you lived along with the letter.

If you wanted to find something out, you had to look it up in a book. You could go to a bookshop and see if you could buy a book on your chosen subject, but that was quite an expensive form of research. Better was to go to a 'library' and look at books there. Libraries were large buildings full of books, organised into categories, run by people called 'librarians' who would help you find what you needed. Schools and universities all had libraries, which anyone who attended the school or university could use. There were also public libraries, paid for by local taxes, which anyone who lived in the area could use. The best books for finding stuff out were called 'reference books'. Some of these were dedicated to specific subjects; others, called 'encyclopaedias', were more ambitious, and claimed to have information about everything. The biggest ones were in 26 volumes, one for each letter of

Maps came in books

the alphabet. You tracked down the information you needed by looking at a list at the back of the book called an 'index', which listed topics in alphabetical order and told you which page of the book they were on. You were allowed to take books home from the library, provided you brought them back after a set period, usually two or three weeks, though this did not apply to reference books, as too many people wanted to use them.

If you wanted to go somewhere outside where you lived and didn't know the way, you needed something called a 'map'. This was a diagram showing the roads, streets or landscape of an area. Maps for smaller areas, designed for use by people who were walking, were usually large pieces of paper that folded down small. Maps for car journeys, or for walking round large cities, came in a book called an 'atlas'. If you were driving somewhere unfamiliar on your own, it was very difficult because, unless you had a very good memory, you had to keep pulling over to check the map. The only drivers who never looked at maps were London black cab drivers. In order to get a licence to drive a cab, they had to pass a test called 'the knowledge'. To prepare for this, they had to spend months or even years driving, cycling or walking round London, memorising all the streets, so that they would instantly know how to get from one place to another without having to look it up. If you invited someone to your house for the first time, or to a drink or a meal in a pub or a restaurant they didn't know, you were expected to give them detailed directions, either by dictating them over the phone, or by sending them in a letter.

If you wanted to travel the world to see a bit more of other countries, you went to a shop called a 'travel agent'. The travel agent had lots of information about flights, hotels, places to visit, etc., and would make all the arrangements for you, in return for a fee. If you were really adventurous, you might go to a bookshop and buy your own travel guide. The travel guide would list the addresses of places in the country you were going to visit, so you could write to the hotels, etc., to make a booking. This would take a lot of time, both to write the letters, and to wait for the reply.

If you wanted to take pictures while you were on holiday, to help you remember where you'd been, you had to use a machine called a 'camera'. There were lots of different kinds of camera. The cheaper ones were fairly small and light, but didn't take very good pictures. More expensive ones would take better pictures, but were also heavier and more bulky. You had to put a roll of plastic film inside the camera before you could use it. Films had a set number of pictures you could take on each roll. When you took

The world began to change

a picture, you had no idea how it would turn out. You had to wait till you had taken all the pictures on the roll, then carefully remove the film from the camera, and either post it or take it to a shop, where, for a fee, they would 'develop' it. This meant they would turn the film into paper prints. If you posted the film, you might have to wait a week to get the pictures back; if you took the film to a shop, you could pick them up faster, maybe even the same day, if you didn't mind paying a premium price for express service. If it turned out any or all of your pictures weren't very good, there was nothing you could do about it. If you wanted to share your pictures with your friends, you could paste them into a photo album, and invite your friends round to your house to look at them.

That was the world of my childhood, my adolescence and, if I'm honest, quite a lot of my adulthood. Some of it has disappeared; some of it hasn't. Round about the end of the twentieth century and the beginning of the twenty-first century, the world began to change.

When it changed

Here are some key dates.

1990 British computer scientist Tim Berners-Lee completes work on a collection of networks he calls 'the World Wide Web'.

1994 Amazon is launched.

1995 Microsoft launches Internet Explorer.

1998 Google is launched.

2001 Apple launches the iPod.

2004 Facebook (now Meta) is launched.

2004 Gmail is launched.

2005 YouTube is launched.

2005 Google Maps is launched.

2006 Twitter (now X) is launched.

2006 Google buys YouTube.

2007 Netflix video on demand is first streamed over the internet.

2007 Apple launches the first iPhone.

2009 Uber is launched.

2009 WhatsApp is launched.

2010 Instagram is launched.

2012 Zoom is launched.

2012 Facebook buys Instagram.

2013 Deliveroo is launched.

2014 Facebook buys WhatsApp.

2015 Apple Music is launched.

2016 TikTok is launched.

Big Tech is bigger than many small countries

Who made it change?

What is sometimes collectively known as 'Big Tech' – particularly the so-called 'Big Five' or 'GAFAM', i.e. Google, Apple, Facebook / Meta, Amazon, Microsoft – has gone from being marginal or non-existent at the start of the twenty-first century to being wealthier and more powerful than many small countries. I'm wary of giving statistics, because they are subject to constant change, and by the time you read this book they will be thoroughly out of date. Below, however, is a snapshot from late 2022 to give you a flavour of Big Tech's power and wealth.

Turnover (total value of sales) of Big Tech companies in 2022

Amazon $469 billion

Apple $365 billion

Facebook / Meta $118 billion

Google $209 billion

Microsoft $168 billion

To give a point of comparison, the Gross Domestic Product (GDP) of Finland (population: 5.5 million) for 2021 was $299 billion. (GDP is the total value created by a country in a given period.) So, in terms of income, Facebook / Meta is just over a third the size of Finland, Microsoft is just over half the size of Finland, Google is just over two-thirds the size of Finland, Apple is about 20% bigger than Finland, and Amazon is 50% bigger than Finland.

How did they get all this money? Amazon, Apple and Microsoft sell stuff; Facebook / Meta and Google look like they're free, but

More than half the people in the world use Google every day

make their money via advertising. To make that much money, they have to have a lot of customers (Apple, Amazon and Microsoft) and a lot of users (Facebook / Meta and Google).

How many (as of late 2022)?

Amazon Over 200 million people subscribe to Amazon Prime.

Apple There are over 1 billion active iPhones in the world.

Facebook / Meta 2.9 billion people use Facebook at least once a month.

Google 4.3 billion people use Google every day.

Microsoft 1 billion people use Microsoft Word software and apps.

The population of the world in late 2022 was 8 billion. So one in eight people in the world have an iPhone and / or use Microsoft Word, over a third are on Facebook, and over half use Google every day.

That is a lot.

Who's running all this activity?

Number of employees

Amazon 1,680,000

Apple 164,000

Facebook / Meta 61,000

Google 163,000

Microsoft 221,000

Each figure sounds like a big workforce, but if you consider them in relation to turnover – how much money they take in – it's not that much. So, for example, the workforce of Google is about 1/35th of the population of Finland, and yet Google is worth almost as much as Finland; the workforce of Apple is about the same size as Google's, and Apple is worth more than Finland. Amazon has a big workforce – because they have to deal with real stuff rather than virtual stuff – but they're still worth 50% more than Finland with about 30% of the population. Does that mean that the Finns need to buck their ideas up and start working harder? Unlikely: Finland is widely recognised as a high-functioning, prosperous, successful country with a strong economy and an excellent standard of living (even if it does get a bit cold in winter). It's more likely to mean that the business model of Big Tech gives a relatively small number of people access to a vast amount of wealth, far more than in the wider economy.

Big Tech is wealthy, powerful and answers to no one

Those were the numbers as of late 2022. Look up what they are now (probably using Google …). They will almost certainly be bigger by the time you read this book.

With wealth, of course, comes power. Who has that power? It is a feature of Big Tech companies that they tend to have highly centralised power structures. The founders and / or owners often structure the allocation of shares so that they have a built-in majority; this means that their decisions about the company cannot be overruled. Even if this is not the case, it is likely that the (very few) people at the top will be able to do more or less what they want with the company, with very little expectation of anyone challenging them.

The Prime Minister of Finland also has quite a lot of power over the 5.5 million people who live in Finland. But if you're Finnish, and you don't like what the Prime Minister of Finland is doing, you can vote her or him out in the next election. However, if you don't like what the CEO of Amazon or Apple is doing with their power, well, there's not a lot you can do about it, unless you can raise a few hundred billion pounds to buy their companies off them. What's more, the Prime Minister of Finland only gets to exercise her or his power over a puny 5.5 million people; the CEOs of Big Tech companies have the power to touch the daily lives of billions.

So Big Tech is:

- Very, very **big**
- Very, very **wealthy**
- Very, very **powerful**
- Run by very **few people**, who are almost entirely unaccountable for what they do with their power.

Then again, maybe they deserve all that money and power. Big Tech has, after all, changed our lives immeasurably for the better.

Has Big Tech changed our lives for the better?

How life is now

Here are some things you can do now you couldn't do before the twenty-first century.

- Send a written message to anyone anywhere in the world instantly, at any time, at next to no cost.
- Talk to and / or see anyone anywhere in the world instantly, at any time, at next to no cost.
- Look for and buy almost anything, and have it delivered to your house within 24 hours.
- Buy anything you need without having to touch notes or coins; see immediately what you have spent and on what, and how much you have left in your bank account.
- Order a meal or groceries and have them delivered to your house within the hour.
- Have a taxi arrive where you are and take you where you want to go within minutes.
- Listen to almost any music you want, or watch almost any film you want, at any time, anywhere, at little or no cost.
- Follow any sports event or any news event anywhere in the world live, as it happens, at next to no cost.
- Express your views on any issue at any time in a way that is accessible to anyone anywhere in the world at any time, without revealing your identity unless you want to.
- Find out anything about anything, at any time, instantly, at next to no cost.
- Carry several hundred books in your pocket.
- Be given step-by-step directions from anywhere to anywhere, instantly, at next to no cost.
- Find out about and book flights, hotels, restaurants, museums, concerts, etc., anywhere in the world, at any time, instantly.
- Take photos and videos anywhere, at any time, edit them in any way you want, and instantly share them with anyone anywhere in the world.

That's a much better world than the one we used to have, isn't it?

Or is it?

That's what we're going to be considering in the next section.

2. THE ISSUES

Online life is a fact of life

Two questions:

- Is the internet good for us or bad for us?
- Who controls the internet, really?

1. Is the internet good for us or bad for us?

If you're under twenty-five, your parents will have often told you that you spend too much time on your phone and that it's bad for you. Don't worry: they were told the same thing by their parents about watching television. And their parents were told the same thing by their parents (your great-grandparents) about watching American films in the cinema. And so on and so on, back down the ages: every generation believes that what was there when they were growing up is both normal and indispensable, anything that was invented between when they were fifteen and thirty-five is exciting and will change the world for the better, while anything invented after they were thirty-five is dangerous and worrying.

But are they maybe right this time?

Online technology is more pervasive and universal than any previous technology. However addicted baby boomers were to television, they couldn't carry a telly round in their pockets, to watch on the bus, in bed, in the bath, on the toilet. Their parents may have swooned at James Stewart and Rita Hayworth more than was healthy, but there was only one place in town they could do it, and only at certain times. What's more, they didn't need a television or a cinema ticket to communicate with friends, family or workmates, travel on public transport, find their way around town, find out stuff, buy stuff, or perform almost any other everyday task.

Online life is a fact of life. But is it good or bad for us?

The answer is: a bit of both. Here are some advantages and disadvantages of online life.

ADVANTAGES	DISADVANTAGES
Freedom	Dependence
Information	Disinformation
Connection	Division
Saves time	Wastes time

A smart phone gives you the world in your pocket

The internet gives us enormous **freedom**. We can access an almost infinite amount of information, carry out a huge range of tasks, and communicate with a vast number of people, very quickly, easily and cheaply. When televisions first became available to the majority of households, people who had grown up without them often commented that it was like having the world come into their living rooms. A smartphone brings the world not just into your living room but into your pocket. You can carry around a device which gives you the whole world in your hand, with access to a far greater range of information than a television could ever give you.

On the other hand, online technology can create a great sense of **dependence**. Ever lost or broken your phone? Remember how scary that is? Some people try giving up social media for Lent; it can be a lot harder than going without chocolate. Beyond the practicalities of needing to take an expensive device with you wherever you go, constantly beeping and farting in your pocket and tugging at your sleeve like a demanding toddler, there is also the danger of addiction. Social media sites, online games and apps are all set up to hook you in and keep you there. They feed you just enough 'likes', just enough in-game rewards, to send the dopamine racing through your brain and making you want more. Of course, ever since the first farmers put their shiniest apples at the front of the stall, people selling stuff to other people have gone to a lot of trouble to make it attractive, but this is on a different scale, at a different level of sophistication, and is much harder to detect while it's being done to you.

This dependence on technology can give those who control the technology a lot of power over users. For commercial companies, this can mean locking you into their systems with every new upgrade, taking away any meaningful freedom of choice. It also has the potential to be used by tyrannical governments as a **means of control**. The Chinese government runs a system of so-called 'social credit', whereby citizens' behaviour is monitored via their online activity. If the government doesn't like what you do, you can be blacklisted, and may be banned from certain kinds of travel, schools or jobs.

The internet is a source of **information**. Previous generations had to wait for newspapers to appear or TV or radio news bulletins to come on to find out what was happening in the world. Now, you can get moment-to-moment updates on news and sport whenever you want. In the olden days, if you wanted to know what your friends were up to, you had to go to some trouble to organise a social event, or, if they didn't live nearby, wait for a letter from them. If you were desperate, you could phone them up, though you'd need to wait till your parents were out to avoid them overhearing the gossip / complaining about the phone bill. Now, you can contact all your friends instantly at any time of day or night, and read about and watch what they're up to anywhere in the world.

Is online life real life?

The internet is a source of **disinformation**. You might have had to wait a while for your news pre-internet, but you could be reasonably sure it was accurate, if you went to the right place. Now, facts are crowded out by lies, some of them dangerous and divisive. Millions of people in the United States believe that the 2020 presidential election was stolen, that Covid is a fraud, and that the Covid vaccine is bad for them, in large part because these lies have gone viral online. The first lie is potentially fatal for American democracy; the second and third lies have been literally fatal for thousands of people. People have always spread and believed lies, but now lies can be spread on a different scale and at a different speed. What's more, they're much harder to call out as lies. This is partly because people with access to sophisticated technology can use bots and fake accounts to make their lies look plausible, and partly because there is just so much information, it is very hard to distinguish between what is true and what is false.

On the level of personal relationships, it might look like we can share more with friends and family, but is the life we see online really their life? Who hasn't retaken or edited a photo to make themselves look better? Who doesn't select the moments they share very carefully to give the best impression of the best time they are having? How often do people admit to being bored or lonely or depressed on Instagram?

The internet creates **connection**; it brings people together. Think back to the Covid lockdowns. Businesses could go on functioning without anyone having to leave their homes. Children could go on being educated, connecting directly with their teachers. Friends and families could stay in touch, providing invaluable moral and emotional support at a time of crisis. Even in normal times, the ping or buzz of a message from a friend or loved one landing on your phone can bring comfort, joy, or just a good laugh. The internet means the people you love are always near you, always contactable. No matter where you are in the world, you need never feel lonely.

Social media can bring people together who would otherwise never have found each other, maybe for a shared cause or project to make the world a better place, mustering people for a

The internet means you need never feel lonely

demonstration or a protest, or alternatively for more intimate and personal relationships. Almost everyone I know under the age of thirty-five met their partner online. Think of all the children in the world who would never have existed without dating apps.

The internet brings **division**. Social media apps deliberately direct us to posts and sites that reinforce our existing views, often in more and more extreme ways, so that we end up living in 'tribes' where everyone we interact with reflects back our own prejudices, and we become convinced that people who disagree with us are either evil or stupid or both. Social media also makes people more aggressive. Users hiding behind anonymous accounts can send abusive messages (often racist, homophobic or misogynistic in nature), or even death threats to people they don't agree with. Online pile-ons and cancel campaigns can make people fearful of engaging in public debate.

Interacting with friends online becomes a competitive sport, pitting friends against each other, as everyone strives to make everyone else think they have the most perfect body, the most friends, the best nights out and generally live the perfect life. From FOMO (fear of missing out) to eating disorders and mental health issues, the consequences of this divisive competition can be immensely damaging.

The internet **saves time**. Your parents and grandparents had to work hard at seeking out the things they wanted to buy, going to the right part of town, walking from shop to shop, making their own comparisons; now you can type in what you want on your phone, instantly see a full selection, and order what you need in minutes or seconds. A song, a film, a taxi, a meal are all just a few swipes and clicks away. We have so much more time to enjoy the good things of life than previous generations.

The internet **wastes time.** Having a phone is like having a small child. It demands constant attention. There is always something to do: check your messages; update your social media feed; make sure you haven't missed the latest update on sport, news or celebrity gossip. And the more attention you give it, the more it demands. All that time staring at a screen stops you interacting with real people in real life; it prevents you from rejoicing at the late afternoon sunlight breaking through autumn leaves; it makes you bump into lamp posts. How long nowadays can you concentrate on one task? When was the last time you finished writing an essay in one go? When did you last spend all morning reading a book, or giving a friend your undivided attention?

Like many things in life, whether the internet is good or bad depends on what you do with it.

Having a phone is like having a small child

2. Who controls the internet, really?

It looks like the answer is simple: nobody.

Pre-internet, commerce and communications were controlled by powerful gatekeepers. If you wanted to tell the world about something that was happening, your only hope was that a journalist would take an interest and that a newspaper would print your story, or that a radio or television company would broadcast it. If you wanted to express an opinion about something, you had to hope that a newspaper would print your letter or, if you were really lucky, accept an article from you. Alternatively, you could find a 'phone-in' show on the radio, and hope that your call would be taken. If your story or opinion didn't fit with the political agenda of the newspaper (or if they just didn't have space for it), or if you couldn't get through to the radio station – too bad.

Now, anyone can post anything anywhere any time at next to no cost without anyone controlling them, because the internet belongs to everyone. No one owns the internet. It is just there, in cyberspace, and anyone can put anything up at no charge. As the inventor of the World Wide Web, Sir Tim Berners-Lee, tweeted at the Opening Ceremony to the 2012 Olympics in London, 'This is for everyone.' So the internet is the most democratic and egalitarian invention in history.

Or is it?

It is of course possible for anyone who owns a device and has an internet connection to post anything for anyone to read. But will they read it? How on earth do you connect the world's eyeballs with your post?

As of late 2022, there were an estimated 1.8 billion websites in the world, (although fewer than 400 million are active). Approximately 500 million Facebook posts were uploaded, 867 million tweets were sent and 100 million photos were shared on Instagram every day. You may have something to say. But how are you going to get people to listen to you, in the midst of all this noise?

Getting people's attention – getting their eyeballs on your site or your post – is not just personally gratifying. It is also **valuable.** It allows you to **sell** things to people, and it allows you to **influence** them. It gives you access to two of the most eagerly sought-

If you're not paying for the product, you are the product

after commodities in the world: **wealth** and **power**. So it is little wonder that there is a whole industry dedicated to capturing and controlling our attention.

Do you carefully read every word of the terms and conditions each time you buy a new device, upgrade to a new piece of software or download a new app, unpicking all the legal implications of each clause, taking professional advice as appropriate? Me neither. If you did, you wouldn't have time to do much else. One investigation estimated that if the average person scrutinised properly the terms and conditions they signed up to for the tech they use, it would take them 76 full workdays a year. There may be a reason those terms and conditions are long and hard to understand. When you tick that box, you are very likely to be agreeing not just to using the device, software or app, but to letting it use you. The **data** you share about yourself may be necessary to make the device, software or app work for you, but it is also immensely valuable to the company that makes the device, software or app. And once you've ticked that box, your data belongs to them. They will know where you like to shop; what you like to eat; what you like to watch; what you like to wear; what you like to listen to; where you like to go; what you do when you get there; what you think about the world. They will have similar information on all your friends and contacts.

What will they do with this information?

One thing they will do is **sell** you stuff. If you download *The Godfather*, you might be interested in other gangster movies, so they'll put some in your stream, making you an offer they'll hope you can't refuse. If you order a vindaloo from Deliveroo, you'll soon be hearing about other Indian restaurants in your area. Buy a new pair of sunglasses online, and ads will start popping up for swimsuits and sun cream.

But it won't be just through your purchases that they will find out about you. Being online isn't just about buying and selling stuff. It's also about expressing yourself. If rising levels of immigration make you angry, and you say so online, you will be directed to sites that are even more angry about immigration. Then those sites will direct you to even more angry sites, saying worse and worse things about migrants. And so on and on and on. If, on the other hand, what riles you up is hostility to migrants, you will be directed to like-minded sites, which say worse and worse things about people who don't like immigration. Either way, you will find yourself living in an **echo chamber**, having your own views repeated back to you and amplified, unable to hear from anyone who doesn't agree with you. Maybe you're not interested in politics. Maybe what you really care about is hand-knitted frogs. In that case, you will be steered towards sites and posts filled with woolly amphibians, where you can meet kindred spirits who believe that nothing matters more than what size buttons you should use for their eyes.

Social media locks you in an echo chamber

This will happen not because the internet companies want you to find moral support for your deeply held beliefs, or new friends to share your hobbies with, but because they want you to keep clicking. The more you click, the more ads you will see; the more ads you see, the more money they make. And they won't just advertise their own stuff. They will sell your data to other companies, so those companies can sell you their stuff.

So having access to your data can make a lot of people a lot of **money**. But it can also give them something else: **power.**

Let's think about how the internet has changed the way democracies work. Voting is the cornerstone of democracy (see Chapter 5, **Democracy**). It's the ultimate expression of freedom. Citizens weigh up the pros and cons of the different parties and candidates, and pick the one they like best. You cast your vote in secret. No one is allowed to know (unless you choose to tell them) how you voted, so no one can intimidate you or bribe you into voting a certain way.

They can, however, **influence** you.

Pre-internet, influencing voters mostly happened openly and in public. Volunteers pushed leaflets through letterboxes. Activists went from door to door, finding out who supported their candidate or party, trying to persuade people to vote their way. Similar conversations might go on between friends, family and workmates. Parties ran meetings. Posters were put up. Candidates gave speeches. Newspapers, TV and radio reported the campaign, informing voters of what the different candidates and parties were saying. Campaigners would still target their message, crafting speeches and leaflets around the particular concerns of an area – this part of town has a hospital threatened with closure, so let's talk about how we'll spend more on the NHS; that area has a high crime rate, so let's promise to put more bobbies on the beat – but, for the most part, the process of debate and discussion that led up to an election was a shared and public experience.

Not any more.

Why bother engaging with people in real life?

Now, if you want to change people's minds, there's a way to do it that's much more individualised, much quicker, much more effective, and much cheaper. Why spend money on hiring a site for a poster which people might never go past, and might not notice if they do, when you can send them a meme via social media (which will probably be funnier and more memorable than the poster ever would be)? Why cajole or hire activists to pound the pavements talking to people, when you can flood their inboxes with messages? Why go up and down the country talking to half-empty, draughty church halls when you can record yourself speaking from your own home and have a million people listen to you (probably feeling more connected to you than they ever would at a public meeting, as you're sitting in a cosy armchair with a picture of your wife and kids in the background and your cat on your lap)? Why hold a mass meeting in the rain, when you can post a tweet that goes viral in seconds? Why hope the media will report you favourably when you can talk to voters directly, via a little device they carry round in their pockets?

What are the advantages for us of these new ways of selling people stuff, and of changing our minds? And what are the problems?

Online marketing might actually be in customers' interests. Perhaps you hadn't heard of that gangster movie, or were looking for a new place to munch a masala, or needed that nudge to refresh your swimwear. Or perhaps you're happy to accept the ads as the price of using the free service, and ignore them. What's more, the internet allows people to set up and market their own businesses at little or no cost, expanding opportunities for budding entrepreneurs, and widening customer choice. Once, Freddie, whose passion is knitting frogs, would have had to save up a lot of money or take out a loan to rent a shop, and hope that fellow frog-lovers would find it and buy his creations. Now, he can set up his own website and soon be dispatching Freddie's Frogs to delighted customers from Croydon to Karachi. He's making a living; frog-lovers have got what they always wanted. What's the problem?

Politics online may actually be even more democratic. All it is doing is what campaigners have always done, that is, reach out to voters. It's just doing it on a larger scale, and this is a good thing for democracy. The internet engages far more people in political discussion and debate than ever before. Pre-internet, it took a considerable level of commitment to give up an evening to travel to a public meeting and hear what the candidates had to say. If you wanted to engage in debate in these meetings, you had to be brave enough to raise your hand in front of a crowd, and then hope that the chair of the meeting would pick you. You could follow the campaign through the newspapers and on TV or radio, but even that demanded setting aside quite a lot of time and energy (and you had no way of engaging with the debate, other than shouting at the telly). Now, you can pull a device out of your pocket while you are sitting on a bus or train, or waiting in a queue at a coffee shop, and immediately be able not just to hear the arguments on both or all sides, but also to engage in active live debate yourself.

Social media can bring down tyrants

What is more, the accessibility and affordability of online campaigning is a godsend in non-democratic countries. Once, tyrants could tear down posters, shut down printing presses and arrest speakers at rallies. Much harder for them to monitor millions of social media messages which expose their iniquities and share people's hopes for the future, and can summon a crowd to a demonstration against their rule in minutes.

It is true that the internet can be a way of widening **choice** and **availability** in the economic sphere, and can be a way of widening **participation** and **access** in the democratic sphere. But there are still issues with its role in both areas. These have to do with **transparency** and **power**.

To start with **transparency**. Marketing existed pre-internet, but you could see it coming. Businesses promoting their products or services used advertisements in magazines and newspapers; slots in the ad breaks on TV and radio; posters; leaflets pushed through your door. You might have resented the interruption to your reading or viewing or listening, or the pile of junk mail on your doormat, but you knew what it was and what it was trying to do to you. Now, your attention is steered and your choices tweaked by stealth, under your radar. The algorithms which Big Tech companies use (and sometimes sell) to mine your data and work out what you might spend your money on are highly complex, unknown and unaccountable. The internet seems to give you infinite choice, but in fact your choices are highly constrained and controlled by these invisible algorithms.

It costs a lot of money to set up and run these systems, so they naturally tend to be biased towards already powerful and wealthy businesses. The lone entrepreneur who wants to share his passion for knitted frogs with the world is actually very unlikely to get anywhere once a big business realises there's money in small amphibians, as they can afford to manipulate the search engine to ensure they are always on the first page. Freddie's Frogs may

You are led by an invisible hand

be better than those sold by a major supermarket chain, but you'll never get to see them.

Transparency also matters in the political sphere. As with commerce, so with politics, the internet is not as open as it looks. You might think that you are free to explore whatever opinions and ideas you like online. But, just as with advertising, there are sophisticated (and expensive) algorithms which will put in front of your eyes ideas and information that will confirm your world view rather than challenge it. Of course this happened pre-internet to a degree. Lefties would read *The Guardian*, and nod along with its liberal views; Conservatives would be comforted to recognise the way they saw things was echoed in the pages of *The Daily Telegraph*. Talking things through in the pub or the cafe with like-minded friends would remind you of how right you were. But in both cases, those were conscious and deliberate choices. You knew which newspaper you were reading, because you'd handed over the money for it; you knew which friends were influencing you, because you could look them in the eye. And you'd decided, of your own free will, to read *The Guardian* or be friends with Adetola. Now, however, you are led by an invisible and unaccountable hand towards sites that influence you without admitting to influencing you, because they just seem like what is out there and available to anyone.

The lack of transparency also makes it harder to check the **accuracy** of what you see online. Is Nora from Neasden, who shares her heartrending story about all the muggings in her area committed by asylum seekers, and urges you to vote for greater restrictions on immigration, for real? Maybe not. Is that picture of the politician who campaigns for restrictions on immigration dressed up in a Nazi uniform at a party genuine? It may be a deepfake. Politicians and their followers have been telling lies since the days of the Ancient Greeks, but pre-internet it was easier to call them out. You could see the person who was telling the lie in the flesh. Newspapers had (have) editors and fact-checkers; TV and radio stations had (have) codes of conduct, and reputations to protect. Outright lies could (can) ultimately be prosecuted under the laws of libel (for written communication) or slander (for the spoken word). But whereas you can challenge and / or sue a publication or a person, you can't do that to a fictional character created online or an anonymised social media page or handle. The stories about mugging migrants and Hitler-loving politicians may or may not be true. You have no way of telling. The danger then is that a healthy scepticism about what is online can turn into an unhealthy cynicism, which refuses to accept any information,

Knowledge is power

even from reliable and trustworthy sources, which does not confirm your existing beliefs. If the government tells you that 40,000 illegal immigrants have crossed the Channel this year, why should you believe them any more or less than a post that says it's really 400,000? Or 4 million? Or none, and that the images you see on the news of dinghies washing up in Dover are all staged by actors? When everything is equally believable, nothing is believable. And when we can't agree on the facts, we can't have the kind of debates and discussions on which democracy relies to function properly.

So the lack of transparency about where and how our attention is being directed by businesses and political campaigners can actually restrict our choice as consumers, and make us less well informed and less engaged as citizens. It puts us less in control.

Then there's **power**.

Knowledge is power. Data – particularly the vast quantities of data about our most intimate thoughts and actions that can be scraped from our multiple interactions with online devices every day – is knowledge about people (about us) on a very large scale, larger than has ever been seen before in history. So the access to your data that you cheerfully hand over when you tick that little box on your new software, device or app, impatient to get on and start using it, gives the companies who own it (and the companies they sell it to) enormous power over you.

How do they use that power?

The way that commerce is supposed to work in a capitalist system is that the consumer has a free choice between different goods and services. Competition will drive out the bad and promote the good. However, if companies own enough data, and can afford to set up sophisticated enough algorithms, they can manipulate that choice by directing consumers' attention (that precious resource) towards their own products. The consumer no longer has a true freedom of choice. Acquiring that data and setting up those algorithms costs money, so that power over consumers is likely to be held by already very wealthy companies, thereby making them wealthier and more powerful still. As a few companies become bigger and wealthier, they can kill off / buy up smaller companies, and you end up with an economy dominated by a very few large, powerful companies – a situation close to (or an actual) monopoly, in which consumers have little or no freedom of choice.

This monopoly of commercial power is particularly evident in the

We have less choice than we think

case of the Big Tech companies. We long ago stopped saying 'look it up on a search engine'; we say 'google it'. A privately owned company has colonised part of the English language. Other search engines are available, but half the world's population googles every day. This gives Google enormous unaccountable power to influence what we see, buy and think, a power made greater by their access to our data. Other Big Tech companies exercise a similar monopolistic power by the way their products are set up. If you love reading, it's wonderful to have hundreds of books in your pocket on your Kindle, but every one of those books has to be bought from Amazon. Once you've got your first iPhone from Apple, you're in it for life; sooner or later your phone will die and you'll have to buy the upgrade. Leaders of these companies would react in horror to the socialist notion that the government should take over parts of the economy and run them, giving consumers no choice. But, in practice, large parts of our lives are run by companies which severely restrict our choices, and which, unlike governments in democracies, cannot be removed by a popular vote.

Politics is, by definition, about power. But, pre-internet, that power was largely out in the open. If a candidate or a campaigner was trying to influence you, you could see how they were doing it. Now, given access to enough data and the right algorithms, it is possible to manipulate people's views, and indeed spread outright and dangerous lies, in a very sophisticated way and on a very large scale. You can target your message very precisely, telling people exactly what they want to hear, whether or not it is true. You can bombard them with so many lies that they stop believing the truth. The successful Leave campaign in the 2016 Brexit referendum was greatly assisted, not by the careful presentation of logical and considered arguments in favour of the UK leaving the EU, but by access to vast amounts of personal data about UK voters sold to it by Cambridge Analytica which enabled them to target ads (many of them highly inaccurate and misleading) in favour of voting Leave to millions of people, each one carefully crafted to appeal to the voter's own personal fears and anxieties. Vladimir Putin's regime in Russia pays hundreds of people to work full-time creating fake accounts on social media to divide and destabilise the societies of Russia's enemies. Those are just two examples of covert misinformation being used to change the world; there are many more, and their number is only likely to grow. The point is that the internet allows people and organisations to spread dangerous misinformation in a sophisticated but completely unaccountable way, giving them enormous unseen power.

Are we truly free online?

On the one hand, the internet is the most open and free space ever invented; on the other hand, it can be (and is) controlled and manipulated by the wealthy and powerful to make themselves even more wealthy and powerful.

3. THE POINT OF CLASH

We're not going to uninvent the internet – it is here to stay. But we can think about how best to use it.

Does the **freedom** and **opportunity** given by the internet outweigh the **dependence** it can cause? Does it make us **better informed** about the world, or does it spread **misinformation** too easily? Does it **connect** people or **divide** them? Does it **save us time** or **waste our time**? Is the **convenience** provided by the internet worth the sacrifice of our **privacy**? Is allowing **powerful** and **wealthy** organisations access to the most intimate information about our lives a price worth paying for having **cheap**, **easily available** goods and services?

Does the **openness** and **immediacy** of the internet help or hinder proper **democratic debate**? How **free** is free speech on the internet? Does it share power more **equally**, or concentrate it in **fewer hands**? Should we find ways to **spread that power more widely**?

The internet is an immensely powerful and all-pervasive force in our lives. The point of clash turns ultimately around how that power is used.

4. THE ARGUMENTS

The internet has improved our lives	The internet has made our lives worse
We have freedom to do more things, see more things, know more things, buy more things.	We are dependent in an addictive and destructive way on our devices.
The internet provides us with a wealth of information.	Much of that information is inaccurate; information online can be manipulated in dangerous ways.
The internet connects people.	The internet divides people into warring factions, and encourages social division.
The internet makes so many tasks so much more efficient.	The internet takes us away from real life by keeping us glued to our devices, and diminishes our powers of concentration.
The internet gives us more choice as consumers.	Access to our data via our internet usage allows businesses to sell us things we don't want or need.
The internet gives us more freedom as consumers.	Access to our data via our internet usage gives businesses enormous unaccountable power over us.
More sophisticated technology gives us more control over our lives.	The concentrated monopolistic power of Big Tech companies gives them more power than most democratic governments.
The internet provides a space for free, open, unrestricted debate.	The internet encourages anonymous abuse, bullying and shaming.
The internet allows people to express their views freely, without the need for powerful gatekeepers.	The internet allows powerful and anonymous organisations to manipulate public debate.
The internet promotes democracy by encouraging the free exchange of views.	The internet has been hijacked by unaccountable organisations and despotic governments which spread division and disinformation.

5. THE MOTIONS

1. This house would make social media companies legally responsible for the content of their sites.
2. This house would ban political advertising from social media.
3. This house would not allow children under 16 / 14 / 11 access to social media / the internet.
4. This house would ban mobile phones in schools.
5. This house would make it illegal for internet companies to retain customers' data.
6. This house would ban anonymous social media accounts.
7. This house believes that the internet is good for democracy.
8. This house believes in free speech on the internet.
9. This house would delete social media.
10. This house would introduce one compulsory offline day every week.
11. This house believes the internet is bad for our mental health.
12. This house believes that the internet has done more harm than good.

Keep thinking...

A selection of further reading and viewing to help you think more deeply about the issues around online life.

Ten Arguments for Deleting Your Social Media Accounts Right Now, Jaron Lanier (Bodley Head, 2018)

The title doesn't pull any punches, and nor does the rest of the book. Lanier has worked in Silicon Valley for many years, so he knows from the inside just how social media is set up, and how it isn't always for our benefit. He makes a passionate polemical argument about the damage that social media, and our addiction to it, can do to us as individuals and as a society. He ends, though, on a hopeful note, imagining a better future.

Clear Bright Future, Paul Mason (Penguin, 2019)

Mason is a very political writer, and an active campaigner himself. He sends a stark warning about the dangers of the immense concentration of power in a few hands that online technology can bring, but combines this warning with a passionate and inspiring plea for the rediscovery of human values.

This Is Not Propaganda, Peter Pomerantsev (Faber and Faber, 2019)

Pomerantsev's parents were dissidents in the Soviet Union, secretly working against the Communist dictatorship, risking their lives in the cause of freedom, until they were forced to flee to England. Pomerantsev follows his parents' example of campaigning against the abuse of power. He reveals how, in the internet age, power is not always exercised by men with guns. It works in a much more subtle, insidious and dangerous way by attacking people's minds via social media, sowing fear, anxiety and division. Pomerantsev gives us examples from countries around the world to show the damage online manipulation and disinformation can do to democracy and to our hopes for a civilised society.

The Age of Surveillance Capitalism, Shoshana Zuboff (Profile, 2019)

Zuboff spent ten years researching and writing this book. The depth of her knowledge and the sophistication and intelligence of her argument make this an essential book for anyone who wants to understand the impact of the digital revolution. She argues that the invention of the internet has, almost by accident, given rise to an entirely new form of economic arrangement, which nobody chose and nobody voted for. The phenomenal quantity and complexity of knowledge about every last aspect of our lives held by Big Tech companies gives them an unprecedented level of power over us. No longer do big companies just sell us stuff; now they tell us how to behave, without us even knowing we're being told. If you read just one book about how the internet has changed our lives, make it this one. It's a challenging read, but worth it.

The Social Network, directed by David Fincher (Columbia Pictures, 2010)

Jesse Eisenberg plays Mark Zuckerberg in this dramatisation of the early days of Facebook, with a razor-sharp script by Aaron Sorkin. It shows how Zuckerberg turned what started out almost as a student prank into one of the most powerful and wealthy companies in history, through a combination of new technology, old-fashioned ruthlessness, and quite a lot of luck. Bear in mind this is a drama, not a documentary; nonetheless, it gives a very good idea of the motivations driving the people at the top of Big Tech.

CHAPTER 15

Climate Change

In this chapter we're thinking about...

- **What is climate change and what needs to be done about it?**
- **How should we respond most fairly to climate change?**
- **How should we respond most effectively to climate change?**

1. THE FACTS

More stuff means more gas

What is climate change?

Climate change is caused by too high a level of **greenhouse gases** in the Earth's atmosphere.

Greenhouse gases are principally carbon dioxide (CO^2), methane and nitrous oxide. They are released into the atmosphere in various ways; below are the most significant ways in which this happens.

- **Fossil fuels** – coal, gas and oil – release CO^2 into the atmosphere when they are burnt. Vehicles, planes, heavy industry and the energy needed to heat or air-condition buildings are the biggest consumers of fossil fuels.
- **Trees** absorb CO^2 from the atmosphere, so the fewer trees there are, the more CO^2 there will be. Cutting down trees to sell the wood and / or to make space for building houses and factories, or to release land to graze livestock, results in more CO^2 remaining in the atmosphere.
- Dumping **waste** in landfill produces methane when the waste decomposes.
- The use of certain **fertilisers** in agriculture produces nitrous oxide.
- **Dairy farming** produces methane (from cows burping and farting).

Since the start of the Industrial Revolution in the early nineteenth century, humans have been releasing greenhouse gases into the atmosphere in increasing quantities, which are now far above levels that the Earth can deal with naturally.

This has been driven by, among other things:

- Increasing prosperity leading to more **stuff** being made (requiring factories to make it, and landfill to get rid of it when we don't need it any more).
- The invention and more widespread use of **cars**, **planes** and other forms of motorised transport.
- People making themselves more comfortable by using **heating** or **air conditioning** in their homes and workplaces.

- Increasing access to and appetite for **meat and dairy products**, leading to much more land being taken up by (burping and farting) animals.
- The growth of the human population, now at more than 8 billion people. In 1804, there were only 1 billion people in the world.

Most of the above developments have been more pronounced in economically developed countries than in less economically developed countries.

What greenhouse gases do

The temperature inside a greenhouse is higher than outside because the glass allows heat from the Sun to pass through, but then traps it inside the greenhouse. Greenhouse gases work in the same way. They allow heat from the Sun to pass through the atmosphere, but when that heat is reflected back from the Earth, rather than escaping out of the atmosphere as used to happen naturally before the increase in greenhouse gases, they trap the heat, like a greenhouse, causing the temperature of the Earth to rise.

How much has the temperature of the Earth risen?

Between 1900 and 2015, average global temperatures increased by 1°C, having remained essentially stable throughout previous recorded history. This increase has gone faster over time. In the sixty years between 1860 and 1920, temperatures increased by 0.2°; in the twenty years between 1980 and 2000, they went up by 0.4°; it then took only fifteen years, from 2000 to 2015, to see another 0.4° rise. The ten years between 2010 and 2020 were the hottest ten-year period on record; 2016 and 2020 were the hottest years on record. In July 2022, the UK recorded its first ever 40° heat. Current predictions give a more than 50% chance of a rise to 1.5° above pre-industrial levels by 2026.

Why does temperature rise matter?

A one-degree rise in temperature doesn't sound like much. You'd barely notice it on a normal day. It wouldn't even be enough to take your jumper off. And if the rise goes to two degrees, three, four, even five or six, so what? Just change into shorts and open the windows, surely? What's the problem?

Scared yet? You should be

Here's the problem.

Here are some changes to the climate caused by global warming.

- A rise in sea level caused by ice melting at the poles.
- An increase in the number of destructive storms.
- An increase in the number of heatwaves.

Here are some of the consequences of those changes in the climate. Some of these have already happened / are happening; others will happen if climate change is not stopped.

- Longer, harder droughts, hitting water and food supplies.
- Flooding of coastal cities (including, eventually, London, New York, Jakarta and Shanghai).
- Destruction of property and infrastructure through storm damage.
- The death and displacement of large numbers of people through storms and flooding.
- Wildfires causing the destruction of large swathes of forest and other habitats, property and infrastructure, while also killing people and wildlife on a massive scale.
- The death of large numbers of people because of extreme heat.
- Many parts of the world rendered effectively unlivable for long periods of time by extreme heat.
- An increase in the spread of deadly diseases such as malaria as pests move into new areas.
- The extinction of an increasing number of species as many animals' original habitats become unsustainable.
- The destruction of crops by flooding and / or heatwaves leading to catastrophic food shortages.
- Mass migration of millions of people escaping the above consequences of climate change, leading to the breakdown of societies and violent conflict over ever-decreasing resources.

Are you scared yet? You should be. Climate change is not something that can or should be ignored. It represents an **existential** threat: that is, the very survival of humanity (and many other species) depends on its being tackled.

Stopping climate change is very simple but very hard

It needs saying, by the way, that one thing that is **not** a matter for debate is the existence of climate change. There are no arguments for the case that climate change is a fraud because there are no facts to support such a case. The scientific evidence – not to mention the evidence before our eyes, as we swelter in heatwaves every summer, and clear up after flood damage most winters – is overwhelming and incontrovertible. Climate denial is a lie: a very dangerous lie. It is like a man who has had a major heart attack and who has been rushed into hospital for emergency surgery getting up off the trolley outside the operating theatre to tell the doctors that all he's got is indigestion from last night's curry, he doesn't need any treatment, thank you very much, he's got a lot of important meetings he needs to get back to, and can he go home now, please? His denial puts his life at risk. Similarly, climate denial puts the future of the whole of humanity at risk, and should not be given airtime.

What can and should be debated is the most **effective** and **fairest** response to the fact of climate change.

What can be done about climate change?

Simple. Reduce to a minimum emissions of greenhouse gases. Easy. Job done.

How are we going to do that?

Ah, now you're asking the hard question. There are a number of possible ways. We will look at the pros and cons of each one in the next section.

What has been done so far?

A global problem needs a global solution: something a bit bigger than printing on both sides of the paper or taking your reusable cup to the coffee shop. In 1994, the United Nations set up the United Nations Framework Convention on Climate Change (UNFCCC). This has convened annual meetings in cities across the world ever since, known as Conferences of the Parties (COP). At the time of writing, there have been 27 COP meetings. Here are the three most significant, and what they agreed.

1997 – COP3, Kyoto, Japan

This established the Kyoto Protocol. The two key elements of the protocol were as follows.

1. **Emissions trading.** Each country has an allocation of permitted emissions. If a country wants to go over its allocation, it can buy permits to do so from less-polluting countries which do not use all of their own allocation. Emissions become a commodity like wheat or oil, which can be bought and sold.

2. **Emissions reduction.** The majority of industrialised countries agreed to a legally binding target of a reduction of 6–8% in emissions below 1990 levels, during the 2008–12 period.

These two major commitments were undermined when the US Congress failed to ratify the Kyoto Protocol, despite support from the president at the time, Bill Clinton. Clinton's successor as president, George W. Bush, withdrew the US entirely from the protocol in 2001. Australia and Russia also refused to ratify it. Between them, these three countries account for over 50% of global emissions of CO^2.

2009 – COP15, Copenhagen, Denmark

The purpose of COP15 was to establish a successor to the (imperfectly implemented) Kyoto Protocol when it ran out in 2012. Hopes were high with the recent election of Barack Obama as US president. However, COP15 broke up without significant progress. It took another six years to come up with an agreement.

2015 – COP21, Paris, France

At COP21, resulting in the Paris Agreement, almost all the countries in the world committed themselves to keeping the rise in global temperatures to 'well below' 2° above pre-industrial levels, thereby preventing some (though not all) of the most extreme effects of climate change. They would achieve this by reducing emissions to net zero (that is, adding no new CO^2 to the atmosphere) by the middle of the twenty-first century. All countries would be obliged to log and share their emissions. There was an aspiration to keep the rise to 1.5°, which would require a 50% reduction by 2030. The US briefly withdrew from this agreement in 2020 under President Trump, only to rejoin in 2021 under President Biden.

COP21 raised hopes around the world. However, more sceptical observers noted that while the targets agreed were admirable, the difficulty lay in enforcing them. Given the very considerable economic sacrifices that they would entail, there would be a strong temptation for governments to backslide on them. As there is no international body with the power to impose significant sanctions for non-compliance, the future survival of humanity effectively depends on a great many powerful people from a wide range of cultures and backgrounds all being willing simultaneously to take deeply unpopular actions with no immediate benefit and at great cost to themselves.

And you thought it was hard getting your mum to turn down the heating.

2. THE ISSUES

The five farmers

Here is a story which will help us to think about climate change.

There is a village, surrounded by five dairy farms. In the middle of the village, there is a big field called a common. It's called a common because it doesn't belong to anyone. Everyone can use it. The dairy farmers round about depend on the common, because it's full of grass, and their cows need to eat grass. Every day, the dairy farmers bring their cows to the common to graze (that is, eat grass). Each dairy farm has a herd of twenty cows. That makes a hundred cows, who spend all day every day eating grass. There's enough grass on the common for the hundred cows to eat their fill every day. The grass that's eaten is replaced by more grass regrowing. The five farmers can look on contentedly at the peaceful scene as the hundred cows chomp on the green stuff, interrupted only by the occasional moo, burp or fart. The cows get on with each other, as cows usually do. So do the farmers. So far.

Why do the farmers have the cows? What's in it for them? What's in it for them is the milk they take from the cows every morning. (If you're vegan, suspend your beliefs for a while to enter into the story.) They can sell the milk, or make the milk into butter and cheese and sell that. That's how they make their living; that's how they support their families.

Then, one day, one of the farmers (let's call him Alex) decides he'd like to do a bit better for himself. He's just had another child (his fifth!) and he wants to move into a bigger house. That's going to cost more money. How will he pay for it? He can't make any of his existing cows produce more milk. So he goes to the market and buys five more cows. He has to pay for them, of course, but before long he's earned that money back in the income he receives from the extra milk production. Soon his earnings are up by 25%. Lucky Alex! He and his family can move into their dream home. Of course, the extra cows need somewhere to eat grass. But that's not a problem. The common doesn't belong to anyone, so he doesn't have to pay to use it. There's no added cost in taking his extra cows to the common every day.

Individual benefit vs the common good

It's not long before the other farmers notice what Alex has done. Word gets round the village pub that Alex and his family have moved into a bigger house. What's more, he's got a new car, and his wife and kids have nice new clothes; he seems to have money to burn these days. What's his secret? Expanding his herd, that's what. The other farmers decide they'd like some of what Alex has got. So, one by one, little by little, they head to the market and buy more cows. They produce more milk, more butter, more cheese. They earn more money. Now they can afford bigger houses, new cars, new clothes. They're spending more in the village shop and down at the village pub: good news for the shopkeeper and the publican, who themselves now have more money to spend. Prosperity all round; everyone's a winner.

Or are they? After a while, Alex and his fellow farmers notice that their cows are getting thinner and the milk yield is going down. Why? The answer is on the common. The grass there is getting thinner and thinner. There's less and less for the cows to eat. When there were just a hundred cows on it every day there was enough to go round. Now there are far more than a hundred, the grass is all used up and there's no time for it to regrow. If the farmers got rid of their extra cows, that would solve the problem; there'd be enough to go round again. But of course if they did get rid of the extra cows, their income would drop. They might have to move out of their big houses, give up their car, skip the fancy meals at the pub. So they keep their cows. And the grass keeps getting thinner. Eventually, there is none left. The common turns to dust and mud. The cows get sick and die of starvation. The farmers go bankrupt. So do the village shop and the village pub. The once prosperous village falls into poverty.

This story of the five farmers illustrates a problem: the problem of balancing **individual benefit** with the **common good**. If the farmers act on the basis of individual benefit, it makes sense for them to get as many cows as they can lay their hands on. The

Keep talking

additional grass needed by the cows costs them nothing, and more cows means more prosperity for them. If, on the other hand, they act on the basis of the common good, they should restrict the number of cows they have, to stop the grass running out for everyone. But acting in the interests of the common good would mean sacrificing the greater prosperity that comes with having more cows. That's hard to do when a bigger house and a new car and fancy meals down the pub (the publican's just hired a new chef) are right in front of you. Much easier to carry on buying cows. Easier until there's no grass left. By which time it's too late.

The obvious answer is for the farmers to sit down in the village pub together over a few beers and agree a limit on the number of cows they can each have. This will ensure that there are never more than a hundred in total and the grass never runs out. Let's imagine they do that. They start with a simple idea: we'll stick to twenty each. Then it gets complicated. Alex says, hang on, I've got five kids to feed and I need a bigger house. Bernadette at the next farm is a single woman; she doesn't need as much as me. Can't I have more cows and she have fewer? Colin butts in and says, well, my farm's been in my family since the twelfth century. My ancestors built the village church and fought at the Battle of Agincourt, so I'm entitled to more cows than anyone else. Denise pipes up to point out that she has a disabled son who needs expensive extra care, so she needs more income, therefore more cows. Eric (who's kept quiet till now) reminds them that he's the best at making cheese. Everyone wants to buy his cheese because it tastes so good. He can't keep up with all the orders; he needs more cows to provide people with what they want. On and on they argue, late into the night, as the beer glasses mount up on the table.

They keep talking. After several evenings (and a lot of beer), they finally reach a compromise they are all happy with. In order to do this, they have had to make a number of **trade-offs**, recognising that not everyone has the same needs or rights, so they can't all be treated exactly equally. Fortunately, they have been able to make those trade-offs in a friendly way.

But that's not the end of it. What if one of them sneakily slips in a few more cows than their allowance? They realise that they need a way of enforcing their agreement. Say they decide that anyone who wants to up their allowance of cows will have to do so by buying somebody else's cow off them, to avoid the common being overgrazed. Or say they agree that anyone who brings an extra cow one year, to up their income temporarily, will have to bring one fewer the next year to make up for it. Both these systems could work, but they require **agreement**, **cooperation** and **trust**, on an ongoing basis. They require the farmers to work **collaboratively**. For the common not to die, and for the cows not to die, and for all of them to avoid falling into poverty, they need to be willing to **sacrifice** some of their individual benefit. But nobody likes sacrifice.

Short-term losses for long-term gains

What has all this got to do with climate change? You've probably worked it out already.

The grass on the common is the Earth's atmosphere, the air we all breathe, which can't be contained within borders or countries, which belongs to everybody and nobody. The cows are all the human activities – running factories, driving cars, flying planes, consuming stuff – that bring us prosperity but at the same time impact on the atmosphere by producing greenhouse gases. Before the Industrial Revolution, when human activity was low, the atmosphere was unaffected by greenhouse gases, so, like the grass before Alex went to market, the atmosphere remained stable. The farmers' spending spree on cows is the increase in human activity in the last two hundred years – it brings more prosperity, but it also damages what we all have in common: the grass / atmosphere. The farmers are the governments of all the countries in the world, who have to agree a fair way to stop what they all have in common – the grass / atmosphere – becoming so damaged that they all fall into ruin. The evenings down the pub are the ongoing international negotiations on climate change, known as COP meetings. The farmers / countries are going to have to put the common good before individual benefit and, just as significantly, **long-term gains** ahead of **short-term losses** – the future ahead of the present.

The five farmers seem to have sorted out their grass problem. The global problem of climate change is a little more complicated, as we are dealing not with five people who all do the same job, live in the same place, and can sit round the same table in a nice pub, but with 193 countries and 8 billion people. And if we get it wrong, it won't just be a few cows that will die; the human race itself might be wiped out.

So what are we going to do? Here are some questions to help us consider different solutions.

- **Is climate change the responsibility of individuals or of the state?**
- **Is climate change better dealt with by markets or by regulation?**
- **Should richer countries sacrifice more than poorer countries?**

Individuals or the state?

1. Is climate change the responsibility of individuals or of the state?

We need to bring emissions down. That's beyond debate. But should it be left up to individuals to reduce emissions through their own choices? Or should the state force them to reduce their emissions by passing laws? Should we inform people about the consequences of flying long haul and eating beef, and then trust them to switch to holidays at home and aubergine curries? Or should we slap taxes on air travel and meat? Or even ration Big Macs and big holidays?

There is a lot we can all do to reduce emissions through our everyday choices. Reuse envelopes. Fill up our water bottles from the tap. Eat less steak. Cycle or walk to work. Holiday in the Lake District, not Los Angeles.

But is that enough? Fishing an envelope out of the bin isn't going to stop the ice caps from melting. And maybe the sacrifice asked for is too great. What if I'm sending in a job application and I need to make a good impression? What if I'm outside in a heatwave and I need a drink? What if the doctor said I need to keep up my iron intake? What if cycling to work is too dangerous and walking takes too long? What if my mum lives in Los Angeles? Why should I do anything? What I do or don't do will make so little difference that there is no point in making these sacrifices.

It is true that reusing one envelope is not going to stop the ice caps from melting. But it is also true that there are a lot of people in the world, and that if they all – or at least most of them – change their behaviour, it will make a difference. The racist apartheid regime in South Africa was eventually forced to grant equal rights to all of its citizens, black and white, in the mid-1990s, at least in part because so many people around the world refused, as individuals, to have anything to do with South African products. One person not buying South African oranges didn't bring down the racist regime. Millions of people not buying South African oranges went a long way towards making the government change its mind. So it is with climate change: individually, we don't make much difference; collectively, by the accumulation of many individual actions, we do.

So should we leave action on climate change entirely up to individuals? Should we educate, advise, encourage, even incentivise people (50p off your next skinny latte if you bring your own reusable cup!) to act in the right way, rather than compelling them by law?

Compulsion can be counter-productive

There are three main advantages that come from prioritising **individual choice** over **state action**.

The first is that it promotes individual **responsibility**. If we hand all responsibility over to the government, people are disempowered and are no longer incentivised to do the right thing. Why shouldn't I fly to the Maldives for the weekend? It's not my problem. If it's such a bad thing, the government will make a law against long-haul flights. Until they do, I can carry on doing what I want. Next week, New York!

The second is that it preserves **individual freedom**. Freedom is an essential part of human dignity. No one likes being told what to do; no one likes being shamed for their actions. Being bossed around diminishes us all. Moreover, it is dangerous. Once you start telling people how to behave, you open the door to tyranny. Giving people tax breaks to buy bikes is one thing. You can still choose whether to cycle or not; you keep your freedom. Banning cars from city centres is a different matter – now the state is telling you where you can and can't go. How long before they introduce travel passes and start putting up walls and fences?

The third is that it may be more **effective**. Compulsion can be counterproductive. Sacrifices which are enforced by law are more likely to be resisted and evaded. People are more likely to sustain behaviour which they have freely chosen. An example is the rollout of the Covid vaccine from 2021 onwards. The UK government judged that making the vaccine compulsory by law would be counterproductive as it would generate resistance and make martyrs of anti-vaxxers. Better to give the public as much information as possible about the benefits of the vaccine (and the absence of any harms), and make it as easy as possible for people to access it: **information**, **encouragement** and **facilitation** over compulsion and threat. This was a very effective strategy; there was over 90% uptake of vaccines across the population.

There are two main problems with these arguments for freedom and responsibility.

The first is to do with **scale**. The climate crisis is so extreme and so urgent that it is not enough to leave it up to individuals. It requires immediate action on a national level. It's no good waiting around for people to get out of their cars; the state needs to stop people from using them. When, in 1940, Britain was in imminent danger of invasion, many basic freedoms were suspended. You couldn't buy what you wanted, go where you wanted, say what you wanted. This incursion on freedom was largely accepted, as Britain faced an existential threat from Nazi Germany. Climate change is a similarly existential threat, and warrants a similar level of intervention by governments. **Survival** is more important than freedom.

The second is to do with **fairness**. Not everyone contributes equally to climate change, and yet climate change affects everyone equally. Actually, that's not quite true. The wealthier you are, the less likely you are to be affected by climate change, because it is easier to protect yourself from it. When a heatwave hits, you can turn on your air conditioning; when the floodwaters are rising, you can move to your second home; when food prices go through the roof, you can still afford your sourdough bread and avocado. A poor person stuck in a crowded, boiling hot flat with water lapping at the door, unable to feed her children, has no such choices. Well, you might say, that's the point of being wealthy: it gives you a nicer life. If you've worked hard and earned enough money to afford air con, a second home and avocado toast, why shouldn't you have them? The problem is that wealthier people, as well as having more choices, also tend to have a bigger carbon footprint (precisely because they have more choices). They are more likely to fly, to live in bigger houses which need more heating (and more air con), and to demand food that comes from around the world. They created the problem, and they are now protected from the consequences of the problem they created, while people who didn't create the problem suffer because of their actions. This isn't fair. The government needs to step in to redress this unfairness.

Of course, the argument is not quite as binary as all that. Just as you can both support the law against theft and at the same time choose not to steal, so it is possible to combine state action on climate change with personal choices. You can both have a tax on plastic bags and decide to reuse the ones you bought as bin liners. Nonetheless, thinking through the issues above will help to clarify just how far the state should intervene to reduce emissions: what the balance should be between the **individual** and the **collective**.

2. Is climate change best dealt with by markets or by regulation?

Nudge, nudge

The state can take no action on climate change and leave everyone to make their own choices. Or the state can take a lot of action, intervening heavily in people's lives. Then there's a third way. The

Do you want a nudge or an order?

state can encourage people to do some things and discourage them from doing others. The state can **nudge**.

To take one example. Electric cars produce fewer emissions than petrol cars. So, a good way to deal with climate change is to work towards ultimately replacing petrol cars with electric cars. There are a number of ways this can be achieved:

A. Make a law against petrol cars.

B. Make a law against petrol cars, but pay all owners of petrol cars compensation for scrapping them, perhaps with a bit extra to make up for the inconvenience.

C. Keep petrol cars legal, but tax them very heavily so they are more expensive.

D. Keep petrol cars legal, but subsidise electric cars from taxes, making them much cheaper than petrol cars.

Each approach has its advantages and disadvantages.

A deals with the problem very thoroughly and very immediately. However, it would be hard to win popular support for it. This lack of support would make it hard to enforce, and might open the door to widespread law-breaking. Also, poor people in remote regions who depend on their vehicles and cannot afford to buy an electric car would suffer far more than people in cities with good public transport, and wealthy people who can afford to buy electric cars.

B would make the measure slightly less unpopular, and would mitigate some of the harm done to people who genuinely depend on cars. However, it would be expensive, and would divert a lot of resources which arguably could be better used elsewhere.

C would be more popular and easier to enforce. It would also be less expensive, and would actually raise money for the state, which might be spent on other things. However, it would advantage wealthy people who could afford the taxes, and disadvantage poor people who couldn't. The hedge fund manager gets to carry on driving her Range Rover when she's shopping in Chelsea, while the district nurse in the Scottish Highlands can't afford to visit his patients any more.

D would be the most popular. Petrolheads would lose nothing by hanging on to their gas guzzlers, while people who want to do the right thing would find it easier. However, the more popular the measure became, the more expensive it would be.

Markets? Or regulations?

A is an example of straight **regulation**; that is, the state telling people what to do, with them having no choice in the matter. **B**, **C** and **D** all, to varying degrees, use the **market**. That is, the state lets people choose what to do, but intervenes in the market – the exchange between people of goods and services – to influence people's actions. Regulation is simpler and more immediate, but sacrifices freedom; using the market protects freedom, but is also more risky and may produce less equal outcomes.

You can use the ideas above about markets and regulation to consider other climate-related measures, such as:

- Taxing meat
- Taxing air travel
- Taxing packaging
- Taxing petrol
- Taxing aviation fuel
- Subsidising home insulation
- Subsidising public transport

Emissions trading

There is another example of using the market to reduce emissions, this time on an international scale: **emissions trading**. This was the measure proposed (though never fully implemented) in the Kyoto Protocol in 1997 (see above).

Emissions trading means some countries can pollute more, and others can pollute less. Each country is given a certain allocation of emissions, with the total quantity of emissions being low enough to slow or prevent a rise in the global temperature. If one country wants to pollute more than its quota, it can buy extra emissions from another country which is happy to pollute less. The US can't kick its SUV habit, so it buys extra emissions from Bangladesh. Bangladesh gets cash to spend on more basic needs like healthcare and education, while Americans can carry on cruising their freeways with a clear conscience, in the knowledge that over the whole world no damage is being done. To go back to the five farmers: Alex wants more cows so he can make more money in the long term, while Bernadette needs immediate cash to repair her cowshed. Alex buys some cow permits from Bernadette, allowing him to have thirty cows while she just has ten, but there are still only a hundred cows on the common, so the grass won't run out.

Emissions trading has the advantage of preserving flexibility and freedom in a way that a universal, uniform cut in emissions doesn't. However, it does depend on a high degree of trust between countries not to cheat or game the system. It also reinforces inequalities between rich and poor countries. Which brings us on to the next issue.

Should the rich pay more?

3. Should richer countries sacrifice more than poorer countries?

The vast majority of the emissions that have caused climate change have been produced by richer, more economically developed countries in the so-called 'Global North'. The 'Global North' comprises North America, Europe, China, Australia and New Zealand, along with countries such as Argentina, Botswana, Israel, Japan and South Korea (although not all of these wealthier countries are in the northern hemisphere).

The vast majority of the damage caused by climate change will be felt or is being felt by countries in poorer, less economically developed countries, in what is known as the 'Global South' (Africa, South Asia).

So the rich countries get most of the benefits of industrialisation and hardly any of the harms; the poor countries get most of the harms of industrialisation and hardly any of the benefits. Is that fair?

Should rich countries have to do more to compensate for the damage they have done historically? Should poorer countries have to do less? How is it fair to expect poorer countries to miss out on the benefits of industrialisation by forcing them to cut emissions, when richer countries have been enjoying those benefits for decades?

One way of dealing with these inequalities would be to make rich countries cut their emissions more, and poorer countries cut them less. This would be a little like progressive taxation. Under progressive taxation, the higher your income, the higher the rate of income tax you pay; if you earn below a certain level, you don't pay any income tax at all. Should it be the same for emission-cutting, so that prosperous countries like the US are forced to create fewer emissions, while poorer countries like Bangladesh are allowed to carry on polluting so they can catch up with them economically?

Freedom or fairness?

Richer countries might say that while industrialisation has brought climate change, it has also brought prosperity and technological advancement, to the benefit of the whole world. Why should they be punished for that? Even if industrialisation was unambiguously wrong, why should people now living in richer countries suffer for the actions of people who lived before they were born? It's a shame that poor countries have to miss out on the benefits of industrialisation, but we still can't let them start building motorways and factories – the climate emergency is too serious. Everyone needs to cut emissions. Is it fair though to expect people in developing countries not to want a TV or washing machine, when people in the Global North have relied on these things for many years?

Emissions trading, as described above, is meant to be a way of managing these inequalities. It is supposed to give countries freedom of choice through the market in how they manage emissions. The problem is that, as often happens with markets, it tends to benefit the already fortunate over the less fortunate. The US can afford to have even more cars; Bangladesh can't afford even a few cars. So the world becomes even more unequal, with growing resentment between rich and poor.

3. THE POINT OF CLASH

Trust or force?

Is climate change the responsibility of individuals or of the state?

Which is more **important**? Allowing people **freedom** and **responsibility** for their actions? Or sacrificing freedom in the interests of the **common good**?

Which is more **effective**? **Trusting** people to act responsibly? Or **forcing** them to act in the interests of the common good, with sanctions imposed if they do not?

Is climate change better dealt with by markets or by regulation?

Which works better? **Incentivising** people to do the right thing via financial rewards? Or **forcing** people to do the right thing through the application of the law?

Is emissions trading a **sustainable**, **fair** and **effective** way of reducing emissions? Or does it increase **inequality**?

Should richer countries sacrifice more than poorer countries?

Is it fair to expect those who **have more** to **sacrifice more**? Or should they be allowed to keep what they have? Is it fair to expect people alive now to accept sacrifices because of actions taken by their **ancestors**? Or should they only have to take the consequences of their **own actions**? Is **increasing prosperity** in poor countries a more urgent need than tackling climate change? Or is climate change such an existential threat that people in those countries should have to accept a **reduced standard of living**? Should richer countries be allowed to have more of the benefits of greenhouse gas emissions because they can **afford** them? Or should all countries make **equal sacrifices**?

4. THE ARGUMENTS

People should be encouraged to take action on climate change	People should be forced to take action on climate change
The free market is a more flexible and responsive way to moderate people's choices than government intervention.	The free market favours the wealthy and the powerful.
Freely chosen actions are more sustainable, and are likely to have a higher uptake.	Using the law is a more certain way to ensure the right actions are taken.
Compulsion is counterproductive.	Compulsion is fairer, because it treats everyone the same.
Giving people responsibility for their own actions empowers them, and makes them more engaged with their actions.	Allowing people free choice means the selfless have to make more sacrifices to make up for the selfish.
Different people have different circumstances and needs, and should be allowed to act according to those circumstances and needs, e.g. someone whose elderly mother lives in India needs to fly long haul more often than someone whose family are all in the UK.	Differences in circumstance give some people unfair advantages over others, e.g. rich people can afford to fly long haul as often as they want, while poor people suffer more of the consequences of the resultant climate change. The law needs to intervene to correct this unfairness.
Unpopular laws will be evaded.	Unpopular laws are sometimes necessary and need to be enforced.
It is not the business of government to tell us how to live our lives.	It is the business of government to protect us from harm.
Human freedom is a fundamental value that must be protected.	Survival is more important than freedom.

Rich countries should make more sacrifices than poor countries	Everyone should make equal sacrifices
Rich countries have benefited, and do benefit, from industrialisation; they should therefore deal with the harms it has caused.	The benefits industrialisation has brought have spread to the whole world; it is unfair to punish rich countries for bringing these benefits.
Rich countries created climate change; they should clean up their own mess.	The mess was created by people now dead; it isn't our mess.
Making rich countries sacrifice more will create greater equality across the world, and therefore greater solidarity.	If rich countries have earned their prosperity, they should be allowed to keep it.
Rich countries already have enough prosperity; they don't need more, but poor countries do.	Encouraging poor countries to industrialise will accelerate climate change.
Rich countries can afford to cut emissions more, so they should.	All countries need to cut emissions.

5. THE MOTIONS

1. This house would tax meat.
2. This house would make vegetarianism / veganism compulsory.
3. This house would ban cars from city centres.
4. This house would ban petrol cars.
5. This house would make public transport free, paid for by taxes.
6. This house would subsidise electric cars / home insulation, paid for by taxes.
7. This house would tax long-haul flights.
8. This house would restrict everyone to one long-haul flight a year.
9. This house would disinvest from fossil fuel companies.
10. This house believes emissions trading is the most effective way to tackle climate change.
11. This house would require richer countries to undertake bigger emission cuts than poorer countries.
12. This house would ban all fossil fuel extraction.

Keep thinking...

A selection of further reading and viewing to help you think more deeply about the issues around climate change.

How to Blow Up a Pipeline, dir. Daniel Goldhaber (Neon, 2022)

This is a kind of green heist movie. A motley gang of climate activists come together to blow up a pipeline, encountering many obstacles and dangers on the way. They're outlaws but heroes. It's a fast-paced, entertaining thriller, nerve-shreddingly tense in places. There's not much light and shade: it does tend to fall into the trap of much climate fiction by pitching uncompromisingly heroic activists against no less uncompromisingly evil fossil fuel interests. However, it will give you a sympathetic insight into the motivations of the more extreme climate activists, and prompt much thought about whether the climate emergency is so serious that it justifies breaking the law. (For more on this last issue, see Chapter 10, **Crime, Punishment and the Law**).

This Changes Everything: Capitalism vs the Climate, Naomi Klein (Penguin, 2015)

For Naomi Klein, capitalism (the economic system followed by most countries in the world) is not, as fans of market-based solutions to climate change would argue, the solution: it's the problem. She argues strongly that the climate crisis will only be resolved by a radical restructuring of our economic model. She does, however, hold out some hope – the crisis could be turned into an opportunity to build a fairer world.

The Wall, John Lanchester (WW Norton & Company, 2019)

It's not too far into the future. Every inch of the coast of Britain is covered by an immense wall, designed to stop climate refugees ('Others') from entering the country. All adult British citizens have to do a tour of duty as 'Defenders' on the wall. If anyone gets in on their watch, they are put to sea in a small boat to face almost certain death.

Lanchester's novel is one of the most impressive examples of 'climate fiction'. The fact that his main characters go on living their lives (falling in and out of love, arguing with their families, going on holiday) in the midst of a catastrophe makes his imagined future all the more plausible, and therefore all the more terrifying.

Our Final Warning: Six Degrees of Climate Emergency, Mark Lynas (Fourth Estate, 2021)

Mark Lynas has read hundreds of scientific studies so we don't have to. Calmly and systematically, fully supported by the evidence, he sets out the consequences of different degrees of global warming, degree by degree. As you would expect, it gets worse. Much worse. Despite all this, he remains cautiously hopeful that it is not too late to save ourselves from the consequences of a warming planet, but only if we take drastic action now.

The Climate Book, created by Greta Thunberg (Penguin, 2022)

Greta Thunberg's personal story is one of the most remarkable of recent times. Starting out as a solitary teenager skipping school in protest at the lack of action on climate change, she has become the patron saint of the climate movement, speaking uncomfortable truths to those in power and inspiring millions of young people to take responsibility for the planet's future. In this book, she assembles a wide selection of experts to present the scientific facts about climate change and its consequences in a way that is both accessible and thorough. This should be your one-stop shop for facts on climate change.

Don't Look Up, dir. Adam McKay (Netflix, 2021)

A meteorite is heading for the Earth. When it lands, its impact will extinguish all human life. It could still be diverted from its course, if the richest and most powerful nations collaborate. So what do they do? Attack the scientists who discovered the meteorite. Pretend it's not happening. Say it's all a left-wing plot. Claim that there might actually be some benefits from a massive meteorite hitting the Earth. Fill the news with celebrity gossip, because who wants to talk about that depressing stuff?

Don't Look Up is by turns hilarious, horrifying and inspiring. It seems like a ludicrous, implausible farce, until you compare it to the actual response to climate change, and then it feels like a documentary. You will laugh and cry in quick succession, but you will also have your eyes opened. The last words of the movie, 'We had something good there, when you think about it', still offer some hope.

6

PART SIX

Life and Death

How to think about life and death

In this last section we think about **life and death**.

So, we think about **abortion**. When does life begin? Is an unborn child a person whose life must be preserved, or just a part of a woman's body? At what point does an unborn child become a person in their own right? When is abortion right and when is it wrong?

And we finish by thinking about the end of life: about **assisted dying**. Should people be allowed to decide how and when they die, even when they have a terminal illness and are in pain? Should other people be allowed to help them die? Is the protection of life an absolute good?

CHAPTER 16

Abortion

In this chapter we're thinking about...

- **Is abortion always wrong?**
- **Might abortion be right in some circumstances, and if so, what circumstances?**
- **Should there be any legal restrictions on abortion, and if so, what should those restrictions be?**

1. THE FACTS

Abortion is the deliberate termination of a pregnancy

What is abortion?

Abortion is the deliberate termination of a pregnancy. Until the development of modern surgical techniques, this was most commonly carried out by the pregnant woman undertaking extreme physical exercise (sometimes amounting to self-harm) to induce an abortion, or taking medicine to have the same effect. Since improvements in anaesthetics and medical hygiene, abortions became more likely to be carried out by surgical intervention.

Stages of pregnancy

There are essentially three stages of pregnancy:

- **Zygote**
- **Embryo**
- **Foetus**

Pregnancy starts with a single cell in an egg that has been fertilised by sperm, usually via sexual intercourse. The fertilised egg is called a **zygote**. During the first fourteen days, the zygote may split, creating identical twins, or even triplets or quadruplets.

After about fourteen days, the zygote becomes an **embryo**. During this stage, the basic physical structures of the body are laid down.

After about ten weeks, the embryo becomes a **foetus**. The foetus is more recognisable as a potential human being. A few weeks later, it also begins moving within the mother's womb, sometimes known as 'quickening'.

The foetus continues to develop and grow up until the moment of birth, approximately nine months after conception. The earliest moment at which a foetus could live outside its mother's womb (with very considerable amounts of medical support) is 24 weeks.

The division between zygote, embryo and foetus is somewhat arbitrary. There is no clear-cut moment when one turns into another, but they are helpful ways of describing the different stages of development of a person from conception to birth.

Babies were routinely abandoned in the ancient world

Attitudes towards abortion

The ancient world

In the pre-Christian western world, newborn babies who were disabled, unwanted or just inconvenient – all grounds for abortion in the modern world – were routinely abandoned and left to die. (Think of the story of Moses in the Bible, and of Oedipus in Sophocles's drama of the same name; both were left to die as babies, only to be miraculously rescued, saving them for great deeds in later life.) This attitude to infant life – either callous or pragmatic, depending on your point of view – carried over to abortion, which was not generally seen as a moral issue.

The common view in Ancient Rome, influenced by the Stoicism of the Ancient Greeks, was that the foetus was a phase of development with no more consciousness than that of a plant, but was then born with a similar urge for self-preservation as an animal. Abortion was therefore considered acceptable up to the moment of birth. The only situations in which abortion was condemned was when it was considered to have infringed on paternal rights. If a woman had an abortion without the permission of the father of her child, she was seen to have deprived him of his offspring. If someone induced an abortion in another man's wife without his permission, they had deprived him of his property.

The Ancient Greek philosopher Aristotle argued that an embryo was not human until it acquired a soul; before that it was not fully alive. He judged this moment to arrive at 40 days after conception for a male embryo, and 80 to 90 days for a female embryo.

Religion and Abortion

The attitude to abortion varies with different religions and their followers. Individual religious believers often diverge from what their faith teaches about abortion, in belief and / or practice. It is simplistic (and wrong) to say 'All religious people are against abortion.' That said, the general tendency is for religions to see abortion as the taking of a life created by God, and therefore to teach that it should be kept to a minimum, if not prevented entirely. Religious faith has been a powerful force throughout history, and is still more significant around the world than is often recognised by people used to living in more secular (less religious) societies. This has had a significant impact on attitudes to and laws relating to abortion.

Early **Christian** thinkers agreed with Aristotle's judgement that the foetus did not become human until the moment of 'ensoulment', so did not rule out early abortions. It was not until 1869 that the Roman Catholic Church formally stated that life began from the moment of conception, and that therefore abortion was always wrong. Currently, the Roman Catholic Church, the Orthodox churches, and most Evangelical churches teach that abortion is wrong in all circumstances. More mainstream Protestant churches take a more nuanced view, tending to regard abortion as regrettable while accepting that in some circumstances it may be a lesser evil. Some more liberal Protestants are actively supportive of abortion rights.

Most religions oppose abortion

The views of **Islam** and **Judaism** on abortion vary depending on the different traditions within each religion. Both religions tend towards the view that the soul does not enter the body until several weeks into pregnancy, and therefore accept early abortions. Neither religion opposes abortion when the mother's life is in danger, and some traditions in each faith accept other extenuating circumstances in which abortion may be acceptable. Both faiths, though, fall well short of endorsing unrestricted abortion on demand.

Hinduism traditionally teaches that life begins at the moment of conception, and that therefore abortion is always wrong.

Attitudes vary within different traditions of **Buddhism**, though the majority view is that any abortion is the killing of an innocent being, and is therefore wrong. However, Buddhists are encouraged to consider compassionately the circumstances that might cause a woman to seek an abortion.

Feminism and abortion

As women have fought for and achieved greater autonomy over their own lives, they have also fought for and achieved greater autonomy over their own bodies.

Many feminists therefore regard abortion as a feminist issue and about the rights of women. They have tended to make the following arguments in favour of allowing women free access to abortion:

- Laws restricting abortion are an unwarranted incursion by (mostly male) lawmakers into a woman's right to choose what she does with her own body.
- The economic, health and personal consequences of an unwanted pregnancy, and still more of an unwanted (and /

Equality for women makes abortion easier

or unaffordable) child, are borne predominantly by women, so women should have the right to choose to terminate their own pregnancies.

- Women who have been made pregnant against their will, by violent partners or partners who have put pressure on them to have unprotected sex, should not be forced to carry to term a child they never wished to conceive.
- Illegal abortions are likely to be dangerous and to put the woman's life at risk.

Attitudes towards abortion in a society are likely to correlate closely with the degree of equality and autonomy achieved by women within that society. The more equality and autonomy women have achieved, the more liberal laws on abortion are likely to be.

Abortion and the law

Around the world

Although abortion may have been associated with stigma and shame for much of history, laws against it only began to appear in the nineteenth century. These laws were prompted partly by moral concerns, but also by concerns over the physical dangers posed to women by abortions (though, of course, making it illegal did not stop it from happening). Another, generally unspoken, reason for outlawing abortion was a concern that it might cause the birth rate to fall, particularly amongst dominant racial groups, or where the population had been significantly diminished by war or disease.

From about the middle of the twentieth century, more liberal laws have emerged around the world. As of 2019, abortion was legal or at least tolerated on the following grounds around the world:

- **To save the woman's life:** in 98% of countries.
- **To protect the woman's physical health:** in 72% of countries.
- **In cases of rape or incest:** in 61% of countries.
- **In cases of serious impairment of the foetus:** in 61% of countries.
- **For social or economic reasons:** in 37% of countries.
- **At the woman's request:** in 34% of countries.
- **To select the sex of the foetus:** in 2% of countries.

The legal time limit for abortion varies between countries from 12 weeks to 24 weeks, with some countries permitting abortion even later in cases of foetal impairment or risk to the woman's life.

Abortion is hugely divisive in the US

The least liberal laws tend to be found in Muslim majority countries, and in Latin America, where the Catholic Church is still very powerful. The most liberal laws tend to be found in Western Europe (though abortion is still illegal in Malta and Andorra, both strongly Catholic countries).

Abortion has been a hugely contentious and divisive issue in the United States, featuring heavily in the so-called 'culture wars', pitting less educated, poorer people from smaller towns and rural areas (often members of Evangelical churches), who are more likely to be 'pro-life' (that is, opposed to legalising abortion), against more prosperous and better educated liberals in large cities, who are more likely to be 'pro-choice' (that is, in favour of legalising abortion). For many voters, a politician's position on abortion is more important than anything they might say or do about economic issues.

In 1973, the US Supreme Court made a landmark ruling in the case of **Roe v. Wade**. 'Jane Roe' was the legal pseudonym of Norma McCorvey, who wanted an abortion when she became pregnant with her third child. In Texas, where she lived, this was illegal. The court ruled that making abortion illegal was unconstitutional, because to prevent a woman from terminating her own pregnancy infringed her constitutional right to privacy. This effectively legalised abortion across the US, as it overturned the laws against abortion that applied in the great majority of states. (The US is made up of 50 states. While most laws are 'federal' – that is, they apply across the whole country – individual states nonetheless retain a high degree of independence, enabling them to set many of their own laws.) Following the appointment of more conservative judges to the Supreme Court by President Trump, Roe v. Wade was overturned in June 2022 on the grounds that the right to privacy was not deeply rooted in the history and tradition of the US. This did not make abortion illegal as such, but it did allow state governments to make abortion illegal in their state. Several states (though not all) immediately enacted laws making abortion either illegal or very highly restricted.

In the UK

Abortion was criminalised in the UK by the **Offences Against the Person Act** in **1828**. Initially, the penalty was death or transportation (to Australia) for life. In **1857**, the punishment was

Abortion became safe, legal, affordable

modified to hard labour as a prisoner in the UK. An **1861** update of the Offences Against the Person Act made it illegal to procure or provide drugs which could induce an abortion (the most common means at the time). Abortion continued to be practised widely: to take one year as an example, it was estimated that in 1914 there were 100,000 abortions in the UK. In **1929**, the Infant Life (Preservation) Act came into effect. This criminalised the 'deliberate destruction of a child capable of being born alive'.

In **1967**, the **Abortion Act** was passed. Its intention was to make abortion safe, legal and affordable, allowing it to be provided by the National Health Service. Many of the arguments made for the new law were essentially pragmatic: abortion is going to happen anyway, so we need to protect women from the consequences of dangerous illegal abortions. The promoters of the law did not envisage that it would usher in abortion on demand. They still thought abortion should be carried out as an exceptional last resort.

The act provided for four grounds for an abortion:

A. Risk to the life of the pregnant woman.

B. Preventing grave permanent injury to the woman's physical or mental health.

C. Risk of injury to the physical or mental health of the pregnant woman or any existing children of her family.

D. Substantial risk that, if the child were born, he or she would 'suffer from such physical or mental abnormalities as to be seriously handicapped'.

Abortion on grounds A, B and D was allowed up to 28 weeks; for ground C only up to 24 weeks. An abortion had to be authorised by two separate doctors.

In 1990, the Human Fertilisation and Embryology Act was passed, modifying the law on abortion. It was now allowed on the following grounds:

A. Risk to the life of the pregnant woman.

B. To prevent grave permanent injury to the physical or mental health of the pregnant woman.

C. Risk of injury to the physical or mental health of the pregnant woman.

D. Risk of injury to the physical or mental health of any existing children of the family of the pregnant woman.

E. Substantial risk that if the child were born it would suffer from such physical or mental abnormalities as to be seriously disabled.

F. To save the life of the pregnant woman.

G. To prevent grave permanent injury to the physical or mental health of the pregnant woman in an emergency.

Abortion is available on demand in the UK

Apart from on grounds C and D, where the limit is now set at 24 weeks, an abortion can be performed at any time during a pregnancy. The authorisation of two doctors is still required.

Neither act applied to Northern Ireland, which continued to have very strict laws on abortion. Attitudes there have tended to be more conservative under the powerful influence of both the Catholic Church and the more fundamentalist Protestant churches. In 2020, during a period when the devolved government was suspended due to the inability of the political parties to agree on forming an administration, the UK government legalised abortion in Northern Ireland, though it remains difficult to access there.

The provision to allow abortion on the grounds of a woman's mental health has, in practice, been very liberally interpreted, such that abortion is effectively available on demand in the UK (contrary to the original intentions of the 1967 act). It remains free, via the NHS. It is estimated that slightly over 200,000 abortions are carried out in the UK every year.

2. THE ISSUES

Abortion raises very strong emotions. This is hardly surprising, as it deals with decisions about life and death, and probes intimately into a woman's relationship with her own body. For some women, the decision to have an abortion is a simple one, and is followed by a sense of relief; for others, it may be a painful, agonising choice. A woman seeking an abortion may be in a situation of profound personal crisis or danger. Abortion is both an intensely private matter and, at the same time, a very public concern. A society's stance on abortion says a lot about its attitude towards many other issues: the role of women; the role of families; the role of children; life; death. Women have always had abortions, and they always will. Abortion will never be 'ended'. How society responds to the fact of abortion has changed over time, however, and may yet change again.

Abortion raises strong emotions

For pro-abortion campaigners, any restriction on abortion is a wholly unjustifiable infringement on a woman's right to do what she chooses with her body; for anti-abortion campaigners, abortion is murder of a defenceless being. Little wonder then that temperatures run so high on both sides. So it's all the more important for debaters (and everyone else) to take a step back and look at the issues in as dispassionate a way as possible, and to remember that people who disagree with them are not necessarily evil and / or stupid. It is also important to realise that abortion is not quite as binary an issue as it may at first appear; there is a bigger middle ground between the two sides than you might imagine.

Some key questions to consider when thinking about abortion.

1. **Is the foetus a person?**
2. **Which should take priority, the mother's rights or those of the foetus?**
3. **Is it possible to argue that abortion is morally wrong, but should still be legal?**
4. **Should there be any restrictions on abortions? Or should they be available on demand?**

1. Is the foetus a person?

There is a very simple binary response to this question.

If the answer is **yes**, then an abortion, however unwanted, however difficult or dangerous the pregnancy, is killing a person. Given that the person in question is utterly defenceless and incapable of agency, killing them can only be regarded as murder. Once you grasp this concept, you can see why some people are so vehemently against abortion. It's no good telling them that a certain woman should be allowed an abortion because she already has five children and can't afford to feed a sixth. Their response would be that, no matter how poor or desperate she is, you would never allow her to kill one of her living children, so why should she be allowed to kill a living child inside her?

If, however, the answer is **no**, and you believe that the foetus is a part of the woman's body, but not yet a person in its own right, then there is no reason why the law should be involved in telling a woman what to do with her body. An individual woman may have many personal, ethical and medical reasons to consider when she makes a decision about an abortion, but they are a matter for her and her doctor, not for the state.

Is abortion about one person or two?

To put it even more simply, the only question to consider is: does an abortion concern **one** person, or **two**? Once you know the answer to this, you know the answer on abortion.

However (as so often) it may be a little more complicated than that.

When does someone become a person? Is it at the moment of conception, when the sperm hits the egg, and a new life becomes possible? This is the position of the Catholic Church. Certainly, a zygote (a fertilised egg) is a **potential** life. But potential is not the same as actual. Are we justified in curtailing a potential life? You could argue that this is what some forms of contraception do, by intervening in a sexual act to prevent the potential for a new life to be formed (one reason the Catholic Church is also opposed to contraception). A fertilised egg is a long way from what most people would regard as a person. It has no recognisable individual characteristics, and indeed hasn't yet made its mind up as to whether it is one person or two (or maybe even three or four), given that identical twins, triplets and quadruplets may be created if the egg splits after fertilisation.

Is an embryo a person? It is starting to lay down some of the features of a person, but it isn't finished yet. It is common for a woman to be quite unaware that she is pregnant, and even to lose her baby without being aware of it, while it is still an embryo.

A woman is not normally physically aware of her baby until it is a foetus, from around ten weeks. This is the time known traditionally as 'quickening', and is the time when the Ancient Greeks and early Christian thinkers believed, and Islam still teaches, that the soul enters the body. It is easy to understand why, as a foetus seen on a scan is recognisably a baby, just very small and scrunched up. Does that recognition make it a person? Or has it been a person all along, and this is the first time we have realised?

Or does the foetus become a person once it is able to live independently? This way of looking at the issue is one reason why abortion is, even under the most liberal regimes, normally banned after 24 weeks of pregnancy other than in the most extreme circumstances. A baby delivered prematurely past 24 weeks has the potential to live and grow old (though not without intensive medical intervention); does that make it a person? You could also argue that the possibility of life at this stage is only real in the context of access to the latest healthcare. The unborn child of a wealthy woman in Manhattan who is six months pregnant has a

When do we become a person?

high chance of living outside the womb; the unborn child of a poor woman in Madagascar has none.

So does a baby become a person only when it leaves the mother's womb, and we can see and touch and hold it? Anyone who has been present at the birth of a child (especially their own) will know the overwhelming instinct to protect and care for the newborn. However, in what sense is a newborn baby a person? They cannot live independently; they cannot express themselves, other than in the most basic ways; they are unable to show any preferences, other than for survival.

The philosopher Peter Singer argues that killing sick or disabled newborns should not be forbidden, as it is no worse morally than aborting them, and has been a common practice in many cultures (and still is in some). Most people would react with utter revulsion to such a suggestion; but it does make us think hard about where and when a person begins. Is our revulsion at the thought of killing babies more about our own feelings than about the interests of the baby? Some people feel the same sense of revulsion at the thought of abortion.

Here's a further point to ponder when considering at what point someone becomes a person, and thereby acquires the rights due to a person. Killing a baby simply because it is disabled would be regarded by almost everyone in our culture as an appalling crime. And yet disability in the foetus is a common reason for abortion. Why is it all right to kill someone for being disabled in the womb, but not out of it? Some campaigners for people with Down's Syndrome claim that as tests for Down's in the womb improve, and abortion of foetuses with Down's (which are legal in the UK right up to the moment before birth) becomes more common, there will eventually be almost no people with Down's left in the world. They regard this as a kind of genocide. Are they right?

2. Which should take priority, the rights of the mother or those of the foetus?

The feminist case for liberalising the law on abortion has focused very strongly on the question of a woman's right to do what she chooses with her body. It is undoubtedly the case that women's physical autonomy and safety has been (and still is) under regular threat from the greater physical, social and financial power of men. In some cultures, women have been (and sometimes still are) treated as little more than the physical property of their fathers or husbands. Before reliable contraception, women could be

Who matters more? Mother or foetus?

burdened with endless pregnancies and more and more children in return for satisfying their husband's sexual demands. Even in seemingly more liberal cultures, men can exert psychological or financial pressure to control women's physical autonomy ('I'm not letting you go out in that dress!'; 'You need to stay at home and look after the kids because I will always earn more than you.') Sometimes the threat to a woman's physical well-being is immediate and explicit, as in the case of domestic violence, rape or sexual harassment. Sometimes it can be more subtle and implicit, as when women are bombarded with messages designed to make them feel insecure about their weight or appearance, or are afraid to walk home alone at night.

This context of a historic (and continuing) imbalance of physical power between men and women can make free access to abortion look like a natural extension of the battle to right this injustice. Laws on abortion have (like most laws) mostly been made by men. (Though that is not to say that there are no women who oppose abortion – some of the most passionate pro-life campaigners are women.) It is always women who bear the physical consequences of pregnancy; it is nearly always women who bear the social and financial consequences of having more children than they can afford. Shouldn't women be allowed to decide what to do with their pregnant bodies?

This argument does, of course, depend on the assumption that there is only one person involved in a pregnancy. Once you accept that a pregnant woman is in fact two people in one person, it gets more complicated. It is possible to be an uncompromising feminist who supports full equality and autonomy for women in work and relationships, but still to believe that abortion is morally wrong, on the grounds that a pregnant woman has another person inside her, who is more vulnerable and deserving of protection than even the most oppressed woman.

Is it possible though to accept that the foetus is a person and still defend a woman's right to an abortion? This could be possible if you take the view that the woman's life is more fully developed and on those grounds should take priority. Imagine a teenage girl who falls pregnant halfway through her last year at school, just as she is about to take her A-Levels and head off to university. The father of her child is unable and unwilling to support her. She has a whole life mapped out ahead of her, full of promise, in which she, and her parents and teachers, have invested a great deal. If she carries her child to term and has to devote several years of her young life to caring on her own for a baby and then a young child, she faces the prospect of wiping out that promising future, perhaps damaging the rest of her life. The foetus inside her has as yet no such life. Shouldn't her rights and her needs come first?

An abortion may threaten a woman's rights

It is also important to remember that there are occasions when a woman's rights may actually be threatened by an abortion. A woman may be pressured to abort a child she wants to keep because her partner does not want the responsibility and expense of a child, or because he is married to someone else, and does not want living evidence of his infidelity. In cultures that value boys more highly than girls, a woman may be pressured into aborting a girl. This practice has led to a significant imbalance between the sexes in India and China, and could even be seen as an example of systemic violence or genocide against women.

So, if a foetus is simply a part of a woman's body, the feminist argument for prioritising the woman's right to choose, and therefore allowing abortion on demand, is pretty much unanswerable. However, when you consider other factors, the situation becomes more complex.

3. Is it possible to argue that abortion is morally wrong, but should still be legal?

This was the basis on which many of the arguments were made around the legalisation of abortion in the UK in 1967.

All the evidence shows that abortion has always happened, in every culture and in every time. Think of those estimated 100,000 abortions taking place in the UK in 1914, when anyone found guilty of procuring an abortion could face a jail sentence. Making abortion illegal is not going to make it go away. What it will do is make it much more dangerous for women. Abortions may be initiated by women themselves, engaging in acts of self-harm such as taking drugs or throwing themselves downstairs; they may be carried out by doctors operating outside the law, without the wider clinical support necessary to ensure the woman's well-being, and with the potential for the abortionist to use the threat of discovery and prosecution to exploit the woman financially or even sexually; they may be carried out by amateurs with no medical training. Whichever way it is done, women will be in much greater danger than if abortions are carried out legally in clean, safe, regulated hospitals. What is more, the burden of danger will fall disproportionately on poorer and more vulnerable women. Rich women have always been able to find a way of disposing of an inconvenient pregnancy. In Ireland in the twentieth century when, under the influence of the Catholic Church, the illegality of abortion was written into the constitution, women seeking an abortion would often get on a plane to London, but they had to be able to afford the plane fare and somewhere to stay. Since the overturning of Roe v. Wade in the United States, a woman in Texas (where abortion is illegal) can drive to California for an abortion (where it is still legal); easy if she has money and time to spare, but impossible if she is a single parent already bringing up several children on a minimum-wage job.

Pragmatism or principle?

Given all the above, it is perfectly tenable to argue both that abortion is inherently wrong, and, at the same time, that it should not be illegal, on the grounds that the harm caused by criminalisation is greater than the harm caused by legalisation.

Taking this view prioritises **pragmatism** over **principle**. In philosophical terms, it takes a **consequentialist** approach (where what is most important is the consequences of an action, not whether the action is right or wrong in itself) over a **deontological** approach (where what is most important is whether an action is right or wrong in itself, regardless of the consequences of the action).

On the other hand, you can take the uncompromising view that abortion is murder, and murder can never be justified. With this view, it is no good arguing that abortion will always happen. Murder will always happen, but we still need laws against it both to minimise its occurrence, and to signal our values as a civilised society.

Then again … the law, and almost everyone – bar the most uncompromising pacifist – recognises that there are times when killing someone may be justified: a police officer shooting a man who is about to detonate a suicide bomb in a crowded place; a soldier defending their country from invasion; someone acting in self-defence, who has to kill their assailant to protect their own life, or the lives of others. It could be argued that, in certain circumstances, abortion is still killing a person, but it is justified killing.

4. Should there be restrictions on abortions? Or should they be available on demand?

If you take the view that the foetus is simply a part of a woman's body over which she should have control, there should be no restrictions on abortions, and abortion should be available on the woman's demand. The only issue (apart from the expense for the health service) for someone who took this view might be that it is

Could abortion be justified killing?

better to prevent unwanted pregnancies than to terminate them, given the stress that any significant medical intervention will place on a woman's body and conscience. So girls (and boys) should be given the best possible education around issues of consent and the practicalities of contraception, and the fullest possible access to contraception, in order to ensure that every pregnancy is a wanted pregnancy.

On the other hand, if you regard abortion as being in some sense the termination of a life, it should be minimised. A negative way of doing this is to have strict conditions for allowing an abortion. This was the original intention of the 1967 Abortion Act, whose conditions implied that a woman should only be allowed an abortion when in physical or mental danger from which she needed to be protected. At one extreme, you could argue that abortion is only acceptable when the woman is in real danger of death if she went ahead with the pregnancy; at the other, you could simply say that the pregnancy must lead to significant harm to the woman for an abortion to be authorised.

A more positive, less punitive way to minimise the number of terminated pregnancies would be to create conditions where women have less need of abortion. Ways of achieving this might include easy access to contraception; a culture of respect and equality in which women are less likely to be pressured (or forced) into unprotected sex against their will; and an economic system in which no woman need fear that she will be unable to provide for her existing or future children.

It is possible to pursue both the negative and the positive approach at the same time.

3. THE POINT OF CLASH

Make abortions less necessary

Should a woman have complete **autonomy over her body**? Or does she become **two people in one body** at the moment she becomes pregnant? If the first, then women should have unrestricted access to abortion. If the second, then abortion should be either illegal or significantly restricted.

Is a foetus a person? If yes, abortion is murder of a defenceless person, and is always wrong. If no, a foetus is simply a part of a woman's body and it should be up to her what she does with it.

When does a person become a person? At **conception**? If yes, then abortion at any stage is murder of a defenceless person, and is always wrong. Or when it changes from an embryo into a **foetus**, after 10–12 weeks? If yes, then abortion in the early stages of pregnancy is acceptable. Or is it when the foetus can **live independently**? If yes, then abortion is acceptable up to the stage when a foetus could live outside the womb, at around 24 weeks.

Is it justifiable to take **one life** in order to save the loss of **two lives**? If yes, then abortion to save a woman's life is acceptable.

Is it justifiable to prioritise a **fully formed life** over one which is still only a **potential life**? If yes, then abortion to protect the physical, social, psychological or financial well-being of the mother is acceptable.

Is it justifiable to accept a **lesser evil** over a **greater evil**? If yes, then it is possible to believe abortion is the taking of an innocent life, but still to keep it legal, because criminalising it will not prevent it from happening, but will only lead to greater harm.

4. THE ARGUMENTS

For abortion	Against abortion
Abortion should be legal because women have a fundamental right to do what they choose with their bodies.	A pregnant woman carries a separate life within her which needs to be protected by law.
Women always carry the consequences of unwanted or unsupportable pregnancies and births.	Women should be helped to avoid unwanted and unsupportable pregnancies and births, not terminate them.
Abortion is nothing more than a medical procedure on a woman's body, a matter for her and her doctor alone.	Abortion is the taking of a life, and should only be allowed in the most exceptional circumstances.
Restrictions on abortion are another example of men controlling women.	The issue is not about controlling women; it is about protecting the unborn child.
Abortion should be legal because criminalisation would bring even greater harm to pregnant women.	Abortion should be illegal because it is murder.
The more developed life of the mother should take priority over the undeveloped life of the foetus.	All life is of equal value.
Abortion is a private decision in which the law should not intervene.	The law has a responsibility to intervene to prevent and / or minimise the taking of innocent life.

5. THE MOTIONS

1. This house would make abortion illegal.
2. This house would allow abortion on demand.
3. This house would reduce the time limit on abortion to 12 weeks.
4. This house would allow girls under 16 to receive abortions without permission from their parents.
5. This house believes abortion is a human right.
6. This house would only allow abortion when the woman's life is at risk / in the case of rape and incest / when the child is likely to be born with a severe disability.

Keep thinking…

A selection of further reading and viewing to help you think more deeply about the issues around abortion.

Human Life, Action and Ethics, G.E.M. Anscombe (Imprint Academic, 2005)

The Oxford philosopher Elizabeth Anscombe was famous for being both terrifyingly intelligent and shamelessly eccentric. (It is said that once, when told by a waiter that women were not allowed to wear trousers in a restaurant she wanted to eat in, she simply took off her trousers and sat down in her knickers.) A Catholic convert, she took up the uncompromising position of opposing abortion in all circumstances. It is well worth reading some of her essays on the subject, as you will never find this unpopular position more lucidly argued.

The Puzzle of Ethics, Paul Grosch and Peter Vardy (Routledge, 1997)

The chapter on abortion is a very accessible, clearly explained introduction to the issues.

About Abortion: Terminating Pregnancy in Twenty-First-Century America, Carol Sanger (Harvard University Press, 2017)

A thoughtful, wide-ranging discussion of the issues around abortion, including the social, political and economic contexts. It is written very much from a US perspective, but most of the issues discussed are of universal relevance. Sanger is firmly pro-choice, but seeks to understand rather than demonise those who disagree with her. The book was written before the 2022 Supreme Court ruling which overturned the constitutional protection for abortion rights, but anticipates many of the issues that gave rise to this ruling.

Practical Ethics, Peter Singer (3rd edition, Cambridge University Press, 2011)

Singer is one of the leading ethicists of his generation, making clear, forceful and often controversial arguments. In his essay on abortion, he makes the case that killing newborn babies may sometimes be justified. However horrifying you find this notion, it will help you to think more clearly about issues around abortion.

An Intelligent Person's Guide to Ethics, Mary Warnock (Duckworth, 1998)

Warnock was a rare example of someone able to combine deep thought and study on ethical issues with a practical grasp of their application in the real world. A professor of philosophy at Oxford, she advised the UK government on the drafting of the 1990 Human Fertilisation and Embryology Act. She was also for a time headmistress of a girls' school, where she sometimes found herself having to advise girls who had fallen pregnant. Her analysis of the issues around abortion are thoughtful, measured and stimulating.

Vera Drake, directed by Mike Leigh (Thin Man Films, 2004)

Imelda Staunton stars as Vera Drake, a working-class woman in the East End of London in the 1950s, who performs amateur abortions for girls who have 'got themselves into trouble' and married women who cannot afford another child. She accepts no payment for her services, acting out of kindness. When she finds herself facing prosecution and imprisonment for her actions, her family and friends cannot believe that someone so good-hearted should be punished for what she does. Meanwhile, the daughter of the upper-middle-class family she cleans for is able to obtain an abortion with impunity (but at a very high price).

The film is a tad sentimental – the upper-middle-class characters are invariably cruel, callous and entitled, while the working-class characters almost all have hearts of gold (except when one of them sells out by aspiring to a washing machine) – but it provides a vivid portrayal of the reality of abortion in the UK before it was legalised, and of the unequal way in which the law impacted women of different socio-economic backgrounds.

CHAPTER 17

Assisted Dying

In this chapter we're thinking about...

- **Is it ever right to end the life of someone who is suffering?**
- **Is it ever right to help someone who is suffering to end their own life?**
- **If so, what rules should there be about how and for whom it is done?**

1. THE FACTS

Assisted dying ends suffering

What is assisted dying (euthanasia)?

Assisted dying – or **euthanasia** – is the act of taking the life of someone who is suffering physically or mentally. **Assisted suicide** is when a doctor gives a person the means to end their own life.

There are two types of assisted dying: **active** euthanasia and **passive** euthanasia.

Active euthanasia

Active euthanasia means ending someone's life by direct intervention, for example by giving them a lethal injection.

Passive euthanasia

Passive euthanasia means ending someone's life by withholding treatment which could prolong their life. It can also be achieved by withholding food and drink.

Both active and passive euthanasia can be further divided into two categories: **voluntary** and **non-voluntary** euthanasia.

Voluntary euthanasia

With voluntary euthanasia, the person whose life is being ended gives their full informed consent for their life to be ended, most commonly if they are suffering from a severe long-term physical health condition or extreme pain from a terminal illness.

Involuntary euthanasia

With involuntary euthanasia, the person whose life is being ended does not give their consent. Normally they are not capable of doing so: they may be a newborn baby or be in a coma. To fit the definition, it is carried out deliberately and in the patient's best interest. If it is carried out by accident, it is regarded in law as manslaughter; if it is carried out for personal gain, it is regarded in law as murder.

Assisted dying (euthanasia) and religion

Christianity, **Islam** and **Judaism** all teach that life is a gift from God, and that we do not have the right to end our life or another person's life prematurely. They regard euthanasia as a

King George V's doctor helped him on his way

kind of murder. However, they also all teach that when there is no possibility of a person recovering from a terminal illness, it is acceptable to withhold treatment and to allow nature to take its course.

Buddhism teaches that we must avoid harm to other people. Killing someone is harming them, so it is wrong.

There are different opinions within **Hinduism**. For some Hindus, all life is sacred and euthanasia is wrong. For others, to relieve someone of their suffering by helping them to die is a good act.

Assisted dying and the law

Assisted dying is, at the time of writing, against the law in the UK, and always has been. Deliberately taking someone's life for them at their request is regarded as murder. Until 1961, suicide was against the law in the UK (making it, bizarrely, a crime for which you could only be prosecuted if you tried but failed to commit it). The 1961 Suicide Act decriminalised suicide, but made assisting someone else with their suicide a criminal offence, incurring a maximum penalty of 14 years in prison.

There is considerable anecdotal evidence that, until quite recently, doctors would often discreetly help dying patients on their way with a lethal injection. This even applied to the highest in the land. On January 20th, 1936, Lord Dawson, King George V's doctor, declared, 'The King's life is moving peacefully towards its close.' The King's death was duly announced at five minutes to midnight on that day. In 1986, fifty years after the death of the King, Lord Dawson's diary was published. This revealed that Lord Dawson had given the King a lethal injection to end his life, partly to end his suffering, but also to ensure that his death was announced in the morning edition of *The Times*, rather than the supposedly less dignified evening papers. Lord Dawson was almost certainly not the only doctor to have practised assisted dying in this way (even if his reasons for doing so were rather unusual), though, given that they were breaking the law, most doctors, unlike Lord Dawson, did not record their actions. Passive euthanasia was also sometimes discreetly carried out in the case of severely disabled newborn babies, simply by withholding care from them.

These practices were helped by a medical culture in which doctors were given a great deal of power to make decisions on behalf of their patients, with little or no consultation. In recent years, that culture has changed, and there is now an expectation that patients should be fully informed and consulted on all important decisions regarding their care. This has probably made the practice of assisted dying less prevalent.

Doctors have to listen to patients

The law against assisted dying in the UK regularly faces tough challenges from high-profile cases. Here are a couple of them.

In April 1989, at the FA Cup semi-final match between Liverpool and Nottingham Forest at the Hillsborough Stadium in Sheffield, police misdirected a group of Liverpool fans, resulting in hundreds of them being crushed against fences. Ninety-five people died. **Tony Bland**, an 18-year-old Liverpool fan, did not die, but damage to his ribs and lungs cut off oxygen to his brain, leaving him in a 'persistent vegetative state' (PVS). He was kept alive only by being artificially fed and given fluids, and by constant care. He showed no awareness of anything or anyone around him; there was no prospect of his ever recovering. As far as his family were concerned, they had already lost him, and they wanted to be able to begin mourning him. For nearly four years, they campaigned for him to be allowed to die. The House of Lords eventually ruled that doctors could stop supplying him with food and drink, on the following grounds:

- A doctor is under no duty to continue treating a patient where such treatment confers no benefit on the patient.
- Being in a persistent vegetative state with no prospect of recovery is not of benefit to a patient.

The doctors duly stopped feeding and hydrating him, and he died in March 1993.

Diane Pretty suffered from motor neurone disease. As her condition got worse, she suffered constant pain and discomfort, and had to have almost everything done for her, though she remained mentally sharp. Her illness was terminal. She had no wish to go on living in these circumstances. She said, 'I want to have a quick death, with no suffering, surrounded by my family.' However, her disability meant that she was physically unable to take any action which would end her life. She asked the Director of Public Prosecutions (DPP) for a guarantee that, if her husband were to assist her in taking her own life, he would not be prosecuted under the Suicide Act. The DPP refused. She took her case to the European Court of Human Rights, arguing that, had she not been disabled, she could have, and would have, taken her own life without anyone else's assistance. Because her disability meant that she could not perform this entirely legal action unaided, she claimed that it

The law is interpreted flexibly

was discrimination against her as a disabled person not to allow her husband to assist her. Disabled people should be entitled to assistance with ending their own lives in the same way as they are entitled to assistance with getting in and out of buildings. Diane Pretty lost her case, and died not long after, though not in the way she would have wished to.

The Tony Bland case was seen by many as having effectively legalised assisted dying in the UK, though the law did not (and has not) changed. Diane Pretty's case aroused great sympathy, with even some religious leaders expressing the view that her wishes about the end of her life should have been respected.

Another challenge to the law on assisted suicide has come from the hundreds of UK citizens who have travelled to Switzerland to make use of the services of Dignitas, an organisation offering assisted suicide. Many of them have been so unwell, or so severely disabled, that they could not travel alone. Anyone accompanying them is effectively assisting their suicide – a criminal offence in the UK. In practice, very few of these people have been prosecuted. The DPP has tended to rule that prosecution 'would not be in the public interest', a way of saying that what they did was a crime, but we're not going to do anything about it.

So, while both euthanasia and assisted suicide remain against the law in the UK, the law has at times been interpreted flexibly.

Assisted dying and the law around the world

Assisted dying and / or assisted suicide is still against the law in the great majority of countries around the world, though the number of countries which have legalised assisted dying is growing. The list below is accurate at the time of writing, but I cannot guarantee that it will be completely accurate by the time you read this book, as the situation is changing fast – you may want to check for the latest situation. Looking at how the law operates in countries which have legalised assisted dying provides a helpful insight into what legalisation might look like in the UK. It is worth saying that each country which has legalised assisted dying has done so only with careful restrictions and safeguarding in place, so that a person cannot be helped to die unless they have expressly chosen this, are of sound mind, and it is not done for another person's benefit. It is also usually the case that no doctor can be obliged to carry out assisted dying against their will.

Switzerland

Since 1941, assisted suicide has been legal in Switzerland, provided the person offering the assistance is not a doctor and has no vested interest in the person's death. So-called 'suicide tourism' has seen thousands of people over the years travelling to Switzerland to take advantage of this law.

Active euthanasia – the deliberate taking of someone's life at their request – remains illegal in Switzerland.

No one has to carry out assisted dying

Colombia

Colombia decriminalised assisted dying in 1997, though the first assisted death did not happen till 2015. In 2021, the law was extended to allow assisted dying for serious injury and non-terminal illnesses, though only in cases of acute physical or mental pain. The inability to lead a dignified life is not a sufficient reason to seek assisted dying.

Australia

Assisted dying was briefly legalised in the Australian state of Northern Territory in 1995, before the federal (national) parliament overturned the law in 1997. Public opinion changed over the years; between 2017 and 2021, five out of the six Australian states legalised voluntary euthanasia.

US states

In 1997, following a referendum on the issue, Oregon became the first US state to legalise assisted suicide. The conditions are as follows.

The patient must:

- Be over 18.
- Be a resident of Oregon.
- Be capable of making and communicating a clear decision.
- Be terminally ill, with a prognosis of under six months to live.
- Make two verbal requests to a doctor, 15 days apart.
- Make a written request to a doctor.

The doctor must:

- Refer any patient she or he considers to be suffering from depression to a counsellor.

The Netherlands has the most advanced laws

- Ensure the patient is fully informed on how palliative care and medication can help relieve their suffering.
- Consult a second doctor.
- Encourage the patient to notify their next of kin of their decision.

At the time of writing, ten other American states have followed Oregon's example in legalising assisted suicide. No American state has yet legalised active euthanasia.

Benelux (Belgium, Netherlands and Luxembourg)

In 2002, the Netherlands became the first country in the world to legalise active euthanasia, though a blind eye had been turned to the practice for many years before that.

Assisted dying is legal in the Netherlands provided the following rigorous conditions are met:

- Assisted dying is carried out by a doctor.
- The patient has explicitly requested assisted dying in a manner that leaves no doubt that the patient's desire to die is voluntary, well informed and well considered.
- The patient has a condition causing protracted physical or mental suffering which the patient finds unbearable.
- There is no reasonable alternative to alleviate the patient's suffering.
- The doctor has consulted with another doctor who agrees with his or her judgement.

A full report on any use of assisted dying must be submitted to a central authority by the doctor who has carried it out. Any doctor who is judged not to have followed all the necessary conditions may be liable to prosecution.

Belgium followed suit by legalising assisted dying later in the same year, while Luxembourg legalised it in 2008. Both countries imposed very similar conditions to the Netherlands.

In all of the above countries, there is widespread support for maintaining the law as it stands. This is helped particularly in the Netherlands by the provision of excellent health care, a cultural willingness to talk openly about difficult issues, and a tradition of patients retaining a strong relationship with one doctor throughout their lives. There is little evidence of people abusing the law – for example, to put pressure on elderly relatives whose care has become a burden, or whose death might provide a lucrative inheritance. There is even some evidence that legalising assisted dying has actually decreased its practice. Many terminally ill people find comfort in knowing that the option of assisted dying is available to them, but do not take it up.

Passive euthanasia is generally tolerated

New Zealand

In 2020, New Zealand legalised voluntary euthanasia for terminally ill people with six or fewer months left to live, in irreversible decline and with unbearable suffering, provided the decision is approved by two doctors. An application takes four to six weeks to process, and the person can change their mind at any time.

Spain

In 2021, Spain legalised voluntary euthanasia, either through the active giving of a lethal injection or by the person taking an administered dose. The person needs to:

- Be over 18.
- Be a Spanish citizen or legal resident.
- Be fully aware and conscious.
- Be experiencing unbearable suffering through a terminal illness or severe medical condition.
- Apply twice in writing, and several days apart.

Canada

In 2021, Canada expanded its existing law allowing euthanasia to permit adults with a serious and incurable "disease, illness or disability" who are in an advanced state of decline and are suffering to seek a medically assisted death even if they are not dying.

In many countries around the world, passive euthanasia is tolerated, when this is achieved by the withholding of treatment from a terminally ill patient with the patient's consent.

No one wants to suffer

2. THE ISSUES

No one wants to suffer; most people don't want to die. No one wants to see someone they love suffer; no one wants to see someone they love die. Sometimes, though, the only way to end our own suffering, or the suffering of someone we love, may be to hasten our, or their, death.

The conflict between the instinctive wish to avoid suffering in ourselves and in those we love, and the no less powerful instinct to preserve life, lies at the heart of any debate on assisted dying. The fundamental question is this:

Are there any circumstances in which it is right to take life in order to prevent suffering?

This fundamental question can be broken down into further questions:

1. Is life inherently sacred?
2. Can we make exceptions to universal laws out of compassion for individuals?
3. Are all kinds of life equally valuable?
4. Which is more important, personal autonomy or the preservation of life?
5. What dangers might legalising assisted dying bring?
6. Assisted dying is going to happen anyway; isn't it better to regulate it?

Let's consider them one by one.

1. Is life inherently sacred?

The word 'sacred' suggests religious belief. It literally means 'made holy'. We have seen above that most religions oppose assisted dying because they believe that life is holy, since it comes from God. However, you do not have to be religious to hold life as a sacred value, to believe in 'the sanctity of life'. You can detach the term 'sacred' from its religious origins, and repurpose it to mean 'of supreme value, important above all other things'. So non-religious people as much as religious people can say that they believe in the sanctity of life.

If you hold this belief, then there can be no circumstances in which it is right to take life, even to relieve suffering. All people, whatever

Is it always wrong to kill?

their age or state of health, must have their lives protected. To suggest that you could take someone's life – or actively assist them to take their own life – is fundamentally inhumane. Of course, when we see someone we love in great suffering, it is only natural, and indeed kind, to want to free them from that suffering. We should do all we can to alleviate their suffering through treatment and care. But we should not alleviate it by ending their life prematurely. To do so is to disrespect their humanity.

Equally, if we ourselves are in great pain, it is entirely human to want to end that pain, even if it means ending our lives. But while no one should be punished by the law for attempting to kill themselves, or condemned by society for succeeding, it is quite wrong to allow doctors to assist people with suicide. A doctor's duty is to preserve life, not to end it; this is even more important than the doctor's duty to alleviate suffering. Nor should a suffering person's loved ones be allowed by the law to assist them in suicide. We can respond to breaches of this law with compassion, and moderate how the law responds, depending on the circumstances. Clearly, a loving wife who gives an overdose to her husband when he is in great pain and has only weeks to live is very different from a manipulative con man who befriends a lonely old woman, gets her to sign her house over to him in her will, and then hands her some pills. We might let the wife off with a minimal penalty, but we must still make it clear that she has broken the law. No matter how good and loving the intention behind the act, once we allow anyone to help another person to kill themselves, we are attacking a fundamental principle of a civilised society: it is wrong to take life. Of course it is hard to maintain this principle in the face of intense and incurable suffering, but there is a wise saying, 'Hard cases make bad law'. That is, you should not base law-making on extreme and exceptional cases.

2. Can we make exceptions to universal laws out of compassion for individuals?

This might be the initial response to the arguments made above. We can accept the fundamental principle that we should respect and preserve life, but argue at the same time that there are circumstances where compassion should take priority. This, you could say, has been the pragmatic response of the UK legal system when it has often chosen not to prosecute people who have accompanied loved ones to Dignitas in Switzerland, even though they have technically broken the law. Of course, depending on the goodwill of the Director of Public Prosecutions is a risky strategy for a would-be practiser of assisted dying; nor is it a satisfactory way for society to deal with an important moral issue. Perhaps we do need to change the law, so everyone knows where they stand. We can still say that life needs to be preserved, but we can allow some exceptions to this general rule. After all, the law already allows soldiers and police officers to take life in order to protect the public, and it is sometimes legal to kill another person in self-defence when your own life is in danger, so it need not be that big a step to allow the taking of life to end acute suffering. As for hard cases making bad law, well, if there are enough hard cases, then maybe it is the law that is bad and it needs changing.

3. Are all kinds of life equally valuable?

Why should we assume that all life is equally valuable? Should we perhaps focus on quality of life rather than quantity? What value does a life with no pleasure, no control, no hope for the future, nothing but pain, really have? You say you want to respect humanity by preserving life – how then is it respecting a person's humanity to subject them to unending indignity and suffering from which they wish to be released?

What about people in a persistent vegetative state, kept alive by machines, with no prospect of recovery? They may be biologically alive, but they are not biographically alive: that is, their organs may be functioning, but they have no consciousness. They have no hope of any future. The case of Tony Bland (see pages 419–420) is very telling. As far as his parents – the people who loved him more than anyone else in the world – were concerned, his life no longer had any meaning, and they wanted it to end. Truly respecting life means respecting the quality of a person's life.

4. Which is more important, personal autonomy or the preservation of life?

Perhaps simply having life is not the highest value. Perhaps autonomy – the ability to have control over our lives – is more important. If we deny someone the right to have assistance with ending their life in a dignified way, we show disrespect for their humanity, because the essence of humanity is the ability to make free choices about our destiny. The case of Diane Pretty (see pages 419–420) dramatises this argument very well. Her human dignity was already compromised by the limitations imposed on her by her disability; it was further compromised by the refusal of the law to allow her freely to ask her husband to end her suffering, without putting him in danger of prosecution. She felt imprisoned twice, first by her disability, then by an unjust law. She did not wish for her husband to risk actual imprisonment too.

What does being alive mean?

Doctors who treat terminally ill people often report that the patients who find it hardest to cope are those who, in their earlier lives, were powerful or important people, used to being in charge. The loss of autonomy that goes with being seriously ill is, for some people, even worse than the pain. For those who feel this way, restoring their autonomy over their own lives will at least restore some of their human dignity. It isn't **being alive** that makes us human, it's **having life**. And if we have something, if we own it, we are surely entitled to stop having it when we no longer want it.

5. What dangers might legalising assisted dying bring?

This is the so-called 'slippery slope' argument, which proposes that a change which is initially well intentioned will slowly but inexorably fall open to abuse. This kind of argument is often fallacious, but in the case of assisted dying it does have validity.

We might start out by seeing assisted dying as a humane way to end unnecessary suffering. If we put enough safeguards around it (in debating terms, have a tight enough mechanism), there should be no danger of abuse. But then an old person who does not really want to die says they do because they feel guilty about the burden they are placing on their children. A wealthy old man is persuaded by his greedy son that his suffering is unbearable. A disabled woman internalises society's negative attitudes towards disability so profoundly that she comes to believe that her life is not worth living. What if the definition of suffering ends up being extended to mental suffering, as in Canada? One symptom of severe depression can be very powerful suicidal thoughts. People often recover from depression, are liberated from these thoughts, and go on to live happy, fulfilled lives. If they had been allowed – perhaps even encouraged – to end their mental suffering while in a depressive episode, they might never have had the opportunity for a happy life. As an example of how all this could happen, look at abortion. When the law on abortion in the UK was changed in 1967 (see previous chapter), the original intention was that abortion would be used as an exceptional last resort; now, it is effectively available on demand. Once something is legal, it is very hard to stop it becoming commonplace.

What is more, just the fact of having legalised assisted dying on the statute books sends out a message about how we value life, and in particular the life of people who are sick, heavily injured or disabled. Changing the law to allow same-sex marriage has done

Changing the law changes attitudes

much to alter wider social attitudes towards gay people, making them feel more accepted and valued. Changing the law to allow assisted dying would have the opposite effect on sick, injured or disabled people, making them feel less accepted and valued.

6. Assisted dying is going to happen anyway; isn't it better to regulate it?

This was the main argument made for decriminalising abortion in the UK in 1967. Once there are strict rules about how and when you can practise assisted dying, it is much harder for an unscrupulous relative or a power-hungry doctor to take someone's life for the wrong reasons. There is a considerable amount of evidence that since assisted dying has been legalised in the Netherlands, its practice has actually decreased. King George V did not consent to his assisted dying after a proper process of request and reflection, fully informed by appropriate medical advice, and the same has very likely been true for thousands of people (and may still be true). The law should be pragmatic, accept that people are going to find ways to end their lives when they are suffering, and protect them from bad choices and exploitation through carefully thought through and properly debated regulations and structures.

3. THE POINT OF CLASH

Is the **sanctity of life** more important than any other consideration?

Or is **autonomy**, the freedom for people to do what they want with their life, even up to and including ending it, more important?

Is all life equally **valuable**? Or are some kinds of life simply **not worth living**?

Is allowing assisted dying a way of introducing **compassion** into the law? Or is it **dangerous**?

4. THE ARGUMENTS

For legalising assisted dying	Against legalising assisted dying
People have the right to do what they want with their lives. If they wish to die, and cannot do it by themselves, they should be helped.	The sanctity of life is more important than liberty. It is never right to take someone's life.
Some kinds of life, e.g. PVS, extreme disability or suffering from an acutely painful incurable illness, may not seem worth living.	All life is intrinsically valuable.
It is inhumane to force someone to go on living when they wish to die.	It is inhumane to legalise killing.
It is inhumane that someone who only wishes to spare someone they love from acute suffering should be threatened with prosecution.	No one should be allowed to kill another person, no matter how good their intentions.
We already allow soldiers and police officers to take life to protect us, and permit the taking of life in self-defence, so the sanctity of life is not absolute.	Taking life to protect innocent people is completely different from taking the life of a sick or vulnerable person.
A doctor's first responsibility is to alleviate suffering; sometimes assisted dying may be the only way to do this.	A doctor's first responsibility is to preserve life.
Assisted dying is going to happen anyway, so it is better to regulate it properly to prevent abuse.	However rigorous the regulations, once assisted dying is legalised, abuse will inevitably creep in.
Legal assisted dying is the mark of a compassionate, humane society.	Legal assisted dying is the mark of a society that believes some people are less valuable than others.

5. THE MOTIONS

1. This house would legalise assisted dying for terminally ill people.
2. This house would legalise assisted dying for severely disabled people.
3. This house would legalise assisted dying for people with severe and incurable depression.
4. This house would legalise assisted dying for people in a persistent vegetative state.
5. This house would legalise assisted dyinge.
6. This house believes in the sanctity of life.

Keep thinking...

A selection of further reading and viewing to help you think more deeply about the issues around assisted dying.

Practical Ethics, Peter Singer (3rd edition, Cambridge University Press, 2011)

In his chapter on assisted dying, Singer argues vigorously in favour of eassisted dying, not just for people at the end of their lives, but also for severely disabled newborn babies. We're willing to practise assisted dying on dogs and cats to save them from unnecessary suffering, he says; shouldn't we treat people at least as well as animals? You may be shocked by some of his arguments, but he will make you think hard.

Easeful Death: Is There a Case for Assisted Dying?, Mary Warnock and Elisabeth MacDonald (OUP, 2008)

Warnock and MacDonald analyse the issues around assisted dying carefully and thoughtfully, basing their arguments both on Warnock's training as an academic philosopher, and on her practical experience in advising the UK government on proposed changes to the law. They come down tentatively in favour of legalising assisted dying, but with much sympathy for opposing points of view.

Dishonest to God: On Keeping Religion out of Politics, Mary Warnock (Continuum, 2010)

In this book, Warnock describes the public and parliamentary debates in the UK in the early twenty-first century around major moral issues, including assisted dying. She was closely involved in these debates, and gives a fascinating insight into how they unfolded. Among other things, she considers how much weight, if any, should be given to religious belief in framing the law.

Whose Life is it Anyway?, directed by John Badham (United Artists, 1981)

Richard Dreyfuss stars in this film as Ken Harrison, a sculptor who has become paralysed from the neck down following a car accident. Though he is still mentally capable, he feels that, without the use of his body, his life has no meaning, and he wishes to end it; his doctor, however, is vehemently opposed to assisted dying. The story reaches its climax with a legal hearing in which Harrison argues for his right to die at a time of his choosing. The film dramatises very effectively and accessibly the moral, legal and ethical questions around assisted dying.

Afterword

If you've finished this book, you'll have done lots of thinking. Don't stop now. Keep curious about the world. Keep challenging everything you hear and read and see. Most of all, keep challenging your own ideas. How do you know that this is true? Why do you think that? What would someone who disagreed with you say?

The world is changing (it is always changing) and you are changing too (you are always changing). As the world changes and you change, your ideas need to change. In the words of the poet Thom Gunn:

At worst, one is in motion; and at best,
Reaching no absolute, in which to rest,
One is always nearer by not keeping still.

Keep thinking. Keep debating.

Keep thinking like a debater.

Acknowledgments

Thank you to Chris Hall for imaginative and creative layout and design. Thank you to Monica Byles for meticulous editing and fact-checking; any infelicities or errors which remain are my fault for not listening to her. Thank you to Tiffany Jenkins for expert advice on the colonialism chapter, and to Zehra Odunayo for expert advice on the race chapter. If those chapters are better for their advice, it is thanks to them; if they are not, it is my fault. Thank you to James Renshaw for invaluable information on free speech in the ancient world, and to George Oliver for tips on statistics. Thank you to Eve Benima-Chow, Imane Benima-Chow, Orla Flutter, Sophie Melzack, Mary Murray and Max Robins for reading and giving feedback on selected chapters. Thank you to the staff and trustees of the London Library for giving me a beautiful place to read, think and write (and also for lots of books). Thank you to Jean and Alina for love and encouragement. Thank you above all to the hundreds of students and teachers I've had the privilege of working with since I became a full-time debate trainer. As with my first book, this book would not exist without you, and is for you.

Printed in Dunstable, United Kingdom

68446267R00246